The Silent Revolution
and the Making of
Victorian England

The Silent Revolution and the Making of Victorian England

HERBERT SCHLOSSBERG

OHIO STATE UNIVERSITY PRESS

COLUMBUS

Library of Congress Cataloging-in-Publication Data

Schlossberg, Herbert.
The silent revolution and the making of
Victorian England / Herbert Schlossberg.
p.   cm.
Includes bibliographical references (p.   ) and index.
ISBN 0-8142-0843-6 (cloth : alk. paper) —
ISBN 0-8142-5046-7 (pbk. : alk. paper)
1. Great Britain—History—Victoria, 1837–1901.
2. Religion and sociology—Great Britain—History—19th century.
3. Evangelicalism—Great Britain—History—19th century.
4. Great Britain—Church history—19th century.
5. Great Britain—Civilization—19th
century.   I. Title.

DA550 .S3 2000   99-056104
941.081—dc21

Text and jacket design by
Robert Tombs.

Type set in Adobe Caslon
by G&S Typesetters, Inc.

Printed by McNaughton & Gunn.

9 8 7 6 5 4 3 2 1

*To Howard and Roberta Ahmanson, good friends
and supporters, without whose help the task
could not have been undertaken*

Contents

Illustrations

Acknowledgments

I AM INDEBTED TO TWO exceptional scholars of nineteenth-century England for valuable advice on various aspects of this book. Josef L. Altholz of the University of Minnesota, who directed my thesis on an unrelated subject a generation ago, once again took up his blue pencil, a task unpaid this time but not thankless, and commented on each chapter. Gertrude Himmelfarb also read and commented on a draft of each chapter. Between their efforts I was saved numerous errors of fact and interpretation. George P. Landow of Brown University also made valuable suggestions. The usual absolution of responsibility applies to each of them.

Steve Kennedy, Jeffry Morrison, and Stephen Schlossberg provided research assistance, with Mr. Schlossberg doing double duty as an editor. Amy L. Sherman, a fine young scholar in a completely different field, taught a much older friend a good deal about organizing a piece of writing and added clarity to the work. Other friends who read the manuscript and made useful suggestions were Harry Bracken and Denis Haack. The critical comments of two readers chosen by the Ohio State University Press, whose identities are unknown to me, were of great help.

I also benefited from an international crew of like-minded friends and critics whose support I am glad to acknowledge: Steve Ferguson, Charlie and Serena Colchester, Luke and Caroline Bretherton, Marsh and Tuula Moyle, Milan and Bozena Čičel, Hermann and Bridget Gschwandtner, Juraj Kušnierik, Miro Jurík, Carol Crom, Sarah Leichty, and others, mainly in Central Europe.

I relied on the libraries of the University of Minnesota, the American University, and George Mason University, and the librarians of the Pohick Branch of the Fairfax County (Virginia) library as well as the Interlibrary Loan staff of the county system. In England I made use mainly of the British Library, but also received hospitality from the University of London library and the Bodleian at Oxford University. Patrick and Rosemary Sookhdeo were gracious hosts during many of my forays into London libraries.

My wife, Terry, as usual, was of inestimable help in many ways. In particular she tracked down the illustrations during a trip to London.

Introduction

THE VICTORIAN PERIOD IN
THE MINDS OF ITS SUCCESSORS

WITH A RHETORICAL FLOURISH, a modern historian has written that the generation born in England around 1790 was the most important in the modern history not only of its own country but of the whole Christian world. He reasons that the revolutionary forces sweeping through France threatened to destroy the political and cultural institutions of many other nations as well and that the success or failure of that prospect had enormous consequences for everything that followed.[1] This explanation is in some ways true, but it has the unfortunate effect of associating revolution exclusively with the violent overthrow of the political and social order, and it obscures the revolutionary changes that occurred in England during the period before the start of Queen Victoria's reign.

This book argues that the culture of Victorianism was set deeply within the English psyche before Victoria was crowned in 1837. Most of the praise and the censure (the latter much more common) that critics have heaped on the Victorian years applies in much the same way to the preceding generation. Therefore, although we are primarily concerned with the early decades of the nineteenth century, we look at those decades through critiques of the years that followed. The features that moderns love and hate about Victorian culture could be discerned very early in the century. "Victorianism," as Muriel Jaeger puts it, "had already prepared the way for Victoria."[2]

Along with and overpowering the nostalgia for things Victorian has been an intense dislike, sometimes seeming to be a visceral hatred. For many of us today, Victorian England conjures up visions of ugly factories belching smoke and soot, of abject poverty, and of a bizarre preoccupation with sex and its repression. But these disagreeable images were commonly remarked upon long before the Queen's death. Leslie Stephen, one of the most illustrious scholars of the period, believed it certain that no matter how strong the currents of nostalgia for the past might run, nobody would want to revive the nineteenth century. Somewhat later, H. G. Wells wrote of the period as "slovenly and wasteful," with its contemptible dwellings, railways, furnishings, art, and literature.[3] Such reactions amount to more than disciplined, measured criticism.

I

Much of the negative thinking about England in the nineteenth century derives from the polemical struggles of the period. The reformers early in the century paraded and exaggerated the evils present in order to generate support for ameliorating them. Indeed, were it not for their protests against the economic and social difficulties under which many ordinary people lived, the parliamentary commissions that investigated conditions would not have been undertaken, nor the consequent ameliorative legislation. The novelists highlighted those same difficulties for dramatic purposes. For others, history served as well as fiction—in fact, was sometimes a form of fiction. In his *History of the Protestant Reformation in England and Ireland* (1824–27), Richard Cobbett, radical journalist of the 1820s and 1830s, painted medieval Europe in the rosiest way to convince his readers that in the Middle Ages happy peasants populated the countryside, lively, prosperous, and free. This provided him with a utopia against which he could contrast modern England, burdened, as he saw it, with a ruling class of rich oppressors.

Apart from the unavoidable fact that fictional and polemical writing distorts the truth, later writers, unable to sympathize with the prevailing religiosity of the period, simply omitted what they did not care about. We have, for example, a scholar writing about Robert Chalmers's scheme for poor relief without mentioning the fact that Chalmers, a Scottish Presbyterian minister, envisioned it as taking place through the instrument of the parish church. Thus, he completely misapprehended the subject he was discussing.[4] During the Victorian period the same kind of distortions took place: the future prime minister William Gladstone was critical of his atheist friend John Morley's *Life of Cobden* because it did not make clear Cobden's religious motivation.[5] Twentieth-century authors such as Lytton Strachey and J. M. Robertson went beyond omission to harsh complaint and ridicule and have exerted considerable influence on the thinking of the public.[6]

In addition to its reputation as a religious period, the Victorian age is regarded as the heyday of capitalism. In historical studies, Beatrice and Sidney Webb and J. L. and Barbara Hammond, leaders in the Fabian socialist movement, emphasized the handicaps under which the lower classes were placed in the burgeoning Industrial Revolution and used the historical material to highlight their current concerns. Not all of their charges have stood the test of time, but they have become embedded in the popular consciousness, and we shall have to examine the issue. Two modern sociologists writing from a similar perspective describe themselves as "heirs of a British radical tradition" that informs their scholarship. They depict many of their colleagues in the same way—outsiders, fringe people who do not fit into the institutions that count in modern Britain. "Almost all looked back on a home dominated by political radicalism." Even their accents—they were "branded on the tongue"—marked them as hostile to the elites and there-fore set the tone of their scholarship.[7] One of the most famous examples of such works, E. P. Thompson's book *The Making of the English Working Class,* has been exceptionally influential, becoming almost the defining doc-ument of that point of view.

Along with whatever ideological baggage modern historians drag into their studies, there is the problem that they are *modern.* Although they are interested in the past, they (we) pursue that interest with minds that have been conditioned to view past events through the lens of modernity. A scholar of nineteenth-century religion tells us that he views the meaning of religion as Feuerbach did, which is to say that theology is, at its heart, an-thropology.[8] This reductionist position makes the views of the people he is studying not just wrong but delusional. Such a scholar can provide valuable help in our search for meaning in the past, and this one does, but it is doubt-ful that he can penetrate very far beneath the surface of what he is describ-ing, since he does not believe there is anything there. Writings from a social science perspective are particularly prone to this difficulty.[9] There are now studies of Victorian England dominated by modern types of antinomian-ism. One of these, for example, treats opposition to prostitution as a form of repression.[10] The point here is not whether one agrees with such views, but rather how much light they can shed on a period with which they are so lacking in sympathy that they seem to stare at it uncomprehendingly.

About a half century ago it looked as if the tide was turning and a new willingness to understand the Victorian period with something like objec-tivity had come. Basil Willey wrote that the days when Lytton Strachey could write scurrilous things about the Victorians to public applause were over, now that the debunking urge was largely gone.[11] Crane Brinton in the same period announced from the Harvard history department that "the Victorian era is coming back into good repute."[12] In Jerome Buckley's ver-sion of the story, now that Victoria had been in the grave for half a century, the easy repudiation of her era had become "outmoded."[13] John Holloway pronounced the end of the fashionable denigration of the Victorians, but like some of the others of his era who were ostensibly rehabilitating the reign, he continued to denigrate them. According to Holloway, we should respect and revere them "for all their blindness and taboos, and for all their wildness and crudity too."[14] At about the same time, the BBC sponsored a series of radio broadcasts about the period, conducted by recognized schol-ars and published under the title *Ideas and Beliefs of the Victorians.* The pub-lic was informed in these broadcasts that the time of reaction against the preceding century was over and that the period of dispassionate considera-tion had come.[15] There was a certain irony in that judgment, since some of the essays in the book seemed to have been written with a full measure of smug self-satisfaction that the writers were not like Victorians, which is to say not smugly self-satisfied, not greedy, not imbued with the capitalist ethic, not religious.

These upbeat, if not unmixed, messages about Victorian scholarship largely came to nought. This is not the fault of the prognosticators, who after all were paid to tell the truth about the past, not the future. Evidently the yearning for normalcy and peace after World War II—these speculations about the Victorian rehabilitation were written in the 1940s and 1950s—was wrecked on the shoals of the cultural revolutions of the next decade, and the newly fashionable ideologies perceived no need to accommodate the predictions of their predecessors. In the 1990s, the same perspectives continued in the scholarly as well as the general literature. An academic book on Victorian sexuality begins by speaking of the "special place" that the Victorian age has in our culture: "More than any other era it awakens in us our capacities to feel hostile toward a past way of life, to perceive the past as alien, unenlightened, and silly."[16] And an article in a journal of popular scholarship informs us that Robert Louis Stevenson was born "in the coal smoke and sea fog and Protestant miasma of Victorian Edinburgh."[17] Enveloped as he was by noxious vapors, both physical and metaphysical, poor Stevenson died early.

But there may be a larger trend working behind the apparent one, a kind of tsunami that could overtake and overwhelm the surface ripples that until then seemed so revelatory. Writing in *Victorian Studies* in 1990, a reviewer of four new scholarly books dealing seriously with religion in Victorian England calls such works "typical for the 1980s, when it is no longer philosophically unrespectable to believe in God."[18] And the author of one of those four books said much the same thing, citing the "revival of evangelical and charismatic worship" as especially worthy of note.[19]

THE GREATER EUROPEAN REVOLUTION

Much of the modern effort to understand English history in the early nineteenth century has been taken up with the question raised by the French historian Élie Halévy before World War I. Why, he wondered, did England escape from the trauma of revolution that had seized much of Europe in the half century or so after 1789? Halévy concluded that the Methodist movement had so changed the lower classes of England as to improve their lives and abate their dissatisfactions and thereby had removed the causes of revolution.[20] The disagreements with Halévy's view have centered largely on Methodism's effects on the population and on whether those effects could have forestalled revolution. I think a more compelling question is suggested by the analysis of a later French historian writing on a different historical period. Paul Hazard summarized in this way the changes in French culture during the thirty-five years after 1680: "One day, the French people, almost to a man, were thinking like Bossuet. The day after, they were thinking like Voltaire. No ordinary swing of the pendulum, that. It was a revolution."[21] Hazard did not mean that there was a political cataclysm but rather that the replacement of one kind of thinking with another was a revolutionary event.

Now, Hazard knew that not many of the French people had heard of either the Bishop of Meaux or the exemplar of French unbelief, but he was onto something important. A generation is not a long time to replace one way of thinking with another, and *revolution* is not too strong a word to describe this phenomenon, even when it includes only a well-educated elite. Looking at England in the half century beginning one hundred years after Hazard's starting point, we might make a similar judgment. The question to be asked is not Halévy's about why the Continental revolutions did not have their English counterpart but rather how such a revolutionary change in English culture could have taken place and how it could have done so without causing a corresponding political upheaval. Moreover, we shall want to consider why the change in thinking was not only among a small elite, as in the case of France in the earlier period, but throughout the great mass of English society. If the American publishers of Hazard's book had translated the title from the French, it would have appeared as *The Crisis of the European Conscience*, which I think describes well what happened in France in the late seventeenth and early eighteenth centuries—and in England a century later.

The idea of the pre-Victorian period as a revolutionary one is not new. When the French social observer Alexis de Tocqueville arrived in England in 1833, he thought the country had experienced a great revolution that was still in progress. The key lay in his meaning of the term *revolution*, which he defined as "any fundamental change in the law, or any social transformation, or any substitution of one regulating principle for another." He explicitly did not mean "a violent or sudden change."[22] He might have gone on to describe that English revolution as a greater one than that of his homeland, which, after all, was followed by a succession of republics, monarchies, and empires. It is hard to see that the life of the typical French citizen (or subject) changed much in the course of this or that political convulsion, if we except the trail of bodies left in its wake, whereas the cultural revolution of which he spoke changed England profoundly and for many decades.

What sort of change did Tocqueville have in mind when he wrote of the English revolution? Consider his account of a luncheon at the Earl of Radnor's house on May 27, 1835:

> Before coming to table Lord Radnor went to his study; Lady Radnor and his daughters went there too; after a moment eleven or twelve women and eight or ten men-servants came in. . . . These twenty people took their places round the room and knelt down looking towards the wall. Near the fireplace Lord and Lady Radnor and Lady Louisa knelt down too, and Lord Radnor read a prayer aloud, the servants giving the responses. This sort of little service lasted six or eight minutes, after which the male and female servants got up and went out in the same order to resume their work.[23]

And Tocqueville described Lord Radnor, because of his political affiliations, as a *radical*. Everywhere Tocqueville traveled in England he saw this sort of devotional exercise, which he knew very well he would not have seen a half century earlier. Of course, if that had been all that had happened, just a little ceremony superimposed upon the same set of habits and relationships, it would have had little meaning. But Tocqueville observed that the culture had changed in profound ways that were symbolized by such ceremonies, and that is why he called the changes revolutionary.

REVOLUTION AND CULTURE

Several modern scholars have used *revolution* in the sense I mean it— G. M. Young, J. Wesley Bready, Gertrude Himmelfarb, Bernard Semmel, and perhaps others as well.[24] This use of the word is much more slippery than its more common meaning. We cannot point to a coup, an election, or an armed rebellion. The events that mark this kind of revolution are mostly private ones, such as took place at Lord Radnor's house, of which we would know nothing if Tocqueville had not been invited to lunch. I am reminded of the study done by E. Digby Baltzell, who was puzzled about why two cities in the northeastern United States should be so different from each other, in particular why one had produced influential leaders over many generations while the other had not. His conclusion may be inferred from his title: *Puritan Boston and Quaker Philadelphia*. The Puritans and Quakers, both Protestant sects that had trouble being accepted by their society, or indeed by each other, molded their respective communities in ways that were dependent on their differing theologies, so that even three centuries later the residue of their cultural differences persisted. This book explores such a contrast, but it is a longitudinal study that shows how change was effected in the society over a period of several decades.

Baltzell was an admirer of the distinguished Harvard scholar of Puritanism Perry Miller, and he adverted to the apologetic insertion in Miller's first book. "I lay myself open to the charge," Miller wrote in 1933, "of being so very naive as to believe that the way men think has some influence upon their actions, of not remembering that these ways of thinking have been officially decided by modern psychologists to be generally just so many rationalizations constructed by the subconscious to disguise the pursuit of more tangible ends." Miller went on to insist that for the subject he was addressing, at any rate, it was necessary to take seriously the claimed beliefs of the principal actors.[25] If anything, the social sciences have become much more domineering since Miller's time, and skepticism about human motivations and beliefs has become more corrosive, but this book is written with the same assumption as Miller's: how people think matters, and the religious worldview (under whatever name it might conceal itself) that shapes their thinking matters most.

The skeptical view about human thought that Miller rejected is not new to the twentieth century but was present in the nineteenth as well. Samuel Taylor Coleridge, who will play an important role in our story, found it necessary to deny that thoughts are less important than actions, holding that even in the world of commerce "the most important changes . . . had their origin in the closets or lonely walks of uninterested theorists."[26] (This calls to mind the oft-quoted aphorism of John Maynard Keynes: "Madmen in authority, who hear voices in the air, are distilling their frenzy from some academic scribbler of a few years back.") John Stuart Mill wrote an article on the "spirit of the age," remarking in 1831 that he did not think that idea could be found prior to a half century before then. He believed that such a concept is to be found only in a period of rapid change, since it is only then that people think much about the oddities of their own age and how they differ from their predecessors'. "A change has taken place in the human mind; a change which, being effected by insensible gradations, and without noise, had already proceeded far before it was generally perceived." When, much later, it was perceived, "thousands awoke as from a dream." I do not think Mill had it exactly right, since he believed that some men clung to the past while others (like himself) had moved into a newer mode of being. He did not perceive that almost everyone had changed with him, despite the wide range of disagreement, or that the change in himself was not as complete as he imagined it to be. Still, he was right about this: "Those were indeed new men."[27]

IDEAS AND THEIR TRANSMISSION

I stress the unconscious nature of the changing spirit, as Mill did, because that seems to be the way it was; perhaps that is the way it usually is with human beings. What we are is not always, perhaps not often, what we think we are. In 1837 a clergyman in Leeds remarked that "the established religion in Leeds is Methodism, and it is Methodism that all the most pious among the Churchmen unconsciously talk."[28] That is, Methodism, which by then had separated from the Church of England, had come to dominate the thinking of the city to the extent that even Anglicans had been swallowed up in its spirit, albeit without realizing it.

We have here the outworking of an assumption about the transmission of ideas. Can it be said that someone who had never heard of, say, Jeremy Bentham, could still be influenced by him? Yes, argued Jenifer Hart, because of Bentham's influence on the climate of opinion. If that were not true, "there would be few thinkers who could be shown to have had any practical influence at all."[29] Christopher Dawson was getting at something very similar when he wrote that a living culture "must possess some spiritual dynamic, which provides the energy necessary for that sustained social effort which is civilization." He thought that this dynamic was generally supplied by a religion but that in some cases it might "disguise itself" as philosophy or politics.[30] Thus, in speaking of a generalized shift in the spirit of an age, we are dealing with what is more amorphous than we might like. Our evidence may come in a poem or a prayer rather than an economic report or a diplomatic agreement. A dialogue constructed by Dickens can be as illuminating as a speech by Peel, a tract written for a near-illiterate audience as a tome by a philosopher. This is especially true for the period we are considering because people with culture-changing ideas were not likely to be professional theorists but were more prone than later generations to have jobs that required them to do their intellectualizing on the side.[31] Mill, to cite one prominent example, like his father (also an intellectual), was a bureaucrat working for the East India Company. Our purposes are also better served by the more informal sources because of our interest in determining the effects of the cultural transformation on the lives of ordinary English people.

CHANGE AND THE PERCEPTION OF PERIL

The stereotype of Victorian society as staid and conservative does not prepare us well for the ferment of the early nineteenth century. This was a period of dynamic change. In 1790, the largest single source of income was agriculture, and landowners were the plutocrats of the age, the wealthiest and most powerful of families. By the middle of the next century, none of this was true. Industrialization had changed the status not only of wealth but of the whole population. There were more goods available, cheaper goods, and more money with which to buy them. Many articulate Englishmen were concerned about the "condition of England" question and what was to be done about it, and we shall have to devote considerable effort to determine why this was so, but there can be little doubt that all classes of the society benefited from the Industrial Revolution.[32]

Yet the late eighteenth and early nineteenth centuries were not entirely a psychologically buoyant period. There was a constant state of crisis for about thirty years due to the French Revolution and the intermittent state of warfare with France. Henry Thornton, one of the leading Evangelicals[33] of Clapham, wrote with an ominous sense of heaviness in his journal on July 31, 1803, as the second Napoleonic war began:

> I now write . . . in the apprehension of an invasion. My wife is advised by some of our friends to leave London for the sake of avoiding the danger of being surrounded by French soldiery, and I am hearing day by day new accounts of slaughter and insurrection in Ireland. Perhaps however the war was not finally to be avoided. I myself suspect that it was not but I was anxious to take at least the best chance of avoiding it. May I and mine be preserved from the perils which surround us, and may we perform our part in sustaining the spirit of the country, and in deprecating that wrath of God which there is too much reason to fear may be denounced against us.[34]

It was not only the war with France that was so determinative of English sensibilities; it was also the French Revolution. Some argue that the almost unbroken Tory domination of English politics from 1783 until 1830 came from the fears of the ruling class that the contagion of rebellion would cross the Channel, fears that were fueled by periodic bouts of violence caused by economic distress.[35] William Wilberforce, leader of the Clapham Evangelicals in the House of Commons, joined with many others in fearing not only the violence of the French Revolution but more especially its source in atheism. Thus, he supported the increasing repression in Pitt's long ministry. Each edition of a Thomas Paine book, each formation of a new radical society, seemed to provide new justification for repressive measures.[36] Distress for some was something close to ecstasy for others, as the revolutionary fires heightened hopes that something like a new world order was in the offing. The three famous Lake Poets, Wordsworth, Coleridge, and

Southey, later known as conservatives, were in their youth flaming radicals who were inspired by events across the Channel to pursue utopian schemes. Looking back on the period from his middle age, Southey explained how they had been affected: "Few persons but those who had lived in it can conceive or comprehend what . . . a visionary world seemed to open upon those who were just entering it. . . . Old things seemed passing away, and nothing was dreamt of it but the regeneration of the human race." He had mixed feelings about who should win the war, for France stood for liberty and England for reaction, or so he thought at the time.[37]

There was indeed a regeneration in England's future, but not the one that the young Southey and his friends envisioned. The "secular" eighteenth century, when we look beneath the surface, turns out to be the start of a profound spiritual revival. As it spread from the Church of England throughout the society, it affected the life of the non-Anglican, or Dissenting, congregations. The chapels in which the Dissenters worshiped increasingly rang with the ideas and hymns of the evangelical movement, even in such unlikely groups as the Quakers, whose distinctive features had been their quietism, their emphasis on separation and contemplation, and their peculiarities of dress and speech.

But within the Church of England, the rise of evangelicalism was far from unchallenged, and the interplay between it and rival movements is an important part of the story. The old "orthodoxy"—to adopt the contemporary terminology—remained despite the opposition from Evangelicals, from liberals, and from a renewed High Church, and we shall have to consider each of these manifestations of opposition to the characteristic complacency of the Anglican church of the eighteenth century.

THE PLAN OF THE BOOK

This book begins with the setting against which the changes it describes took place, the spiritual condition of England in the eighteenth century. Chapters 2 through 6 describe the various manifestations of the religious renewal: the eighteenth-century beginnings (chapter 2); then the three main renewal movements in the Church of England—the Evangelical (chapter 3), the Tractarian or High Church (chapter 4), and the movement that began with Thomas Arnold at Rugby School (chapter 5); and then the spread of evangelicalism to the Dissenting (non-Anglican) religious groups (chapter 6).

The next three chapters deal with the relationship between the religious revival and various aspects of the society that are often thought to be of little relevance to religion: Samuel Taylor Coleridge and Thomas Carlyle as important intellectuals who exemplify very different parts of the cultural spectrum (chapter 7); the place of religious activity in the rapidly changing social and economic situation brought about by the Industrial Revolution and associated factors (chapter 8); and the puzzling extent of agreement between the two opposing contenders for intellectual domination in the period, evangelicalism and utilitarianism (chapter 9).

Our examination of the pre-Victorian period must explain the transformation of English sensibilities and institutions in such a way as to justify the contention that this was indeed a revolutionary period. We shall have to consider the changes in the way people thought and felt (chapter 10), the changes in moral sensibility and practice (chapter 11), and the remaking of English institutions (chapter 12). Finally, chapter 13 will summarize and synthesize the arguments, showing how England discarded the skepticism, immorality, and frivolity of the Enlightenment century, during which people had been content to enslave people of another race and had been largely unmoved in the face of widespread poverty and misery, and became a more humane, generous, and livable society.

The Georgian Slide

DECADENCE IN

EIGHTEENTH-CENTURY

ENGLAND

UNDERSTANDING A PERIOD OF RELIGIOUS revival requires us to consider the period that spawned it. Many people in the pre-Victorian period consciously reacted against what they considered to be an idolatrous and immoral age, and not a few of their predecessors in the eighteenth century thought the same. There were good reasons for that.

THE ECLIPSE OF CHRISTIANITY

With the restoration of the monarchy in 1660, there began a serious decline in the public expression of Christian faith. It was not just that the religious rigor of Cromwell's regime had engendered a backlash. The character of the new king and his court made an important contribution to the decline, and the legislation that ensued removed incentives for the moral life that had existed earlier—the example of the upper classes and the restraining influence of a vigorous religious life. Before his return to England, Charles II had signed a declaration that guaranteed amnesty to the "tender consciences" that declined to follow the Established religion. But the election that followed brought to ascendency the Cavalier sentiments that had been crushed during the Commonwealth period, and with them the urge for revenge. The bodies of Cromwell and his associates were ripped from their graves and publicly hanged, a number of people responsible for the execution of Charles I were themselves executed, many prominent Puritans were cast into prison, and it seemed that every government office in the land sought its own way to stamp out the last vestige of the Puritan Commonwealth. Another wave of repressive measures ensued from the Glorious Revolution of 1688. A number of High Church clergy refused to accept the legitimacy of the reign of William and Mary, arguing that James II was still the Lord's anointed king to whom they owed loyalty. These nonjurors, as they were called, lost their clerical jobs on February 1, 1690, after first suffering suspension, and the Church lost their services. Thus, the leadership of the "Catholic" wing of the Anglican Church was gone in 1691 just as the "Protestant" wing had been cast out thirty years earlier. The result was an emasculated church. "The 'moderate,' 'reasonable' men, the time-servers, self-seekers and pluralists—these all were left: but the wings of faith were gone. Had the 'National' Church studied how best to extinguish all spiritual fire within the realm and to crush all crusading initiative, she could have devised no better plan than these two tragic expulsions."[1] English life thus entered the eighteenth century, as one historian describes it, "like the surface of the moon . . . pockmarked with extinct religious volcanic craters."[2]

That judgment may seem overstated, but contemporaries were saying similar things. Here is Bishop Butler in the Advertisement to the first edition of his *Analogy of Religion,* published in 1736:

> It is come, I know not how, to be taken for granted, by many persons, that Christianity is not so much as a subject of inquiry; but that it is, not at length, discovered to be fictitious. And accordingly they treat it, as if, in the present age, this were an agreed point among all people of discernment; and nothing remained, but to set it up as a principal subject of mirth and ridicule, as it were by way of reprisals, for its having so long interrupted the pleasures of the world.[3]

Two years later, Bishop Berkeley, writing in his *Discourse Addressed to Magistrates and Men in Authority,* declared that the state of religion and morality had utterly collapsed, and to a greater extent than had ever been seen in any Christian country. "Our prospect is very terrible and the symptoms grow worse from day to day."[4] That same year Thomas Secker, bishop of Oxford, lamented in an episcopal charge that the open detestation of religion had become "the distinguishing character of the age."[5] Across the Channel, Montesquieu wrote in 1730 that "there is no religion in England. If anyone mentions religion people begin to laugh."[6] Although the generalization gradually became obsolete as the decades wore on, in pockets at least the same phenomenon could always be found. When in the 1790s Hannah More's efforts to reform Cheddar ran into fierce opposition, the *Christian Observer* claimed that it was not her supposed Methodism (she was never, in fact, a Methodist) that inflamed her detractors but the hatred of religion among the wealthier people in the district.[7] William Wilberforce confided to John Harford that his *Practical View of the Prevailing Religious System of Professed Christians* of 1797 was motivated largely by his daily meeting with MPs, men of education, wealth, and position who were largely ignorant of the faith most of them professed.[8]

The educational institutions retained traces of the legacy of unbelief, or at least suspicion of religious zeal, until the 1830s and perhaps later. Six evangelical students were expelled from St. Edmund Hall, Oxford, in 1768 for their religious zeal, and undergraduates were prohibited from entering St. Mary Magdalene Church, which was the only Evangelical church in the city. Cambridge was worse, and Evangelicals found it very difficult to get their candidates for holy orders admitted.[9] The public schools were a religious desert. Near the end of the century, Charles Simeon, who was to lead the Evangelical renewal at Cambridge, found that religious instruction at Eton was virtually nonexistent, even though the staff was clerical.[10] William Gladstone, born in 1809, recalled his days at Eton: "The actual teaching of Christianity was all but dead, though happily none of its forms had been surrendered."[11] George Moberly, who later became headmaster of Winchester, wrote of his undergraduate days at Oxford University in the 1820s that "the tone of young men, . . . whether they came from Winchester, Eton, Rugby, Harrow, or wherever else, was universally irreligious."[12]

Although the official religious establishment of the country was and remained Protestant Christianity, there were other religious manifestations. Even well into the Victorian period (and perhaps up to the present day), there was plenty of evidence for what is often called "folk religion," a mixture of pagan beliefs and practices that are common in primitive societies but show up also when the formal religion of the respective regions is very different. When school inspectors began visiting out-of-the-way locations during the Victorian period, they discovered the persistence of this sort of thing in rural England. One of them found in the Pottery district "wild forms of religious belief" as well as infidelity. Another discovered odd and unexpected religious phenomena in his travels to Norfolk: "Here a wizard terrifying his neighbors by the power of inflicting injuries by his charms; there . . . a quack curing all diseases by his knowledge of the stars."[13] In South Lindsey, even where Christian worship was well attended, it often coincided with ideas and practices that had nothing to do with Christianity or that retained the form while investing it with something contrary. The countryman might regard the Sabbath as lucky rather than holy, or he might make the sign of the cross in order to nullify the bad luck that would come after he had seen a magpie or been so careless as to wash his hands in water that a preceding washer had used. A girl bent on finding whom she would marry would mutter incantations over a Bible, inside of which she had placed a house key. A striking feature of this folk religion, even when it was based on Christian elements, was the absence from it of Jesus Christ, who was, of course, the central figure in the Christian faith of the official religion.[14] Since folk religion lacked a settled body of teaching, there was no part of life where applications for it might not be found. The country was full of soothsayers of various kinds and medical experts whose extrascientific cures found ready customers. We have accounts of parents bringing tubercular children to the scaffold to be cured by running the hands of freshly executed criminals over their bodies; another remedy for the same disease was rubbing the patient with the body of a suitably prepared toad.[15]

In Cornwall, Methodism made strong inroads, particularly in the mining and fishing villages. But the old paganism continued side by side with the Methodists among those who practiced these dangerous trades. Sometimes its manifestations seemed to mark it as anti-Christian. Miners would not allow their comrades to make the sign of the cross while they were underground; fishermen would not push off from shore if a clergyman was in sight. The Cornish called underground spirits "knockers." They could bring good luck for those they favored by indicating the presence of rich ore with knocks of their hammers, but for skeptics they had only serious woe in store. Villagers might employ a witch to induce the knockers to bestow favor on them.[16]

None of this is to say that folk religion was an exact parallel to the official religion of the country. There were similarities, and for many people the first acted as a substitute for the second. But the collection of myths, remedies, occult practices, and other manifestations of folk religion did little more than provide protection against the contingencies of a difficult life. It had no explanation for the great issues of life and death, never explained human existence or held the promise of a future life. One specialist in this subject described it as "a collection of miscellaneous recipes."[17] It seldom penetrated to the educated because it had no intellectual content and because its many nostrums could not be reconciled with the science that was known.

Yet there were paganisms favored by the upper classes. Sometimes these were attempts to keep up with the fashions of the day, which, as we shall see, ran to unbelief, especially in the early eighteenth century. The infamous Medmenham Abbey group of "Franciscans"—named after their leader, Sir Francis Dashwood—mocked Christian ceremonies by holding their own pagan versions. (Aldous Huxley may have gotten from this group his idea for the communion services held in honor of "Our Ford" in *Brave New World*.) One young gentleman was described by the journalist Richard Steele (d. 1729) as "so ambitious to be thought worse than he is" that he debated in favor of atheism in the coffeehouses all day but was known to be saying his prayers morning and evening. Many of the upper class officials of the East India Company went native and, for political motives or out of sincerity, adopted Indian customs and religion. Job Charnock, the founder of Calcutta, openly adopted pagan practices and annually sacrificed a cock on the tomb of his native wife. Later on, officials trooped to pagan shrines to offer sacrifices of thanksgiving to the goddess Kali. Evangelicals, in particular, were incensed at the casual acceptance by these Englishmen of the most ferocious and bloody pagan customs, including widow burning.[18]

THE DEPRAVITIES OF ENGLISH LIFE

English society for much of its history has been exceedingly violent. The concern about crime that one sees in modern British newspapers is not something entirely new to the country but is rather a reversion to the conditions of a previous age.[19] In the eighteenth century, smuggling in the coastal areas and robbery almost everywhere were elements of daily life. Unaccompanied women were always in danger. A memoir of Oxford around 1790 speaks of the prevalence of highway robberies. Travelers learned to travel with pistols at the ready, and those who had banknotes sewed them into the lining of their clothing.[20] Blood sports were not confined to hunting and stalking but involved the joyful contemplation of animals and human beings inflicting suffering on each other. Scotland was much the same. Thomas Carlyle noted in his memoirs that his old hometown of Annandale had long been part of the lawless Border country and that in his youth the people had still showed the effects of that heritage. "The 'gallant man' of those districts was still a wild, almost animal man."[21]

It is hard to find an account of life in eighteenth-century England that does not speak of the disaster alcohol caused to millions of lives. Beginning in the reign of George I, the taste for gin became characteristic of the English palate. When it reached the lower classes, the public menace could no longer be hidden. In 1736 the Justices of the Peace of Middlesex County expressed their alarm in a petition to Parliament, pointing out that "the drinking of Geneva had for some years past greatly increased, especially among the people of inferior rank, and that the constant and excessive use thereof had destroyed thousands of people, that it had contributed to the spread of thieving and other enormities, and that it had resulted in the halter gracing the necks of many."[22] Contemporary accounts blamed alcohol for extraordinarily elevated death rates and also for diminished birthrates. A high percentage of infants born to drinking mothers were and remained sickly, many dying while very young. The liquor trade was encouraged by the corruption of the Parliament, as distillers were spared onerous provisions of the law that hobbled other businesses.[23]

When the Puritan regime ended after Oliver Cromwell's death, the licentious period for which the Restoration became famous had its beginning. Debauchery became fashionable, from the court of Charles II to each succeeding layer of rank below. The libertine ideal captured the imagination of the opinion molders and their followers. That set the style for the remainder of the seventeenth century and the one that followed as well. The notion that married people were to be monogamous had been completely cast aside by the upper classes. In the reign of Queen Anne it was said that "if men had gone into mourning for the immorality of their wives, sisters and daughters, half the Court would have been continually in black," and matters became worse under the Georges. Diaries and novels from the period show the abandon of the nobility.[24] With the indignation of a late Victorian, the historian George Otto Trevelyan wrote of the Whig politician Charles James Fox (d. 1806) that the peculiarity of his period was "that men of age and standing, of strong mental powers and refined cultivation, lived openly, shamelessly, and habitually, in the face of all England, as no one who had any care for his reputation would not live during a single fortnight of the year at Monaco."[25] Trevelyan did not mean that the Victorian ideal of chastity was the historical norm but rather that it was an aberration that men who were in the light of public scrutiny should so openly live as Fox and his contemporaries did.

The story of Sir Walter Scott's great-aunt Mrs. Keith of Ravelstone has been told many times. In the 1820s she asked Scott if he would procure for her the novels of Aphra Behn, which she had enjoyed when a young woman and which she and her friends had read aloud to each other. Scott demurred on the grounds that the books were not proper, but when she insisted, he sent them to her in a package marked "private and confidential." When he saw her next, she turned the books over to him and recommended that he burn them. She had found it impossible to finish the first novel, and she mused how odd it was that at more than eighty years of age she felt ashamed to read alone what high society had been reading openly sixty years earlier. Francis Place, known as the "radical tailor," noted in his autobiography a similar sort of experience, although he was on the opposite end of the social spectrum. By the age of thirteen there was little he did not know about sex, since there was far less reticence on such things at that time than in the England of his maturity. "Conversation on these matters was much less reserved than it is now, books relating to the subject were much more within the reach of boys and girls than they are now, and I had little to learn on any part of the subject."[26] Place drew a dismaying picture of the London of his youth in the 1780s and 1790s, so dissolute that he was apprehensive that modern people would not believe his story. And he was speaking of ordinary lower class people, not those he considered to be the dregs of society:

> The circumstances which it will be seen I have mentioned relative to the ignorance, the immorality, the grossness, the obscenity, the drunkenness, the dirtiness, and depravity of the middling and even of a large portion of the better sort of tradesmen, the artizans, and the journeymen tradesmen of London in the days of my youth, may excite a suspicion that the picture I have drawn is a caricature, the parts of which are out of keeping and have no symmetry as a whole.[27]

Place feared being taken as a limner of caricatures, but we get the same picture in the work of a real caricaturist. The prints of William Hogarth (d. 1764) show a variety of terrible scenes that could have been used to illustrate Place's autobiography, though he lived earlier.[28] Halévy, among others, wrote graphically of the degradation into which miners of both sexes had sunk: "The miners lived . . . like absolute savages both in the dirty and ruined villages in which they spent the night and in the subterranean galleries where of necessity there was less supervision than in the workshops of a factory . . . haggard faces and ruffianlike figures. . . . the most bestial debauchery."[29] The miners may have been an exaggerated case, but the morals of the lower classes improved only gradually during the pre-Victorian period. There is no reason to doubt the judgment of Place and others that the situation was much improved by the 1830s, but even then there were plenty of concerns. The Factory Commission in 1833 reported that the workers did not seem to be more immoral than people in other lines of work, but the impression one gets is that the general level was still lower than the authorities would have liked. Immorality among domestic servants and dressmakers was reputed to be high, and among plaiters prostitution was rife. Evidently the common element among them was a lack of moral teaching in the communities.[30]

Hannah More, the most prolific and possibly the most effective of the Evangelical writers, tied the state of morals to the low esteem for Christianity among the populace. She said that since virtues are the product of "secret habits of self-control," they do not come without effort and training and that where those are lacking, moral life suffers.[31] More, however, was not denouncing ordinary people; rather, she was demanding that the upper classes conduct themselves in a manner that would provide a decent model for others to follow.

Moderns have often disdained the Victorian penchant for respectability, sobriety, and cleanliness, but they should examine the corruption and brutality against which their forebears were reacting. Beginning under Charles II, bribery of government officials became commonplace, and Walpole's remark about the members of Parliament that "all these men have their price" was a fair description of the situation, including Walpole's own part in it. The savagery of the legal system may be judged by the fact that more than 150 offenses were capital crimes—including picking pockets, shoplifting, animal stealing, breaking a young tree, snatching a piece of fruit, poaching, and appearing on a high road in blackface. Charles Wesley once visited a jail in which fifty-two felons, among them a child of ten, were awaiting the noose. A parliamentary committee in 1728–29 found that the "gross cruelties" under which prisoners suffered, even those in prison as debtors, were tantamount to "deliberate torture." But reform did not follow until many years later, when John Wesley's disciple John Howard awakened the conscience of the nation.[32] Accounts of Cornwall in the mid-eighteenth century—"West Barbary" in the popular vernacular—reveal public flogging, hangings as popular entertainment for all classes, lunatics displayed in cages to amuse the public, and a variety of ills caused by widespread drunkenness. Wakes were scenes of great revelry, with all-night drinking parties taking place alongside the corpse.[33]

The ill effects of widespread drunkenness persisted until well into the nineteenth century. This was partly because unsafe drinking water prompted the use of alcohol to quench the thirst. Even hospitals in London fed their patients intoxicating beverages for this reason. Drink also served important social functions. It was supposed to impart extra energy for demanding occasions; for men, drinking provided a demonstration of virility, and getting a lad drunk was the way for a father to celebrate his son's coming of age. Public speakers, preachers as well as politicians, received confidence from a few drinks.[34] There were many reasons why people allowed alcohol to wreck their lives, but when drinking heavily became an act required for social acceptance, it passed from an individual problem to a social pathology of great significance for the country.

INTELLECTUAL FACTORS IN THE DECLINE

Tendencies in eighteenth-century intellectual life further weakened the Christian heritage of the country. The emphasis on the "Author of Nature" in the Newtonian worldview furthered an Arian doctrine of Christ as the subordinate messenger of the Father, facilitating the wider acceptance of Unitarianism.[35] The universities, formally Anglican, were in a state of advanced decrepitude, such that a modern *defense* of Oxford and Cambridge in the eighteenth century acknowledges that degree requirements were "farcical . . . a joke even to contemporaries," with the graduates for the most part remaining ignorant. One candidate for a Cambridge doctorate was caught off guard at being asked whether it was the sun that turned around the earth or the reverse. Unsure of the answer, he assumed a confident air and replied: "Sometimes the one, sometimes the other." Struck by the hilarity of the moment, the examiners made him a doctor on the spot.[36] The universities improved in the next century, but slowly, and not decisively until around midcentury. The dyspeptic Mark Pattison, rector of Lincoln College, Oxford, recalled of his student days at the university in the 1830s that even the best students had "no inner life, no capacity of being moved by poetry, by natural beauty." They were not intellectually alive, "never haunted by the ideal, or baffled by philosophical perplexities."[37] Speaking of an earlier period, Leslie Stephen said much the same of the intellectual life of the whole country when he wrote of the "strange decline of speculative energy" in the last half of the eighteenth century.[38]

The eighteenth century is often thought of as coldly rationalistic, a characteristic succeeded by Romanticism and Victorian sentimentality. But studies of the literature of the period suggest that almost the opposite is true. Some analysts are impressed by the self-indulgence of the fiction of the earlier period, an egoistic and complacent self-concern. "Tears are too facile, too enjoyable, and the sensible heart is too much like an Æolian harp, designed to be susceptible and placed in the position where it will be most affected."[39] Poetry tended to a sentimentality that was the opposite of the Christian thinking that, as we have seen, lost ground early in the century. It was tied to a non-Christian anthropology that saw man as fundamentally good rather than fundamentally flawed. As the century wore on, the paganism of the poetry moderated, perhaps under the influence of the slow spread of the evangelical revival and the loosening of rationalism's grip on the English spirit. The sentimentalist might even call himself a Christian, but analysis of the poetry reveals "Christianity sentimentalized, or the cult of feeling with a Christian tinge."[40]

THE STATE OF THE CHURCH OF ENGLAND IN THE EIGHTEENTH CENTURY

Given the low level of vitality of the Christian religion in much of eighteenth-century England, it is only natural to wonder about what the

Church of England was like in the period. It was the Established religion, and its temporal head was the king. There were other Christian bodies, but their status was expressed in negatives—"nonjurors," "Dissenters," "Nonconformists." One way to describe the Church's posture in that age is to reflect on the use of the word *enthusiasm*. This was taken to be not a praiseworthy description of zeal in the execution of a good work but rather a byword for spiritual self-importance, for zealous execution of a task that one has presumptuously taken as a commission from God. And the virtue that corresponded to this vice seemed in practice to be a sluggish acceptance of whatever mode of thought and action one's predecessors found acceptable. An Anglican assessment calls the era "the Glacial Epoch in our Church History."[41] When William Wilberforce's sons wrote of the conversion that had set their father on his life's course, they said—as no doubt they had heard him say—"He had been roused out of a deadly lethargy."[42] An observer from the 1830s looked back on the previous century and concluded that the Church then had valued "a regard to decency—a sort of ecclesiastical decorum" in which the gospel could not be easily discerned.[43] Gladstone wrote a letter to his father in which he expressed his sense of unity with the Evangelicals, while desiring a "more comprehensive" system than theirs. But the kind of religion with which he had no sympathy at all, one that had plagued the Church of England in the eighteenth century, was the Protestant Anglicanism that "lowered and almost paganised doctrine, loosened and destroyed discipline, and much defaced, in contempt of law the decent and beautiful order of the Church."[44]

Gladstone's complaint was that the teachings of the Church had come to comport little with the heritage of the centuries. The famous jurist Sir William Blackstone told of visiting the churches of note in London early in the reign of George III and hearing not a single sermon he would identify as Christian. For all he could tell, the preachers might as well have been followers of Confucius or Mohammed as of Christ.[45] An exaggeration for effect, no doubt, but still indicative of the impression the experience made on Blackstone. The turning of the century worked no magic on the preaching of the Church. Leigh Hunt, radical journalist, recalled the clergymen who preached at his school and who made no impression whatever on him or his fellows, except insofar as their speech mannerisms could be imitated and ridiculed.[46] Other writers had similar memories. J. A. Froude, disciple and biographer of Carlyle, was the son of a rector and archdeacon. His father was a clergyman, a magistrate, a member of the landed interest, and an expert on art and antiquities. "About doctrine, Evangelical or [Anglo-] Catholic," Froude recalled, "I do not think that in my early boyhood I ever heard a single word."[47] (Froude was the younger brother of Hurrell Froude, the Tractarian leader at Oxford, of whom we shall hear later.)

Modern analysts have arrived at the same view of the spiritual Establishment as did those contemporary voices. A Roman Catholic historian puzzled over the fact that in England, unlike France, there was no violent outburst against the Church from the Deists of the eighteenth century. He concluded that such hostility would have made no sense in England because the two parties were so close in spirit. Churchmen and Deists alike were passionate believers in progress, optimism, and political and social reform, and not much else.[48] The Hammonds had not the slightest respect for evangelicalism—"That movement would have embarrassed any Church"—but they did not think it a mystery that it was resented and feared by the "sleepy . . . Establishment of the eighteenth century, with its languid and polite piety, its sensible and conventional sermons, and its free pagan life."[49]

If the teaching of the Church of England did not center on its historic message, if it was known more for its complacency than its fervor, how did it conceive of its mission? Its mission, though unstated by some central authority, was to improve the morals of the nation. At least, that is the gist of the reports we have of the era. Eighteenth-century religion had become for many merely a practical rule of life. Since the old sanctions seemed to be losing their force, being no longer believed, how could society maintain its cohesion? Numerous philosophers addressed this question—Locke, Hume, Smith, for example—and so did Churchmen, often to the exclusion of other matters. But morality to the exclusion of other matters was no longer connected with the moral teachings of the Christian tradition. Something was missing. Gladstone thought back to his childhood and noted that morality in those days was taught "without direct derivation from, or reference to, the Person of Christ," which should have given pause to more Churchmen than it did.[50] For, even apart from the question of the integrity of the Christian message, the preaching of morality apart from any deeper *basis* for the teaching appeared futile, as the course of society's morality seemed to prove. "We have preached morality so long," exclaimed a Methodist preacher, "that we have hardly any morality left."[51]

James Boswell once confided to Wilberforce that Dr. Johnson had never known a single clergyman he would consider religious.[52] Some time about 1835, Sydney Smith, the canon of St. Paul's who seemed never to be without a wry quip, remarked to Gladstone at a dinner party, "Whenever you meet a clergyman of my age you may be quite sure he is a bad clergyman."[53] And by that time the quality of the clergy had much improved! The poet George Crabbe, who was himself a clergyman, wrote of the parson of the Vale of Belvoir:

> A jovial youth, who thinks his Sunday's task,
> As much as GOD or Man can fairly ask;
> The rest he gives to Loves and Labours light,
> To Fields the morning and to Feasts the night;
> None better skill'd the noisy Pack to guide,
> To urge their chase, to cheer them or to chide;
> A Sportsman keen, he shoots through half the day,
> And skill'd at Whist, devotes the night to play;
> Then, while such honours bloom around his head,
> Shall he sit sadly by the Sick Man's bed,
> To raise the hope he feels not, or with zeal
> To combat fears that ev'n the pious feel?[54]

These lines of Crabbe's were not marked by poetic license. Pastoral positions—"livings" in the apt terminology of the time—were mostly at the disposal of persons, usually laymen, who dealt them out as they saw fit—to sons, to friends, to the sons of friends, to repay some obligation or other. Sometimes livings were offered to men with genuine religious vocations, but that qualification was not often deemed necessary. Henry Hunt, the well-known radical orator, was offered by his father a living from which he would receive £1,000 a year and "have nothing else to do for six days out of seven but to hunt, shoot, and fish by day, and play cards, talk scandal with the old maids of the parish, and win the money of the wives and children of your parish at speculation. . . . All that will be expected of you is to read prayers and preach a sermon, which will cost you threepence once a week, or by a visit to the metropolis you can lay in a stock of manuscript sermons which will last you for the whole of your life."[55]

The Anglican Evangelical newspaper, the *Record*, published the sad numbers of nonworking clergy for the year 1814. The paper found that 5,088 clergymen were discharging their duties in the parish, though not all were resident in them. The number of nonresident clergy doing no service in their parishes was 4,803. These were all *beneficed* clergy, receiving the livings from the parishes, whether or not they were doing anything to earn their pay.[56]

The reaction of ordinary English people to the state of the Established Church was just as we should expect. Working people favored the churches with their absence, and later on, when the Establishment revived, it was faced with the problem of attracting families who had not in living memory darkened its doors. Bishop Butler of Hereford compared Church attendance in his diocese in 1792 with the numbers from 1747 and found a substantial decline. In 1800 in the diocese of Lincoln, England's largest, Evangelical clergymen found that of 15,000 persons in seventy-nine parishes, fewer than 5,000 were known to attend Church; of these, only 1,800 were communicants. Many of the nonattenders had gone over to Dissent, but there was still a very low level of religious participation. In 1799, Bishop Cleaver of Chester, a highly industrial region, discovered a parish of 40,000 in which nobody attended religious services of any kind.[57] Thomas Arnold of Rugby later concluded that the reason for the Church's great unpopularity was the widespread disgust with abuses and corruption, the patronage that induced parsons to incline to the aristocracy and gentry rather than to the souls of the masses.[58] Modern analysts, too, conclude that organizational matters were primary. The Church's position as the Establishment is a particular villain in this view, largely because it put the Church under the control of the state, a relationship that had the effect of placing handcuffs on its ministry.[59] Others point to the internal migrations that left newly settled industrial regions bereft of churches.[60] But these assessments do not consider adequately the spiritual impoverishment of the clergy and the ineffectiveness of institutions that were not corrupt. Francis Place recalled that in his school the teaching of religion was done by someone who evidently believed in none of it, an observation that was influential in his own rejection of religion.[61] The authors of the bicentennial history of the Society for Promoting Christian Knowledge (SPCK) entitled Chapter 15 of their book "Evangelization of the Masses," but they should rather have entitled it "The SPCK Refuses to Evangelize the Masses." Among the few poor entries in the chapter, there is nothing for the period between 1703 and 1825, which is a good indication of what the organization had become. But the very existence of the chapter shows a bad conscience about the fact.[62]

What of Dissent? If the Church was cold and ineffective, perhaps those who were religious but refused to be part of it had the determination and resources to accomplish their mission. That seems not to have been the case. William Jay, a Dissenting minister born in 1769, thought that the Dissenters were to blame for the growth of Methodism. Their ministers were well educated and well spoken, in contrast to the rank and file of Methodist lay preachers, but their sermons were, "with a very few exceptions, pointless, cold, and drawled off from notes." Instead of seeing the successes of the "boisterous, rude, coarse, incoherent" Methodist preachers as a judgment on their own proud ineffectiveness, thus leading them to repentance and reform, they maintained their disastrous course.[63] John Newton, former slaving captain who became an Evangelical parson and loyal Churchman, wrote in a letter that the Dissenters of the seventeenth century had been more serious Christians than their counterparts in the Church. But in the eighteenth century they had turned to Socinianism (the common term for Unitarianism), which Newton called "another word for infidelity."[64] The Presbyterians, more than any of the other Dissenting groups, turned their backs on their own reformed heritage and became Unitarian.[65] The general decay of Dissenting orthodoxy was widely remarked at the time, and some observers held it to be much more serious than in the Church because Dissent lacked the structures of authority that might have worked toward correcting the situation.[66]

Our interest here is principally in England, but we may note in passing that the situation was little different in Wales and Scotland. Dissent was especially strong in Wales, but by the end of the eighteenth century the decline was evident. In Carw Hill at that time, there was said to be only one communicant member left. In one town of 500 there were reputed to be 80 who made a profession of religion, our informant adding, "and among these not unlikely some hypocrites, tho' I hope not very many." Those numbers increased in the first two decades of the next century, but at a rate below the population increase. According to the testimony of the Welsh themselves, the land was in the eighteenth century a place of almost unrelieved ignorance, vice, and drunkenness.[67]

In Scotland the situation was similar. Some of Wilberforce's Clapham colleagues were of Scottish origin, and they have left us testimony about their younger days. Zachary Macaulay reminisced about his student life in Glasgow and the way in which older students used their influence "in eradicating from my mind every trace of religious belief." Some of those men had gone into the Christian ministry, and Macaulay recalled sadly that their beliefs were unchanged. James Stephen reported rarely staying home of an afternoon or evening; he spent his time in hard drinking and gambling. Being able to hold one's alcohol was in his circles a "matter of emulation and boast."[68] The Presbyterian Establishment for the most part resembled its counterpart south of the Tweed in apathy and neglect.[69]

In summing up the spiritual temper of the country, we shall not go far wrong in quoting Halévy, providing we recognize a bit of rhetorical exuberance: "An Established Church apathetic, sceptical, lifeless; sects weakened by rationalism, unorganized, their missionary spirit extinct. This was English Protestantism in the eighteenth century."[70] Riding in a stagecoach, a traveler heard this fragment of a conversation: "Well, what *is* the Church of England?" "The Church of England," came the reply, "is a damn big building with an organ inside." That is the way William Gladstone remembered the conversation and the way he told it at innumerable dinner parties for the remainder of his life.[71] And that is the way English people tended to regard their Establishment in the waning years of the eighteenth century and for some time afterwards, which is the point Gladstone was making. When Wilberforce wrote his *Practical View* in 1797, it was not to persuade the skeptic to mend his ways but rather to "point out the scanty and erroneous system of the bulk of those who belong to the class of Orthodox Christians."[72] *Orthodoxy* used in this sense became a common expression in the next half century. It did not refer to a standard of truth as against heresy, which is the common meaning, but rather to the low standards of the Georgian Establishment, with its latitudinarian ersatz theology and its moral failure. The widespread use of this term indicates the impression that the bulk of the Church made on observers like Wilberforce. Even in 1818 there was considerable pessimism about the Church, and Southey, the poet laureate, in a conversation with Wilberforce referred to the clergy as "marrying and christening machines."[73]

I suggested earlier a bit of rhetorical excess in Halévy's description of English religion in the eighteenth century. That qualification comes from stirrings during the period that foreshadowed the revolution that would be coming. One Victorian analyst, whose work was much quoted at the time, believed that the Church of England had reached its lowest point during the first thirty years of the reign of George III, which is to say 1760 to 1790. During that dreary period, he said, the Church was in its period of "frozen lifelessness. . . . The spirit was expelled, and the dregs remained."[74] But even then, the multitudes of ordinary people, neglected by the Church that was appointed to care for their souls, came under the ministry of the Wesley brothers as the Methodist movement was born in the 1730s and spread throughout much of England and Wales and even across the ocean to the North American colonies. Here and there in the parishes of England as well—in Truro, in Huddersfield, in Olney, and elsewhere—a parish priest would regain the vision that had so long been lost, and a spiritual renewal would begin. As the century wore on, such parsons became less isolated, began informal associations, started publications, and ultimately changed their culture. How that began is what we need to consider next.

First Bounce

EIGHTEENTH-CENTURY
ORIGINS OF THE REVIVAL

ALTHOUGH ENGLAND AFTER THE RESTORATION of the monarchy began imitating an increasingly dissolute court, it was not left without the means for renewal. There were rich resources in the national religious tradition that had the potential for lifting it from the state into which it had descended. When the long process toward reform began before the middle of the eighteenth century, it did so in two streams. The Methodist stream begun by the Wesley brothers organized small groups of poor people into local "classes" over much of the kingdom, although in clumps rather than evenly. At about the same time, in scattered parishes from Yorkshire to Cornwall, dedicated clergymen caught a vision for what the Church of England could be that had seemingly departed from the land. Both streams arose out of the Church of England, and both were evangelical in theology, but only the second of them was firmly based in the Anglican parish system.

ANTECEDENTS OF THE RELIGIOUS REVIVAL

It would be surprising if Restoration decadence should not have provoked a backlash of some sort. The turn toward morality, eventually Victorian morality, is sometimes interpreted almost exclusively as an equal and opposite reaction, much like the reactions that Newton discovered for physical forces.[1] There is in these formulations a sense of necessity, as if people behave in the same predictable ways as physical forces. The documents available to us do not seem to provide much evidence of that. Yet the society at its worst moments had within itself the seeds of its own regeneration. Gordon Rupp points to a lively reforming literature in the Restoration period, both Puritan and orthodox Anglican, and to the lay organization of religious societies. Thus the Evangelical revival did not arise ex nihilo but had roots in the preceding period. One such group that formed in the late seventeenth century, the Society of St. Giles, came mainly from the artisan class; it was composed of skilled workers, young and moderately literate, and all members of the Church of England. Their first rule was "that all that entered . . . should resolve upon a holy and serious life, that the sole design of this society being to promote real holiness of heart and life, it is absolutely necessary that the persons who enter into it do seriously resolve to apply themselves in good earnest to all means proper to make them wise unto salvation." Their meetings were led by clergymen of the Established Church, using the Liturgy and Psalter. They paid sixpence a week for their membership and assessed themselves fines for missing meetings, giving most of the money so raised to charity.[2] These societies, Rupp concludes, "were the soil in which the Evangelical Revival was rooted."[3] More than twenty years after he founded the Methodists, John Wesley linked his movement to predecessors who provided the example of the small group dedicated to spiritual growth that he was to put to such effective use.

However eclipsed the old Anglican Puritans were by the reaction of 1660, their thinking was never far from the surface. The introspective piety, the reliance on biblical teaching, the demand that the whole society reflect the godly inheritance of the faith broke out from time to time, usually without creating more than a local stir. But the evangelical revival that began in the eighteenth century bore more than a trace of the same characteristics. David Bebbington's definition of the traits of evangelicalism seems to have received general acceptance. He lists four qualities that set evangelicals apart from other Protestants of the period: (1) conversionism, the belief that people can be changed fundamentally through repentance and faith in Christ; (2) activism, the readiness of the converted person to vigorously pursue courses of action in keeping with the mandates of Christian faith; (3) biblicism, a reliance on the Bible for religious authority; and (4) crucicentrism, a stress on the sacrifice of Christ as grounds for forgiveness for sin. These four characteristics are not unique to any one party in the Church of England or to any other Christian body. As Bebbington recognizes, often the only thing that distinguishes evangelicals from others is how this or that point is emphasized.[4]

The Dissenting minister William Law (1686–1761) put some of the elements of the old piety into contemporary form and had an extraordinary influence on people of widely divergent perspectives: the Wesley brothers, Samuel Johnson, and the Tractarians of the next century, for example. His books criticized sharply the latitudinarianism of the society and appealed to those who were seeking something deeper. Most often quoted was the *Serious Call to a Devout and Holy Life* (1729), which offered an ascetic approach to Christian faith. Law's later work was more mystical in its emphasis, an outlook that found fewer followers, perhaps because Law seemed to find dispensable the keystone doctrine of the Atonement. In the year that Law published the *Serious Call,* Wesley and the "Holy Club" began meeting at Oxford. Wesley used to walk all the way to Putney to see Law. Later, Law's failure to affirm the Atonement led Wesley to caution his followers against his writings. In 1749, Wesley wrote about Law's new book *The Spirit of Prayer:* "It is another gospel."[5] One of the best known of the early Evangelical clergymen, Henry Venn, followed Law as a young man but eventually realized that the way of moral reformation contradicted the evangelical understanding of the way of the cross and so jettisoned his former master's teachings.[6] Nevertheless, the "serious call" aspect of Law's *Serious Call* appealed to evangelicals for many decades after his death, and if they did not continue with him, many were happy to give him the credit for starting them on the right path. Thomas Coke, one of Wesley's right-hand men, referred to Law as "the great forerunner of the Revival which followed, and did more to promote it than any other individual whatsoever."[7] That is why John Walsh calls Law "an awakening rather than a converting influence."[8]

THE EARLY METHODIST MOVEMENT

The revival started in Wales even before the Wesleyan movement began. It was largely the inspiration of Griffith Jones (1684–1761), an Anglican priest, whose base remained for much of his life the parish of Llandowror. In the 1730s, while the Society for Promoting Christian Knowledge (SPCK) was founding English-language schools in Wales, Jones began to build Welsh-language schools, teaching literacy through the use of the Welsh Bible. By the time of his death, according to some estimates, he had founded more than 3,000 schools, taught some 150,000 people to read, and distributed 30,000 copies of the Welsh Bible. These schools republished many of the old Puritan devotional books in Welsh, including Bunyan's *Pilgrim's Progress.* Jones, good Churchman that he was, opposed the itinerancy of the Welsh lay preachers but still remained a mentor to the young evangelists.[9]

Whatever reservations the later evangelicals may have developed about William Law, when they first read the *Serious Call,* it was like a beacon on a dark night. The Wesley brothers and their friends at Oxford took to it with enthusiasm, following its advice in their Bible studies and prayer meetings. Formally Anglican, Oxford was in the main godless, and this odd group was given such names as the "Bible Moths" or "Holy Club" until a name was dredged up from antiquity that seemed to fit their regular pious habits, and they became the *Methodists.* By 1735 there were fourteen of them meeting at Oxford, at first in John Wesley's quarters at Lincoln College. With the activism that would later characterize the movement, they began to minister to the prisoners at the Oxford castle, first obtaining the permission of the bishop. They read aloud from *The Country Parson's Advice to His Parishioners*. They used the Litany on Wednesdays and Fridays and began Sunday afternoon services with a sermon. From the castle they expanded to Bocardo and the debtors' prison and also started a school in the slums of Oxford.[10]

On May 24, 1738, having returned from a dispiriting stint as a missionary in Georgia, John Wesley had his famous experience in a Moravian meeting on Aldersgate Street, not far from St. Paul's cathedral. Wesley had earlier met the Moravians aboard ship on his outbound journey to the colonies and had been impressed by their piety. Now he heard something on Aldersgate Street that changed the rest of his life, and English history as well. As the leader read from Luther's preface to St. Paul's epistle to the Romans, something was happening in Wesley's consciousness. "About a quarter before nine, while he was describing the change which God works in the heart through faith in Christ I felt my heart strangely warmed, I felt I did trust in Christ, Christ alone, for salvation, and an assurance was given me that he had taken away my sins, even mine, and saved me from the law of sin and death." Thus the classic evangelical conversion experience, which Wesley and his followers, the Evangelical parsons, and innumerable Dissenting ministers preached and to whom many thousands responded. The life-changing impact of this experience explains why Wesley and so many others held firmly against doctrinal teaching that made conversion seem dispensable. The calls to moral reformation without reliance on God's grace seemed only to bring people to a state of frustration at their inability to reform themselves. This was the conclusion Wesley reached after two years of preaching Law's treatises. Wesley wrote to Law to inquire why he did not counsel his readers to rely on Christ rather than on their own righteousness. "If you say you advised other things as preparatory to this, what is this but laying a foundation below the foundation. . . . I beseech you, sir, by the mercies of God to consider . . . whether the true reason of your never pressing this upon me, was not this, that you had it not yourself?"[11]

Wesley's most famous colleague on the Methodist preaching circuit was George Whitefield, a member of the original Holy Club at Oxford. Whitefield was also an Anglican priest, and his itinerancy covered much of England, Wales, Scotland, and the American colonies. He became a close friend of men of renown who did not agree with his religious position—Benjamin Franklin, for example. Lord Bolingbroke had many private conversations with him, although remaining a Deist. He wrote to Whitefield's sponsor that Whitefield "is the most extraordinary man in our times. He has the most commanding eloquence I ever heard in any person."[12] In addition to

JOHN WESLEY.
By courtesy of the National Portrait Gallery, London.

his eloquence, he had the sponsorship of Lady Huntingdon, the daughter and wife of earls, whose conversion was followed by a lifetime of struggle to extend the gospel to her fellow peers. She arranged for chapels to be built in Bath, Brighton, and elsewhere, staffed by Evangelical clergymen, and for Whitefield to preach to her friends in her home. That probably accounts in part for Horace Walpole's remark in 1749 that Methodism, the religion preached to and by the poor, was in London highly fashionable, especially among the ladies.[13] On special occasions, such as funerals, tickets had to be issued for the high-born to enter the chapels. When some of the peers complained to George III about Lady Huntingdon, he replied, "I wish there was a Lady Huntingdon in every diocese of the kingdom."[14]

Whitefield's wing of Methodism eventually was mostly lost to the Anglican church, many of his adherents becoming Dissenters. Lady Huntingdon was forced to register her chapels as Dissenting places of worship. Her chaplains thereupon resigned, and her followers gradually lost contact with the clergy. Almost from the start there was considerable strain between the Wesleys and the bulk of the Methodists on the one hand and Whitefield and his followers on the other. The main cause was that the Wesleys were Arminians, believing that the sacrifice of Christ was for all men and that all who repented and believed could receive its benefits. Whitefield's Calvinism put the emphasis on another doctrine in the New Testament, that of *election*, which held that God would determine who was saved by an act of his sovereign will, which no human action could change. For something like a half century, this controversy divided the Methodists and later performed the same disservice among the non-Methodist Evangelicals. It finally died away in the nineteenth century, when there remained very few who were willing to be identified with the strict Calvinist position. When Wesley preached Whitefield's funeral sermon at the Tottenham Court Road Chapel in November 1770, he alluded to their differences as mere opinions and affirmed that on the essential doctrines of the faith he and Whitefield were as one. He would regard himself as a "bigot" if he were to attack a man on the basis of an opinion. He also expressed doubt that there was any difference between his own thinking and Calvin's, making it seem as if Calvin himself would not have been a Calvinist.[15]

Some idea of the ambivalence with which Wesley has been regarded by the Church of England may be seen in the thought of Sabine Baring-Gould, a remarkably productive clergyman (160 books, fifteen children) who was born in 1834 and lived until after World War I. He became known not only as a controversialist but also as a novelist and hymn writer, having written the immensely popular hymn *Onward Christian Soldiers*. Baring-Gould was a convinced High Churchman. He knew many of the leaders of the High Church Tractarian movement and was highly learned about virtually everything connected with the recent history of the Church of England. He wrote a history of the Evangelical movement but was largely hostile to it. He read Wesley's sermons and saw little of interest in them, concluding that Wesley must have been a hypnotist to secure the genuine religious conversion of so many English people. He disagreed with Wesley's doctrine of conversion, complaining that it followed Luther too closely, and—more remarkably—that it resembled something found in paganism. Baring-Gould had more complaints about evangelicalism, and Wesley's in particular, but that is enough to give the flavor. Yet he was completely unambiguous about the necessity of Wesley's work for the health of the Church of England and of the nation itself. "What stands out as an unimpeachable fact is that under the teaching of Wesley, multitudes of homely English folk who hitherto had not given much heed to religion at a bound attained to what appeared to them, and what actually was, a new life, the acquisition of a new faculty, like the opening of the eyes of one who had been born blind. They may not have seen correctly, may have seen men as trees walking, nevertheless they saw, who had never seen before." [16]

Observers of Baring-Gould's convictions might have withheld all praise from Wesley had his loyalty to the Church of England not been so complete. Unlike later Methodists and unlike many in Lady Huntingdon's circle, he refused to consider joining Dissent. "If ever the Methodists were to leave the Church, I must leave them," he wrote in 1783, and again in 1787: "When the Methodists leave the Church of England, God will leave them." Charles Wesley's journal contains even stronger determination than his brother's never to desert the Church, even insisting that he be buried in the parish church rather than at the meetinghouse, as some of the Methodists preferred. [17]

Although Wesley broke with the Moravians on the grounds of the quietism and antinomianism that was prevalent among their number in England, he was convinced by their example that he could remain a faithful clergyman in the Church of England while building the Methodist organization. Count Zinzendorf had led the Brethren in Germany as a church within the church and had divided his followers into bands. Wesley adapted much of their practice to the Methodist movement within the Church of England. Hence the solution that has seemed anomalous to many observers but which to Wesley was completely coherent: his complete loyalty to the Church of England and to his calling as a priest therein, along with the "Puritan" sentiments—as some termed them—that seemed incompatible with it. But any incompatibility was a matter only of historical precedent, not of internal contradiction. Wesley believed he was simply reviving an ancient tradition of the Christian church that had been allowed to fall into desuetude. [18]

Ultimately, of course, there was a separation. There is no doubt that many ordinary Methodists felt nothing of the loyalty that their leaders had for the Church, a Church that they believed had never done anything for them. And Churchmen in many ways showed their contempt for this movement within. From the start, the Wesleys and their followers ran into opposition. The preachers were physically assaulted by mobs of people who were often instigated by the upper classes. They were stoned, shot at, soaked by firehoses, and beaten. The clergy, on whose work the itinerant preachers cast at least an implicit criticism, were especially hostile. Wesley's *Journal* for April 17, 1743, records this experience at a preaching service: "While I was speaking a gentleman rode up very drunk; and after many unseemly and bitter words, laboured much to ride over some of the people. I was surprised to hear that he was a neighbouring clergyman!" [19] Apart from physical assaults, books and pamphlets by journalists, politicians, and literary people from almost every sector of the writing public assailed the various aspects of the revival. This pressure worsened after 1789, as fears of revolution and invasion from France put any kind of dissident movement under intense suspicion. In 1790 Lincolnshire magistrates unanimously confirmed a fine of £20 against a Methodist who had allowed a society meeting in his home. They ruled that the Act of Toleration did not apply in that case because they were Church attenders.[20] Thus, de facto, the Methodists eventually were expelled. But many did not go willingly. In 1811, when Lord Sidmouth was attempting to place restrictions on Dissent, the Methodist leader Adam Clarke testified before Parliament that Methodist preachers should not have to be licensed because *"we are not dissenters. In our doctrine, both religious and political, we are the same as the Established Church."*[21] Even at the end of the nineteenth century, there were Methodists who called themselves loyal members of the Church of England. But long before then, such people were anachronisms; the severance was complete.

REASON AND EXPERIENCE IN METHODISM

Emotion and reason, revelation and experience: these categories have been put forth by religious thinkers at least since the most logical and argumentative among the Apostles wrote, "Has not God made foolish the wisdom of the world?" (1 Cor. 1:20). The Puritans of the seventeenth century had dealt with the issue by emphasizing the intellectual heritage of the faith, reserving the emotional content for private contemplation. Their emotional literature has been called introspective rather than meant for public persuasion. The Wesleyan approach was different. John Wesley's preaching was among the least histrionic of the preachers of the revival, but the emotional content of the gospel message was not hidden; if this was to be a life-changing experience, it could not be treated as just another event. The hymns of Charles Wesley provide a musical version of his brother's sermons: they contain doctrinal teaching, public worship, a call to turn one's life over to God, and the frank recognition of the emotional excitement that it all entails. He was at once musician, preacher, teacher, transmitter of high culture from several languages, and cheerleader of the revival.[22] That ability to bring the whole person—mind, emotions, and spirit—into the orbit of his thinking and to persuade him or her to forsake all and follow Christ, as the Wesleys put it, is perhaps why the future poet laureate Robert Southey regarded John Wesley as "the most influential mind" of the eighteenth century.[23]

What intervened between the time of the Puritan ascendency and the more unrestrained nature of the revival of the eighteenth century? It has become apparent from recent scholarship that the philosophy of John Locke was a primary reason for the change, not least because Wesley was a close and dedicated student of the prophet of empirical epistemology. Richard Brantley, who has made the major recent contribution to our understanding of Locke's role in the revival, concluded that the Lockean emphasis on experience as the source of knowledge was a major component of Wesley's theology and subsequently of the Romantic revolution in sensibility. Locke's theory of knowledge formed the intellectual grounding of the Wesleyan movement, lending to it the conviction that true knowledge came from sense perception along with reason. The senses and the intellectual components of the process together made real knowledge possible. "Locke's rational empiricism (i.e., his epistemology of sense perception attended by induction and deduction) directly informs the religious 'epistemology' whereby Wesley claimed the saving faith he felt was his." Brantley believes that because of their prejudices over the last two centuries, students of the Enlightenment have ignored Wesley entirely, regarding him as a kind of obscurantist anachronism, and that this is why his role in the more intellectual history of the times is so little appreciated.[24] In another work Brantley elaborates on why Locke was so important for understanding Wesley:

> Although empiricism is "natural" and evangelicalism is "spiritual," the great principle of empiricism, that one must see for oneself and be in the presence of the thing one knows, applies as well to evangelical faith. Each of these two methodologies operates along a continuum that joins emotion to intellect; each joins externality to words through "ideas/ideals of sensation," that is, through perception or grace-in-perception or both. While *empiricism* refers to immediate contact with and direct impact from objects and subjects in time and place, *evangelicalism* entertains the notions that religious truth is concerned with experiential presuppositions and that experience need not be nonreligious.[25]

Moreover, Brantley shows how the *natural* experiential emphasis of Locke combines with the *spiritual* experiential emphasis of Wesley to provide the "central dialectic" of the Romantic poets who were to come in the next century. "Not only does the almost religious quality of their emotion relate to Wesley's emotional faith, but a Wesleyan blend of 'spiritual sense' and a posteriori reason forms part of what they all retained from the century and the place in which all of them were born."[26]

If we are born with blank slates for minds, as Locke taught and as learned opinion in the eighteenth century believed, then experience counts for everything, for without it our minds remain blank. Hence experience is honored in religion also, and those who took religion seriously on its own terms would look favorably on the experiential version of it, which is to say the evangelical version, although they might use the more common expression *experimental* religion. This is the familiar manifestation known as "the religion of the heart." It was found in various modes of expression, from hymns—not only of Charles Wesley but of many others—to children's literature. Isaac Watts became famous in both those fields, and his dependence on Locke is evident in his whole corpus.[27] In that respect Watts became typical of Dissent as Locke took over the thinking of the Dissenting academies, which flourished because of the prevailing requirement that only members of the Church of England could receive university degrees. Later in the century, the more orthodox Dissenting ministers blamed Locke's influence in the academies for the drift toward heresy.[28] But the firmness in orthodoxy of so many of Locke's disciples makes that a doubtful proposition.

The Wesleys did not countenance the free play of religious emotion without limits. They were loyal Churchmen who tried to keep the movement in the broad stream of Church tradition. University men, they fraternized with the poor members in the Methodist societies but also with the leading intellectuals of the day. They were close friends of Dr. Johnson, and a modern scholar finds interesting parallels between Boswell's *Life of Johnson* and John Wesley's *Journal* that reflect their friendship.[29] Later on, people could speak of Methodist "ranters," but the most egregious examples of this did not occur until after the turn of the century, and even then those given to emotional disturbances tended to split off into splinter groups.

Organization was not the only check on emotions in the Methodist system. The leadership stressed the importance of reason. Wesley advised one of the more rambunctious of his preachers to exercise restraint: "I dislike something that has the appearance of *enthusiasm* . . . overvaluing feelings and inward *impressions:* mistaking the mere work of imagination for the voice of the Spirit . . . and undervaluing *reason, knowledge* and *wisdom* in general." Other Methodist leaders repeated those exhortations.[30] Of course, if their warnings were universally heeded, there would have been no need to keep repeating them; whatever Wesley thought about "enthusiasm," it was to be the standard complaint of all those who attacked him. Still, his emphasis on serious study and the exercise of reason bore fruit long after his death. Methodist class meetings in the next century often formed reading and study groups, and these sometimes developed into schools. Instruction took place within families or between neighbors who formed cooperatives for educating children.[31] Within the Methodist conception, then, there was no contradiction between reason and emotion, and in Wesley and others like him they were held in complementary balance. What happened in the hinterlands, where the meetings might be led by the newly (and barely) literate, could be another matter. Moreover, the meetings imparted discipline; none could remain in the society while leading an irregular life, and expulsions took place along with recruitment. In 1748, Wesley undertook a purification process in the Bristol society that reduced it from 900 to 730 members. As John Walsh puts it, "Wesley's societies were not intended as modern free-expression psychotherapy groups but as disciplined pilgrim companies pressing along a strenuous path to perfection."[32]

The evangelical revival elicited criticism from those who disagreed with its emphasis on experience. *Conversion,* for those participating in revivals, is always perceived subjectively, regardless of what objective realities may lie beyond the perception. Even within the revival milieu, there are disagreements about the place and meaning of experience. A recent biography of Whitefield contrasts his understanding of this with his predecessors in seventeenth-century Dissent. Dissenters, with their theological sophistication, understood conversion as being connected with proper doctrinal teaching. In this way experience was tempered by understanding and was expected not to break loose from its tether. But Whitefield, and many others as well, reversed this. Rather than the conversion experience being validated by teaching that showed where it fit in the religious life, the experience validated the teaching. God would not provide this great blessing, it was said, in connection with false teaching. The experience was the fruit of the doctrine and of the faithfulness to the doctrine.[33] The Anglican High Church has had a particular aversion for the elevation of feelings over doctrine, but it has often misunderstood what it was criticizing. Sabine Baring-Gould spoke for many when he said that justification by faith for Wesley became justification by feelings.[34] But such a view would have been repugnant to Wesley—and to Whitefield as well.

THE EARLY PARISH EVANGELICALS

Samuel Walker of Truro, in Cornwall, was probably the best known of the early Evangelical clergymen, and his case will serve as an example of what the breed was like. He arrived in Truro in 1746, a courtly and charming member of an old family of the West Country, as curate with an absentee rector. He was a brilliant conversationalist and eloquent preacher. Although his doctrines were more or less faithful to the teaching of the Church, there was no spiritual life to his ministry. He was brought face to face with the emptiness of his life and teachings by the Truro schoolmaster, who, as he described it, was "the first person I ever met possessed of the mind of Christ." That meeting led to others and eventually to Walker's conversion. He explained his new understanding from the pulpit, preaching repentance and faith and the necessity of the new birth. This brought him enemies, who appealed against him to the bishop. But there was no charge that could be leveled against him. The enemies then turned to the rector, who was induced to dismiss his curate. The rector called on Walker but was received with such graciousness that he retreated in confusion, unable to complete his mission. Arriving a second time at Walker's home for the same purpose, the rector again withdrew without dismissing the curate. Taken to task by the dissident parishioners, the rector responded: "Do you go and dismiss him, if you can. I feel in his presence as if he were a being of a superior order."

Walker disapproved of itinerant preaching and stayed in his own corner of the realm. But what he accomplished in that corner! Almost all of Truro turned out of a Sunday, the moral laxity so common in the England of the period—Cornwall especially—more or less disappeared, and the spiritual life of the parish prospered. After five years he wrote in a letter, "The number of those who have made particular application to me inquiring what they must do to be saved cannot have been less than eight hundred"—this in a town of 1,600. When he died in 1761 it was said that he left Truro the most Christian town in England.[35]

William Romaine was reputed to be the only Evangelical clergyman in London when he began lecturing with evangelical emphases at St. Dunstan's-in-the-West in 1749. He roused the fury of the churchwardens, who did what they could to obstruct him with a number of annoying acts. They changed the hour of lectures to seven in the evening but refused to light or heat the church or to allow the people to enter it before the service began. Thus Romaine lectured with the only light in the church coming from a candle that he held in his hand. When he finally received a living, it was by vote of the parishioners of St. Andrew-by-the-Wardrobe, where he remained until his death in 1795. (He was also one of Lady Huntingdon's chaplains until she left the Church for Dissent.)[36]

The conversion of Charles Simeon prepared the way for one of the most influential Evangelical careers in the first third of the nineteenth century. Arriving at Cambridge University in 1779, the young Simeon was dismayed to learn that he would be required to take Communion. Feeling himself to be wholly unworthy of this step, he set about to prepare as best he could. He bought a copy of *The Whole Duty of Man*, an anonymous work that had been published more than a century earlier, "the only religious book that I

CHARLES SIMEON.
By courtesy of the National Portrait Gallery, London.

had ever heard of, and began to read it with great diligence; at the same time calling my ways to remember, and crying to God for mercy; and so earnest was I in these exercises that within the three weeks I made myself quite ill with reading, fasting, and prayer." Simeon's relief came through a reading of Bishop Wilson's exposition of the Lord's Supper, which explained that the Old Testament sacrifices were accomplished with the conscious transfer of the worshiper's sin to the head of the animal. He realized that the gospel meant that his sins had been transferred to Jesus. "From that hour peace followed in rich abundance into my soul." [37] We have numerous stories such as Simeon's, and this confirms the observation sometimes made that the Evangelical revival owes much more to the High Church tradition than to Dissent or to Methodism. As in Simeon's case, the sacraments, the liturgy, and the literature of the Church of England combine to bring the person to repentance and faith.

Simeon's reception as a clergyman in the Holy Trinity parish in Cambridge was singularly hostile. Evidently it was his passionate preaching that earned him the dislike of many of his parishioners. In 1829, by then highly respected by the multitudes, he cast his mind back to his beginnings in the ministry: "Thirty years ago, . . . it was a university crime to speak to me, and was reported to parents."[38] In fact his early successes at Cambridge were among Dissenters, who had fewer prejudices than members of the Establishment. Dissent itself split under the example of the revival. The Presbyterians for the most part continued into rationalism and Unitarianism, but Independents and Baptists became mostly evangelical.[39]

Halévy viewed the Evangelicals in the Church of England as just so many Methodists whom Wesley's followers, forced out of the Church by defenders of the status quo, had left behind as a kind of "rear-guard." Methodists were, so to speak, the "High Church of Nonconformity," and the Evangelicals in the parishes constituted "a species of Anglican Methodism."[40] The trouble with Halévy's conflation of two different movements is that it does not comport well with the understanding of the people it claims to describe. The Wesley brothers and some of their chief lieutenants, as we have seen, would have abhorred the notion that they were any sort of Nonconformists. It is true, as Halévy says, that their enemies tarred the Evangelicals with the title of "Methodist" as a kind of taunt, but that did not make them Methodists. The Evangelicals were much more cautious about venturing outside of the parish structure than Wesley was, and some of the staunchest of them—Walker of Truro, for example, whom Wesley admired greatly—tried in vain to persuade the Methodists to refrain from coming into their parishes. In addition there was the matter of "Christian perfection," which the Wesleys believed and taught and which few Evangelicals accepted. Calvinism also retained some residual hold on the Evangelicals, although less so than some commentators have asserted, and that made for a separation from the Wesleyan side of the Methodist movement.

It seems to be the case, rather, that the Evangelical movement of the eighteenth century arose in the main stream of the Church of England quite apart from the Methodists. Biographical studies show numerous examples of this. By the middle of the century it was even possible that the example of the Methodists hindered conversion of Anglicans because of the checkered reputation they were acquiring.[41]

The Evangelicals were sometimes called Puritans because some of their emphases were similar. The necessity of being converted through faith in Christ, the reliance on biblical revelation for religious truth, the pessimistic anthropology that was a necessary consequence of the doctrine of original sin, and the aversion to certain amusements were characteristic of both movements. But the Evangelicals were much more accepting of the Church order, sacraments, and liturgies; cheerful rather than gloomy; more fruitful in doing good works as an outcome of their faith; and much less theologically innovative.[42]

ASPECTS OF THE SOCIAL DIMENSIONS OF THE REVIVAL

Few aspects of the revival showed up on the complaint lists of its opponents more often than its supposed individualism. High Church critics disliked the individualistic aspects of the evangelical teaching about faith because it was not dependent upon the administration of the sacraments, which was done in corporate acts. It is true that the old saying attributed to Luther, to the effect that everyone must repent for himself just as everyone must eventually die for himself, was one of the characteristics of the evangelical teaching. But the revival emphasis on the individual's accountability to groups of fellow believers, and the effect of those groups in reinforcing changes of behavior, requires some reassessment of the old charges. Wesley's formation of societies to nurture converts was based upon his conviction about the unchristian nature of solitude. He decried the mystics and hermits who sought to achieve sanctification in the desert. "The Gospel of Christ knows of no religion but social, no holiness but social holiness."[43]

From the start the sermons of both the Wesleys and Whitefield revealed the moral reformation of society as one of their highest priorities. They were seeking, as one of the Wesleys put it, "a reformation not of opinions . . . but of men's tempers and lives; of vice in every kind." John Wesley told the assembled dons of Oxford in June 1738 that only the doctrine of salvation by faith could "give a check to that immorality which has overspread the land as a flood." Whitefield contended in 1739 that any improvement in the moral order that is brought about by coercion will be "only outward and superficial," but improvement that comes by spiritual renewal "will be inward and lasting." The Methodists by this argument showed the weakness not only of moral coercion but also of the moralistic preaching so prevalent in the churches.[44]

Moral reformation in the Methodist system was enhanced by the organization of the people in class meetings because it afforded mutual encouragement and accountability. The small groups met weekly to study the Bible and to discuss their spiritual problems and progress. There were usually only a dozen or so members in the class, which enabled the members to get beyond the superficial. Each class had a lay leader who was expected to exercise spiritual oversight over the members. Many of the class meetings spawned offshoots, such as reading circles, a natural outgrowth of Wesley's attempt to encourage reading and learning. The class meetings sometimes also started Sunday schools and day schools, and libraries along with them. Some of the groups studied not only secular books along with the theology but also books written by their adversaries, including Tom Paine's *Age of Reason* and *The Rights of Man*.[45]

The reformers took advantage of one of the characteristic institutions of the early eighteenth century, the association, or club. Given the itinerant nature of the Methodist ministry, the class meetings had to be led by members of the local society, which means spiritual direction was given by people with little education or training. Hence the importance of Wesley's constant admonition that reading and education were vital for the success of the movement. The local leader might be a farm worker or a plumber, and he exercised leadership over friends and neighbors. His role, lacking formal authority, had to be validated by a kind of mutual submission and a bonding of community spirit. The family, valued in its own right, also served as nurturing grounds for Christian discipleship. It functioned in complementary fashion with the society, each reinforcing the other's teaching and discipline.[46]

It is almost a constant effect of religious revivals in the Christian West that they are accompanied by attempts at educational reform. When the Society for Promoting Christian Knowledge (SPCK), founded in 1699, tried to stem the rising tide of moral lawlessness, one of its strategies was to encourage clergymen to establish schools for poor people and to print Bibles and other religious literature. By 1723 the organization claimed to be running 1,329 schools, with more than 23,000 pupils. The journalist Richard Steele called this achievement "the greatest instance of public spirit the age had produced." Later on, the figures burgeoned; by 1761 Wales alone had almost 3,500 schools with 150,000 pupils. The early charity school movement was largely a creation of the Established Church. But along with clerical encouragement, the laity, both men and women, played an important role in both leadership and instruction. Eventually the example of the charity schools led to the establishment in 1785 of a central coordinating body for the Sunday schools, the Sunday School Society. Its first president was the London banker Henry Thornton, who was to become famous as one of the leaders of the Clapham Evangelicals. The society, like many in the coming heyday of evangelical societies, but unlike the SPCK, had no formal connection with the Establishment, drawing support from a number of denominations. In spite of the hostile reception with which much of the Establishment greeted evangelical endeavors, the Sunday schools met with almost universal approval. The bishops of Llandaff and Salisbury welcomed them with enthusiasm; the dean of Lincoln commended them to the clergy. The Unitarian minister and scientist in Birmingham, Joseph Priestley, was enthusiastic.[47] Beilby Porteous, bishop of Chester, saw the Sunday schools as an alternative to the bloody penal code, which was thought by many to be the only antidote to the epidemic of crime to which the country was subject. His argument was that laws are futile when people lack the underlying disposition to do good and that disposition could not "otherwise be regulated than by a right education, by impressing on the minds of youth principles and habits of piety and virtue." Porteous exemplified what was true of most of the Sunday school advocates—the primary motivation was social and religious, not educational.[48]

As with so many of the movements of the period, this remarkable burst of charitable energy had its beginning with the dedication and energy of one man. Robert Raikes was an Anglican layman, a journalist in Gloucester who founded the first Sunday school in 1780. He had the children taken to church twice on Sundays to be taught to read and to learn the catechism. The roughness of the age and the class of scholars presented formidable challenges to the teachers and directors, who sought to impart not only knowledge but changes in behavior. "The great principle I inculcate," said Raikes, "is to be kind and good natured to each other; not to provoke one another; to be dutiful to their parents; not to offend God by cursing and swearing."[49] Raikes owned the *Gloucester Journal* and found many opportunities to publicize the work of the schools: for example, he published Bishop Porteous's letter explaining their advantages to the country. The idea caught on rapidly and spread to other cities. The Manchester Sunday schools were launched in 1784 and placed under a committee composed of Churchmen, Dissenters, and Roman Catholics, thus copying a system already in use in Leeds. A year later, 2,300 pupils were attending classes, and the committee had to field inquiries from all over the kingdom.[50] By 1820 the number of children attending the schools was thought to be nearly 480,000.

Halévy believed that the organization of the Methodists into classes and then annual conferences was the secret to their success. He contrasted with it the role of the Dissenting ministers, whose freedom of action was sharply constrained by the congregations that employed them. The Dissenters were also constrained financially because they had no mechanism for pooling resources for the sake of spreading the gospel such as the Methodists had.[51] That centralization has marked Methodist bodies to the present, although there has been nobody with the prestige to be called "Pope John," one of the nicknames by which Wesley was known.

It has been argued of late that this ability to nurture leadership from the bottom rungs of society combined with the Arminian theology urged by the Wesleys to provide the underpinnings for the development of English liberty and democracy. Tocqueville may have been the first to point out the differences between the French and English revolutionary impulses and to identify English religion as the main reason for them. Bernard Semmel has built on this insight, paying particular attention to the theology of perfectionism, which laid emphasis on the *worth* of the individual, as contrasted with the characteristically Calvinist emphasis on sin. Thus liberty and equality became realities to countless people, first in their hearts and then in their meetings and chapels, and made the transition to political liberalism possible later on. In this way Methodism "proved a strong support to a society which, almost uniquely, sought to extend liberty, and was able to enjoy that liberty because it had mastered, again almost uniquely, a large measure of self-discipline."[52]

MORALISM AND ANTINOMIANISM

There is a curious paradox in that the movement that ended up in the Victorian period and later with the reputation for moral rigor in the narrow-minded, intolerant sense should have begun with its enemies making the opposite charge. As we saw earlier, the governing ethos of the day preached morality (or moralism) in the Church while much of the society's behavior was grossly immoral. Moralistic preaching was long associated with the influence of the archbishop of Canterbury, John Tillotson (1691–94), and in the course of explaining to someone his family influences, William Wilberforce remarked that his mother had been an "Archbishop Tillotson Christian."[53] The learned High Church historian Baring-Gould called the tendency the *sirop Tillotsonien* and believed it to be common among the Methodists.[54] As the beliefs of the original Reformers were recovered, the doctrine of justification by faith alone—to the exclusion of good works and of keeping the law—naturally came to the fore. And just as naturally, if keeping the strictures of God's law was thought to be superfluous to salvation, some people would justify their lawlessness on the basis of Christian doctrine. Such is the reason for the charges of antinomianism against the revival. Southey regarded antinomianism as the natural concomitant of the doctrine of justification by faith, although he acknowledged that Wesley always opposed it. In fact, he opposed it so strenuously that some of the Calvinists took him to have crossed the line into works-righteousness, which would make the Atonement superfluous.[55] These charges probably bore some relationship to those that pinned the "individualistic" label on the Methodists. If Wesley's followers really did spurn social bonds it would have been natural for them to disassociate themselves from the laws that made social life both safe and pleasurable. Evidently his refusal to countenance law breaking was the main source of Wesley's early break with the Moravians, who had been such a strong influence in his spiritual development. When in 1746 the Methodist London Tabernacle had to deal with inner contention and "antinomianism grew to a strong head," the difficulty was said to have come from "Brother Cennick's drinking into the Moravian spirit."[56] Probably because of the progress of the revival, toward the end of the century preaching in Tillotson's way was disdained by a broad range of parties: Church and Dissent, evangelicals, nonevangelicals, and Methodists. "Merely moral" became a common term of reproach because it implied that the gospel was deprived of all but its moral implications.[57]

If it is possible to specify a point at which the beginnings of national revival began to coalesce from the scattered communities of renewal that this chapter deals with, it may be the royal proclamation of June 1, 1787. King George III issued a Proclamation for the Encouragement of Piety and Virtue, under the urging of a little-known parliamentarian, William Wilberforce, then only twenty-seven years of age. The king noted the "rapid progress of impiety and licentiousness" and enjoined his subjects to mend their ways; the upper classes in particular were to set a good example for others. His proclamation urged persons in authority to punish drunkenness, blasphemy, lewdness, profanation of the Sabbath, public gambling, and immoral books. We do not have much reason to suppose that the issuance of the royal proclamation itself had a profound effect on the spiritual life or morals of the country, but its very existence suggests that something fundamental was going on in the country of which the king was taking note. He was endorsing a trend that was already well underway, and that is what we shall have to consider next.

The Odyssey of the Anglican Evangelicals

THE MID-EIGHTEENTH-CENTURY evangelical movement in the Church of England was scattered thinly and unevenly across the realm, had no influence in the Church and no support among the bishops, and faced almost universal disdain. A century later the movement had become the dominant voice in the Church. (In later chapters we shall have to examine its effect on the broader society.) Even when it became dominant, it did not constitute the majority of Church people, and it always faced opposition, but by the time of Victoria's coronation in 1837 the opposition had taken on some of its characteristics, as had indeed the whole society.

EVANGELICAL THEOLOGICAL EMPHASES

Our definition—any definition—of evangelicalism must be hedged by qualifications. The Evangelicals recognized that often only a shift in emphasis separated them from someone in another party of the Church, and there was considerable disagreement among the Evangelicals themselves concerning a number of issues. Contemporaries usually had little trouble distinguishing a partisan of the High Church from an Evangelical, but there were Evangelicals whose conception of the Church was little different from that of a High Churchman. The divisions were blurred on other issues as well. Henry Thornton, of the Evangelical community that lived in the London suburb of Clapham, had a conception of God that emphasized the stern aspects of the divine character, while his pastor John Venn's preaching was more concerned to communicate the love of God made available to the sinner by Christ. Thornton would have done away with the word *Trinity* if that would have advanced the cause, and he paid no attention to the current theological controversies.[1] The next generation would not be so tolerant. Some evangelicals were so different than others that it is only with some strain that we comprehend them as part of the same movement. Comparing the *Christian Observer,* the voice of "moderate" Evangelicals in the

Church of England, with the *Record,* which began publication in 1828, reveals not only differences of opinion on this or that issue but a radically different psychological orientation.[2]

It is easier to define what the Evangelicals were by showing what they were not. One commonly sees them referred to as the Low Church party in the Established Church, but that use of the term probably only dates from the 1830s. Prior to that time, *Low Church* meant latitudinarian, and it represented a set of ideas that the Evangelicals abhorred, being a theological justification for the excesses they were trying to root out of the society.[3]

The Arminian-Calvinist struggles among the Methodists did not have their counterpart among the Anglican Evangelicals, except in a weak, half-hearted way, especially after the turn of the nineteenth century. The Evangelicals may have learned a lesson from the earlier battles, or they may, like Henry Thornton, simply have had what they considered more important work to do. Older historical works stressed the Calvinism of the Evangelicals, contrasting them with the Wesleyans, with whom they otherwise had much in common.[4] But the available records do not provide much support for this. In fact, surprisingly, Dissent retained much of the Calvinist spirit that the Evangelicals had left behind, with many Dissenters calling themselves Calvinists, some *strict* Calvinist, until near the end of the nineteenth century.[5]

Calvinism had an early foothold among the isolated pioneers of eighteenth-century Evangelicalism. The first Henry Venn had been an Arminian, but, largely in contemplating his own unworthiness, he became convinced that only the grace of God could rescue him, and he became a Calvinist.[6] Venn and Charles Simeon believed that Wesley had failed to take sin seriously enough and so had made too much of the human capacity to repent and reform. Venn's son, John, thought the controversy was much overblown and should be allowed to die a quiet death. He had moved from his father's Calvinism toward a more moderate position, and so had others of the Claphamites—Thornton, for example.[7] Wilberforce seldom had anything to say of contentious doctrines, and his example in that respect was largely followed by the leadership among the Clapham Evangelicals. His friend James Stephen said that Wilberforce was not a Calvinist and "dislikes all such controversies." To Stephen's knowledge he had hardly ever mentioned them in either conversation or writing.[8] In 1805 Wilberforce, in a personal letter to a friend whose daughter had just died, explicitly rejected a Calvinistic explanation that might have helped him comfort the mother.[9]

In its first year of publication, the *Christian Observer,* which for many years was virtually the voice of the Clapham Evangelicals, pronounced itself in favor of evangelical teaching, without wishing to take sides, being "little anxious" about matters relating to Calvinism.[10] Two years later, the magazine mildly defended Calvinism and disassociated it from Puritanism, which still suffered in reputation from the memories of the Commonwealth.[11] By 1810, the subject seemed to present itself to the *Observer* not as a matter of truth to be discovered and taught but rather as an obstacle that prevented unity and excited the disapprobation of others in the Church of England. But the *Observer* thought the two factions were being reconciled.[12] In any case, according to the magazine, evangelical preachers rarely mentioned the matter at all.[13]

The main Cambridge Evangelicals, more clerical, theological, and pastoral than those at Clapham, were no less ambivalent about Calvinism. Isaac Milner at Queens College thought it unfair that the Evangelical clergy should be taken as nearly all Calvinist. Still, he was unwilling to be cut off entirely from the teacher of Geneva. "There are, in Calvin, a number of expressions which I totally disapprove—yet, in general, I may agree with him."[14] His colleague Charles Simeon told of a conversation on the subject he had had with John Wesley in which he had concluded that they were virtually in agreement and that the dispute was mostly over words, since Wesley's Arminianism was hardly different from his own Calvinism.[15] Someone recorded a conversation in which Simeon said, "Sometimes I am a high Calvinist, at other times a low Arminian, so that if extremes will please you, I am your man; only remember it is not *one* extreme that we are to go to, but *both* extremes."[16] The task of resolving the paradox of election and human responsibility was beyond the Evangelicals' interest, and given the nature of their sense of calling and the opposition they faced from outsiders, they saw nothing but frustration and failure in trying to fathom the truth of the matter.

Calvinism was not only a set of doctrines stemming from the Protestant Reformation but also a polemical device. It sometimes seemed that the enemies of Evangelicalism seized on it as a convenient way to discredit the whole movement. When the *Christian Observer* reviewed a pamphlet by Robert Fellowes of St. Mary Hall, Oxford, entitled *The Anti-Calvinist; or Two Plain Discourses on Redemption and Faith,* they were surprised to find not the attack on Calvinism that they expected but an attack on Evangelicalism. Fellowes's most telling arguments were actually against antinomianism, in which the *Observer* was happy to join with him.[17]

The cardinal Evangelical doctrine of conversion provided a similar opportunity for opponents. But the Evangelicals were generally less dogmatic about the matter than their critics often acknowledged. Writing about the famous revival in Cane Ridge, Kentucky (1801)—one of the major early events of the Second Great Awakening in America—the *Observer* rejoiced at the mass conversions but disagreed with the reports that implied some theological virtue in the physical manifestations that accompanied them. It feared that such an emphasis would lead people to despise "the more slow and ordinary methods of instruction." Emotions were apt to be spurious and in any case short-lived.[18] Later on, the less conciliatory *Record* responded to an attack in the *Edinburgh Review* that claimed that Evangelicals taught the damnation of those who could not point to a dramatic conversion experience. The *Record* denied that the *Review* had accurately portrayed evangelical teaching. There are a wide variety of experiences possible, it said, all legitimate.[19] That is no more than the mainstream of Evangelicalism had always taught.

Fellowes's assault on the Evangelicals for their supposed antinomianism was a common ploy. The radical writer Leigh Hunt stooped to this in his attack on the Methodists, and by implication on all evangelicals. Hunt, a friend and business associate of Byron and Shelley—poets whom many contemporaries regarded as libertines—and Dickens's model for the parasite Harold Skimpole in *Bleak House,* charged that the doctrine of justification by faith alone led to antinomianism.[20] Notwithstanding the injustice of the charges, the evangelicals were not entirely clear of the fault: Wilberforce once complained to his journal about hearing a "sad Antinomian sermon."[21] The *Christian Observer* was concerned not only about antinomian preachers but also about those who were not antinomians but whose preaching was uncertain enough to engender antinomianism in their hearers.[22]

WILBERFORCE AND THE POLITICAL INFLUENCE OF THE EVANGELICALS

To speak of the political influence of the Evangelicals in the first third of the nineteenth century is to speak of William Wilberforce. And to speak of Wilberforce is to speak of the Evangelical community that lived in Clapham. He was a member of the House of Commons for several decades, first as a Tory, then as an independent, but he never held office. The extent of his influence was due solely to his personal qualities—sincerity of faith, intelligence, deep humanity, love for his fellows, scrupulous honesty, and a lively and fascinating speaking style, both in personal conversation and in parliamentary speeches. He was one of the most widely loved personalities of his age. His personal magnetism and his dedication to causes that were already gripping the imagination of highly motivated people drew to him the friendship and service of an extraordinarily gifted band of fellow laborers without whom he would have been able to accomplish very little. Plagued by ill health for most of his life, he often had to stop his arduous labors because his congenitally weak eyes failed him. His stomach ailments led him to become dependent on the only remedy the medicine of the day could provide, opium, and that also may have slowed him down. "I am now scribbling whilst ready to faint," he wrote to a colleague, "and must lay down my pen." [23] It was a theme that would turn up often in his letters. At the age of fifty-two, he required assurance by his close friend and brother-in-law, James Stephen, that he was not going senile.[24]

Born into a wealthy Yorkshire merchant family in 1759, Wilberforce lived for a time in his uncle's house, where he came under the influence of an aunt who was a devotee of George Whitefield. This alarmed his parents, who brought him back to the paternal home as soon as possible. At the age of thirty-seven he looked back and attributed these experiences to divine providence, for he came into contact with the gospel in his relatives' house, but rather than being cut off from society there as a "bigoted despised methodist" he had been drawn back to where he might become connected with politics and thereby be "useful in life." [25] The turning point of his life came after his graduation from Cambridge. On tour of the Continent with the Cambridge Evangelical Isaac Milner, Wilberforce, with his ready wit, jousted with his more serious companion until, in February 1785, the two men together read Philip Doddridge's book *The Rise and Progress of Religion* (1745). In the course of the discussions that accompanied their reading, Wilberforce experienced the classical evangelical conversion. He always dated his real spiritual life from that time.

The esteem in which the man was held was almost universal. On the stump in Yorkshire during the election of 1784, the small and frail Wilberforce once spoke without knowing that James Boswell, on the road from Edinburgh to visit the ailing Samuel Johnson in London, was among his auditors. Afterwards Boswell described the occasion to the Scottish politician Henry Dundas, later first Viscount Melville: "I saw what seemed a mere shrimp mount upon the table; but, as I listened, he grew, until the shrimp became a whale." [26] By 1814, he was so generally esteemed that when he entered a room a path would clear before him so that he might proceed unimpeded. When he rose to speak, the assembled crowd greeted him with loud applause.[27] John Henry Newman wrote to his mother: "I was much taken with Mr. Wilberforce. It is seldom indeed we may hope to see such simplicity and unaffected humility, in one who has been so long moving in the intrigues of public life and the circles of private flattery." [28] At his death in July 1833, the House of Commons vetoed the family's plan to give him a quiet funeral, insisting that he be buried in Westminster Abbey. When the

WILLIAM WILBERFORCE.
By courtesy of the National Portrait Gallery, London.

funeral party reached the abbey, the entire House joined it, the Speaker having canceled the session out of fear that none of the members would be present.

There is, of course, another side to the matter, as there would have to be for a man in the thick of the most contentious political controversies of the age. The slave-owning interests were completely opposed to Wilberforce's attempts first to end the slave trade and then, when that was successful, to ban the owning of slaves. But the most strident opposition to him came from political radicals; they had a particularly virulent hatred for him, possibly as intense a feeling as borne by his admirers. This was partly due to his reverence for the ancient English constitution and his conviction that the nation's numerous ills could be put right without overturning all its traditions. The traumatic effect of the French Revolution on English sensibilities led to the muzzling of radical opinion and the imprisonment of writers, publishers, and booksellers, and Wilberforce's acquiescence in these policies, especially the Combination Laws of 1799–1800, which banned unions, infuriated the radicals. His leadership in the Evangelical movement increased the ire of some of these critics, many of whom were proponents of radical religious views or outright atheism. William Cobbett, a former army sergeant who had become well known as a radical journalist, wrote from his temporary exile about how agreeable living was in the United States. Among the wonderful features of the life he was enjoying, Cobbett included with exultation the fact that there were in the new world "no Wilberforces—think of that—NO WILBERFORCES."[29] Francis Place, who rose from poor tailor to prosperous merchant and was a friend and colleague of Bentham and the Mills, called Wilberforce "an ugly epitome of the devil"[30]—the devil, that is, who Place did not believe existed. In a litany of praise for Wilberforce—not untinged with irony—William Hazlitt averred, in *The Spirit of the Age,* that all he lacked was an "economy of good parts. By aiming at too much, he has spoiled all. . . . The graces and accomplishments of private life mar the man of business and the statesman."[31] That is a curious statement, a holdover from the spirit of the previous age, when a man's private vices might enhance his public reputation.

The key to understanding Wilberforce's political activities is to recognize that his view of everything in life, including statecraft, was related to his understanding of the will of God, for himself, for Great Britain, and for all humanity. When he became gloomy about the state of the nation, it was not so much because of this or that setback but because the nation persisted in its wickedness, refusing to repent and mend its ways. "Above all, we do not recognise the hand of God, though so plainly lifted up. . . . There is nothing like humiliation, nothing like an acknowledgment of the government of God."[32] Wesley evidently viewed Wilberforce's mission as standing against what the society had become and as a force for reforming it. In what is reputed to be the last letter Wesley wrote, just before his death, he urged Wilberforce on "as Athanasius contra mundum."[33]

Wilberforce wrote only one book, but it was a blockbuster. His publisher was pessimistic about its prospects, on the grounds that there was little demand for religious works at that time (1797). (What a difference a generation would make!) Cadell suggested they might print five hundred copies of the book and seemed surprised that Wilberforce intended to affix his name to it. Wilberforce thought the publisher was treating him as "an amiable enthusiast." Formidably entitled *A Practical View of the Prevailing Religious System of Professed Christians in the Higher and Middle Classes in this Country Contrasted with Real Christianity,* the edition was sold out within a few days. John Newton, famed clergyman and good friend of the Clapham Evangelicals, wrote to say, shrewdly, that while others would write books to which nobody would pay any attention, Wilberforce's book would get a hearing just because of who he was.[34] At the six-month mark, 7,500 copies had been sold, and the run was only beginning. By 1826, fifteen editions in England and twenty-five in America had passed through the booksellers' hands, and there were French, Dutch, Italian, Spanish, and German translations.[35] The old statesman Edmund Burke was on his deathbed as the book appeared, and one of his attendants testified that he spent much of his last two days reading it, with considerable appreciation.[36] Thomas Chalmers, the great Scottish reformer who would leave his mark on the age, was converted upon reading it in December 1810.[37]

Wilberforce's thesis in the *Practical View* is clearly stated in the title: the prevailing religion in Great Britain was supposed to be Christianity but was in fact something else. His justification for taking that position was moral. The conduct of professing Christians was little different from that of unbelievers; hence their religious status was no different. The general view that to be born in a Christian country makes one a Christian is badly mistaken.[38] This was an idea he returned to again and again. "Christianity is not a geographical, but a moral term. It is not being a native of a Christian country: it is *a condition, a state;* the possession of a *peculiar nature,* with the *qualities* and *properties* which belong to it" (p. 298). Repeatedly attacking the loose morals of the upper classes, he nevertheless rejected moralism, regarding it as a substitute for true religion (pp. 246–72). The *Practical View* would not have been an Evangelical book had it not contained a clear exposition of the gospel and an argument for the necessity of conversion, and such it had (pp. 300–348). Wilberforce married his spiritual concerns with his concerns for the fate of the nation, as was common among the Clapham politicians. Evil was rampant in the land, and only the fruits of genuine Christian faith could nullify its effects and bring about hope (pp. 403–6). Wilberforce addressed his book to the upper orders because their bad example was leading the masses to imitate their immoral behavior; the general reformation of the country would have to be preceded by the moral reformation of those with wealth and influence (pp. 372–73).

Wilberforce's admonition to the upper classes was not the first Evangelical word on the subject. His friend Thomas Gisborne had written a book three years earlier that considered the specific duties of people occupying positions of authority. By that, Gisborne did not mean only political authority. Rather, he argued that anyone in a position of wealth, leisure, or expertise owes to the divine favor all that he has and therefore lives with the burden of obligations placed upon him. The purpose of his book was to spell out those responsibilities in separate chapters for peers, MPs, government ministers, lawyers, magistrates, clergymen, physicians, businessmen, and "private gentlemen" (who do no work but derive income from properties). Gisborne even had a chapter that advised the king on *his* particular responsibilities. A final chapter offered the usual evangelistic appeal.[39]

LIBRARY AT BATTERSEA RISE.
Private collection; photograph,
Courtauld Institute of Art, London.

This was the room in Henry Thornton's house at Clapham where Wilberforce and Thornton along with others in the group made their plans for the ending of the slave trade. The figure in the center is said to be Wilberforce, and the others members of Thornton's family.

THE CLAPHAM COMMUNITY

In 1792, Wilberforce agreed to move into the house of his relative Henry Thornton, which was located in the community of Clapham, a few miles south of London. The house was called Battersea Rise and was to be the center of innumerable planning and strategy sessions over the next couple of decades.[40] The two men, both still bachelors, complemented each other perfectly. Zachary Macaulay, one of the original Clapham team, wrote of this in a letter:

> In point of talents, doubtless, there is a splendour about Wilberforce which quite eclipses the other; but then the soundness of Thornton's judgment, and the extreme considerateness and painful scrutiny with which he is accustomed to view every subject that requires his decision, serves as a counterbalance. . . . Wilberforce's active love flies immediately to the relief of an object in distress, and gives almost instinctively. Thornton's consideration leads him to weigh the best mode of imparting relief so as to raise no false hopes, and to produce no future unhappiness, and to join, if possible, the interests of eternity to those of time.[41]

Macaulay himself was more in the Thornton mold. Without much of a sense of humor or personal warmth, he nevertheless drew the affection and loyalty of his friends and fellow workers. He was known for his prodigious memory and the indefatigable way he attacked the documents that were the substance of his political work, particularly that relating to the antislavery issue. With the intellectual brilliance that would be even more evident in his famous historian son, Lord Macaulay, he was a walking encyclopedia. Wilberforce would sometimes say, when they were pressed for some factual information, "Let us look it up in Macaulay."[42]

This "Clapham sect" was not a sect but a unique set of relationships that has been called the "brotherhood of Christian politicians." That "Clapham sect" appellation and the further one, "the Saints," that was applied to their parliamentary members, were ironic terms used by enemies to make them objects of ridicule. James Stephen the younger lamented in 1845, when the original group were all dead: "Oh, where are the people who are at once really religious and really cultivated in heart and understanding—the people with whom we could associate as our fathers used to associate with each other?"[43]

With Battersea Rise their headquarters, Thornton's daughter, Marianne, was in a good position to see them in action:

> He [Wilberforce] was as restless and as volatile as a child himself, and during the long and grave discussions that went on between him and my father and others, he was most thankful to refresh himself by throwing a ball or a bunch of flowers at me, or opening the glass door and going off with me for a race on the lawn "to warm his feet." I know one of my first lessons was I must never disturb Papa when he was talking or reading, but no such prohibition existed with Mr. Wilberforce. His love for,

and enjoyment in, all children was remarkable, and he had a strong reason for his affection for all of us.[44]

When Isaac Milner, by then dean of Carlisle, came to visit, he would be-come vexed at the inattention of his host, who might be flitting around after a book, a child, or perhaps a cat. "Now Wilberforce listen," he would roar, "for no power will make me repeat what I am going to say."[45]

The domesticity revealed by the memoirs and correspondence of the Clapham group is very different from the stereotype of family life in the Victorian period, for here the female side of the household was omnipres-ent. There was no segregation by age and sex. Wives and daughters were never far from the center of household life where the men and boys were.[46]

The community of publicly minded Evangelicals widened considerably beyond Clapham after 1802, when the group, along with friends, founded the *Christian Observer*, a monthly publication devoted to a religious under-standing of British culture, in the widest meaning of the term. It encom-passed not only religion and politics but virtually every other aspect of social life. It impresses the modern reader as nothing so much as an Internet forum almost two centuries before the time, with its continuous assertions and responses, the closest one might come in those days to a long-range general conversation with numerous participants. The debates must have been bracing as well as clarifying, and valuable for increasing the unity and advancing the various aims of the Evangelicals.

Although the Clapham Evangelicals are known largely for their political activities, they were conscious of personal responsibilities to do good and be generous with their possessions. They instituted a great age of philan-thropy, and a modern study of the subject credits them with reforging the link between philanthropy and religion that had worn thin in the preceding century.[47] Before he married, Wilberforce, always a soft touch for a hard-luck story, gave one-fourth of his income to charity. Inglis started out the day with a bag full of coins, returning at night with the bag empty, hav-ing distributed its contents to needy persons. Every winter Babington ran a soup kitchen in Clapham. Thornton's carefulness in giving, as Macaulay recounted it, did not make him parsimonious in charity. He gave away as much as six-sevenths of his income before he married, and afterwards at least one-third. Thornton left behind records that show his practice:[48]

	£ Charity	£ All Other Expenses
1790	2260	1543
1792	3960	1817
1793	6680	1988

The kindness of the Clapham group extended to persons of other races. When the family of the unfortunate late King Henri Christophe of Haiti (to whom Wilberforce had written long letters of advice on the administration of his government) arrived in England, Thomas Clarkson, who regarded himself as a "slave to the slave," gave them hospitality in his home for several months.[49] The son of John Shore (Lord Teignmouth) recalled his childhood in Clapham, when for several months he had no schoolfellows except six black boys for whom the community was providing.[50] Granville Sharp, along with Zachary Macaulay, headed up a project, mostly underwritten by Clapham Evangelicals, to resettle in Sierra Leone several hundred free blacks living in destitution in London.[51]

Their extension of love went beyond mere strangers. When the radical Richard Carlile was imprisoned for publishing infidel literature, he was visited by a kindly stranger who tried to interest him in the Bible. They talked for a long time without Carlile budging from his hostility to religion. Later on, Carlile was listening to a sermon by a Dissenting minister and was astonished to discover that his visitor had been Wilberforce, who had privately recounted the incident to his friend, the minister. Carlile is said eventually to have professed adherence to Christian faith.[52]

THE POLITICS OF CLAPHAM

The common interpretation of Clapham politics concludes that it was completely Tory. Sometimes this is taken to mean that the group sought an England in which the few rich dominated and profited, corruption ruled the land, and privilege had its way in every sphere of life.[53] It is true that there was a strong propensity among Tories to uphold the traditions of church and state and to assume the permanence of social relationships that were in fact going to change in the near future. The Evangelical Tories made some of the same mistakes as others, although few adopted the set of opinions that the parodies alleged. In the manner of conservatives everywhere, they ran the risk of confusing contingent relationships with eternal ones. The French Revolution solidified the Tory bias by raising fears of a bloodbath in London on the order of what was happening in Paris. In July 1, 1791, tumultuous riots erupted in Birmingham. Mobs of boys followed Joseph Priestley, scientist and Unitarian minister, chanting "Damn Priestley, damn him for ever." Dissenting meeting houses went up in flames, and Priestley's house was sacked. He left the city permanently.

Clapham supported the general crackdown against radicalism led by Pitt's government. The antireligious fervor of the French revolutionaries had convinced almost everyone that the forces of unbelief and sedition were united in their determination to overturn the society. Tom Paine's atheism and his revolutionary politics were held to be inseparable, and neither could be tolerated; hence the persecution of printers and booksellers for producing and distributing radical literature. The battle cry of church and state under attack rallied many supporters and became the Tory watchword. But Clapham did not blindly follow the Tory government. Wilberforce was determined that his conversion must make a difference in his political conduct as in every other area of life. He and Pitt had been at Cambridge together and had subsequently become very close friends. He wrote to Pitt and told him that he would always have strong affection for him and would generally support him but that he would not be the party man he had been before. Wilberforce described the reply: "It was full of kindness—nothing I had told him, he said, could affect our friendship; that he wished me always to act as I thought right."[54] That close relationship lasted until Pitt's death in 1806, interrupted only by a short period of estrangement when Wilberforce could not support Pitt's policy of continuing the war with France. The major recent study we have of the politics of the Clapham group and its allies in Parliament concludes that "the complete independence which they maintained from all ties of party or faction was undoubtedly the characteristic of the Saints which most struck contemporaries and which distinguished them most strongly from many of their colleagues in parliament. But hardly less striking was their independence from ties of influence and place."[55] Wilberforce's moral presence in Parliament was such that one analyst calls him "a kind of uncrowned king of the House of Commons."[56]

There is in the position of the Clapham Evangelicals a duality or paradox. On the one hand, the kingdom of God was for them an overriding presence and loyalty that relativized all other loyalties, including those that pertained to government and nation. On the other hand, since they rejected an eremitic existence, lesser loyalties continued to have a legitimate claim on them. How to reconcile the two loyalties in the midst of the practical issues of the day posed unavoidable tensions. The *Christian Observer*, in its March 1803 number, praised a sermon entitled "The Unrivaled Felicity of the British Empire."[57] But the same issue warned about the "real danger. There is a degree of corruption in the land, which, if left to produce its own natural consequences, may . . . bring on the most tremendous evils."[58] The almost instinctive Toryism of the Clapham group would seldom be allowed to override higher loyalties.

Although they were sometimes taunted as Methodists, the Claphamites remained firm Churchmen. But their Toryism was not such as to wish to condemn Dissenters. When Lord Sidmouth proposed a new law that would impose hardship on Dissenters, the *Christian Observer* opposed the measure.[59] Later on, the much less conciliatory *Record* favored the repeal of the discriminatory Test and Corporation Acts, which it said would restore to the Dissenters the "unfettered enjoyment of their civil privileges."[60] After Wilberforce's retirement from the Commons in 1825, the leadership on the most pressing issues, principally slavery, was taken by Thomas Fowell Buxton, owner of a brewing company, and the political complexion of the movement shifted. Buxton was an Anglican, but he had been strongly influenced by his Quaker mother, and he was a Whig. Thus the movement began looking with more favor on issues relating to liberty, such as the Reform Bill of 1832, rather than order. Of course, by then the wars with France had receded into the past, and the nation had embarked on a long period of peace.

The leadership of Evangelical politics was changing in other ways. Wilberforce had never commanded the votes of parliamentary Evangelicals but rather had relied on his enormous prestige to win support. After his retirement there was no leader of comparable influence, and the relatively homogeneous center of Evangelical political thinking splintered. The flexibility of the Wilberforce style of leadership seemed to some observers as unnecessarily compromising, and they grew increasingly restive under that mode of proceeding. Led by a businessman of Scottish origin, Andrew Hamilton, these bolder types began publishing the *Record* in 1828. The first issue stated its role as a "political journal . . . conducted on moral and religious principles. . . . The religion we profess is the professed religion of this country."[61] Thus the paper was firmly in the Establishment camp, and by "religious principles" it meant Evangelical principles. Several months later, a financial crisis was resolved by an infusion of capital and the appointment of another Scot who would guide the paper for many years: the twenty-eight-year-old barrister Alexander Haldane.[62] In its fourth year of publication, the editor was moved to reply to criticism about the mixing of the religious and the secular. Some readers were "offended" that the sacred should be considered along with the profane, and the paper was sarcastic about such views. "Religion in a newspaper! I am for every thing being kept in its proper place. Religion, and news, and accidents, and offences, and advertisements, all mingled together. What an incongruous mixture! How derogatory to the dignity of celestial truth!" The *Record* adopted the same views on this issue as Wesley and the Clapham group had: the truth of Scripture points the way to political, social, and economic health in the society, and they would not allow that truth to be forced into some irrelevant "spiritual" nook where it could safely be ignored.[63]

After Wilberforce's retirement from politics, the strong Tory constituency among the Evangelicals became increasingly distrustful of the Evangelical leadership in the House of Commons, who, it was widely feared, were becoming gradually secular. These fears were expressed in particular by the Evangelical clergy. The *Record* and the large public for which it spoke were determined to reverse the progressive trend to which the Clapham party had acquiesced. With Wilberforce gone from the fray, the argument was, his faction had gone over to the enemy.[64]

The labors of the Clapham group were extraordinary. If they are remembered for only one thing, it is for their efforts to end the slave trade, which finally bore fruit in 1807, after two decades of hard work. Finally, within days of Wilberforce's death in 1833, slavery was banned everywhere in the British empire. The organizing of research, the travels to Africa and elsewhere for evidence, the endless planning meetings, the lobbying, and the mobilizing of public opinion were feats calling for enormous dedication and tireless devotion. Thomas Clarkson on a visit to Paris wrote a letter of some fifteen to twenty pages every day to a French official to keep him abreast of the latest events of the slave trade. Once he needed the name of a sailor he had seen but whose name he did not know. He tracked the man down from port to port until finally locating him on the 317th ship he visited. Well did Pitt remark with admiration that the group meeting at Battersea Rise were Wilberforce's "white negroes."

THE EVANGELICALS AND CHURCH REFORM

Although politics was high on Clapham's agenda, reforming the deficiencies of the Church of England was not. They were laymen, and their idea of their calling had to do with statesmanship. To the extent that they participated in other kinds of reform activities, these were in the evangelical societies that started to proliferate in the late eighteenth century. Yet Evangelicals were at the forefront of the Church reform movement, or at least one side of it. Perhaps because they were so critical of the Church's weaknesses, they were very unpopular in many quarters.[65] Beyond the Evangelicals' criticisms of Church dereliction, there was also the effect of evangelical doctrine on the conception of Church order. Although there were High Church Evangelicals, the doctrine of justification by faith necessarily derogates from the views held by some High Churchmen; faith, according to the Evangelicals, is accessible to the penitent without regard for the presence or absence of priest, sacrament, or hierarchy. This doctrine as much as any attitudinal differences rules against a consistent High Churchmanship such as the Tractarian movement of the 1830s would find acceptable. However, the boundaries of these parties are impossible to set with precision, and the Churchmen of the period were as capable as any-one else of holding contradictory ideas simultaneously.[66]

Convinced Protestants in the Church of England feared the High Church as the stalking horse for Roman Catholicism. The *Christian Observer* warned against the "dangers of papism" within the Church of England.[67] The *Record* was even less subtle. In its inaugural issue, it set the tone by which it would henceforth be known when it spoke of "that anti-christian Hierarchy, which, under the pretense of keeping, has taken away, the key of knowledge, and which systematically teaches, for the doctrines of God, the commandments of men."[68] Two years later, declaiming on the subject of Church reform, the *Record* allowed as how the clergy might think the subject unimportant, but the editor had not found a single layman who disagreed with the paper's opinion. Still later, Lord Shaftesbury, by then the most prominent Evangelical layman, was much less a Churchman than those two publications. He preferred the Church of England but had little more regard for it than that. He was suspicious of bishops, even though through his relative by marriage, the Prime Minister, Lord Palmerston, he had considerable influence in how they were chosen.[69]

The Evangelicals were excluded not only by the hierarchy—their first bishop was not named until 1815, when Henry Ryder was appointed to the see of Gloucester—but also by the old societies. Venn, Thornton, Macaulay, Grant, Wilberforce, Simeon, and Pratt subscribed to the Society for the Promotion of the Gospel and the Society for Promoting Christian Knowledge (SPCK) but were unable to obtain any influence in them. As late as 1824, Simeon was blackballed when advanced for membership in the SPCK.[70]

As Clapham was the venue for the Evangelical attempt to influence the political life of England, so Cambridge was home for the effort on its ecclesiastical life. Isaac Milner, who had traveled with the young Wilberforce on the Continent and discussed religion with him, became professor of natural philosophy and then president of Queens College, Cambridge, afterwards dean of Carlisle. A brilliant scholar, he was sometimes called (perhaps with more hope than accuracy) an Evangelical Dr. Johnson.

More influential yet, if not quite as brilliant, was Charles Simeon. Called to the ministry at Holy Trinity, Cambridge, he faced great opposition because of his evangelical views. He began with a high view of the Church's prerogatives and for that reason began to give special lectures in 1782. "If those whose minds were impressed by my preaching had not some opportunity of further instruction, they would infallibly go to the dissenting meetings, and thus be gradually drawn away from the church." He hired a private room to meet with parishioners for preaching and prayer. That soon proved to be too small, and he rented another in an adjacent parish.[71] He did this, he said, not only for the sake of the parishioners, "*but chiefly for the preservation of the Established Church.*"[72] "Otherwise the clergyman beats the bush and the dissenters catch the game."[73] Like many of the Evangelicals, Simeon did not see his allegiance as being to a party, a concept he disliked intensely. If he had wanted to declare allegiance to a system of human thought, it would not be to Calvin or Arminius but to the documents that defined the Church of England.[74] The future Lord Macaulay, who took his Cambridge degree in 1822, had plenty of opportunity to watch the man at work. "As to Simeon," he wrote to a sister in 1844, "if you knew what his authority and influence were, and how they extended from Cambridge to the most remote corners of England, you would allow that his real sway over the Church was far greater than that of any Primate."[75]

In addition to his parish responsibilities, Simeon worked hard to bring spiritual teaching to the undergraduates of the university. By 1811, he thought he was spending two-thirds of his time with them, rather than with his parishioners. This was work that he considered well rewarded, as he saw good numbers of students come to faith in Christ. His outreach was indefatigable, and he regularly went far beyond his formal responsibilities. Starting in 1796, he arranged annual summer house parties for clergymen and their wives. Two or three score would gather in a large country house for two days. In the morning they would meet in conference, with Simeon presiding, and discuss texts relating to the spiritual life. The women were provided for in their own morning session, and these were evidently times of great profit to the participants, as well as a great enjoyment.[76]

Perhaps Simeon's most effective contribution was to compensate for the failure of the Church to provide professional training for the ministry. Ordinands were admitted to ministry normally upon taking an Oxford or Cambridge degree, but their preparation (such as it was in that period before university reform) was in the classics or mathematics. They would begin their ministries with either no training at all or such as they could receive informally from experienced clergymen. Simeon met with undergraduates aspiring to be parsons every other Friday evening. These "conversation parties" knit the students together into a band of future clergymen who could overcome the natural isolation that geography and convictions would otherwise impose on them. They also had the benefit of Simeon's instruction in sermon preparation and delivery.[77] Although Simeon died in 1836, Evangelical students at Cambridge were known as "Sims" until the 1850s.

Simeon is chiefly known as the controlling trustee of "Simeon's Trust." This activity, which from some points of view seems to be an absurdity, was possible because of the peculiar nature of the right to appoint church rectors and vicars. As a *property* right, the "advowson"—the power to nominate incumbents to parishes—was owned and, like any other piece of property, could be sold or passed on to heirs. This practice led to one of the difficulties of Evangelical ministries; when the incumbent died or retired, he was replaced by a successor chosen by whoever owned the advowson. (For that reason the ministry of Samuel Walker, to cite one example, failed to have lasting results in Truro.) John Thornton, father of Henry Thornton of Clapham, had left funds for the purpose of purchasing advowsons that would be used for appointing Evangelical clergymen, and the power to accomplish this eventually fell into Simeon's hands. In the 1820s Simeon began to put his own money into the project and whatever other funds he could raise. Hence evangelical views, which for decades were enough to deny livings to clergymen, gradually became a way to gain a living. Simeon's Trust was especially important to the Evangelicals because they were so discriminated against in the making of appointments. Bishop Marsh of Peterborough, for example, devised his famous "trap" in order to keep them out of the parishes. This was a series of eighty-seven questions designed for the sole purpose of smoking out evangelical views in prospective clergymen in order to exclude them from the diocese. It was a clever (or dishonest) Evangelical candidate who could navigate past that roadblock.

Simeon's High Church convictions were apparently of crucial importance in keeping the Evangelicals within the fold of the Church. As his biographer put it, it was he "more than any other single individual, who taught the Evangelicals to believe in the Church of England and steer clear, not only of the Scylla of academic latitudinarianism, but also of the Charybdis of that pastoral enthusiasm which walks disorderly in its indiscriminate and unthinking zeal."[78]

THE BRISTOL CENTER: EVANGELICALISM AND THE TRANSFORMATION OF A LOCAL CULTURE

If we wish to see Evangelical politics in action, we go to Clapham. For the reform of the Anglican clergy along Evangelical lines, we watch the lectures, meetings, conferences, and preaching of Milner and Simeon in Cambridge and the placements of the Simeon Trust. To see how Evangelicals in action could transform a local community, we go to Bristol near the west coast, where the More sisters lived.

Hannah More was born in 1745, the fourth of five daughters of a schoolmaster. A precocious young woman, she was writing plays while still in her twenties and making trips to London, where she made friends in literary

HANNAH MORE.
By courtesy of the National Portrait Gallery, London.

and artistic circles. She was close to Dr. Johnson, David Garrick (at the time England's most celebrated actor) and his wife, and Horace Walpole. She came under the tutelage of John Newton, the former slaver captain and curate of Olney when the poet William Cowper lived there. Some have regarded Newton as the real founder of the Anglican Evangelical party. He was rector of St. Mary Woolnoth in London when Hannah More met him, one of the few Evangelicals then occupying pulpits in the capital. She was not unacquainted with the doctrines she heard from Newton, which were old hat in the Church of England and which she had long accepted. But her correspondence with Newton shows that she had not possessed the consciousness of the reality of God of which the Evangelicals spoke. When she fell in with the Evangelicals, she did not lose her attractiveness to her literary friends, and numerous people in the public eye trooped to Cowslip Green, her home near Bristol, to meet her. The man of letters Thomas De Quincy, son of an Evangelical mother who had known the More sisters years before, said that he visited in Somersetshire each year in order to meet interesting political or literary figures at Cowslip Green.[79] General Howe, back in England in 1779 after an unsuccessful record in the American colonies, complained to her of his treatment by the authorities.[80]

She met Wilberforce in 1787, when he was twenty-eight, and two years later their long collaboration began in earnest. In August 1789, the young MP visited Cowslip Green for a few days along with his sister. The More sisters urged their guests not to leave without visiting the cliffs of Cheddar, which were one of the most esteemed sights of the district. When the Wilberforces returned, the cold chicken and wine they had been given for lunch were untouched, and Wilberforce disappeared into his room, dismissing even his reader. When he came down finally it was to speak of the dire poverty and wretchedness of the common people he had seen. He had found no resident minister, no industry, no basis for either material or spiritual comfort. Wilberforce insisted that something had to be done about the situation. "If *you* will be at the trouble, *I* will be at the expense."[81] Hannah More later gave further details in a letter to Wilberforce: The vicar of Cheddar was absent, living in Oxford, where he had duties she could not ascertain. The curate lived twelve miles away and was only present once a week. The incumbent of the neighboring parish was drunk almost daily and frequently was unable to preach because he had black eyes; evidently his will to fight was stronger than his skill. In another letter she reported, "We saw but one Bible in all the parish, and that was used to prop a flowerpot" (p. 19). In two mining villages to the north of Mendip, Shipham and Rowberrow, lawlessness was complete. A constable who arrested a Shipham man could expect to disappear forever in one of the mining pits; there were few arrests. "The people savage and depraved almost even beyond Cheddar, brutal in their natures, and ferocious in their manners. They began by suspecting we should make our fortunes by selling their children as slaves" (p. 28).

Hannah and Martha More began visiting the farmers of the area to get their support for starting schools for the children of the laborers. Their method was to teach reading and practical household skills. By 1792, they had 168 children enrolled in Cheddar (p. 54). By the end of 1793, they were claiming ten villages, with 1,000 children in training (p. 99). From the children they proceeded to the parents, holding classes and also worship services. They also taught women how to order their households and provided opportunities for them to gather for fellowship. Although some of her writings were for the higher classes, Hannah's concern in her home district was for those on the bottom. She explained in a letter of 1796: "I desire to have little to do with the great. I have devoted the remnant of my life to the poor, and to those that have no helper; and if I can do them little good, I can at least sympathize with them, and I know it is some comfort for a forlorn creature to be able to say, 'there is somebody that cares for me'" (p. 178).

The establishment figures in the district did not welcome the Mores' efforts. One rich and influential farmer "assured us religion would be the ruin of agriculture" (p. 14). The sisters grew adept at massaging the egos of those whose opposition might have been fatal to the project. "Miss Wilberforce would have been shocked," Hannah wrote to Wilberforce, "had she seen the petty tyrants whose insolence we stroked and tamed, the ugly children we fondled, the pointers and spaniels we caressed, the cider we commended, and the wine we swallowed" (p. 17). In Draycot, a wealthy woman offered gin for children and their parents if they did not attend the Mores' school (p. 60). After the effort was underway, criticism continued from various sources. Some of the local gentry remained hostile (pp. 210–14). The High Church Hannah More was accused of being a Methodist, and one of the local clergymen who felt constrained to blunt the charge testified to the prosperity of his ministry as a result of the Mores' work, with attendance more than quadrupling.[82] Yet the Methodists criticized her for her refusal to be counted as one of them "in order to prove her own sincere attachment to the Church."[83]

For Hannah and Martha More, the trials were worth it because they could see the kind of results for which Wilberforce had first approached them. In their eyes, and not theirs only, the district had seen remarkable improvement. Besides the statistics of pupils in schools, attendance in church, and the like, there were the usual stories of transformed persons. For example, the brother of the great man of Cheddar: "Profligate, abusive, depraved, this proud man—this haughty sinner—this gentleman of Cheddar—is brought to confess, with joy and gratitude, that Jesus Christ came into the world to save sinners, and he is likewise brought to confess this truth amidst a congregation of poor people, over whom he has power, and over whom he has too often exercised it."[84] Many years later, Wilberforce wrote to her of his satisfaction at the small part he had played in initiating the work, but especially at her labors "for the benefit of your poor cottagers. . . . There is no part of your life on which I reflect with more pleasure than on the payment of your debt to the Barbarians, after settling your account so honourably with the Greeks—the polished inhabitants of the London squares."[85]

A modern historian has judged rightly the significance of the experiment at Cheddar: "The achievement proved that in certain areas, at least, Anglicanism could have a religious-cultural impact on a previously neglected community comparable with that which Methodism and New Dissent achieved in many industrial communities."[86] Another modern critic, whose hostility to evangelicalism has already been noted here, nevertheless re-marked on "the Evangelical superiority to the serene spectators of suffering, destitution, vice and helpless degradation" who were so numerous in the pe-riod.[87] Hannah More outlived all her sisters, and she remained in harness for the rest of her life. At the age of eighty-two, six years before her death, she wrote to a Claphamite ally: "I never had so little leisure in my life, now that I ought to have the most. Letters which I cannot answer; applications that I cannot comply with; company that I cannot refuse."[88] Yet one sus-pects that she would not have had it any other way.

THE EVANGELICAL SOCIETIES

The More sisters made a profound difference in their own community. The generality of Evangelicals found that they could band together into societies of special interest and make analogous contributions to the whole nation.

Gladstone observed in his article on the growth of Evangelicalism that the movement was too individualistic, more so even than Dissent, and that this was a "besetting weakness."[89] Gladstone did not specify what he meant by that, but the charge against evangelical individualism has been made many times before and since. Some High Church partisans could make such a statement and mean by it that the evangelical doctrine of justification did not need church or sacrament, but only the individual's faith; but that is not likely to have been Gladstone's meaning, for his doctrine of justification was not far from the Evangelical one. If the meaning is that the Evangelicals thought the company of others was dispensable, there is no justification for the charge, for the movement accomplished much of its mission through the development of voluntary societies, indeed made them a dominant form of social action in nineteenth-century England. The constitutional scholar Walter Bagehot later on wrote as if such societies were a funda-mental part of English life, in contrast to, say, France, where nobody could do anything without gaining first the permission of the *préfet*.[90] Bagehot at-tributed this phenomenon in England to the ancient powers of the munic-ipalities, which exercised a check on the central authority, but I think it doubtful that he would even have noticed it had not he been preceded by the extraordinary proliferation of Evangelical and then other societies in the two or three generations preceding his own.

The societies that became the dominant mode of Evangelical social action in the nineteenth century had predecessors. We have already seen the SPCK's beginning as the seventeenth century drew to a close, and there were others as well. The Eclectic Society, though neither well known nor open for public participation, may have been the most important of the new societies. Founded by two Oxford men, Henry Foster and Richard Cecil, along with a few colleagues, the group met once a fortnight for the purpose of mutual fellowship and exchanging ideas. The first meeting was held at the Castle and Falcon Inn on Aldersgate Street on January 16, 1783. Considering all that came out of this society, it is surprising to learn that it comprised not much more than a dozen persons. Along with the clergymen, there were a few laymen and even a Dissenting minister or two.[91] This society gave the hitherto few and scattered Evangelical clergymen an opportunity to break out of their isolation—one might say out of their individualism—and set the stage for the formation of the societies that would do the real work of the movement. For example, the minutes show that on February 4, 1799, the Rev. Josiah Pratt proposed as the question for discussion how much utility there would be in establishing a periodical to further the "interests of religion." There were no additional notes taken on the content of that meeting, but the editor noted that the result was the formation of the foremost Evangelical publication for at least thirty years, the *Christian Observer*, which first saw the light of day in January 1802. The periodical was, in effect, the voice of the Clapham branch of the religious revival.[92]

The Church Missionary Society (CMS) was another feather in the cap of the Eclectic Society, having been founded out of discussions at the latter between Charles Simeon and Charles Grant. They met with colleagues (again at the Castle and Falcon Inn) on April 12, 1799, and the CMS was born.[93] In 1813–14 the CMS conducted a highly successful campaign by sending preachers out all over England in pairs to attract support to the missionary effort. (This should not be confused with Methodist itinerancy; they preached only in churches.)

After the turn of the century, the roster of societies grew. The Bible Society, the Lord's Day Observation Society, and the CMS were obvious evangelical interests. Perhaps less obviously so were the British and Foreign Temperance Society and the Royal Society for the Prevention of Cruelty to Animals. The evangelicals, within the Church and Dissenters as well, were interested in more than a narrowly religious agenda, although their motivation remained gospel centered. They sought and received increasing clerical and episcopal support, but the societies were dominated and funded by laymen. This may have been the reason for some of the "Low Church" charges that arose against Evangelicals, especially after the Tractarian movement got under way. As the evangelicals trooped into the societies, they spilled over into yet more societies; seemingly there was not an ill in

England that was not attacked by an evangelical society. By 1821, the annual index to the *Christian Observer* took half a column just to list the societies about which the journal had written during the year.

The formation of the Bible Society suggests the reason evangelicals of all affiliations believed the new societies were necessary. A religious awakening in the early 1790s had increased the demand for the scriptures. Repeated pleas to the SPCK for large press runs went unanswered, even with the inducement of financial guarantees. After a small printing by the SPCK in 1799 was quickly swallowed up by demand, the evangelicals gave up on the old organization and formed the Bible Society. By 1804 the list of supporters looked like a roster of Clapham: Wilberforce, Sharp, Grant, Macaulay, Teignmouth, and Thornton. Shrewdly, the organizers decided that the only role the society would play would be the distribution of Bibles. To gain the widest possible support, the thirty-six-member governing committee was to be made up of fifteen Churchmen, fifteen Dissenters, and six representatives of foreign churches. There would be no doctrinal teaching and no interpretation; thus they secured support for the venture from both Church and Dissent.[94] In fact, the breadth of support would later call on them the denunciations of the *Record,* which could not countenance the presence of Socinians in evangelical organizations.

It is easy to underestimate the enormous effect of Bible distribution on religious communities, which is usually to deepen religious fervor and make it more informed. After 1809, local auxiliaries to the Bible Society sprang up all over the country and thereby were able to meet local demands better than any centralized body could do. With good reason, if perhaps also with some hyperbole, the Bible Society has been described (surprisingly) by an unfriendly critic as "the greatest single agency of moral reform under the Christian dispensation that the world has seen."[95]

In addition to the broad-based societies, others were formed to correspond with special interests. In 1819, for example, the *Christian Observer* reported the establishment in the year previous of the Seamen's Bible Society. Members of the society boarded outbound ships to sell Bibles at subsidized prices. An interested seaman who could not afford a Bible would have one loaned to him for the duration of the voyage. In the year just ended, the society had supplied 1,200 ships, manned by a total of 16,000 sailors. They sold about 400 Bibles and Testaments and gave an additional 4,100 for general use by the crew. And those numbers do not count privately owned Bibles placed by individual donors.[96]

Later on, when psychological interpretations of human behavior came into vogue, it would be said that the philanthropical and missionary efforts of the evangelicals came out of a sense of guilt. These middle-class people had so much and were surrounded by such misery that a little largesse was needed to assuage their consciences. But reading the correspondence and publications of these evangelicals turns up little evidence for such an interpretation. Much more in keeping with the sources is the judgment of a social scientist who has argued that the societies were not examples of a philanthropy of guilt but rather of a "philanthropy of confidence." That is, they felt a confidence in the rightness of their cultural and social values and a responsibility to share those values with others—for the benefit of those others.[97]

EVANGELICALS AND THE ESTABLISHMENT

To some extent Evangelicals were so much involved in the societies because the state of tension between them and the leadership of the Church lasted until well past midcentury, forcing them to deflect their activism into other channels. Moreover, the Church itself was running into difficulties. Its status as the religion established by law gave it undeniable advantages. But those advantages carried with them liabilities that the Church found it difficult to overcome. For if the power of the state was the Church's ultimate sanction (for those who took seriously the Church's theology, of course, it was only penultimate), then anything that discredited the state also discredited its creature. Radicals from the period, William Cobbett for example, associated the Church with the repressive state. Cobbett claimed on the basis of observations made during his famous "rural rides" that ordinary people in the countryside had come to distrust the Church as profoundly as they did the state.[98] Because of the Church's status as a political actor on the local scene, it was often drawn into the normal disputes that interrupted the smooth amity of the community. The parson was frequently the magistrate as well, and he often was beholden to the local squire for his living. Studies of local communities show the political elite sometimes divided along religious lines, with the Church on one side and Dissent on the other.[99]

Such challenges to the Church's legitimacy were compounded by implicit or explicit claims that the Church was not fulfilling her spiritual function. After all, it was, as Wilberforce's title had it, the "prevailing religious practices" that the Evangelicals were calling into question, and the fact that they were loyal Churchmen in a way made the experience more galling for the Establishment. For it was only to be expected that the Church should bear criticism from its enemies, but it was much worse that its loyal members should parade its faults before the whole world. When the *Record* began publishing, it was with an unequivocal statement of loyalty to the

Establishment: "But we conceive the Church of England to be a true Gospel Church, built upon the foundation of the Apostles and Prophets, Jesus Christ being the chief cornerstone. Whatever be its defects, it has the power to remedy them."[100] By the 1840s it was saying openly what was implicit all along: the religious principles of the Evangelical clergy "are in more exact harmony with those of the confessor and martyrs of our Church . . . than those of any other section of the Church whatever."[101] Still, there is in the strongest protestations of loyalty to the Established Church an implicit threat of disloyalty. For if the putative loyalists were so much more loyal than those who wielded power in the Church, a day might come when being under the same roof as the leadership would become intolerable. When the *Christian Observer* opposed Lord Sidmouth's imposition of restrictions on the Dissenters in 1810, that seemed to some observers to imply its siding with Dissent against the Established Church to which it had always professed its loyalty.

In its annual survey of 1825, the *Christian Observer* was optimistic that the Evangelicals' cause was on the rise in the Church of England. But it was sensible of the fact that "the most vociferous denunciations" against them came from Anglicans who did not accept what the Evangelicals considered to be the basic principles of Christian faith.[102] The remnants of the old High Church were especially alarmed at the increasing respectability of the Evangelicals. Their periodical the *Anti-Jacobin* in 1816 spread the old church-and-state-in-danger alarm with special urgency because it found "puritans" in the Parliament and the army; only the blind could fail to see the dangers of "a second *usurpation* without the chance of a second restoration."[103] It was not clear who the new Cromwell would be, but presumably the movement could give birth to its leader as well as the other way around. When Granville Sharp died in 1813, the vicar of Fulham would not permit a funeral sermon to be preached for him in the church because of Sharp's connection with the Bible Society.[104] And, as we have seen, even in the 1820s, when Simeon was one of the most influential members of the Church, he was blackballed when he tried to join the SPCK. (A little over a century later, the same organization published his biography.)[105]

Relations with the bishops were marked by some of the same hostility but also the beginning of something else. In its first issue, the *Record* announced that it was not going to be an arena for religious disputations and that it would not "wound the feelings of any class of Christians." There was to be only one exception to that noble intention. "We shall, however, feel no obligation to extend similar forbearance to that antichristian Hierarchy" that directs the affairs of the Church of England.[106] Such hostility was the fruit of a long period of snubs, and worse, from the bishops. By 1810 the CMS had still been unable to count on the formal support of a single bishop. We have already seen Bishop Marsh's "test," designed to prevent Evangelical incumbents from defiling the diocese. In 1815 and 1816, the bishops of Lincoln, Chester, Carlisle, and Ely opposed the Bible Society in the charges to their clergy.[107] John Venn's son, Henry (secretary of the CMS for thirty years), recalled that one day a close relative of the bishop of London came to call on his father at the Clapham rectory. The vicar's two sons were required to wait for the woman at a public house three hundred yards from the rectory. Henry Venn concluded: "The truth being that the Bishop of London could not allow his carriage to be seen to draw up at Mr. Venn's Rectory, though it might be seen to set down a lady at a small public-house."[108]

Wilberforce had tried to gain the confidence of the bishops as early as 1787, at the time of George III's Proclamation for the Encouragement of Piety and Virtue. He communicated with them individually, lest the opposition of a few should poison the rest against the venture to make the proclamation effectual. The Wilberforce brothers cited the *Morning Chronicle* as evidence that their father was successful in that venture.[109] Bishop Porteous of London, who became a good friend of Evangelical ventures, wrote a congratulatory letter to Wilberforce on the publication of the *Practical View*. "I am truly thankful to Providence that a work of this nature had made its appearance at this tremendous moment."[110] John Henry Newman complained that a later bishop of London, Blomfield, offended the Tractarians at Oxford with his introduction of Evangelicals to positions of trust.[111] With the accession of Henry Ryder to the see of Gloucester in 1815 (Lichfield in 1824), the Evangelicals were finally represented on the episcopal bench. John Bird Sumner became bishop of Chester in 1828 and archbishop of Canterbury in 1848. His younger brother, Charles Richard Sumner was appointed bishop of Winchester in 1827, where he remained for more than forty years. Later on, Evangelical bishops were no longer an oddity, and during Palmerston's prime ministry (with the Earl of Shaftesbury breathing into the PM's ear) it became common to see Evangelicals with miters. Notwithstanding the gradual shift of opinion in the hierarchy, the *Record's* hostility in 1828 suggests there was still considerable opposition to them at that time.

THE PLACE OF THE EVANGELICALS IN ENGLISH HISTORY

The Evangelicals have been variously judged from their own time onward. Gladstone perhaps occupied an ideal position in that he was in basic agreement with much of the Evangelical stance but was unconnected with the *party* that went by that name and could see its strengths and weaknesses more clearly than a partisan of either the party or the opposed group. He viewed the Evangelicals as "restorers" of certain emphases that had been part of the Church but had been lost or neglected. They did their work imperfectly, however, and were sometimes guilty of using a "false method of presenting the true," thus giving the gospel "the air of a bargain in a shop."[112] Gladstone's critique of methods and airs suggests he was taking issue with accidents rather than essences. As late as the second half of the twentieth century, some studies, even by well-regarded historians, have been so ideologically tinged as to make them completely unreliable.[113]

The growth of the Church Evangelicals was quite dramatic when one considers the very weak beginnings—a few clergymen thinly dotting the English countryside. The Evangelicals were sensible of the way their numbers had grown. John Venn adverted to the modest beginnings when William Romaine began his work in 1749 and knew of perhaps only a half-dozen like-minded parsons. When he died in 1795, he knew of more than five hundred.[114] The historian Lecky, responding to criticisms that Gladstone made in the essay cited above, acknowledged that Gladstone was right in correcting his account of the number of Evangelical clergy at the close of the eighteenth century; they were actually of a much smaller number than he had previously thought. But he held firm to the larger point of cultural domination, which he thought had largely been accomplished long before Gladstone's date for that circumstance, the 1840s. Lecky called attention to a distinction that is not often enough drawn: that between the Evangelical *party* and Evangelical *influence.* Although their number may have been small in 1800, they had already made serious inroads in the way people thought and felt. Counting both its Dissenting and its Church manifestations, he believed, evangelicalism had become "the chief centre of religious activity in England." It had "attracted to itself nearly all the fervour, the activity, the spirit of religious propagandism and of religious enthusiasm that was circulating in the community." Lecky mentioned the poetry of Cowper, the politics of the Clapham group, and the popular theology that dominated the literature of all classes. He thought that four-fifths of all the literature produced came from evangelical sources.[115]

Leaving the question of quantity, we turn to quality. The early part of the nineteenth century may have seen the evangelical movement at its strongest internally. The vigor of its leadership in Clapham, Cambridge, and Bristol had not yet succumbed to old age, and the internal strife was limited. A later observer put his finger on the problem that occurred when the movement became more mature: hypocrisy started to become a problem because the growing respectability of the movement brought in adherents who only had to learn a few stock phrases to become part of it. These terms were very real to the people who had experienced the reality behind them but then "had become a convention, almost a shibboleth, and like all shibboleths, were capable of being imitated by the indolent and hypocritical."[116] Thus the well-known charge of hypocrisy that has dogged the movement for so long is something that was always extrinsic to it but was still observable in many of its adherents—the hypocrisy that attends all popular movements with exalted statements of purpose. That lent a sort of paradoxical quality to the evangelical movement that justified the description of it as "highly susceptible to abuse by charlatans, but . . . also [as] produc[ing] some of the noblest Victorians."[117]

As evangelical literature, terminology, and categories spread through the public consciousness, the sharp frontiers of doctrinal emphases and verbal expression that had made evangelicalism so easily identifiable gradually softened. The blurring of the boundaries was intolerable to those whose vision of the relationship between the common religion of the Established Church and the Evangelical movement was the same as Wilberforce had expressed in the title of his book: the former was the "prevailing religious system of professed Christians," and the latter was "real Christianity." But the society had shifted in the years since 1797, when the *Practical View* was published. The public consciousness had become much more in keeping with the vision Wilberforce was articulating, the numbers of Evangelical clergy and parishes were increasing, and it may have been possible to step away from the hostile stance toward society without giving up anything vital.

One of the most unusual episodes during this period was a manifestation of this dissatisfaction with the gentrification of the Evangelical spirit: the London career of the Scottish minister Edward Irving. Irving was never part of the Church of England, and he fits into our story only because he was at the center of an enormous controversy that inflamed the Church for several years. He had started his ministry as assistant to the celebrated Thomas Chalmers at St. John's, Glasgow. In 1822, at the age of twenty-nine, he became the minister at the Caledonian Chapel in London. A brilliant preacher, he soon attracted the attention of fashionable society, and the chapel was packed, Sunday after Sunday. After five years a new building in Regent Square was constructed. Thomas Carlyle, close friend of Irving from early manhood until the minister's untimely death, thought that the untoward adulation of the upper classes—including the Prime Minister, Canning—worked in some way to destabilize Irving, inasmuch as a certain naiveté or credulity marred his judgment.[118]

Irving's fall into general disfavor came about through his association with two disreputable points of view. One was an eschatology that contrasted with the general optimism of the times. Premillennial in orientation, this position was based on a biblical hermeneutic concluding that Christ would return at the end of a time of serious troubles, which were even then upon English society. Second, Irving began to allow a Pentecostal movement to take root in his church, and the building began resounding with the noisy manifestations of tongues and prophecies. This was not unique for the period, but Pentecostal manifestations had hitherto been confined to fringe groups that the higher classes did not frequent. The controversies in which Irving became engaged may have unhinged him further. When Chalmers heard him preach in Edinburgh in 1828, he was disturbed by the way his former assistant used a "mysterious and extreme allegorization. . . . I have no hesitation in saying it is quite woeful."[119]

Evangelical opinion on Irving was divided as early as 1823. In a review of his book on oracles, the *Christian Observer* noted that to mention his name within ten miles of London was to call forth "the language of exalted praise or excessive vituperation." Although disgusted with the abuse Irving was receiving, the review was unhappy with the "coarseness" of his writing and a style that seemed to invite criticism. Still at that time the paper was harder on Irving's enemies than on the man himself.[120] By 1829 the paper was grieved at Irving's intolerance of other points of view, in particular his lack of appreciation for the Evangelical societies, which, it said, might have been expected in a Roman Catholic or Unitarian. In short, it said, drawing on the Old Testament story of the banishment of Abraham's son, Irving had become "the Ishmael of the Christian world, his hand being against every man."[121] By the time the *Record* began publishing at the beginning of 1828, the hue and cry against Irving had already been given, and the new hardline paper quickly joined in. But the extent of Irving's support was such that years later, long after Irving's death, the editor commented that "at no time in the history of this Journal, were we exposed to so much obloquy and reproach as when we assailed the embryo heresies of Mr. Irving."[122] And by the time that was written, the *Record* had already been engaged heavily in the polemical wars with the High Church Tractarians at Oxford.

Irving in the end was defrocked by the Church of Scotland. He fought the action and lost the fight; two years later he was dead, and with him the movement. The *Record*, far from trumpeting over the fallen, soberly contemplated the defrocking. "Our personal feelings are those of sorrow, regret, and mortification. We sincerely mourn over Mr. Irving."[123] Carlyle was to mourn much more. "No man I have known had a sunnier type of character, or so little of hatred toward any man or thing. . . . Noble Irving! He was the faithful elder brother of my life in those years; generous, wise, beneficent."[124]

Part of Irving's appeal was his call for a more serious, less accommodating relationship, one that took seriously what was still considered by many to be the debased moral situation in which society found itself. The shift in eschatological expectations was part of this, with the gradually improving postmillennial hopes seeming pallid and unconvincing for those who saw disaster looming. The most visible institutional opposition to the blander version of Evangelicalism was the founding of the *Record* on the first day of 1828.[125] In a short time there was something approximating open warfare between the main publications of the two sides. The *Record,* for example, took umbrage over the *Christian Observer's* criticism of an Evangelical MP named Gordon. They were not surprised that the secular newspapers were unhappy with Mr. Gordon, but they read the *Observer's* attack with "grief." They concluded that the *Observer* had "slid into the evil temper of the age."[126] This was code language: to display the spirit of the age is worldliness, which means to leave the service of God and go over to his enemies. So characteristic was this of a subset of Evangelicals that they have been given a name—the Recordites.

The split in Evangelicalism did not mean the powers of the movement had come to an end. The Claphamite successors' accommodationist position, if that is what it was, could lead to such a blurring of lines that the distinctiveness that made the movement what it was would be lost. The Recordite solution to that required the Evangelicals to erect a kind of protective shield against the contamination of what they considered to be a godless society. But the more impermeable the shield, the less influence the proponents of that position could have on the wider community, and the more shrill and useless would be its denunciations. There is never a simple answer to the dilemma posed by this situation, nor is it unique to the Evangelicals of the early nineteenth century. All dissident groups, political, religious, or moral, face the same kind of quandary.

As is the case for many aspects of the society of the period, we lack good statistics about the Evangelicals. Under Gladstone's criticism, Lecky backed down from what he acknowledged was an exaggeration of the number of Evangelical clergymen at the beginning of the century. In 1853, one critic reckoned Evangelicals to be about one-third of the clergymen in the Church. Owen Chadwick believes that is too high and points to an Evangelical estimate of a few years earlier that counted about 3,000 Evangelicals out of a total of 13,000. But there were both rosy analysts and doomsayers among the Evangelicals, and Chadwick thinks a better measure might be the clerical subscribers to the Church Pastoral Aid Society, which provided Evangelical curates and lay workers to needy parishes. This society numbered 1,700 in 1841, and two later crises added perhaps another 400.[127] Needless to say, figures derived from a methodology of that kind need to be taken very lightly.

Whatever the truth about the numbers, Gladstone, like Lecky, believed that in the early movement at least, the effectiveness of the Evangelicals was all out of proportion to their numerical strength and their lack of clerical preferment. "In activity and moral influence, they counted for a good deal more. The vessels of zeal and fervour, taken man for man, far outweighed the heroes of the ball-room and the hunting-field . . . who supplied so considerable a number of the clerical host."[128] Sabine Baring-Gould, who spent most of his book on the Evangelicals describing their weaknesses, held a position on that point almost the same as Gladstone's. He spoke of an "incalculable debt of gratitude" owed to the Evangelical revival because of the "marvellous change in English social life," referring to the refinement of speech, the use of prayers, the increase in personal piety, the Sunday schools, the hymns, and the improvement of preaching.[129]

These assessments were anticipated by Wilberforce's own reflections as he neared death. Calling the Dissenting minister William Jay to him for a final interview, Wilberforce said: "I see much in the state of the world and church which I deplore, yet I am not among the croakers. I think real religion is spreading; and, I am persuaded, will increasingly spread, till the earth is filled with the knowledge of the Lord."[130]

It was not only people fitting comfortably under the "Evangelical" rubric who exemplified the spirit implied in that word. Lecky, who could not have been happy with the phenomenon, believed that the doctrines stressed by the Evangelicals came to be taught much more in other quarters than they had previously. He even quoted Gladstone to the effect that the moralistic preaching so common in his youth was now largely gone, replaced by the teaching of the whole gospel message. "The doctrine of justification by faith, which in the beginning of the Hanoverian period would have sounded almost like a paradox," said Lecky, "had a century later become a commonplace in the Anglican pulpit."[131] Hence the number of Evangelical clergymen is a question that fades in significance: a dissident movement is never so effective as when its adversaries begin singing the same tune.

Oxford and the Search for the Ancient Catholic Vision

ROOTS OF THE TRACTARIAN MOVEMENT

For about seven years, beginning in 1833, a group of academics and academically inclined clergymen connected with Oxford University issued a series of writings called Tracts. These bore no resemblance to the Evangelical tracts distributed by the millions for the previous forty years or so. Rather, they were mostly sophisticated academic writings that were intended to restore to the Church of England some of the emphases their writers believed had been neglected over the years. Because of these writings and their place of origin, the program went under the name of the *Tractarian* or the *Oxford* Movement. The tracts proved to be extremely contentious, some more so than others, and the brouhaha that erupted after the issuance of the last of them, the ninetieth, effectively ended the movement, at least in that form. Yet the influence of the writings and, possibly even more, the personalities that issued the writings were so powerful that it spread out over much of the country, lasting far longer than the movement itself, even to the present day.

The significance of the movement for our story is that it represents a major part of the religious reaction against the Enlightenment century—against the conscious secularity of the high-born and educated, against the antisupernaturalism that was widespread in the Church, and against the time-serving clergy. The Tractarians differed from other elements of the renewal in that they believed they were recovering certain ancient teachings about the Church: its status as the repository of the gospel, the efficacy of the sacraments and the powers of the priests that administered them, and the role of the bishops as the heirs of the apostolic succession. The movement also represents a reaction against the Erastian tendencies that the Tractarians saw taking place in England, the increasing domination by functionaries of the state in religious matters, which lowered the high position they believed was due the Church. Because their attention was riveted on the Church rather than the society, the social effect of the Tractarians is not immediately apparent. It is to be found partly in the parishes that

JOHN HENRY NEWMAN.
By courtesy of the National Portrait Gallery, London.

adopted the High Church teaching and manner of worship, partly in the labors of the ritualist priests of the next generation, toiling in the slums, and partly in the changed mode of discourse of the Victorian period, to which the Tractarians contributed along with the other elements of the religious revival.

The name with which the movement is chiefly associated is that of John Henry Newman (1801–1890), a young tutor in Oriel College, but he had three close associates. Edward Pusey (1800–1882), an orientalist trained in Germany, became Regius professor of Hebrew at Oxford. John Keble (1792–1866), at the start of a brilliant academic career, took a double first at Oxford, which was almost unheard of. He was elected a fellow of Oriel at age nineteen, his reputation for both brilliance and piety serving to draw many to the college. He resigned his fellowship in 1823 to be the curate of his father's country parish and then in 1835 became vicar of Hursley near

Winchester, where he lived out his days. He accepted the Oxford professorship of poetry reluctantly and in 1827 published one of the most famous poetry books of the early nineteenth century, *The Christian Year*, only upon the urging of friends. Richard Hurrell Froude (1803–1836) was a graduate and fellow of Oriel College and in spite of his early death exercised considerable influence upon the other members of the movement and the students of Oxford.

The Church of England was the product of two traditions that bifurcated in the sixteenth century. When Henry VIII separated the Church of England from Rome, it was for political and dynastic reasons. His minor son and successor came under the influence of advisors who influenced him to move the Church in a Protestant direction. For more than a century after that, the nation oscillated between Catholicism (sometimes covertly) and Protestantism. The most visible religious conflict in England in the 1830s and 1840s was between those who were trying to recover the Catholic emphases that had been lost and those who were trying to preserve its Protestant character. Even after the connection with Rome was definitively broken, there remained as a part of the Church a school of thought that saw the Anglican Establishment as a form of Catholicism—even the highest form, because it was stripped of the "superstitions" of Rome. This High Church position persisted up to the start of the Tractarian movement, when it was absorbed into the energies released by the Oxford activists. High Churchmanship laid great emphasis on the Church of England as a branch of the universal (catholic) church; the supreme value of Scripture as interpreted by the creeds, the prayer book, and the writings of the early fathers; the validity of the sacraments; the necessity for good works; adherence to the Tory values of continuity with the traditions and institutions that had been inherited; and the religious Establishment.[1]

Prior to the Tractarians, the best organized group of High Churchmen was centered in a London suburb called Hackney and for a time was known as the "Hackney Phalanx." Their clerical leader was Henry Handley Norris (1771–1850), a wealthy clergyman and philanthropist. Norris's brother-in-law, Joshua Watson (1771–1855), was the most prominent layman in the group. A wealthy wine merchant, he retired in 1814 and devoted himself to church and charitable work. He organized the National Society for the Education of the Poor and helped found the Church Building Society. In a manner similar to the Evangelical leaders, he was also associated with a number of other societies. The Hackney Phalanx has been given the "High and Dry" label of the High Church of the previous century—that is, maintenance of the prerogatives of the Church and its sacraments, while failing to add genuine piety to the formal adherence—but in recent years historians have questioned whether the expressions of contempt ever were fair.[2]

The Tractarian movement did not come about *ex nihilo* but was undoubtedly related to the general climate of feeling in England that gave rise also to other manifestations of religious interest. John Henry Newman, writing as the movement crested, thought that Catholic feeling had been increasingly manifest in Britain for some years before the movement began. He emphasized that he meant a "feeling" independent of any intellectual basis for it, before people knew what they ought to believe or what actions to take as a consequence. He did not profess to be able to explain exactly how that general feeling had come about, but he cited the influence of two writers who had much to do with it. He was far from endorsing their work as a whole, but he thought the literature of Sir Walter Scott and Samuel Taylor Coleridge was seminal in preparing the public for a more systematic exploration of the consequences of Catholic thinking. Scott prepared the way by sensitizing the feeling, and Coleridge laid "a philosophical basis" for Catholic philosophy and "succeeded in interesting [the age's] genius in the cause of Catholic truth." But Newman regarded these writers less as causes of the Catholic revival than "as indications of what was secretly going on in the minds of men."[3]

EVANGELICAL ORIGINS

It is a plain fact, which was sometimes embarrassing to the Tractarian leaders, that many members of the movement were Evangelicals before they became convinced of High Church principles.[4] The most celebrated example was Newman himself. At the age of fifteen, he came under the influence of Walter Mayers, an Evangelical clergyman of Calvinist leanings, through sermons, conversations, and books that Mayers put into his hands. As a result he experienced an evangelical conversion. As Newman told the story many years later, when he was long out of the Anglican fold and a Roman Catholic priest, the experience was as valid for him then as when it had first taken place. He still regarded Mayers as an "excellent man . . . the human means of this beginning of divine faith in me." He no longer believed the typically Calvinist doctrine of final perseverance that he had learned from Mayers but stated that of the experience of conversion, "I still am more certain than that I have hands and feet."[5]

Other Tractarians also had Evangelical roots. Edward Pusey's family on both sides was from the nobility. Although we do not have any account of a conversion in his story, his family had Evangelical leanings. Henry Manning, a Tractarian who would later become the leader of English Roman Catholicism, was converted in 1831 as a result of his relationship with an Evangelical family that had befriended him. "All this made a new thought spring up in me," he wrote, " . . . not to be a clergyman in the sense of my old destiny, but to give up the world and to live for God. . . . It was a turning point in my life."[6] R. W. Church, later dean of St. Paul's, went to Redlands, an Evangelical school near Bristol. Although he was later to recall the school without saying anything about fond memories, it is not unlikely that some of its teachings sank in to have some later effect.[7] Gladstone had been a fervent Evangelical until reading High Church theology during a vacation in 1830, when he became fascinated with the idea of the Church as the visible institution of God's revelation. Thenceforth he threw his lot in with the Tractarians, becoming a good friend of many of them. Keble once called him "Pusey in a blue-coat."[8] But it was principally his idea of the Church that changed; his Evangelical convictions remained largely intact. Henry Liddon, Pusey's disciple and biographer, viewed the Tractarian movement as a "completion" of Evangelicalism that compensated for the latter's one-sided fixation on the Pauline epistles to the exclusion of the rest of Scripture. Pusey himself regarded the Evangelicals as the most fervent spark of religion in the first three decades of the century and "to the last day of his life . . . retained that 'love of the Evangelicals' to which he often adverted."[9] Of Wilberforce's four sons, three studied at Oxford during the years of Tractarian ascendancy, and all of them were strongly influenced by the movement. Robert and Henry, their father having been safely laid to rest in Westminster Abbey, followed Newman to Rome. Samuel, sorely grieved by his brothers' decisions to leave, remained in the Church, becoming one of the most energetic and effective bishops of the century, with most of his episcopal tenure as bishop of Oxford.

LITERARY ROOTS OF TRACTARIANISM

The Enlightenment and the French Revolution, as well as the marching armies that followed that revolution, made it appear as if the Catholic Church was soon to perish, but the following decades saw its revival. The affinity of some forms of Romanticism for religion is often noted, and the Catholic revival in the nineteenth century throughout much of Europe has long been associated with that movement. Much of the Romantic preoccupation with religion on the Continent was explicitly anti-Protestant. The Reformation was taken to have been an offensive episode that broke the unity of Europe, including the aesthetic spirit that had produced the Continent's finest art.

The genius of Fra Angelico could not be explained, it was said, except by the content of his faith; hence German painters became Roman Catholic in droves. It was not only Catholics who despised both Reformation and Enlightenment; noted non- and even anti-Catholics like Carlyle, Cobbett, and Disraeli showed the same attitude toward the Reformation.[10]

As on the Continent, literary influences on religion made themselves felt in England as well. Wordsworth was the main influence on Keble, who was the poet of the movement. Wordsworth praised Keble's *Christian Year*, as most people did, but there was something faint about his encomium: the book was so good he wished he had written it so that he could make it still better. The *Christian Year* bore the stamp of Wordsworth's influence, as did Keble's *Lectures on Poetry,* published in 1844. Perhaps the most signal benefit Wordsworth performed for Keble was modify the hold that the empirical psychology of Locke and Hartley held over much of his generation. In place of the blank mind, passively receiving what impressions the senses placed on it, Wordsworth (and to a lesser extent Coleridge) saw the human mind as active, creative, doing original things, and this was communicated to Keble and then to Keble's readers. It was for good reason, and little enough payment, that Keble dedicated the *Lectures on Poetry* to Wordsworth.[11] Evidently Coleridge was responsible for Keble's reworking of the old High Church formulations with which he had grown up into aesthetic metaphors. The Church, besides what traditional formulations might be adduced, was also *poetic;* it was a "work of art."[12] Liddon believed that Coleridge's main contribution to the Tractarians was the introduction of a method rather than specific philosophical content. Although he was a dreamer who seemed to have accomplished little—"projecting schemes which were never carried out"—Coleridge was instrumental in making men dissatisfied with the superficial thinking that preceded him and so disposed them to listen to the new Oxford school.[13] Carlyle, who thought little of Coleridge, especially after meeting the poet in his opium-sodden dotage, called him the "father of Puseyism," which by then was the derisive name attached to the Tractarian movement.[14] When R. W. Church first considered attending Newman's afternoon sermons at St. Mary's, he dismissed the idea because he thought there was nothing there but hero worship of Newman and a fashionable kind of religious philosophy that Church called "evangelico-Coleridgian."[15]

Walter Scott's influence was a spiritual presence rather than a set of ideas. Newman had always loved his novels of the Middle Ages, and his friends were of the same mind. We have a report from Elizabeth Sewell, the prolific Tractarian novelist and devotional writer, of a dinner in 1840 on the occasion of the dedication of a new church. Newman, Keble, Williams, and others of their colleagues talked with animation and verve of *Guy Mannering*. Many of those who denounced the Tractarians included Scott in their anathemas.[16]

Scott was both the product and the progenitor of the fascination with the medieval epoch that characterized the era. There is no doubt that this contributed to the increasing interest in the Catholic aspects of the High Church. *Gothic* had had distinctly negative connotations for many decades, but with the new sensibilities, and especially the reaction against the prejudices of the Enlightenment, the word was rehabilitated, along with regard for the period it symbolized. The architecture that went by that name took on new charms, whereas the eighteenth century had been able to see only barbarity in it. The pointed arch came to symbolize freedom; it was thought to resemble the intertwined branches of the tree and therefore to be natural and good.[17] With the church-building program of the early part of the century, gothic-shaped churches dotted the countryside. Conservatives like Southey naturally took to the new assessment of the medieval with enthusiasm, but even those who derided the new obsession might still reflect it. John Stuart Mill praised the medieval romances for "keeping alive the chivalrous spirit . . . giving to the aspirations of the young and susceptible a noble direction, and keeping present to the mind an exalted standard of worth."[18] This interest in the medieval was not the driving motivation for the Tractarian leaders but rather was important for the climate of opinion that made so many people receptive to their arguments.

There is one additional writer to be mentioned in this context, and that is Keble himself. Modern readers seldom are able to show much enthusiasm for his book of poetry, *The Christian Year*, published in 1827, but its appeal can be seen in the great variety of people who were enthralled by it, including multitudes who had no use for the Tractarian movement, for which it was a defining document. Newman's praise might be suspect, did it not reflect the thinking of the multitudes: "It is not necessary, and scarcely becoming, to praise a book which has already become one of the classics of the language. When the general tone of religious literature was so nerveless and impotent, as it was at that time, Keble struck an original note and woke up in the hearts of thousands a new music, the music of a school, long unknown in England. Nor can I pretend to analyze, in my own instance, the effect of religious teaching so deep, so pure, so beautiful." He learned from his "new master," said Newman, two major intellectual truths: first, the sacramental system, which is to say, that material phenomena represent real unseen things; second, the intellectual and spiritual necessity to affirm by faith and love doctrines that do not have evidential corroboration.[19]

JOHN KEBLE.
By courtesy of the National Portrait Gallery, London.

THE START OF THE MOVEMENT

I have devoted so much attention to the movement before getting to its beginning because, more than most, its essence consisted principally of a moral and spiritual atmosphere rather than a series of events. Although Tractarianism was a species of the genus "High Church," its nature partook of something that was in the air in the 1830s, but not much earlier. Some have denied the uniqueness of the Tractarians by highlighting the existence of the High Church all the way through the previous century.

According to this interpretation, ensuing generations have been misled by self-serving Tractarian writers who for their own purposes overemphasized their uniqueness by ignoring or downplaying their immediate predecessors.[20] But it is difficult to imagine the movement taking place much earlier than it did because the culture was not prepared to receive it. Even in the 1830s it was hard for the Tractarians to get a fair hearing among the Oxford Establishment; a half century earlier it would have been almost unthinkable.

On July 14, 1833, Keble, as professor of poetry and fellow of Oriel College, preached in the university pulpit the sermon for the Assize Court meeting, published under the title "National Apostasy." He took as his text the passage in 1 Sam. 12, in which Israel turned away from God to worship the pagan idols, and he drew the conclusion that England was repeating the apostasy in their own day. The general disrespect shown to the successors of the apostles (the current bishops) was symptomatic of the apostasy of the Church and of the nation, and only a return to real piety—to prayer, humility, and renewed zeal—could right the situation. Evidently, the sermon as it was preached made little impression on the assembled judges and guests, but Newman's opinion seems to have carried the judgment of most future historians: "I have ever considered and kept the day, as the start of the religious movement of 1833."[21]

The immediate occasion for Keble's concern was the suppression of the ten Irish bishoprics by the new Whig government, but the real issue was the change in relationships within the Establishment that this event portended. It seemed to High Church people a high-handed, presumptuous move of the state, one in which the ancient prerogatives and traditions of the Anglican Church were being overthrown. It followed soon after the repealing of the Test and Corporation Acts in 1828, which relieved Dissenters of some of the restrictions to their public life, and the Roman Catholic Emancipation Act in 1829. These acts seemed to ensure that parliamentary decisions affecting the Church of England would be made by non-Anglicans.[22] Added together, they seemed to indicate that the Church was going to be under the complete subjection of the state, an Erastian overturning of the balance that had persisted since the Restoration. Keble's biographer notes that the issue of Erastianism was poorly addressed by his harping on the Irish Bishoprics' Bill, since it tied a real issue—the independence of the Church from illegitimate interference by the state—to the defense of a condition of manifest injustice, the forced support by Roman Catholic Irish people of a Church for which they had no respect or loyalty.[23]

WHAT WERE THE TRACTARIANS AFTER?

The Tractarian movement has been called a "clerical counter-reformation," a reaction against the original reformation, which was supposedly (as James Anthony Froude maintained) a revolt of the laity against the clergy.[24] The justification for such a claim lies in the fact that every one of the leading Oxford reformers was a clergyman. The Tractarians themselves would not have subscribed to this interpretation, which would make of their movement a merely sociological occurrence or a quest for personal power. Newman himself said the main item on their agenda was "the principle of dogma: my battle was with liberalism." The operative word in that description was *principle*. Newman did not mean they were dealing with various doctrines that, taken together, added up to a superdoctrine called liberalism. No, the differences were more profound than that, as he made clear. By *liberalism*, "I mean the anti-dogmatic principle and its developments." This principle, Newman suggested, treated religion "as a mere sentiment," which "is to me a dream and a mockery," something on the order of filial love without a father.[25] As aggressive as the Tractarian movement might appear to outsiders, from the inside it was regarded as a defensive response. Newman spoke about defending against "the assault of Liberalism upon the old orthodoxy of Oxford and England."[26] Liberalism was more of an *ur*-doctrine than a doctrine and as such led to various doctrines that the orthodox opposed. They opposed many of the social and political events of the period for reasons that transcended politics. Rather, they saw agitation for such innovations as the great Reform Bill as attempts to build the Kingdom of God out of purely earthly materials. This made for bad policy because it was first bad theology, an example of the self-salvation of the Pelagian heresy.[27]

Along with the theology and ecclesiology that informed whatever they did, the Tractarians were impelled by personal motivations. Their writings convey a certain emotional quality that sometimes seems to be compounded of bitterness and resentment; occasionally it appears close to hatred. R. W. Church spoke of the older Oxford liberals as either "intellectually aristocratic" or "poor in character." In the first case they held their position "from the zest of sneering and mocking" at the received opinions; in the second they were motivated by "the convenience of getting rid of strict and troublesome rules of life," by which he evidently meant the moral requirements incumbent on orthodox Christians.[28] When Church contrasted the Tractarians with the remnant of the old High Church, he said of the former that "a great anger possessed them."[29] Newman admitted that the Liberal successes "fretted me inwardly. I became fierce against its instruments and its manifestations." In this passage he writes of sighting a French vessel at Algiers on his return home from Italy. "I would not even look at the tricolor." When he had to stop in Paris for a day, he refused to go out of doors to see what he acknowledged was a beautiful city because he associated everything French with the progress of liberalism.[30] Froude's *Remains* contain the comment, "Really I hate the Reformation and the Reformers more and more." And Froude wrote of the devastation that came from their work in terms that came from the Apocalypse.[31] Keble's sermons (and to a lesser extent Newman's) had about them an apocalyptic flavor such that one specialist compares them to those of the Scottish preacher Edward Irving. Keble was wont to invoke visions of the impending end of the world in order to encourage repentance and right conduct.[32]

THE TRACTARIAN APPROACH TO THE SPIRITUAL LIFE

Taxed by charges of being stalking-horses for Roman Catholicism,[33] having a medieval approach to religion, and, later, being excessively infatuated with ritual, the Tractarians were actually motivated principally by a concern about inner spirituality. If the Evangelicals were concerned primarily with the doctrine of justification, the Tractarians were similarly preoccupied with that of sanctification. The old texts that informed them were mainly not those of the Middle Ages but rather those of antiquity. Their central focus on the Eucharist was related to that kind of spirituality: the contemplation of the Savior's sufferings would engender in the worshiper a concomitant feeling of surrender to God and willingness to suffer in obedience.[34] If this sounds similar to the emotionalism of the more pietistic manifestations of religion, that is misleading. The Oxford group rejected the kind of intellectualism that informed their Oriel College contemporaries, the "Noetics" whom they thought of as liberals, but for the most part one reads them in vain to discover emotional appeals. (Some of Newman's writings and especially his sermons were another matter.) For them the dogmas of the Christian religion, the *facts* of which the sacraments were representations (although they were not only that), were things that engendered the right response, which included an emotional response. The heart would embrace what the mind had come to understand, but the understanding, of itself, was barren.[35]

One of Newman's complaints about evangelicalism was the same that he levied against liberalism: it is too subjective, focusing its attention on "the heart itself, not to anything external to us."[36] The problem for Newman was not the emotion but the substitution of the emotion for the realities that lie beyond it. This was as unfair a generalization as any levied against Newman and his friends, but there is no doubt that he sincerely believed it. Nor is there any doubt about Newman's own susceptibility to words that stir the heart: we have already seen the stunning effect *The Christian Year* had on him.

That antipathy for Evangelical emphases also lay behind the related Tractarian doctrine on *reserve* in religious teaching. This was systematically introduced in Tract #80, written by Isaac Williams in 1837 and entitled *On Reserve in Communicating Religious Knowledge.* Williams says in his autobiography that he composed the tract specifically to refute the Evangelicals by exposing "their hollow mode of reasoning." It was widely understood to advocate the withholding of the gospel message, sometimes with the inference that only the elite (that is, the Tractarians) could understand the real message, but Williams says that was a misunderstanding. His meaning was that a certain reticence had to be kept in teaching the gospel; it was to be not withheld but taught with reserve, so as to avoid presumption.[37] There were antecedents to the Tractarian doctrine going back a long way. Locke taught something like it, counseling parents, for example, not to be too forward in acquainting their children with the knowledge of God. This was picked up by eighteenth-century evangelical stalwarts like Isaac Watts and Philip Doddridge, although the idea eventually petered out among the Evangelicals.[38] Many others doubtless had the same attitude, perhaps without being able to specify a doctrine to justify it. When Jane Austen lay dying, her spiritual counselors found her composed; they were surprised that one who had shrunk from religious speech during her life should have such settled convictions about such matters.[39]

Although Williams wrote the tract on the subject, the mainspring of the Tractarian teaching on reserve was Keble. This product of the piety that belonged to the High Church tradition was nevertheless very far from the prevalent "High and Dry" school. When the Wilberforce brothers arrived in Oxford, they were looking forward to conversing with this reputed saint and were nonplused at his refusal to discuss spiritual matters with them. Robert Wilberforce once wondered aloud to Williams how Keble could keep Law's *Serious Call* hidden away in a drawer instead of displaying it where it could influence others and do some good. Keble felt deeply but considered it unseemly to speak what he felt. He once turned the irrepressible Froude to serious reflection: "Froude, you thought Law's *Serious Call* was a clever book; it seemed to me as if you had said the Day of Judgment will be a pretty sight."[40] In the *Lectures on Poetry* Keble asked, "Do we not find that men of loftiest piety are reserved and reverent as regards holiest things; they bear themselves religiously in religious worship, and only in the narrow circle of intimate friends ever speak of God's forgiveness or their hopes of heaven?"[41] As characteristic of the Tractarians as reserve came to be, it was not universally applied. Newman was a substantial holdout, and his heart could frequently be found on his sleeve. The future poet Arthur Hugh Clough, then an Oxford student, was disgusted with Newman's emotional "Methodism."[42]

THE TRACTARIANS AND THE ESTABLISHMENT

The tension between the movement and the Establishment was clear from the very beginning. If the country was indeed undergoing "national apostasy," as Keble's assize sermon put it, then the Established Church must have something dreadfully wrong with it. It was inevitable that conflict would break out into the open. Hurrell Froude had seen something like this at firsthand when returning alone from the trip to Italy he had taken with Newman. In France the enemy he saw was not a weak liberalism but the remains of a fierce anti-Catholic revolutionary fervor. It was perhaps this background that made him so contemptuous of the Anglican High Churchman. The Roman Catholic historian Christopher Dawson concluded that much of the ethos of the movement came from Froude's experiences in France, including the break with the Tory traditions that still captivated the old High Church; this made it possible to recruit from a wider selection of young men at Oxford who did not fit into the usual upper class structure. He thinks it possible that the tracts themselves were suggested to Froude's imagination by the publication *L'Avenir,* founded by the priest Lamennais, leader of the French Catholic revival.[43] A frank recognition that a state of spiritual warfare existed was congenial to his ardent type of personality. His uncompromising nature became clear after his death in 1836, when Newman and Keble published his papers. There the Establishment read that the decay in the Church was caused by the hypocrisy of the clergy: Church discipline could not be enforced because the parsons were trying to keep up the "show" that there was a national Church; hence heresy was buried out of sight.[44] Froude's papers also revealed to the Church that disestablishment was not out of the question for these conservative revolutionaries. He had moved to the West Indies for a time in a vain effort to cure the debilitating illness that soon would kill him and there observed the Methodist missionaries at work among the slaves. He mused about the lessons this might hold for Anglicans. "If the Church was thrown on the voluntary system, and left to make its way as the Wesleyans do among the poorer classes, it would make sure as it went, though perhaps the progress might at first seem slow."[45]

Newman and Keble evidently expected that publishing Froude's writings, which were mostly intended only for private reading, would further their cause. This was perhaps naive, but they had some idea of the dangerous waters into which they were sailing. Their preface anticipated that they would be accused of advocating "Romanism," but they dismissed those charges in advance by adverting to anti-Roman remarks in the text.[46] This was somewhat disingenuous, however, for the anti-Romanism seemed generally to be yoked with anti-Protestantism. When Froude declared that he wished for the "total overthrow" of Roman Catholicism, it was in the same sentence in which he branded as a "base calumny" the remark that he had become a "staunch Protestant."[47] And that was in the same volume as a widely circulated statement to the effect that the Reformation "was a limb badly set—it must be broken again in order to be righted."[48]

CRITICS OF THE TRACTARIANS

Opposition to the Tractarians included the old High Church, which, rightly, felt itself included in the attacks on the Establishment coming from Oxford. Hugh James Rose, rector at Hadleigh, who originally figured into plans for the new movement, increasingly became disenchanted with it. He and his colleagues objected to Pusey's *Tract on Baptism*, believing that it overemphasized the consequences of postbaptismal sin. And the anti-Protestant material in Froude's *Remains* further offended them, as did the spiritual exuberance, which was very different from the sober piety of the High Church.[49] The publication of Froude's *Remains* gained for the editors the wrath of much of the Church. Newman and Keble published Part II the year after the first part and in the preface to the former called attention to this. They described the reaction as "the quantity and variety of censure" that had cascaded down upon them and given them pause before they went on with the work.[50] But still they proceeded.

The most persistent and influential of the Tractarian critics were those who went by the title of "liberal," although it may have been chiefly Newman's later copious use of the word in the *Apologia* that makes it seem so common. When Newman arrived at Oriel College in 1822, the college was the most prestigious at the university, a distinction it would later give up to Balliol. He was an Evangelical then, but most of his colleagues were of an advanced group sometimes called the Noetics (although he would later attack them as representatives of liberalism), the best known of whom were Thomas Arnold, Richard Whately (future archbishop of Dublin), and R. D. Hampden; also numbered among them were the college provost, Edward Copleston, and his successor after 1828, Edward Hawkins. Chiefly under the influence of Keble and Froude, Newman became gradually more convinced of the High Church position and drew away from his former attachment to the Noetics. Although the Noetics were always, for Newman, representatives of the despised liberals, they were in fact quite conservative compared to those of the next generation who would wear the mantle of the Broad Church. They were mostly Whig in politics, and they questioned the range of doctrines that ought to be considered dogmas, but in other ways they were not radicals.[51] As we saw in the last chapter, Charles Simeon regarded Copleston as a soulmate on the matter of Scripture.

Arnold left Oriel early for marriage and eventually for the headmastership at Rugby, where he would rule for his remaining years and where he would make his mark by remaking the English public schools. For him the Tractarians would always be the "Newmanites," his version of the more common "Puseyites," and one that was more in accord with the facts of the case. In private letters Arnold would use terms like *folly* and *wickedness* to describe his erstwhile Oxford colleagues. According to his favorite pupil and biographer, Arthur Stanley, he held Newmanite supporters in "absolute repulsion." In Arnold's words, "I doubt whether I should be a good person to deal with anybody who is inclined to Newmanism." The movement was teaching nothing new, said Arnold, just the same tired old errors.[52] Arnold's main complaint against the Tractarians was apparently their elevation of the priesthood and hierarchy and the sacraments to an inappropriate level. He may also have been unhappy about their lack of interest in the social and economic issues that occupied a central part of concerns for the nation. The most energetic and notorious of Arnold's sallies against the Tractarians was his article in the *Edinburgh Review* of April 1836, on which the editor bestowed the title "The Oxford Malignants." Stanley, whose opinions of his old headmaster sometimes bordered on the sycophantic, recalled that this article, and the title in particular, not only brought down on Arnold's head the wrath of his enemies but also caused a scandal among his friends.[53]

As with Arnold, so with the Evangelicals. Less than five months after Keble's assize sermon, the *Record* noted the existence of the new group. The paper said that its own purpose was directed toward "the same end" as the Oxford reformers, which was "the preservation of the church." The editor had eight tracts in front of him and was preparing extracts of them for the readers.[54] But the ensuing three days brought sudden enlightenment, and in its next issue the paper concluded that the Tractarians were papists, whose idea of the Eucharist was "conveying THE SACRIFICE to the people," of the Church as "INTRUSTED WITH THE KEYS OF HEAVEN AND HELL," and "above all" using words that appeared to accept transubstantiation.[55] That was the start of a steady drumbeat of fire directed at the Tractarians, mostly in connection with the threat of papism taking over the Church. The publication of Froude's *Remains,* for them as for many others, proved that they had been right all along about the anti-Protestant nature of the movement.[56] Still, the paper could be cooler than others; as late as November 1840, it denied that the Puseyites were Jesuits or Roman Catholics in disguise, a concession that not all the critics would accept.[57] With Newman's conversion to Rome, however, the *Record* congratulated itself on its prescience: "From the first . . . we predicted and declared that their lucubrations, resting on the doctrine of Rome . . . could lead, fairly carried out nowhere else but to Rome. How were our *ultra-Protestant* notions ridiculed and contemned!"[58]

Samuel Wilberforce, like his brothers Robert and Henry, fell under the spell of the Tractarians but unlike them drew back. He liked their elevation of episcopal authority and their call to holy living. On the second of these emphases, he was a good Claphamite. Wilberforce liked the primary emphases of the Tractarians but disagreed with a number of the doctrines superadded to them. He called these "peculiarities," these additions to the corpus of High Church theology handed down from the seventeenth century, possibly doing so ironically, since in Hurrell Froude's code language the Evangelicals were known as the "peculiars." Under this rubric he included the doctrine of reserve, the overemphasis on sanctification at the expense of justification (the mirror image of the Tractarian criticism of Evangelicals), and the unwarranted stress on postbaptismal sin (Pusey's obsession).[59]

As for Wilberforce's liking for the Tractarian emphasis on the bishops, it was a later but almost contemporary High Church priest and scholar, Sabine Baring-Gould, who said that the great mistake of the Tractarians was that they trusted the bishops, putting a "halo" around them, as if they were truly like the ancient bishops: "The Early Tractarians looked for what was not to be found, and were staggered not to find it. They supposed that bishops would be as war-horses rushing into the battle, and when, instead, they found them halter-led along the high road by a Prime Minister, they reeled back, bit their thumbs, and jumped over the hedge."[60] The later ritualist movement, a product of the Tractarian teaching, was from the first attacked by the bishops, and they did not make that mistake.

The Tractarians were not as woolly-minded as some of their critics thought, but there was something of an air of unreality in their failure to comprehend why the opposition would be so outraged. How could they have been surprised at the ferocity with which Froude's *Remains* were greeted? How could they have been surprised *again* when a year or two later the public outcry against Newman's Tract #90, *Remarks on Certain Passages in the Thirty-Nine Articles,* became almost hysterical? The *Record* may have absolved the Tractarians from being secret Jesuits, but here was a piece of work worthy of that order.[61] For Newman claimed to have found a way to interpret the Thirty-Nine Articles so that they were consistent with Roman Catholic teaching. This was the beginning of the end of the movement. The successive blows of the Evangelical reaction to Williams's tract on reserve, the Froude *Remains* uproar, and now the crowning touch of Tract #90, which convinced many people of good will that Oxford was sponsoring a Romanization of the English Church, ultimately provoked an official response. The university's judicial machinery went into action, and it was only a matter of time before the Tractarian base of operations was lost. Newman resigned his fellowship and moved out of town to Littlemore, a retreat center he had begun earlier. His explanation in the *Apologia* said it all:

> I saw indeed clearly that my place in the Movement was lost; public confidence was at an end; my occupation was gone. It was simply an impossibility that I could say any thing henceforth to good effect, when I had been posted up by the marshal on the buttery-hatch of every College of my University, after the manner of discommoned pastry-cooks, and when in every part of the country and every class of society, through every organ and opportunity of opinion, in newspapers, in periodicals, at meetings, in pulpits, at dinner-tables, in coffee-rooms, in railway carriages, I was denounced as a traitor who had laid his train and was detected in the very act of firing it against the time-honoured Establishment.[62]

But if Newman's place in a movement conveniently, if cunningly, called *Newmanism* (by Arnold, among others) was at an end, what could be left of the movement? Not much. Froude was dead, the somewhat otherworldly Keble was out of touch in his rectory at Hursley, and Pusey was enveloped in gloom and a hair shirt ever since the death of his wife in 1839. (He had determined never to smile in public, and he kept his pledge faithfully.) It was all over, perhaps to be reborn shortly in different form. What was killed at Oxford found life elsewhere; the academic center died to allow the parish progeny to spread.

PERSONALITIES THAT PERSUADE

Contrary to what might be inferred from their name, the Tracts for the Times, from which the movement drew its name, were mostly intended for the few, the chosen, the learned. Newman ensured that their tone was measured, sober, and gentlemanly, but when the group took over the *British Critic* in 1838, a move that one historian calls a "coup," their tactics changed. They turned the magazine into a High Church version of the *Record*. Newman explained the policy in a letter: "We want a Review conducted, i.e. morally conducted, on the Catholic temper—we want all subjects treated on one and the same principle or basis—not the contributors of a board of men, who do not know each other, pared down into harmony by an external editor, but our editor must be the principle, the internal idea of Catholicism itself, pouring itself outwardly, not trimming and shaping from without." [63] It was not that an irenic Newman had turned militant. He had always been militant and now was making only a tactical shift, perhaps because he sensed that their brilliant run was nearing its end. When the movement was still young and he had hoped to enlist the High Church clergyman Hugh James Rose into it, he had used a military metaphor to describe for Rose how he envisioned the Tracts would be composed. They would not resemble anything like magazine articles but rather would be separate publications: "We do not want regular troops, but sharpshooters." [64]

Contemporary accounts suggest that the main avenue of influence was not the writings of the Tractarians but their persons, mainly Newman. Undergraduates flocked to hear Newman because he was pulling the beards of his elders with his "popery" or because his sermons at St. Mary's taught them the Christian religion in a serious way they had never heard before. They imitated his gestures, argued his doctrines. No matter what the subject, Newman came up in the conversation. Archbishop Whately opined that by October 1838, two-thirds of the undergraduates at the university were Puseyites, which may have been another example of the gloomy exaggerations to which he was prone. [65] R. W. Church concluded that Newman's four o'clock sermons at St. Mary's, which he began in 1828, were more powerful in drawing students to the movement than the tracts. Without the sermons, "the movement might never have gone on, certainly would never have been what it was."

> Plain, direct, unornamented, clothed in English that was only pure and lucid, free from any faults of taste, strong in their flexibility and perfect command both of language and thought, they were the expression of a piercing and large insight into character and conscience and motives, of a sympathy at once most tender and most stern with the tempted and the wavering, of an absolute and burning faith in God and His counsels. . . . They made men think of the things which the preacher spoke of, and not of the sermon or the preacher. [66]

The praise of a disciple, of course, but it is hard not to accept Church's complete sincerity.

If another sort of testimony is desired, let us consider that of James Anthony Froude, Hurrell's younger brother, later a famous historian:

> No one who heard his sermons in those days can ever forget them. . . . Newman, taking some Scripture character for a text, spoke to us about ourselves, our temptations, our experiences. . . . He seemed to be addressing the most secret consciousness of each of us—as the eyes of a portrait appear to look at every person in a room. . . . A sermon from him was a poem, formed on a distinct idea, fascinating by its subtlety, welcome—how welcome!—from its sincerity, interesting from its originality, even to those who were careless of religion; and to others who wished to be religious, but had found religion dry and wearisome, it was like the springing of a fountain out of the rock.

Froude also described the rapt attention with which students listened to Newman at his weekly tea parties and the devotion with which they regarded him: "The simplest word which dropped from him was treasured as if it had been an intellectual diamond."[67]

To keep this in perspective, one should bear in mind that the preaching standard against which judgments were made of Newman's sermons was almost uniformly dismal. One former student noted in his memoirs that the preachers went by the name "the Oxford hacks." One of these hacks boasted that he was the best paid preacher in the kingdom, receiving the unheard-of price of a guinea for each member of the audience—the preaching fee was four guineas, and there were three or four people occupying the pews![68]

Pusey's disciple Henry Liddon believed that Keble was the real originator of the movement and attributed words to that effect to Newman. Liddon also said that Pusey believed the *Christian Year* was the progenitor of all that followed because of its elevation of the sacramental principle and of the deeper meaning of Scripture. (Some have called it the Bible of the movement.) As a High Churchman for his whole life, unlike Newman, he always settled on the apostolic succession as the "essential bond" that united the Church of England with the ancient and primitive catholicism.[69] Keble's modern biographer is appreciative of the strengths of character and abilities as poet and scholar that informed the Tractarian movement, but she subtitled her book *A Study in Limitations,* by which she referred to his uncritical Toryism, his failure to appreciate anything that might be termed a liberal tendency, his lack of acquaintance with the scientific knowledge he might have gotten had he gone to Cambridge instead of Oxford, and his lack of understanding of what the industrial north was like.[70] For the most part his colleagues had the same limitations. But Keble's quiet strength and humility affected students in somewhat the same way as Newman, although Keble's personality and strengths were very different. One former student, late in the century, recalled matriculating at Oxford and being greeted by him: "During the two hours I was with Keble his manner and kindness and certain influence, which I hardly can describe, came over me."[71] His piety was of a very deep but undemonstrative sort, very different from the Evangelical kind that was becoming more prevalent, so that the Wilberforce brothers found it difficult at first to figure him out. The seriousness was always there, but people were startled by the playfulness that kept breaking through his reserve, and his gardener commented once that he was "the greatest boy of them all."[72]

A modern scholar has noted that despite the "Puseyite" label pasted on the Tractarians, there has been relatively little written about Pusey. Liddon's monumental work stands as the only biography, although Keble has modern biographers and Newman studies are an industry in themselves.[73] It may be that Pusey's greatest contribution to that generation of High Church leaders was the effect of his life on Newman: "His great learning, his immense diligence, his scholarlike mind, his simple devotion to the cause of religion, overcame me."[74] He lent an immediate aura of respectability to the movement because of his reputation as a scholar; his birthright as scion of a noble family also did not hurt. "Without him," said Newman, "we should have had little chance, especially at the early date of 1834, of making any serious resistance to the Liberal aggression."[75] After Newman's departure for Rome, eleven years later, Pusey filled the leadership vacuum.

Froude's death in 1836 at the age of thirty-three was a disaster for the movement, not only because the others were deprived of his gifts but because they were deprived of him. Keble's biographer has expressed it well: "The brightness fell from the air." Even Keble's writings lost their sparkle and went dull.[76] Froude had been a ferocious combatant but a fair and generous one, and the gaiety of his spirit had supplied something found wanting in the others. He once said that his main accomplishment in life had been to bring Keble and Newman together. Those two did nothing for the movement by publishing Froude's miscellaneous scribblings, nor did they do anything for Froude's reputation by broadcasting to the world half-formed ideas that were never intended for other eyes.

THE MOVEMENT DIES BUT SPREADS ANYWAY

Anyone dependent on Tractarian writings for an understanding of what the Church of England was like in the 1830s will have a badly distorted view of the subject. It was past its long period of both moralism and antinomianism. It still had clergymen of the old school, there were still politics in the administration of the diocese, and pluralism and indifference persisted, but conditions were much better than they had been. They continued to improve, partly because of Tractarian influences.[77]

What the movement actually did to Oxford was subject to various interpretations. The *Record* could see nothing salutary about the movement, but when Samuel Wilberforce visited Oxford in 1836 he thought the spiritual conditions were noticeably better than during his student days.[78] Mark Pattison's view was very different. He had been raised in an Evangelical home and had embraced the Tractarians at Oxford, later turning away from them in great bitterness, which may have been simply a product of his changing conviction combined with his dark personality. Pattison became rector at Lincoln College years later and enveloped the place with the black spirit that had overcome him. Looking back at his Tractarian days at Oxford, he concluded that "fanaticism was laying its deadly grip around me."[79] He said that if someone had gone to sleep in Oxford in 1846 and had awakened four years later, he would not have recognized the place. In the first period one saw fierce debates between different types of Toryism. In 1850 it was all changed "as if by the wand of a magician." The main advantage in the later period seemed to be that "theology was totally banished from Common Room, and even from private conversation."[80]

But Oxford was no more to be the focus of the Tractarian movement. Although the mechanism for its spread is difficult to trace, the ideas of Oxford began moving out through the parishes of the kingdom, there to change the nature of much of the English Church. Baring-Gould, who was born during the movement's second year, likened the debacle of 1845 to the seedpod of a touch-me-not plant exploding and scattering its seed all over the countryside.[81] Edward FitzGerald, translator of *The Rubáiyát of Omar Khayyám*, had no love for the Tractarians but reported what he had seen in Dorsetshire: "I found the churches much occupied by Puseyite parsons; new chancels built, with altars and painted windows that officiously displayed the virgin Mary, etc."[82] Gladstone, who was close to the Tractarian leaders, concluded that the movement, far from ending with Newman's conversion to Roman Catholicism, carried on under its new name—ritualism.[83] A long debate has taken place on this issue. The problem is that the parish priests who followed a ritualist bent used practices common to Roman Catholicism that seemed to be a natural outgrowth of the High Church school at Oxford but that were never advocated by the Tractarian leaders. Pusey would marvel at the "Puseyite" rituals and clerical costumes in which he never had the slightest interest. "What exactly is a chasuble?" he wanted to know. Keble was even less sympathetic to the use of Roman rituals. "I acknowledge that I do not even *know* what constitutes the difference between High and Low Mass."[84] The resolution to the anomaly seems to be that these post-Tractarian clergymen were invested with a spiritual energy and determination that was very different from the tepid timeserving of much of their cohort and that even surpassed the strong motivation of the Evangelicals. The opposition to the Roman-style rituals approached the level of persecution (some of the parsons spent time in jail), and active measures were taken by the government to end the movement.

A German scholar questions whether the rituals were really the heart of this movement, despite its name. He sees, rather, the spiritual life brought about by the slum priests in regions of the towns where few clergymen were prepared to minister: "The message of the Incarnation and of the Body of Christ and of the splendour of the sacraments was to be made visible to the simple, often still very primitive, because neglected, mass of the people. In the dreary monotony of the nineteenth century slums the services of the Ritualists were, together with the enthusiastic revival meetings of the various sects, like sunbeams piercing the fog; and these services were crowded to bursting point." He calls this movement "Catholic Evangelicalism" because it possessed an important quality that was the same as in the evangelical movement—the overwhelming motivation to get out and tell the gospel story to all who would listen and to adopt new forms to make it persuasive.[85]

With the work of the ritualist priests, the High Church movement beginning at Oxford at last seemed to deserve the Puseyite label it had been given as a form of ridicule. For although Pusey did not agree with the use of ritual for its own sake and disliked the signs of arrogance he sometimes saw in the ritualist priests, the mission as it developed on the ground in the parishes came close to the vision for the Church's mission to the poor that he had articulated: "We need missions among the poor of our towns; organized bodies of clergy living among them; licenced preachers in the streets and lanes of our cities; brotherhoods, or guilds, which should replace socialism; or sisterhoods of mercy. . . . We need clergy to penetrate our mines, to migrate with our emigrants, to shift with our shifting population, to grapple with our manufacturing system as the Apostles did with the slave system of the ancient world."[86]

Yet even in the countryside the effects of the Tractarian movement were visible. Many of the Oxfordshire clergy had little sympathy for Newman and his friends, but the Church began changing in the region, especially after Samuel Wilberforce became bishop of Oxford. Priests did what they had to in order to bring about spiritual reformation in the parishes. This often involved more frequent and more reverent celebration of the communion service, taking special interest in the problems of the parishioners, including their hygiene and health, taking much better care of the physical facilities of the church, being diligent in teaching communicant classes, and in general asking what a faithful clergyman ought to be doing.[87]

One gets the impression of a quiet spread of ideas through the parishes of the land not only from the friends of the movement but also from its enemies. The *Record* noted Puseyite ideas and practices spreading to the Society for Promoting Christian Knowledge and the Society for Building and Repairing Churches and Chapels; people were dating documents by referring to saints' days, a Romanist practice (April 23, 1840). Puseyism was spreading from clergy to laity, from tracts to newspapers and magazines (March 15, 1841). Critical of Pugin's revival of Gothic churches, the paper denounced the "sudden revival of the Romish apostasy" as "a remarkable sign of the times" (May 25, 1840). Of all the flourishing Evangelical societies, only the Church Missionary Society "keeps itself pure from the deadly leaven of Tractarianism" (July 21, 1842). In the diocese of Exeter, young men indoctrinated at Oxford "began to change, according to Tractarian model, this goodly order of things" (June 19, 1845). The bishop of Chichester wrote a letter legitimizing Tractarian practices (August 4, 1845). By 1845, if the *Record*'s account is trustworthy, the Oxford colleges counted twenty-five tutors who were Tractarian, twenty-three who were "anti-Romanist" (i.e., holding the *Record*'s position), and sixteen who were neutral (February 27, 1845).

This creation (or *re*-creation) of a new way of functioning for the Church of England has been suggested as the natural outgrowth of Newman's original vision. A recent study calls attention to a little-quoted passage in the *Apologia* in which Newman says, "I wanted to bring out in a substantive form, a living Church, made of flesh and blood, with voice, complexion, and motion and action, and a will of its own." This suggests that the oft-repeated statement that the Tractarians were just defending the Church and the society against liberalism is not the whole story. If the Church truly could be made the Church, in fact as well as principle, then the actions of the state and the question of establishment would assume the secondary character they deserved. "The remedy for national apostasy was to realize the Church. This became the hidden agenda of the Tractarians."[88] There is another reason to take with a bit of skepticism the Tractarians' unrelievedly bleak portrayal of the current state of the Church: the state of the Church was much better than it had been a few years earlier. Reform movements, and in particular the Evangelical revival, had modified the worst of the abuses and replaced many of the timeservers with real pastors. Thus the Tractarians were less a new broom sweeping clean than a part of an ongoing reform process.[89] The bleakness of the Tractarian view may be related to the condition of the Church in Oxford, which was evidently much worse than in many other parts of the realm. The young Gladstone wrote in March 1829, "The state of religion in Oxford is the most painful spectacle it ever fell to my lot to behold."[90]

Although in the *Apologia* Newman understated his role in the Oxford renewal, he explained plausibly the way the movement spread within and far beyond the University. "It was through friends, younger, for the most part, than myself, that my principles were spreading. They heard what I said in conversation, and told it to others." When undergraduates departed, they took elsewhere what they had heard. Many became country curates. They placed tracts and other publications into local bookshops, had extracts published in newspapers, and converted their rectors and fellow curates. "Thus the Movement, viewed with relation to myself, was but a floating opinion; it was not a power."[91] That is the impression one gets from reading the correspondence of the period: people exchanged ideas and encouragement, and so the movement grew. It was more a matter of personal relationships than of formal position. Gladstone and Keble, for example, had a constant and close relationship. Gladstone was only a minor politician at the time, seventeen years younger than Keble, but the older man, a world-famous author and professor of poetry, could write in a letter that "if I cannot quite agree with all his views I really look on it as a great misfortune."[92]

R. W. Church looked back from a vantage point three decades in the future and said that the Establishment might be better off because of all the clergymen and others that followed Newman to Rome after 1845 than it would have been without those terrible losses. The reason was that the defections convinced the authorities that something dreadful was afoot and that reforms were urgently needed.[93] Evidently the clergy, many of them living in poverty and under the thumbs of lay patrons, began to esteem their office more highly as they read tracts assuring them that the clerical dignity was worthy of respect and honor.[94]

Besides the formal writings of the Tractarians themselves, there grew up a tradition of novels that popularized the viewpoint, counterparts to a lively group of Evangelical novelists. Most famous of them was Charlotte Yonge, Keble's disciple, who came under his influence when fifteen years of age and never wavered until her death as she was nearing eighty. Her motto was *Pro Ecclesia Dei,* and late in life she described what was behind her numerous novels: "I have always viewed myself as a sort of instrument for popularising Church views."[95]

In 1848, a schoolboy visited a friend in Hereford and met a young High Church clergyman who acquainted him with Tractarian teachings and literature. In the late 1870s, Sir Edward Burne-Jones, by then a well-known artist and designer, wrote to a friend about that experience: "When I was fifteen or sixteen [reading Newman's works] taught me so much that I do mind—things that will never be out of me. In an age of sofas and cushions he taught me to be indifferent to comfort, and in an age of materialism he taught me to venture all on the unseen. . . . So if this world cannot tempt me—and it can't—or anything that it has in its trumpery treasure house, it is most of all because he said it in a way that touched me—walking with me a step in front."[96]

The real effect of the Tractarian movement can only be judged by the number of times Burne-Jones's experience was repeated in the ensuing years if we could possess that knowledge. That is separate from another question, which is the extent to which the theology of the Church of England was affected. Owen Chadwick has drawn that distinction between the religious and the theological. Later on, there were theological consequences, but in the beginning it was the spiritual life of those who were affected by the movement that was the important thing. "They succeeded, far beyond the expectation of many, in transforming the atmosphere of English worship, in deepening the content of English prayer, in lifting English eyes, not only to their own insular tradition, but to the treasures of the Catholic centuries, whether ancient or modern."[97]

V

School, Church, and Society

DR. ARNOLD'S QUEST

FOR RENEWAL

THE EVANGELICAL MOVEMENT was powered by two engines: the motivation supplied by conversion and the drive to bring about social improvement through active participation in both politics and voluntary activities. Not content to allow the persistence of what they believed to be the deteriorated moral and social state of England, evangelicals became involved in societies and projects without number in an effort to mirror inner spiritual transformation with outer social improvement. As the individual experienced new life, so the society must also be transfigured. But the evangelicals were not the only ones with this perspective. The headmaster at Rugby during the second quarter of the nineteenth century had a similar vision for societal improvement and influenced numerous pupils—and *their* pupils—to pursue similar ends.

Thomas Arnold (1795–1842) seems to have been remembered chiefly for two accomplishments: reforming the English public schools and fathering the poet and literary critic Matthew Arnold. Often one sees reference to him as the father also of the Broad Church movement, which came into prominence around the middle of the century and increasingly thereafter set the tone for some of the most influential elements in the Church of England.[1] Educated at Winchester, Arnold took his degree at Corpus Christi College, Oxford, afterwards becoming a fellow and tutor at Oriel College, where he was ordained. He was associated there with the Noetics: men of somewhat unconventional theological views whom Newman called "liberals." By this, Newman meant people who disbelieved in the principle of dogma, who examined skeptically even those basic precepts of the faith that he thought they should have simply accepted and not held up to public doubt. Arnold left Oriel after only a few years to marry. He earned his living as a tutor to university entrants until 1827, when his application for the headship of Rugby school won him the position. He remained there for fifteen years until his sudden death at the age of forty-seven.

Arnold was a complex man and more than most was the subject of greatly

THOMAS ARNOLD.
By courtesy of the National Portrait Gallery, London.

contrasting evaluations. Newman once answered a question by asking one of his own: whether Arnold could be considered a Christian. This exchange was widely publicized and caused Newman considerable embarrassment. It also colored perceptions of the schoolmaster even among those familiar with the much later half-hearted retraction in Newman's *Apologia.* Curiously, Arnold's place in history has been established more by the efforts and convictions of people on whom he had some later influence than by what he himself said and did. Since the Broad Church movement looked to his memory for inspiration, it is sometimes taken for granted that he must have shared its outlook. Many Broad Church leaders were latitudinarian in moral outlook; hence, it was sometimes said, Arnold belonged to the latitudinarian "school."[2] But Arnold explicitly repudiated the latitudinarian thinking that he believed was all too prevalent in the Church of England, and the later applications of his influence by Broad Church leaders did not always make fair use of what he intended.

ARNOLD AND HISTORICAL CHRISTIANITY

If the "latitudinarian" label really described Arnold, he might be expected to embrace whole-heartedly the establishment of London University as a more or less secular alternative to the two ancient seats of higher learning that were Anglican and, as it then seemed, unalterably so. When the Chancellor of the Exchequer offered him a fellowship in the senate of the new institution, he accepted it in the hope of assisting it to become Christian without being sectarian, part of Arnold's attempt to unite the Christians of the realm. But the new university had come into being with the influence of not only Dissenters but also unbelievers, and he faced an uphill task in bringing that vision to fruition. The sticking point came over the question of including an examination in Scripture as part of the arts degree. This was opposed by Dissenters fearing the effects of Establishment bias, as well as by the strong utilitarian contingent in the leadership of the university. As Arthur Stanley, Arnold's pupil and biographer, described the delicacy of Arnold's position, he was condemned in Oxford as a latitudinarian and in London as a bigot. Isolated in the senate, he withdrew from the position. As Arnold told it in a letter, he alone held out for the inclusion of the Scripture examination for all candidates for degrees; he thought the senate was using Christianity as window dressing for what was essentially a secular institution.[3]

The heart of Arnold's religious motivation, according to Stanley, was his devotion to Christ. "Above all, it was necessary to a right understanding, not only of his religious opinions, but of his whole character, to enter into the peculiar feeling of love and adoration which he entertained towards our Lord Jesus Christ." By this, Stanley meant not only Arnold's objective appreciation for the work of Christ but his feeling toward "Himself, as a living Friend and Master."[4] A typical modern study examines his use of the Scriptures in the "spirit of Christ" and treats it as an exercise in "moral guidance," an approach that exemplifies the liberal concerns of the author but not of Arnold.[5] Arnold's constant preoccupation with religious matters was the theme of the sermon Stanley preached in Rugby on August 14, 1842, at Arnold's death: "Here was a man to whom, with the liveliest sense of earthly happiness and with the deepest interest in all that is most exciting and attractive in all the varied pursuits of human life, the thought of God and of death was ever present."[6] For some observers, this obvious religious sensibility gave his advocacy for an all-inclusive Church of England a credibility that it would otherwise lack. Sabine Baring-Gould, staunch High Churchman that he was, averred that he could have much in common with an Evangelical, even with a Dissenter, but not with a member of the Broad Church, which he regarded as a cover for disbelief in Christian truth. He described Arnold as being of the Broad Church but excepted him, along with F. D. Maurice and Charles Kingsley, from the generalization. Arnold's teaching and preaching, Baring-Gould said, "were marked by devotion to our Blessed Lord."[7]

Arnold disliked many traits of the Evangelicals, but that has served to mislead people about his convictions. He was one of the few Englishmen of the day who read German and was familiar with the turn that Continental theology and philosophy were taking. He thought Evangelical rigidity on scriptural interpretation—the Evangelicals called it "plenary inspiration"—would ill prepare the Church for the general reception of German biblical scholarship, which would overwhelm an overly literalistic hermeneutic; the Evangelicals believed they were sustaining the authority of Scripture, but Arnold thought they were actually setting the stage for its undermining. He was not an accomplished theologian but had a strong interest in biblical interpretation and exposition, and some scholars have suggested that he was most impressive in that role.[8]

Several of Arnold's themes were as close to Evangelical teaching as could be found. Some people, he said in a sermon, are quite familiar with the gospel message from their childhood on. "But it is quite needless to say that our congregations are not such as these; but that a large proportion of them forever require to be told afresh what is the very foundation of Christian life."[9] Not only are the congregations full of people who need to become acquainted with the gospel, but Arnold assumed that such was common knowledge. The central idea in that passage, that people in the Established Church did not understand the gospel, is another way of expressing the contention in Wilberforce's book title that the "prevailing religious system of professed Christians in the higher and middle classes" should be "contrasted with real Christianity." Even Arnold's way of formulating the gospel could sound like the emotion-laden expression common to the Evangelicals. Arnold contended that the most spiritual Christians in the realm needed to bow before the throne of God and say: "I was by nature and inclination a sinner ready to perish forever; and low! [*sic*] my sins have been washed away, and I am purified by the blood of Christ, and born anew by his Spirit, and whereas I was a child of wrath, I am now the reconciled child of God, and an heir of his everlasting Kingdom."[10] When he preached on the fruits of conversion, Arnold said that "it is not improvement that is required, but a change of heart and life; a change of principles, of hopes, of fears, of masters; a change from death unto life; from Satan to God."[11] A visitor could have attended that sermon, closed his eyes, and imagined that Charles Simeon or John Newton was the preacher. In a document found thirteen years after his death, Arnold left instructions for the upbringing of his children in a memorandum for his brother-in-law, Trevenen Penrose. Arnold thought the Evangelicals were overly strict in the raising of their children but nevertheless desired that the children be given an Evangelical foundation for their lives.[12]

Although Arnold's name was never associated with the Evangelicals, the latter did not regard him as an enemy, the way they did the Tractarians, even though they were sometimes at loggerheads with the schoolmaster. The most notable case occurred in 1836, when the Evangelicals and Tractarians combined (probably for the last time) to try to prevent the Noetic—liberal in Newman's lexicon—Renn Dickson Hampden's appointment to the Regius chair of theology. (It was this incident that led to Arnold's notorious "Oxford Malignants" article in the *Edinburgh Review*.) In its review of Stanley's *Life of Arnold*, the *Christian Observer* noted that there were errors in his thinking but reacted very favorably to some of his writings:

> Many passages, and especially the references to our blessed Lord, are so beautiful and touching, that it may seem as unjust as it is painful to imagine anything of latent doctrinal error in the opinions of the writer. We find him speaking of the love of Christ, walking watchfully after him, loving him, coming before him with earnest prayer for his mercy and his help, desiring to do his will and promote his kingdom, and making him the centre of all moral and religious convictions.[13]

The *Observer* believed Arnold's views improved as he aged. "But in his latter years his views of the Gospel would appear to have become more clear and—what word can we use but evangelical?"[14] The *Record*, if not quite so fulsome, also saw much good in Arnold's influence. It spoke of Arnold's errors, particularly his "religious perceptions," his aversion to conservatism, and his refusal to learn from others, but still had high praise for his talents, his powers of investigation, his enthusiasm, his kindness, his loyalty to friends and family, and his desire to serve his age and his country.[15] Halévy thought that Arnold's convictions became what they were because by the time of his maturity Evangelical thinking had become so strong in forming the national ethos.[16]

ARNOLD AND THE REMAKING OF THE ENGLISH PUBLIC SCHOOL

Since not long after his death, Arnold has been credited with setting the example that led to the virtual reinvention of the English public schools. This view has not gone unchallenged in recent years, as we shall see, but it is important to understand why contemporaries would be led to embrace it. The schools were deplorable until about the middle of the century and had been for many years. Numerous educated Englishmen had only to consult their memories to compare the schools after Arnold's time and thus draw some conclusions about what had been accomplished. The main problem was the state of morals in the schools. They had become centers of brutality, rebellion, and sexual vice. When Charles Dickens published the book-length version of *Nicholas Nickleby,* he wrote a preface defending his description of the execrable school in Yorkshire he named Dotheboys Hall. Replying to the criticism he had received when the novel was published in serial form, he said he could easily find a number of schools in Yorkshire that were worse than the one he had portrayed. E. A. Cooper, younger brother of the man who would serve in Parliament as Lord Shaftesbury for much of the century, was beaten lifeless at Eton in 1825, and the event swept under the rug by the school, which attributed the death to the boy's drinking. Shaftesbury himself was sent at the age of seven by neglectful parents to Manor House School in Chiswick. There he was continually terrorized by older pupils. Later in life, Shaftesbury recalled the experience and concluded that his school was similar to Dotheboys Hall. He told of the filth, bullying, neglect, and hard treatment. "The memory of that place makes me shudder; it is repulsive to me even now." [17] The eminence of the school made no difference in the way these republics run by boys were conducted. The historian James Anthony Froude looked back to his school days at Westminster in the 1830s with horror. There, he found himself

the drudge and sport of my stronger contemporaries. No one interfered: it was the rule of the Establishment, and was supposed to be good for us. . . . I have had my legs set on fire to make me dance. When I had crawled to bed and to sleep I have been woke many times by the hot points of cigars burning holes in my face. I was made drunk by being forced to swallow brandy punch, which I hated. My health broke down and I had to be removed for a few months. . . . When I was sent back to college, it all began again.[18]

Religion was virtually a dead letter at these schools, despite the fact that most of the teachers were clergymen. At Eton, Charles Simeon was given almost no Christian teaching. J. B. Sumner, who would later become the first Evangelical archbishop of Canterbury, as a member of the staff at Eton was virtually prohibited from mentioning God or Christian faith. W. E. Gladstone, an Old Boy from the same school, recalled that the teaching of Christianity was absent, although he was able to draw some comfort from the fact that some of the forms remained.[19] The *Record* claimed in 1830 that for more than a century "religion has been almost as much neglected in these institutions, as though the Gospel had never been propagated."[20] George Moberly, headmaster of Winchester from 1835 (and future bishop of Salisbury), was recruited by Stanley to write a letter for inclusion in the biography of Arnold, in spite of Moberly's strong Tractarian sympathies. Moberly testified that when he attended Oxford, the young men who arrived from Winchester, Eton, Rugby, Harrow, or other schools were "universally irreligious." He attributed the great change that had occurred since then to Arnold's influence, which attribution, of course, was Stanley's motive in publishing the letter.[21] The Evangelicals were perfectly aware of the reputation of the public schools and mostly kept their sons away from them.[22]

CHRISTIAN GENTLEMEN IN A CHRISTIAN SCHOOL

Arnold's judgment that religion should be central to a public school education was a natural result of his view of religion as central to life. He preached regularly to the boys, but it was only in 1841 that he combined in his own person the role of both headmaster and chaplain. "It seems to me the natural and fitting thing . . . that the master of the boys should be officially as well as really their pastor."[23] Arnold revised the usual place of intellectual training in his hierarchy of goods at Rugby. The intellect came third among his priorities, after religious and moral training and the inculcation of gentlemanly conduct. "He is not well educated," said Arnold, "who does not know the will of God or knowing it, has received no help in his education towards being inclined and enabled to do it."[24] He was quite pessimistic about his ability to induce the boys to act as he wished, as he wrote in a letter upon assuming the headmastership, but he had high hopes that when they were grown the fruit of the training he offered would become apparent.[25] Still, he would not accept moral failures with a wink. Once when he had expelled a few boys for misbehavior, he addressed the assembled school and said, "It is not necessary that this should be a school of three hundred, or one hundred, or of fifty boys; but it is necessary that it should be a school of Christian gentlemen."[26]

Arnold's role as preacher in the chapel was one of his more effective methods of building character. The effect of his sermons on the pupils reminds one of the way Oxford students responded to Newman's preaching at St. Mary's. Stanley quotes one Old Boy in this way: "I used to listen to [Arnold's sermons] from first to last with a kind of awe, and over and over again could not join my friends at the chapel door, but would walk home to be alone; and I remember the same effects being produced by them, more or less, on others, whom I should have thought hard as stones, and whom I should think Arnold looked at as some of the worst boys in the school."[27]

Arnold's views predominated even in the more strictly academic part of the life of Rugby. He reformed the teaching of the Scriptures in the lower forms. In the sixth form, he introduced two lectures on the Bible during the week, in addition to the Sunday lectures. A boy who remained at the school for three years would have read much of the Bible and also memorized a good deal of it. Arnold insisted on a high level of biblical competence; a boy would have to know not only a passage of Scripture but also its context, the recipient of an epistle, and the exact meaning of the original language. He also gave lectures on church history. In describing all this, Stanley said that more important than the details of the teaching was "the union of reverence and reality in his whole manner." The boys received not only academic instruction but a tacit recognition that the headmaster thought all this was vital for their lives.[28] Arnold put his own stamp even on the teaching of the classics, which was the staple of all English education. He had the boys learn the ancient authors not only for their own sakes but as a means of instilling in them the moral and spiritual lesson he wished them to carry for the remainder of their lives.[29]

ARNOLD'S LEGACY TO THE ENGLISH PUBLIC SCHOOL

A recent school of thought holds that the former view of Arnold as the great school reformer has been greatly exaggerated. Even in the nineteenth century, some questioned the intellectual capabilities of the headmaster.[30] Another approach has been to hold, against all evidence, that the schools were quite religious before Arnold's time, thus rendering nugatory the claims made for Arnold in that area and treating him as something of a religious fanatic.[31] Some have disparaged contemporary testimony about Arnold's effectiveness, with only limited persuasiveness.[32] T. W. Bamford has analyzed the history of other schools after Arnold's tenure at Rugby and has ended up doubting that Arnold had any influence at other schools. At most he believes it possible that Harrow somehow received the stamp of Arnoldian influence. He even doubts that Rugby was much changed by the headmaster.[33] In one way at least Bamford is right. Arnold continually complained that the boys were impious, with questionable morals, and he seemed to believe that he had failed to make much difference in that respect.[34] How, then, did Arnold gain the enviable reputation that has usually been awarded him in the century and a half since his death? The reason, says Bamford, is that Arthur Stanley made the reputation with his biography of his old master, although he acknowledges that other Old Boys contributed to the grand task of misleading the historians.[35] The Old Boys out of personal loyalty no doubt exaggerated Arnold's strengths, but Bamford's cavalier dismissal of some of the witnesses who do not support his debunking treatment is not convincing. Some Old Boys were very critical of Arnold. Most of this sort of criticism seems to be centered on the alleged propensity of their classmates to become self-righteous prigs.[36]

Some of Arnold's modern critics do not sufficiently consider the almost uniform contemporary testimony of the schools being hellholes up to about the middle of the century. Against that background, Arnold's work at Rugby seems almost revolutionary. One scholar has said that the most informative way to look at the effect of Arnold's tenure is to recognize that although he had no special love for the Evangelicals, nor they for him, with Arnold "Evangelicalism began its conquest of the public schools." The argument is that to the extent that evangelicalism could be subsumed under the description of religious seriousness plus moral seriousness—this is not a definition that would satisfy the evangelicals—that is what Arnold brought to Rugby and the public schools in general as his reign there was imitated elsewhere.[37]

One of the Old Boys who did possibly even more than Stanley to increase Arnold's fame was Thomas Hughes, whose novel *Tom Brown's Schooldays* was a fictional treatment of Hughes's recollections of his school. "It was no light act of courage in those days," he wrote, " . . . for a little fellow to say his prayers publicly, even at Rugby. A few years later, when Arnold's manly piety had begun to leaven the school, the tables turned."[38] Arnold's elevation of the importance and use of the chapel also became widely imitated. A less important but still influential and long-lasting reform of Arnold was the use of pupil monitors, or *prefects,* to restrain the habitual anarchy that otherwise terrorized the younger and smaller boys.[39]

THE ROLE OF RELIGION IN SOCIETY

The dark apocalyptic expectations of the Scottish firebrand Edward Irving found scant reception in the admiring elite of London society who formerly crowded the Caledonian Chapel, but Arnold was saying some of the same things at about the same time. "We are engulfed, I believe, inevitably, and must go down the cataract." "My sense of the evils of the times, and to what prospects I am bringing up my children, is over-whelmingly bitter. All in the moral and physical world appears so exactly to announce the coming of the 'great day of the Lord,' i.e., a period of fearful visitation to terminate the existing state of things." [40] The source of Arnold's concern was not a particular interpretation of the prophetic portions of Scripture but rather his observations of society through the moral lens that he habitually used. Just as his expectations for the behavior of his pupils was far higher than the standard of behavior of the public schools, so were his expectations for the whole society. Since the standard came from Scripture, it was consistent that the nature of the retribution should also.

Evidently the main cause of Arnold's pessimism was the general condition of the lower classes, what Carlyle would make famous as the "condition of England" question. In 1831, he began a publication called the *Englishman's Register,* intended to address related issues, but it folded almost immediately, largely because he could not devote sufficient time to it. He then wrote a series of long letters addressing the matter, which the *Sheffield Courant* published. Arnold was exercised not so much by the fact of poverty as by the way it was treated. Using arguments that to the modern ear sound strangely contemporary, he opposed the Speenhamland system of relief, which was especially prevalent in the south of England. This custom (more than a system) started in 1795 and made up the difference through the parish poor rates between what a worker earned and a figure that was set according to what it was determined he needed, based on the number of his dependents and the current level of prices. The abuses of the practice were not hard to predict and were not long in coming. Arnold's concern was not primarily about the fraud that inevitably took place, nor about the consequences for the local poor rates and the willingness to pay them, but rather about the effects on the supposed beneficiaries. The practice continued, he said, "under the mask of kindness to the poor" but was "really one of the most degrading systems of oppression." Since the workers are not paid according to the value of their work but rather by reason of extraneous factors, such as family size, this is akin to slavery. Just as the slave receives enough to keep him alive, regardless of the quality and quantity of his work, so the English worker. "His maintenance is proportioned to his need, not to his exertions; and as a necessary consequence of this want of a stimulus, he is kept to work by the fear of punishment." [41] This concern is in keeping with Arnold's efforts at Rugby. Just as he wished to create conditions that would enhance the moral prospects of the boys, so he hoped the nation would do the same for its citizens.

But the reform of the poor laws would not be sufficient to alleviate what Arnold considered to be social dysfunction. He thought the separation of the classes was a far more serious problem than economic disparity. This came about because of the customs of years long past and extended even to such matters as the spoken language. It was the social and cultural gulf between classes that Arnold thought would do the most damage to English society.[42] This radical tinge to Arnold's thinking was upsetting to his friends as well as others. In a letter Arnold explained to Hawkins at Oriel College that he wanted to avoid revolution in England but also said he admired the revolution that had just taken place in France (1830). Arnold thought Churchmen should take public stands to bring about social renovation in English society. The whole purpose of a national Church is to "Christianize the nation" and bring about justice in its laws.[43] That provides an important clue for understanding Arnold's social ethic. He was completely opposed to any dualism that would separate spiritual from material concerns. He would have nothing to do with the kind of thinking that gives lip service to the principles of Christian faith while refusing to admit "its principles in the concerns of common life, in matters belonging to their own trade or profession, or above all, in the conduct of national affairs." He was very hard on people who "will not tolerate its spirit in their every day practice, but ridicule it as visionary and impracticable."[44] There is on this point and in much else of Arnold's thinking the influence of Samuel Taylor Coleridge, a man who also looked to the influence of the Church to lift the nation to a higher plane.[45] The work of societal reformation was to be accomplished through a renewed understanding of the Bible, not as a collection of pious stories or even as a moral textbook, but rather through an apprehending of the relevance of its teaching to modern life. In this, too, he was indebted to Coleridge's influence.[46]

Arnold was strongly criticized by the Tractarians, and by other loyal Churchmen, for his desire to so conceive the Church of England that Dissenters would be both welcome and willing to be members. (He excepted Unitarians from this invitation on the grounds that they were not Christians.) This could be accomplished without compromising vital theological principles, Arnold believed, because on the most basic points of the faith, all English Christian groups were united.[47] Baring-Gould, who elsewhere expressed his admiration for Arnold, called this conception of the Church "sterilized frog-spawn; which would inspire disgust, but not love."[48]

The Church that Arnold designed to make Christian faith transform English society was one that any High Churchman would detest. In 1833, he published his *Principles of Church Reform,* which proposed a big-tent Church of England in which all Christians except Roman Catholics might be at home. Such a Church would necessarily be "Low," or it would not pass muster with Dissenters, and for that reason also would devalue the importance of dogma. After his death those features would be picked up by the Broad Church, although without the concessions that would attract the

Dissenters; it would also usually remain silent on the devotional aspects of the faith that were so important to Arnold. He wanted to make the Church more hospitable to the working classes, a necessity if the potentially fatal fissures in the society were to be healed. He thought it was "both wicked and impossible" to destroy Dissent by means of persecution (not a radical statement, in view of the repeal of the Test and Corporation Acts just a few years earlier) but sought to "extinguish it by comprehension" into the Church of England. He used a military analogy to make the case: "The different tribes [of Christians] should act together as it were in one army, and under one command, yet should each retain the arms and manner of fighting with which habit has made them most familiar." [49] The analogy reveals his pessimism over the terrible conditions into which he believed the nation had descended. It also shows why the High Church should so detest Arnold: the Church is transformed in his thinking from a divine institution to accomplish God's work to a federation entered into as a kind of joint-stock company, for the convenience and profit of the investors.

The formula that would make the transaction work was contained in a model creed in Arnold's *Principles of Church Reform*. They include a belief in God, with a brief list of his attributes; the deity, death, and resurrection of Jesus Christ; and the authority of the Bible as the rule for faith and life. [50] Arnold even found a way to include some of the Unitarians in the reformed Church, notwithstanding their exclusion elsewhere in his writings: he separated those who were really unbelievers but unwilling to say so from those who believed the essential tenets of Christian faith without believing that the Bible taught the Trinitarian formulations of the Athanasian creed. The latter but not the former would be welcome into the Church of England reformed according to Arnold's principles. [51] Later, Arnold called for the reception into the Church of "all nominal Christians," which he said would "greatly increase its efficacy." Evidently anticipating criticism that this would have serious effects on the Church's authenticity, Arnold said that later on its "purity" could be expected to increase, without specifying how that was to be accomplished. To discredit what he anticipated would be the opposition of many Dissenters, Arnold called attention to the "bad passions" that inflame the most obdurate sect that trumpets its own purity. [52] The great sin that this comprehensive Church had to overcome was that of "the spirit of sectarianism," which he likened to an extreme individualism. [53]

To those who, like Arnold's old friend and mentor John Keble, feared that Erastianism was becoming more and more a feature of modern Church life, there could hardly be a worse solution to the problems of society. For if this reformed and comprehensive Church really were supposed to deal directly with the ills of the society, and do so in the name of all Christians in the realm, it would clearly be impossible to keep the hands of the state off its inner workings. And when that was combined with Arnold's oft-expressed disdain for "priestcraft," there appeared to be no countervailing force to oppose further government interference into ecclesiastical affairs.[54] In general Arnold detested such dualisms as the division of humanity into clerical and lay, and he once wrote in a letter of "the Popery of Canterbury."[55] He treated the sacraments with what a High Churchman would call disparagement. Baptism, he believed, was for many people "a little superstition; a notion that baptism is a sort of charm."[56]

If the High Church had good reason for being dubious of Arnold's teaching, the liberals in the Church had even more, despite Newman's habit of treating Arnold as the prince of liberalism. Or perhaps it would be better to say that Arnold's liberalism was typical of the Noetics of his younger days at Oriel College, rather than the liberals who would come later under the banner of the Broad Church. For Arnold's Christ-centered theology and biblically based morality would have little appeal to those whose thinking would be informed increasingly by the debunking influence of German scholarship. His subordination of intellectual formation to moral behavior as a focus of the educational process would seem old-fashioned and unappetizing to the Oxford dons within a decade or two of his death. One scholar concludes that Arnold "appears as the Hebrew prophet, humble before his God, stern and commanding before man, solemnly exhorting boys to become virtuous and be saved. Sin was ever at his shoulder ready to fasten upon those who for a moment relaxed from duty."[57] Liberalism past the midcentury had a very different mien, and some of the scoffers at the Tractarians and Evangelicals would have similarly low opinions of Arnold and his followers.

But for those who knew and respected him, Arnold's impact was immense. The *Record* might say that Arnold had admirers but not followers,[58] but if that was true, it was true only of his specific policy ideas, such as the Church of England composed of all Christians. His most lasting influence came from the way the boys perceived him and the effect that perception had on them for the remainder of their lives. Stanley, while still at Rugby, expressed in a letter the force of Arnold's personality: "What a wonderful influence that man has over me! I certainly feel that I have hardly a free will of my own on any subject on which he has written or spoken."[59] Theodore Walrond, head boy at Rugby at the time of Arnold's death, wrote the article on him for the *Dictionary of National Biography*. He concluded that Arnold's hold on the boys came from their perception of his spiritual insight, his "extraordinary sense of the reality of the invisible world."[60] In Hughes's

Tom Brown's Schooldays, Tom Brown, now an Old Boy, rushes back to Rugby from a fishing expedition on hearing of Arnold's death and stands before the tomb. There follows a scene of what Hughes acknowledges is hero worship that seems almost too embarrassing to read 150 years later. But Hughes brings to the event a theological perspective that was fitting in one who reverenced Arnold. "Such stages have to be gone through, I believe, by all young and brave souls who must win their way through hero-worship, to the worship of Him who is the King and Lord of heroes."[61] A recent analysis of this novel concludes that the most significant body between its covers does not appear at all in the text—the body of Christ. For the incarnation provided for Hughes the basis of all human solidarity and equality, an idea that was a legitimate inference from Arnold's introduction of theological reflection into the social world.[62] Hughes's simple Christian faith carried him into the leadership of the short-lived and misnamed Christian Socialist movement, and for a time into Parliament as a liberal. The Arnoldian spirit continued to motivate him: "I tell you that all the miseries of England and of other lands consist simply in this and in nothing else, that we men, made in the image of God, made to know Him, to be one with Him and His Son, will not confess that Son, our Lord and Brother, to be the Son of God and Son of Man, the living Head of our race and of each one of us."[63] Hughes may not have been the best judge of what was happening in the England of the high Victorian period, but he seemed to be recalling Arnold's warnings of the dire things that would befall the land if there were no repentance.

Many of Arnold's pupils went to Oxford, predominantly to Balliol College. There they combined with a group of brilliant Scottish disciples of Carlyle to assist Balliol in surpassing Oriel as the preeminent academic center of the university.[64] The effect of Arnold's pupils at Oxford is best seen through the eyes of those who did not appreciate what they stood for but nevertheless could not help admiring them. In the letter of George Moberly that Stanley published in the *Life of Arnold,* Moberly acknowledged that he and his Tractarian friends "disapproved" of their principles but still noted that "they were thoughtful, manly-minded, conscious of duty and obligation. . . . We cordially acknowledged the immense improvement in their characters in respect of morality and personal piety, and looked on Dr. Arnold as exercising an influence for good, which . . . had been absolutely unknown in our public schools."[65]

R. W. Church wrote of Arnold's influence as bespeaking "a new kind of Liberalism. It was much bolder and more independent than the older forms, less inclined to put up with the traditional, more searching and inquisitive in its methods, more suspicious and daring in its criticism." So far so bad, from the Tractarian perspective. But Church continued: "But it was much larger in its views and its sympathies, and, above all, it was imaginative, it was enthusiastic, and, without much of the devotional temper, it was penetrated by a sense of the reality and seriousness of religion." It lacked sympathy with the Tractarian ideal, said Church, "but these younger Liberals were interested in the Tractarian innovators, and, in a degree, sympathised with them as a party of movement who had had the courage to risk and sacrifice much for an unworldly end."[66] There was in this encomium an error of interpretation that perhaps summarized much of the disagreement between Tractarian and Arnoldian: the idea that the Rugby Old Boys would admire anything directed exclusively toward "an unworldly end." It was precisely that dualism that Arnold, and presumably his most devoted disciples, rejected. Arnold saw no contradiction between his unembarrassed devotion to Christ and his demands for societal reform; that something should have an unworldly end would be enough for him to declare its irrelevance and move on to something more important.

Newman's view of the Arnoldian presence at Oxford was in keeping with those of his friends. He reported sadly that during his whole tenure at Oxford the liberal party grew in numbers, in strength of view, and in power. "And, what was a far higher consideration, by the accession of Dr. Arnold's pupils, it was invested with an elevation of character which claimed the respect even of its opponents."[67] Yet the Newman-Arnold tensions gripped the university at the time. "Everybody in Oxford who does not believe in either Newman or Arnold," declared an Arnold enthusiast in 1843—after the one was in what amounted to exile and the other was dead—"cares for nothing but Greek verbs."[68]

Of Arnold's broader influence we can do little more than make informed conjectures. Lord Melbourne, Victoria's first prime minister, commended his sermons to the young queen, although he confessed that the headmaster was "too vehement" for him.[69] Perhaps more to the point is the fact that of the boys who were at Rugby during Arnold's tenure, some 1,500 to 1,600 of them, at least 300 took holy orders, most of them becoming parish priests. Of the thirty boys in Arnold's sixth form in 1834, eighteen became schoolmasters. No less then eighteen of Arnold's pupils became headmasters.[70] Arnold would not have been happy at some of what came later, supposedly inspired by him. The Broad Church movement that was reputed to be largely a creation of his would not resemble the account left by a biographer who had read his diary: "There we read of the gloomy forebodings of a man over-conscious of his age mixed with religious fervour carried to the point of ecstasy."[71]

Perhaps that last word is too strong to use when speaking of Arnold's influence to the next generations. But his friends and his adversaries alike testified to the zeal of his pupils, their moral earnestness, and the favorable impression they made on both their elders and their contemporaries. With so many of them departing the university for the pulpit and schoolroom, it is not hard to imagine their contribution to the broadening stream of the religious revival.

The Recovery of Belief and the Rejection of Establishment

DISSENT

WE HAVE BEEN CONSIDERING the various manifestations of religious renewal: first the thinly scattered outposts of Evangelical parishes and Methodist meeting places; then the Evangelical forces gaining strength and coherence and becoming a movement with its own leadership, publications, and societies. After this came the High Church movement at Oxford and the spread of Dr. Arnold's pupils making their way through the universities and into the parishes and schools of the nation. Now we must consider the Protestant Dissenters who shunned the embrace of the Church of England. Our main concern here will be not the internal aspects of Dissent but rather its relationship to the ongoing changes taking place in the nation.

The eighteenth-century deep freeze that afflicted much of English religious sensibilities affected the Dissenting groups as well as the Church of England. Although the Dissenters suffered legal discrimination until well into the nineteenth century, after the Toleration Act of 1689 they were able to live and worship more or less as they pleased. The Test (1673) and Corporation (1661) Acts imposed legal disabilities related to the holding of public office, but these had loopholes that removed much of their sting. Still, there was a palpable decline in the religious life of Dissent. R. W. Dale, one of the most influential Dissenting ministers of the nineteenth century, wrote a posthumously published history of Congregationalism in which he spoke of the period around the death of Queen Anne (1714) as "showing a want of spiritual energy" in the ranks of the Dissenters, a condition that caused "gravest anxiety" among their leaders.[1] Isaac Watts, the Dissenting hymnodist who lived through that period, pointedly compared his contemporaries in Dissent with their predecessors and found his own age wanting in reverence, assiduity in worship, personal piety, regularity in wholesome habits, family life, industry and frugality, and spiritual seriousness.[2] The fourth decade of the century may have marked the nadir of spiritual life for Dissent as well as for the Church of England. During the 1730s, there were fewer new Baptist and Independent chapels than in any decade since such beginnings began to be registered. Philip Doddridge, whose book *The Rise and*

Progress of Religion later played an important role in the conversion of William Wilberforce, was especially concerned about the decline of Dissent in the west and south of England. Doddridge wrote in 1740, when the movement was showing some of the first signs that it might be coming back to life.[3]

Dissent's revival was not uniform, and scholars speak of a bifurcation between denominations that continued in decline (chiefly Presbyterians) and "New Dissent" denominations (mainly Congregationalists and Baptists) that experienced the quickening of the evangelical movement. The latter group by the 1780s were growing much faster than the still-moribund Presbyterians and Quakers. To a large extent this growth was fueled by the example and influence of the Methodists. The increasing liveliness of New Dissent was accompanied by internal upheaval: the Baptists, for example, split in 1770, with the General Baptist New Connection departing to leave behind a largely Unitarian rump. Such breakups normally began with theological controversy but also included differences over such matters as propriety, order, and formality.[4] Of the three major Dissenting denominations, the Presbyterians remained least affected by evangelicalism, became gradually Unitarian in outlook, and declined in number throughout the period. In the half century after 1772, according to figures compiled by R. W. Dale, Congregationalists increased from 380 congregations to 799, and Baptists from 390 to 532; during the same period, the Presbyterians declined from 320 congregations to 252. Much of the Congregationalist growth came from Calvinistic Methodists coming over from the Whitefield-Lady Huntingdon chapels and from orthodox Presbyterian congregations reacting against the growth of Unitarianism in that denomination. Alarmed by the waxing of Dissent, the House of Lords in 1811 commissioned a survey of houses of worship to be accomplished by the bishops. Considering only towns housing more than one thousand persons, the bishops' officers found 2,547 churches but 3,457 Dissenting chapels.[5]

NEW DISSENT AND THE EVANGELICAL MOVEMENT

In time, the rejuvenated Dissenting denominations recognized formally what had been the case for several decades: they were in fact evangelical in orientation. In 1832, the Baptist Union defined itself officially as a body consisting of churches and ministers "who agree in the sentiments usually denominated evangelical." The next year the Congregationalist Union issued an affirmation called the "Declaration of Faith and Order" that said much the same.[6]

The Quakers, with their long history of quietism and spiritual contemplation, were eventually overtaken by the evangelical flood. By the 1830s the movement led from within by Joseph John Gurney had caused a split among them, and evangelicalism (called "Gurneyism" by its detractors) had largely won control of the denomination. This effectively broke down the long-standing isolation of the Quakers by allying them with an outside movement. In the 1850s, the evangelicals within led them away from their distinctive patterns of speech and dress and the prohibition against marrying outside their own ranks. Evangelical Quakers came to have much more in common with outside evangelicals than with the quietists within their denomination.[7] One effect of this change was to make the Quakers much more active in the ameliorative activities of the evangelicals; rather than expending all their efforts in contemplation and fellowship within their own number, they began to take an active interest in such matters as prison reform, an avenue of service in which they became leaders.[8] The English Quakers were much alarmed over the slide from quietism to deism that had happened to the American Quakers in the Hicksite disruption of 1827. Isaac Crewdson, an ally of Gurney in the Manchester meeting, warned his fellows against repeating that calamity: "Between mysticism and the religion of Christ there is this essential difference—the former is chiefly a religion of *feelings*, the latter is a religion of *faith*, for it is founded on the *testimony of the Spirit of God* transmitted to us in Holy Scripture. . . . Setting up the light within as 'the primary rule of faith and practice,' we believe, lay at the very root of Hicksism."[9]

If we find it surprising that the Protestant quietists should have been swept up by the evangelical tide, it will seem astounding that even the Unitarians were not entirely immune. Some of the most biblically oriented people of the revival found themselves doubting the doctrine of the Trinity because they could not find it in the Bible. A number of such traditionalists were Methodists, mostly geographically isolated, living in hamlets far from easy reach of theological mentors.[10] Such people had very little in common with the rationalist Unitarians like Joseph Priestley, and, as we have seen, Thomas Arnold regarded them as orthodox enough for his big-tent Church of England. Even Priestley had convictions that one could search hard for among modern Unitarians without result. In common with many Unitarians he was a necessitarian; such determinism was perhaps a natural outgrowth from a Calvinist denomination that had gone to seed. It was inevitable, said Priestley, that the glorious reign of the kingdom of God would come to fruition. "Whatever was the beginning of the world, the end will be glorious and paradisaical beyond what our imaginations can conceive." Wilberforce could have spoken the words, which date from 1771, and Wilberforce could also have given Priestley's reason for such convictions, although not its occasion. "As a believer in revelation and consequently in prophecy, I am led by the present aspect of things to look forward to events of the greatest magnitude and importance, leading to the final happy state of the world." Those words of Priestley's came after the French Revolution, which he took to be the triumphant fulfillment of the prophecy of the prophet Isaiah, more than two millennia earlier.[11]

As an evangelical, Dale was happy that the revival had rid the Congregational churches of the indifference and spiritual coldness of the earlier period. But he was conscious of unwelcome changes that accompanied the evangelical renewal. The influx of dissatisfied Presbyterians had filled the chapels with people who had no idea of the basis of the congregational polity—namely that Christ was so identified with the congregation that in effect it was *he* that was choosing the leaders that the people chose. For theologically minded men of the old school, like Dale, this was a palpable loss. Dale also thought he saw the character of the people change for the worse during his own century; they no longer exhibited self-restraint, resolution of effort, interest in theology and politics, or intellectual awareness. One of the characteristics he thought had been lost was "reserve," a watchword for the Tractarians, whose meaning was evidently the same. He was also saddened by the Congregational departure, virtually complete by the 1830s, from Calvinism and its enlistment in the Arminian camp.[12]

DISSENT AND THE ESTABLISHMENT

After the Act of Toleration (1689), relationships between the Establishment and Dissent varied according to local circumstances. The French Revolution brought about a serious turn for the worse. Dissenting opinion of all sorts was taken to be sympathetic to the revolution, and fear that the conflagration could spread to England spurred repression. The Dissenting minister George Burder made ready to flee after Joseph Priestley's meeting house was burned to the ground because of the rumor that Priestley intended to take refuge with him. Burder's son believed that the riots "were planned long before, and were intended to intimidate the Dissenters."[13] He may not have been right in that judgment, but it shows something of the sense of siege under which the Dissenters lived. These tensions lasted a long time because the wars with France lasted a long time.

Meanwhile, the evident successes of the Dissenting bodies threw the Establishment on the defensive. Between 1750 and century's end, the Baptists had grown from 25,000 to nearly 60,000. From 1780 to 1820 the number of churches in the two Baptist Associations doubled, as did the number of members per church. Moreover, the count of "hearers"—attenders who did not join—increased spectacularly, in at least one case numbering five for each member. In 1767, the first year Methodist statistics were recorded, the hearers numbered 22,410. From that point they went to 88,334 in 1800 and 232,074 in 1830. During this period the Church of England apparently lost communicants, and after 1800 its membership declined in proportion to the population.[14] But the bare numbers do not reveal adequately the mortification suffered by the Church of England. When a Church Evangelical incumbent died or retired, he frequently was replaced by a successor of a different sort, and the active parish members might desert en masse to a local evangelical chapel. This happened to some of the most illustrious of the early Evangelical parishes in England—Henry Venn's Huddersfield and Samuel Walker's Truro, for example.

In the generation following the French Revolution, Dissent made striking gains not only in numbers but in the influence implied by the numbers. The intensity of the public opposition to Lord Sidmouth's bill restricting itinerant preaching (1811) may be taken as indicative of this shift in public sensibilities. The pressure on the Establishment mounted after this period, leading to the legislative acts of the 1820s—the repeal of the Test and Corporation Acts—that so exercised the High Churchmen at Oxford and thereby contributed to the Tractarian movement.

The gains of Dissent invited responses of various kinds. Some of the preachers drew upon themselves persecutions similar to those suffered by the Methodists. The Dissenting minister William Jay recalled that even when the ministers followed what they had been taught in theological school, to speak kindly and humbly to their auditors, they were not always treated in corresponding fashion. A preacher might find himself with maimed horse or burgled house, and often—mistakenly in Jay's opinion—allowed the malefactors to escape without prosecution. Jay was convinced that the "village peasantry," who often received them courteously, would have given them no trouble at all had they not been egged on by clergyman, squire, or farmer.[15] This was identical to Wesley's experience.

The universities, especially Oxford, were hotbeds of anti-Dissent feelings, at least until Dissenters were admitted for degrees, which was after our period. One memoir writer recalled attending services at St. Mary's during his undergraduate years at Oxford in the first decade of the nineteenth century. He would go whenever a "great gun," as the noted preachers were called, "was expected to fire away (as was then their wont) at a methodistical or a dissenting target."[16] Even Evangelicals often showed surprisingly little regard for their fellows outside the Church. John Newton once wrote to Wilberforce that Unitarianism had "overrun" the Dissenting ministers: they were "departing with the greatest speed from the purity and truth of the Gospel" simply because they had the wrong form of government.[17] This was almost exactly the opposite of the truth, since Newton made it clear that he was speaking of the generality of Dissenting ministers and not merely the Presbyterians (who were, indeed, moving toward Unitarianism).

If Evangelicals sometimes had little patience for the Dissenters, one can imagine how radicals reacted to them. Leigh Hunt's title *An Attempt to Shew the Folly and Danger of Methodism* (1809) gives the flavor of that work. William Cobbett, with his customary pungency, averred his mixed judgment on Old Dissenters: they were fanatics, but they were honest and courageous men, unlike their successors. The "mongrel 'SAINTS' of our days," by contrast, were out for their own welfare, in it for the money. They were "as much like the Dissenters of old times as a *horse-dung* is like an *apple*."[18]

Dissenting successes at the expense of the Church of England naturally resulted in some soul searching among the Establishment. Thomas Arnold in 1832 took the growth of Dissent as an indictment of the failures of the Church and called urgently for Church reform. "What an organisation for a religious society!" he exclaimed, when speaking of the failures of the Church. "And how natural was it that men should form distinct societies for themselves, when that to which they nominally belonged performed none of the functions of a society." He even used the early Dissenting bodies as an example for Church reform.[19] Three years later Prime Minister Peel said much the same in a letter. He expressed wonder that Trinity College, Cambridge, should receive £2,000 a year from a parish and remit £24 of it to an incumbent as a stipend, cramping the services that could be afforded the parish. "Every post brings me statements which, if they are true, convince me that the deepest responsibility attaches to the Church for the present state of this country in regard to the progress of Dissent."[20] Wales was taken to have been a major failure of the Established Church, which had had a monopoly of religious influence in the century after the Restoration and had done nothing with it. Thus it had fallen to Dissent after the mid-eighteenth century to rescue people from the misery of self-indulgence and drunkenness.[21]

Implicit—sometimes explicit—in such criticism was the notion that if only the Church had done what was right during the years of quasi-monopoly there would have been no need for Dissenters to leave it. Reformers like Coleridge and Arnold thus thought it was feasible for a reformed Establishment to attract Dissenters and so unite the body of Protestant Christians for the benefit of both Church and society. But that was never realistic because it mistook religious convictions for mere expressions of dissatisfaction with the status quo. The principled nature of much Dissenting thought disabuses one of the idea.

"Congregationalism is not like Methodism," wrote a Dissenter of the 1830s, "a system of compromise and adjustment, formed in deference to the prejudice and feeling of the hour. It is the effect of a devout and firm-hearted appeal to the exact nature and design of Christianity. . . . Derived from what is unalterable in the injunctions and spirit of our benign and holy religion, it has itself been permanent."[22] These are not the words of a man amenable to submission to a bishop merely because the worst abuses of the episcopal system have been reformed away. After repeal of the Test and Corporation Acts in 1828, Dissenting gravamina were varied but in general came in one of two forms. The more radical simply opposed the idea of Establishment and campaigned against it. They were not content with correcting the disabilities placed upon Dissent but insisted on ending the constitutional arrangement that made it possible for the disabilities to be imposed. By the 1830s the Wesleyan Methodists were split between those, mainly laymen, who considered themselves enemies of the Establishment and a leadership that was far more conciliatory. Even at this late date many Methodists still considered themselves loyal members of the Church of England.

The more moderate Dissenters in all denominations believed that their complaints stood a better chance of being addressed if there were no attempt to muddy the waters with debates about disestablishment. In 1833–1834 they formed a committee to present a slate of five grievances for which they demanded relief. These related to restrictions placed on non-Churchmen with respect to baptism, marriage, burial, payment of church rates, and the granting of university degrees.[23] Of these issues the one most pressing on the minds of Dissenters was church rates. This was a charge imposed on all parishioners to maintain the local parish. Each vestry voted the rates annually and assessed the parishioners, whether or not they were believing members of the Church of England. Church rates were especially burdensome to the Dissenters at this time because their own communions were flourishing and the costs of building and maintaining the chapels fell squarely on them. Why should they be forced as well to support a religious establishment in which they did not believe? The injustice of the situation was manifest to them. But the Dissenters were not so appalled at their forced membership in the Church of England that they were unwilling to take advantage of it. In some parishes they managed to gain a majority on the vestry and proceeded to sabotage the running of the parish by refusing to impose any church rate at all, or at least by being very selective about the projects that would gain their approval.[24] In time the disabilities that plagued the Dissenters were removed, but that did not occur until well into Victoria's reign.

The great issue of disestablishment had its day in the sun before disappearing. The Religious Freedom Society was founded in 1838 to unite all anti-Establishmentarians under one banner—Church and Dissent, Protestant, Catholic, Jewish. It lasted only five years. At about the same time the Evangelical Voluntary Church Association was organized to seek the ending of religious establishment by uniting Dissenters to speak with a single voice. It too disappeared in a few years.

A longer lasting group formed in 1844 around an energetic Congregational minister from Leicester, Edward Miall, who had resigned his pastorate three years earlier and moved to London to found a paper and who advocated the ending of the Established Church. Called the British Anti-State Church Association, this group borrowed strength from Miall's character, which was compounded of fearless devotion and personal winsomeness and warmth. He had a powerful intellect, adept at both abstract speculation and practical skills. He was also a skillful orator, and as an editor he made the *Nonconformist* one of the most readable papers of the day. He differed from most of the anti-Establishmentarians in that he favored the more radical political solutions of the day, plumping for universal male suffrage, equal electoral districts, and other measures widely regarded as revolutionary.[25] Miall had the reputation for being a gentle opponent, but when it came to the Establishment he could be fierce, and the vehemence with which he expressed his views shows the difficulty in effectuating the dream of Coleridge and Arnold to fuse all Protestant Christians into a single Establishment: Three-quarters of the Anglican ministry, said Miall, could be charitably judged as "practically ignorant of the great spiritual principles of the gospel." Go to almost any parish in the kingdom to preach the gospel, "and your bitterest foe, your most energetic and untiring opponent, will prove to be the clergyman." The Church of England represented what Miall called "political religionism," its parishes being not really churches, some of them "devoid of a single member whose heart is in living sympathy with God."[26] One analyst has called the publication Edward Miall started in 1841 "mainly a paper of political propaganda" in spite of its ostensibly religious character. The whole idea behind it was to destroy the establishment of religion and place all denominations in a condition of equality before the law. In Miall's words, the *Nonconformist* was intended "to show that a national establishment of religion was vicious in its constitution, philosophically, politically, and religiously."[27]

DISSENT AND CLASS

When Puritan clergymen were cast out of their livings wholesale at the restoration of the monarchy, Dissent came to include many members of the aristocracy, as well as gentry and people of wealth and influence. This was particularly true of Independents, Presbyterians, and Quakers, less so of the Baptists. But the privileged orders quietly left in the next few decades, and at the turn of the eighteenth century most of the nobility had departed; by the 1730s, many of the gentry had followed the peers into the Church of England.[28] The Methodists, by dint of Wesley's sense of calling, ministered almost exclusively to the poor, the main exception being Whitefield's mission to Lady Huntingdon's noble friends. Thereafter, Dissenters were composed of people of many occupations, but most accounts suggest that skilled artisans were most numerous. *Artisan* can admit of different meanings but seems to have encompassed the more skilled and prosperous of the lower classes as well as the lower middle class.[29] Over the generations, poor people constantly enjoined to read and study, to avoid wasting money on drink and fripperies, to work hard and diligently, to attend to their families, and to teach their children the same virtues eventually find they are not so poor after all. And their children and grandchildren are able to accomplish much more than the first generation could. Many of these middle-class people were the scions of poor people who were the original evangelical converts.

Mid- and late Victorians of advanced views often lampooned Dissenters, partly because they were thought, with good reason, to be so attached to middle-class ethical values. By the mid-nineteenth century, the Dissenters had become largely middle class. Somewhat after our period, the historian Hippolyte Taine, visiting from France, entered a Dissenting chapel in the west end of London and found that the pews "are not filled by the common people, but by respectable middle-class people very correctly dressed, and with serious, sensible faces."[30] It was commonly recognized that social status was not to be found in the chapels, and families becoming prosperous often migrated to the Established Church. But many did not; those who retained their Dissenting convictions tended to stay where they were, foregoing the increased status that the membership in the Established Church would confer. Even the Methodists, in their dominant Wesleyan faction, had left the ranks of the poorest. Statistics from early in the nineteenth century suggest that about 13 percent of Methodists engaged in middle-class occupations, and some them had become wealthy. In Sheffield a substantial number paid pew rents, an overt indication of prosperity.[31]

The failure of the Church to attract more of the middle class, which consequently went to Dissent, was a frequent lamentation of the clergy. Arch-deacon Henry Manning, later to be the Roman Catholic Cardinal Manning, admitted to the clergy of Chichester in 1846 that the Church had not sufficiently served the great bulk of Englishmen. "I need not say what this middle class might do for the Church if it were drawn into its ministry and service."[32]

Although Dissenters had long been discriminated against by exclusion from the universities, they had not thereby been deprived of higher education. Oxford and Cambridge were academically poor in the eighteenth century, and their revival as seats of learning began around the time the Tractarians were finding themselves out of sympathy with the prevailing ideas in Church and university. The Dissenting academies, though they focused on preparing young men for the ministry, gave them a decent education. And those in the chapel from the lower classes achieved a level of learning to which they otherwise might not aspire. One modern scholar has opined that the best education such people could receive was as members, and possibly lay preachers, in Dissenting congregations.[33] Others have explained the active role of Dissent in the new industrial economy as a function of the quality of its education, which made Dissenters among the most learned of the middle classes; the success in England as industrialists of Scottish Presbyterians is sometimes used to support this contention.[34] In Lancashire, especially Liverpool and Manchester, most of the industrial elite belonged to Unitarian chapels,[35] and the same was true in general with respect to the textile factories in the Midlands.[36]

The common contemporary (and later) criticism of evangelicalism that it was individualistic is most patently false in the case of many of the Dissenting groups, especially those that began as "cottage meetings." Friendly gatherings around the hearthstone of a neighbor, these societies provided an intimacy of fellowship that few parish churches could emulate. Many never became organized chapels but instead continued as informal, evangelical fellowship groups. In those cases they may not have shown up in the census of 1851. Traces of them have been found in parts of Shropshire, for example, where there is no other evidence of organized Dissent. These groups afforded their members opportunities for deepening communal and family experiences, although it might also be said that the sundering of the parish into rival religious factions had less fortunate effects.[37]

One strength of Dissent in its often bitter rivalry with the Establishment lay in its greater ability to adapt to social changes, particularly the growth of towns and cities, which contrasted with the static nature of the rural strength of the Church of England.[38] Some historians have exaggerated this difference so as to reduce the theological differences between Church and chapel to a mere function of this geographical difference.[39]

DISSENT AND POLITICS

Apart from looking out for their own interests with respect to the Establishment, the Dissenters could be mobilized in common evangelical causes. Accounts of the antislavery struggle commonly underestimate the contribution of Dissent by concentrating their attention almost entirely on Clapham. Examination of the antislavery petitions shows a majority coming from chapels, and most of those from the humbler ones. One study based on the petitions notes "a fierce anti-slavery sentiment" in the working-class chapels of the midlands and north.[40]

Because of their continuing grievances, the sense of the injustices of the society, and perhaps other reasons, the Dissenters were associated with radical reform in the second half of the eighteenth century. And because many of them were educated and affluent—they were dominant, for example, in the literary and philosophical societies—they had considerable influence. Their businessmen and journalists played an active role in the radical societies of the 1790s. This was especially true in localities where Dissent was numerically important, such as Norwich, which became known as a center of intellectual Jacobinism.[41] One consequence of antirevolutionary sentiment was the sporadic outbreak of mob action of the sort that burned out Joseph Priestley's chapel. The Dissenters suffered much from this sort of reaction.

After 1820, Dissent's forays into radical politics were led by the Methodist groups that split from the dominant Wesleyans. Having learned how to organize and lead local assemblies, they used those skills in the political sphere. That is principally where the biblical language of denunciation and calls for justice came from, and the Chartist movement of the 1840s retained some of this flavor.[42] This combination of biblical language with radical politics later led Bishop Samuel Wilberforce to interpret Chartism and socialism as secularized forms of Dissent. (He said this not in a spirit of denunciation but rather to highlight the fault of the Church in failing to take seriously the just complaints of the people.)[43] Still, it would be a mistake to think of the Dissenters as simply radical in politics. There is no doubt they wanted fundamental constitutional changes with respect to the Establishment of religion, but divisions in their ranks prevented many political ventures that might have been expected of them. The evangelical factory reformer Richard Oastler was surprised and disappointed that they remained silent in the face of the evils he was so concerned to correct.[44]

With the exception of the Wesleyans, the Dissenters had always looked to the Whigs to oppose the Anglican religious hegemony. This had been the case ever since the days of William and Mary. In the 1830s the Whig government enacted measures that satisfied some of the Dissenters' demands, including the commutation of tithes and the regularizing of birth, marriage, and death services in the chapels. Included in these acts, with support from some Tories, was the appointment of an Ecclesiastical Commission, which we shall examine in a later chapter. There was an irony in this appointment inasmuch as the Church reforms stemming from the commission helped revitalize the Church of England, which was not an aim of the Dissenters.

THE INFLUENCE OF DISSENT IN ENGLAND

The most important effect that Dissent had on English politics may have been to prepare people to engage in the process who would have been unable had it not been for chapel influences. Many of the chapels were self-governing entities; some functioned as part of larger bodies. In either case, decisions were made that required study, discussion, and compromise. These skills had little further formal outlet until the Reform Bill of 1832, followed by later acts, broadened the franchise. But even without being part of regular political life, there were some Dissenters who took part in other kinds of activity, such as Chartism, after having tasted and practiced political life on the scale of the chapel. Later, Dissenting influence grew very strong in Gladstone's ministries, and later still Dissenters made up much of the leadership of the trade unions and the Labour Party.[45] One modern scholar has confessed it difficult to assess just how influential Dissenting groups have been on English political life, "for no one can conceive English politics without them." His argument is that the liberal temper of English life comes from the Dissenting tradition and even looks further back to seventeenth-century Puritanism.[46] Like much in the culture, ideas and attitudes developed through the Dissenting experience have embedded themselves so deeply in the modern psyche that it is difficult to step back far enough to assess them objectively.

During the long years when Dissenters suffered under sharply circumscribed political rights, they devised a substitute known as the Protestant Dissenting deputies. Presbyterian, Independent, and Baptist congregations in the London area each chose two members for the purpose of protecting their civil rights. From these was elected a committee of twenty-one, which in turn chose officers. Lacking a constitutional base for working directly in the political structure, these Deputies had to content themselves with whatever informal activities and means of pressure they could bring to bear. Their purpose from the start was to work for the repeal of the Corporation and Test Acts, but the organization also lent itself to whatever political remedies might be sought. After the offending acts were repealed, thus releasing the Dissenters to participate actively in political life, the Deputies turned their attention to other matters. From the 1830s the subject that took most of their attention was church rates, followed by the aforementioned matter of recognizing in law chapel rights in the registration of births, marriages, and deaths.[47]

If the Dissenters still had little direct influence on the national political scene by the 1840s, their position could be quite different in the localities. To be sure, much of the old Tory hegemony was still in place, including numerous Anglican clergymen serving as magistrates. But in many places Dissenters did not seem to know they were subservient to the Establishment. The Methodists in particular were so powerful in some localities as to come close to justifying Halévy's remark that they were "a second national church by the side of the first."[48] This was especially true in the new towns constructed around the mining and manufacturing industries. Typically there was no church in such communities and no established means of spreading the work of the diocese there. This vacuum was often filled by itinerant Methodist preachers, and before long, chapels were established as founding institutions of the village. Thus in Hetton-le-Hole, described by a historian as a typical mining village, there were separate chapels for Wesleyans, Primitive Methodists, and the Wesleyan New Connexion. By the middle of the nineteenth century, almost every coal community in the country had at least one chapel, and the money for it usually came from the pockets of the miners.[49] A study of Shropshire during the period concludes that in many ways Methodism was "the established church of the Shropshire coalfield." In the census of 1851, the three Methodist groups had more than half of all the attendance at worship services.[50] Whole regions of England seemed to fall to the march of Methodism, perhaps none more so than Cornwall, where one scholar says the movement became a "popular establishment, a *Volkskirche*."[51] By this time the Methodists had suffered two major defections, both after Wesley's death. The New Methodist Connexion, favoring a more democratic polity and separation from the Church of England, broke away in 1796. In 1811 the Primitive Methodists separated because the dominant Wesleyans would not countenance the camp-meeting form of evangelism that had been imported from the United States.

The pattern was similar in various cities. In London in the period from 1800 to 1840, the number of Methodist ministers grew by 320 percent.[52] In Birmingham, which had been a center of Dissent since the seventeenth century, the affairs of the city came to be governed by a "civic gospel" of Dissenting business leaders who knew each other intimately, often inter-married, and dominated the city's social as well as political life.[53] Middles-brough, which sent iron and steel all over Europe and whose products spanned the American continent in the form of rails, was founded, city and industry alike, by Quakers.[54] Leeds was a Methodist town, not only in numbers but also in ethos. "The established religion in Leeds is Method-ism," as a local clergyman put it in 1837, "and it is Methodism that all the most pious among the Churchmen unconsciously talk."[55] The many local strengths of Dissent were in keeping with the dominant thinking about localism in their assemblies. State power in London was associated in the minds of Dissenters with the centralized powers of the religious Estab-lishment supported by crown and Parliament. As a Congregational minis-ter put it in the widely published Crosby Hall lectures, "State power in religion, state power in education, state power in inspectors, state power in Whitehall, reaching over England, are all, as kindred influences, against Dissent, against liberty, against national spirit, against allied interests of self-governed and self acting people." It did no harm to the concept that it was in keeping with the parallel drive by political economists to keep the power of the central government to a minimum, particularly with respect to economic life.[56]

Of the effect of the chapel on the culture of England we must speak in a later chapter. But perhaps it would not be amiss to end this one by quoting scholars with little sympathy for the chapel or what it stood for, particularly Methodism's, on the effect of the chapel on the people who belonged to it:

On this population, partly neglected, partly dragooned by the Church, there descended a religion that happened to supply almost everything that it wanted. The Church offered no function to the poor man: his place was on a rude bench or a mat, listening to sermons on the importance of the subordi-nation of the lower classes to the grand family worshipping amid the spacious cushions of the squire's pew. The Chapel invited him to take a hand in the management of the affairs of his religious society: perhaps to help in choos-ing a minister, to feel that he had a share in its life, responsibility for its risks and undertakings, pride in its self-government and social life, the Chapel occupied a central place in the affections and the thoughts of people who had very little to do with the government of anything else. The management of common enterprises, involving relations with others bringing in their train friendships, quarrels, reconciliations, all the excitements that spring from the infinite surprises and subtleties of human character, brought to the exchange of ideas and prejudices, not only within a small circle, but outside: the diplomacy and agitation of controversy, the eager and combative discussion of rival doctrines.[57]

We may wish to discount the authors' cynicism about the Church, but they caught something about its alternative that is important to bear in mind.

The Prophets

COLERIDGE, CARLYLE, AND
THE SECULAR INFLUENCE OF
RELIGION

A RELIGIOUS REVIVAL either spreads through the society or affects only its own adherents and is eventually stifled in its isolation, ingrown and stagnant. An evangelical revival is expansive as a consequence of its emphasis on taking the gospel to where it is not known, and English evangelicalism was no exception. But Methodist preaching missions, Evangelical clergymen, innumerable mission societies, and untold millions of copies of tracts did not exhaust the means whereby religious messages were distributed. One reason this revival penetrated so deeply into the English consciousness was that it had a profound influence on intellectuals whose writings in turn were widely embraced by people who did not listen to (or read) sermons, disdained tracts, and did not attend worship services. We consider now two of the most important of these, Samuel Taylor Coleridge and Thomas Carlyle. Their religious beliefs and influence cannot be categorized as coming from one of the religious parties we have considered, but that made it possible for them to reach a broader segment of influential Englishmen than would otherwise have been the case.

THE PROPHETIC VOICE

The Old Testament prophets were not primarily foretellers of the future but rather functioned as mouthpieces for God, speaking eternal truths to the time-bound. The earthly powers habitually shunned them, hounded them, and, where they found it expedient, killed them. As one of the New Testament writers put it, in a long, eloquent passage commenting on his Hebrew predecessors: "They were stoned, they were sawn in two, they were killed with the sword; they went about in skins of sheep and goats, destitute, afflicted, ill-treated—of whom the world was not worthy" (Heb. 11:37–38). They were thus treated except when they were heeded, and they were heeded when people were disposed to heed them. The important story of the early nineteenth century is that people were disposed, for a change, to listen to their prophets rather than to stone them.

To use the term *prophet* when speaking about people like Coleridge and Carlyle is not to employ it in its loose, colloquial sense. In their day it signified something very close to the biblical meaning. In both periods prophets arose who saw that things were not right in the society and who sought to convince people that serious moral reformation was required to restore it to health. These prophets had no formal authority to bring about the change they desired. They spoke, and that was enough; or it was not enough but was all they could do.

Prophets become numerous in the land either when matters have become so terrible that the prophetic voice is all that can rescue the nation from utter corruption or when the powers are disposed to pay attention, thus encouraging the prophetic activity. Our period is one of the latter, and we focus on Coleridge and Carlyle not because they are the only ones available but because they were so well known and so influential—and also because they were so different from each other that they illustrate something of the variety that can be found in the prophetic office.

Our two prophets were not contemporaries, although they overlapped. Coleridge was born in 1772, son of a clergyman and headmaster. He was educated in Christ's Hospital and later left Cambridge University without taking a degree. He was a radical in his younger days and with his college friend Robert Southey planned to found a utopian community in Pennsylvania, a project that was abandoned when Southey had a change of heart. After Southey became engaged to Edith Fricker, he persuaded Coleridge to marry her sister, Sara, a disastrous union that plagued both husband and wife to the end of their days. Coleridge was also troubled by bad health; an autopsy performed after his death in 1834 found that his heart and lung diseases were of long standing and belied his reputation as a hypochondriac.

Perhaps the most important of Coleridge's relationships were his friendships with Southey and especially William Wordsworth, who was also a close friend of Thomas Arnold. (Arnold built his home, Fox Howe, in the Lake District to be near to Wordsworth.) Coleridge's good friend the essayist Charles Lamb once referred to this relationship by writing that Coleridge was off on a visit to the north country to "visit his god Wordsworth."[1] His long and famous poem *The Rime of the Ancient Mariner* was part of a collaborative work with Wordsworth. Together the three are often called the Lake Poets because of the district in which they lived, Coleridge only sporadically. Also noteworthy for Coleridge's development was his study tour in Germany from 1799 to 1800, when he learned the language and something of the philosophy that would be so influential in molding his think-

SAMUEL TAYLOR COLERIDGE.
By courtesy of the National Portrait Gallery, London.

ing. Generations of schoolchildren have known of Coleridge as a poet because of the popularity of the *Ancient Mariner,* but his contemporaries and
those who came immediately afterwards knew him as that and much more.
His outward appearance could make him seem much less, however, so that
a modern scholar, an admirer, refers to him as "an opium-addict, and a
ruined man."[2] Coleridge resented the prominence given to his addiction,
claiming that it came about due to his medical problems, averring that it
was common among the better sort of people, and noting with an air of
resentment that William Wilberforce was not taken to task for having the
same affliction.[3]

Thomas Carlyle was born in 1795, the same year as Thomas Arnold, but
lived nearly forty years longer before his life ended in 1881. He was born
to Scottish parents of strict Calvinist beliefs and, although his own convictions departed early from theirs, remained devoted to his family. Evidently

he lost his orthodox Christian beliefs while he was a student at the University of Edinburgh, and although religious faith seemed to dominate much of what he wrote, it is not easy to say with confidence just what it was; sometimes he seemed to write as an orthodox Christian, other times as a pantheist or as a believer in the life force. While he was teaching at Kirkcaldy in 1816, he met Edward Irving, with whom he maintained a devoted friendship until the minister's death. He spent a number of lean years trying to earn a living as a writer before moving to London in 1834. He settled in Chelsea and remained in his rented house on Cheyne Row until he died.

Carlyle was an acute observer of the English scene and commented acidly on many topics of national interest. He also became a noted historian, particularly for his studies of the French Revolution and of the reign of Frederick the Great of Prussia. Like Arnold and Coleridge, he learned German and read widely in philosophical and historical writings in that language. He was not an original thinker but wrote with such force and brilliance that he could not be ignored. Walt Whitman endorsed James Anthony Froude's description of Carlyle as a prophet in the Old Testament sense of men who have "interpreted correctly the signs of their own times." Carlyle regarded himself in this way and sometimes cited the Old Testament prophets to explain what he was up to. "When a Nation is unhappy, the Old Prophet was right and not wrong in saying to it: Ye have forgotten God. . . . It is not according to the law of Fact that ye have lived and guided yourselves, but according to the law of Delusion, Imposture, and wilful and unwilful Mistake of Fact." [4]

The harshness of Carlyle's persona may have been partially a cover for a certain tenderheartedness. The radical journalist Leigh Hunt, who for a short time lived only a few hundred feet from Carlyle's Cheyne Row house and came to know him well, spoke of the antipathies that seemed to motivate the Scot—"a love for the pleasure and exaltation of fault-finding"— but also described him as the most compassionate of men. [5] The painter William Holman Hunt showed the ambivalence toward him felt by so many Englishmen: "Although I did not subscribe to all that his worshipers demand, he was to me one of the real greatnesses of England." [6] Edward Caird, the idealist philosopher, reminisced in 1892 of the great influence Carlyle had on him and concluded that "no English writer . . . has done more to elevate and purify our ideas of life, and to make us conscious that the things of the spirit are real, and that, in the last resort, there is no other reality." [7]

One reason for Carlyle's immense influence is possibly also the reason the star of his renown sank: his inveterate dogmatism, the bullying and

THOMAS CARLYLE.
By courtesy of the National Portrait Gallery, London.

harassing of those of differing viewpoint, the imputation of bad motives to wrong opinions. Carlyle's dyspeptic nature caused him often to lash out publicly at friend and foe alike. In his memoirs he described William Wilberforce as "the famous Nigger-philanthropist, drawing-room Christian, and busy man and politician."[8] Many of those he attacked remained unabashedly his admirers.[9] In Carlyle, the strongest possible statement of conviction is often accompanied by a singular lack of argument or evidence, so that his polemical work sometimes seems mere bombast. He evidently adopted this mode of discourse because he did not believe that convictions are arrived at dispassionately on the basis of evidence; rather they rise out of the moral condition of the heart. He made this explicit in the midst of a historical essay on the St. Edmundsbury Monastery. "How can a man, without clear vision in his heart first of all, have any clear vision in the head? It is impossible!"[10] For a certain type of writer—Carlyle's type of writer—this style enhances his appeal, arguably making him much more effective than a more rational approach would do.[11] But it does not wear well, and readers can find themselves wearied by the constant harangue. Crane Brinton, in an uncharacteristically cynical passage, referred to this "trick of Carlyle's temperament, the last step by which he secured himself in his pulpit," as "his alliance with God." This saved him, according to Brinton, from having to explicate his views in the normal way, using a hypothesis, evidence, and reason. "What he knew he knew once and for all by a revelation superior to caviling logic."[12]

The two men did not know each other well. Carlyle visited Coleridge when the poet was long past his prime, sunk in opium dependency and ailments, and living on the charity of admirers. Carlyle, who it is sometimes said valued work more than anything else and was himself a prodigious laborer, was unimpressed by the "fat flabby incurvated personage" he found at the house in Highgate. "His cardinal sin," he wrote to his brother, "is that he wants will; he has no resolution, he shrinks from pain or labour in any of its shapes."[13] That was a description that might have fit Coleridge throughout his life, but a more balanced assessment would have mentioned the prodigious amount of work Coleridge had turned out in the previous decades.

THE PROPHETS AGAINST THE BACKGROUND
OF MATERIALISM

The reaction against the Enlightenment was typically religious, having High Church, evangelical, and liberal manifestations, but it was also philosophical and literary. In the early nineteenth century, the defenders of Enlightenment thinking, which is to say materialism and atheism, appealing to science, were associated with Jeremy Bentham and his followers, the utilitarians. Bentham's influence was minimal until James Mill, Scottish historian and philosopher, met him in 1808 and gave it new life. Mill's son, John Stuart Mill, became one of the premier thinkers of the century. His father raised him in what amounted to a nineteenth-century version of the "Skinner box," the closed environment in which the Harvard psychologist B. F. Skinner was said to test his theories of human behavior by confining his newborn daughter. Mill did not trust the schools to educate his son, and the boy grew up instructed by his father in the scientific principles that Bentham had worked out. John Stuart Mill came to recognize that, whatever the merits of the Benthamite philosophy, it failed to uncover the richness of human experience, and his own journey included much suffering until he found a way to transcend its limitations. He believed that Bentham and Coleridge were "the two seminal minds of the age," and he was appreciative of Coleridge's efforts to complement the incompleteness of Benthamite materialism. Writing in 1840, Mill described Coleridge as "one of the two English names of our time which are likely to be oftener pronounced, and to become symbolical of more important things, in proportion as the inward workings of the age manifest themselves more and more in outward facts. . . . For no one has contributed more to shape the opinions of those among its younger men, who can be said to have opinions at all."[14]

One of the buttresses of Enlightenment rationalism was the reduction of human action to epiphenomena of impersonal forces from the environment. Locke's idea of human knowledge, amplified by Hartley, was that the blank slate that was the human mind at birth became imprinted by various experiences mediated through the senses. There seemed to be no way to account for characteristically *human* action under those circumstances, so human beings appeared to be little more than automatons reacting to stimuli. This was devastating to the idea of human personality and was evidently part of the reason John Stuart Mill entered his period of crisis, having little beyond Bentham's ideas to fall back on. Coleridge made good use of his German studies by bringing Kant's distinction between pure and practical reason into play. This caused him to emphasize the freedom of the will as a necessary correlate of practical wisdom that enabled the person to function beyond the category of necessity, thus preserving the integrity of the human personality.[15]

Evidently, the human personality was the linchpin of much of Coleridge's thinking. Just as the mechanistic anthropology of Enlightenment psychology impedes clear thinking about personality, so Enlightenment historiography does the same about human society. Coleridge thought Gibbon's style in *The Decline and Fall of the Roman Empire* was "detestable," but that was not the worst of it. He was unable to discern any understanding of human motivation or of causation in Gibbon, finding in his work little more than a string of "splendid anecdotes." "When I read a chapter in Gibbon I seem to be looking through a luminous haze or fog, figures come and go, I know not how or why, all larger than life or distorted." The problem Coleridge saw was that although Gibbon was immensely learned, he had no philosophy to add meaning to his collection of anecdotes. But he had prejudices, particularly against Christianity, and all that amounted to was "that poor piddling scepticism—which Gibbon mistook for Socratic philosophy."[16]

Holding forth in his lengthy monologues before visitors at his Highgate retreat, Coleridge dissected the main prop of the Benthamite public policy—the use of the state power to produce the greatest happiness for the greatest number of people. He considered the criterion absurd because the variety of values and motivations makes it impossible to ever come to general agreement on what might produce happiness. A savage would find happiness in collecting scalps, and a savage Bentham would insist on policies that produced the greatest number of scalps for the most people. The sovereign producer of happiness for the multitudes would find the multitudes seeking to escape his vision of happiness. Coleridge took the Benthamite proposal as a means of circumventing the "standard of Reason and Duty," which circumvention would ensure that happiness would never be attained.[17]

Like Coleridge, Carlyle was a Germanist and also learned in the philosophy of Kant. He thought the Enlightenment understanding of reason led people into oppression and instead urged a more "German" way of approaching it. The understanding is stifled by a mechanistic use of its faculties—that is, a French way of using them—and Carlyle preferred instead the dynamism of Kantian idealism, which recognized internal growth and spiritual ascendancy over the merely material.[18] As early as 1827, in his thirty-second year, he confided to his diary that Jeremy Bentham had significance only in an intellectual sense, being part of a class that was "important only for their number; intrinsically wearisome, almost pitiable and pitiful."[19] His school would come to no good end: "Utilitaria will pass away with a great noise."[20]

The English public first became aware of Carlyle's views on utilitarianism in the weird novel *Sartor Resartus*, part autobiography, part attack on almost everything the Enlightenment stood for. In the maundering of Prof. Diogenes Teufelsdrökh (devil's dung), Carlyle opposed the rationalism of the materialists—"logic-choppers, and treble-pipe Scoffers, and professed Enemies to Wonder; who, in these days, so numerously patrol as night-constables about the Mechanics' Institute of Science, and cackle"—but also was part of the tradition that exposed the failings of the clergy.[21] This mixing of opposition to utilitarianism with anticlericalism made for an odd combination and probably intrigued an audience that found Carlyle hard to pigeonhole. The trouble with rationalism is not that it is reasonable, said Carlyle, but that it is stupid and proud—the "vacant mind furnished with much talk about Progress of the Species, Dark Ages, Prejudice, and the like; so that all were quickly enough blown out into a state of windy argumentativeness; whereby the better sort must soon end in sick, impotent Scepticism."[22] The Benthamites are antihuman with their "Profit-and-Loss Philosophy" because, being materialists, they do not understand "that Soul is *not* synonymous with Stomach . . . and that the loss of his religious Belief was the loss of every thing."[23] The style of *Sartor Resartus* came to be vintage Carlyle: the vivid denunciations with little in the way of argument, the wildly imaginative evocations, the extravagant imagery. Those without faith ("worldlings") do not weaken; they "puke up their sick existence."[24] The apostate clergy do not counsel loose living; they advise "as the solution of such doubts, to 'drink beer, and dance with the girls.' Blind leaders of the blind!"[25]

The early nineteenth century is often considered to be the heyday of Romanticism, but our prophets were opponents of one of the main features of the Romantic impulse—that is, what they considered to be the wild and untrammeled individualism of such poets as Byron and Shelley. The prophetic writers spoke of duty, of responsibility to society, of the recovery of the moral standards that the preceding generations had been wont to ridicule. Walter Scott was a novelist who joined them in this and by his example helped turn the novel toward an exemplifying of morality that would be more in keeping with the values of the new century.[26] Coleridge referred to this shift when he contrasted the last two kings. George IV was an immoral man, as the whole kingdom knew, but Coleridge was proud of his country because of the "influence of [its] private morals," which deplored the king's behavior. "The old King, [George III] in spite of his homeliness, his obstinacy and his craziness . . . was almost universally beloved and popular; George IV has counted his months with victories and yet not one ray of the public glory fell on him!"[27]

COLERIDGE'S RELIGION

In general the Lake Poets were much more orthodox than many have supposed. Older works often associate them with pantheism, largely because of their preoccupation with nature. During Wordsworth's lifetime, the Irish poet and critic Aubrey de Vere, who knew him well, regarded him as an orthodox Christian, increasingly so as he grew older. De Vere was once amazed to see Wordsworth's portrait among those of the saints in a Cistercian monastery. The abbot explained that he had placed it there in gratitude for Wordsworth's spiritual help. He had decided to enter monastic life partly as a result of reading *The Excursion*. De Vere said that Wordsworth had once told him that he wrote of religious matters with diffidence because just as there were matters too low for poetic expression, there were others too high.[28] It may not be coincidental that Wordsworth, who exercised such strong influence over John Keble, should have expressed an idea that found fuller expression in the Tractarian notion of reserve in religious matters.[29]

Coleridge is said to have stepped back from boldly examining the grounds of his faith because as an unhappy man he lacked the inner strength to question the only grounds of his security.[30] Even on the face of it, this formulation of the issue seems highly implausible, and more so when we consider the content of the poet's writings on religion. For, apart from his early work, there is little that he wrote that does not fit squarely into the framework of orthodox Christianity. Nor does any of it have the ring of insincerity or fearfulness of what alternatives might be true. On human nature, for example: "I profess a deep conviction that man is a fallen creature . . . not by accident of bodily constitution or any other cause, but as diseased in his will."[31] We do not have much information on the sources of Coleridge's faith, but a few facts have come to light. Wesley's example evidently had some effect on him, particularly as it was mediated through Southey's *Life*.[32] The *Record* published Coleridge's last letter and treated it as a kind of deathbed confession. In it he declared "eminently blessed" those "who begin early to seek, fear, and love their God, *trusting wholly in the RIGHTEOUSNESS and MEDIATION of their Lord, Redeemer, saviour, and everlasting High Priest Jesus Christ.*" The paper was unhappy with much of Coleridge's thinking but nevertheless welcomed him into the Evangelical ranks because of this understanding of the gospel.[33] Later in the century, John Tulloch agreed that Coleridge was part of the "Evangelical School," but with this interesting caveat. Tulloch believed that the Evangelicals, from Cowper to Chalmers, despite the virtue and accomplishment of their lives, had falsely destroyed the unity of human existence by separating religious life from the rest of life, treating it as "super-added" to humanity. It was Coleridge's achievement, according to this analysis, to restore the human unity and make it possible for the religious to comprehend and purify other human attributes.[34]

COLERIDGE'S RELIGIOUS THINKING

Coleridge's theology was centered on sin and atonement; in this he was little different from the Protestant Reformers.[35] But he also kept the Incarnation central to his thinking in a way that was more common among High Churchmen. He did better than many Evangelicals in separating himself from the twin traps that ensnared so many others: antinomianism and moralism. One reason he was able to do this was that he separated "sin" from "sins." The former is the human condition; the latter is the particular deeds that flow from it. With this understanding good people can be rescued from both self-righteousness in their separation from "sins" and excessive self-reproach in their identification with "sin."[36] Coleridge's proximity to Evangelical thinking is not the invention of later scholars. It will be recalled that when R. W. Church was reluctantly considering whether to attend Newman's sermons at St. Mary's, he was put off by the notion that Newman was preaching a religious philosophy that Church called "Evangelico-Coleridgian."[37] Recent scholarship has made it seem evident that Coleridge's theology and philosophy cannot be abstracted from his poetry, even though they come at a later period. His ideas were transmitted in both poetry and prose and they influenced people together.[38]

Perhaps the main reason the Evangelicals distrusted Coleridge was what they thought to be his denigration of the Bible. In fact, what he denigrated was the idea that the Bible was handed down from God as a ready-made primer that was protected from any error and therefore to be interpreted literally, a view for which he invented the term *bibliolatry*. Yet he was far from passing over to the other side, for he continued to uphold the Bible as the reliable guide to faith and life. He wrote a book entitled *The Statesman's Manual*, which is reminiscent of works by Evangelical writers like Gisborne, More, and Wilberforce in that it directed moral instruction explicitly to "the higher classes." The statesman's manual, as Coleridge explained it, is the Bible, "the main lever by which the moral and intellectual character of Europe has been raised to its present comparative height."[39] Just as Wilberforce had written that Christianity was only the nominal religion of England, and just as Arnold would later preach that the gospel was little known in English homes considering themselves Christian, so Coleridge wrote that "the main hindrance" to the use of the Bible as the statesman's manual was the mistaken idea that Englishmen knew what it contained.[40] A decade after Coleridge's death, the *Christian Observer* published a letter he had written to a clergyman that expressed strong support for the Bible Society, with only the one reservation: the society was too expectant of immediate result. Still, he considered it "probable" that "the written word will have a large share in the conversion of the nations to the living and eternal Word."[41] Coleridge paid considerable attention to the Old Testament and believed that virtually all of its messianic passages pointed to a spiritual savior to come; had it been otherwise, there would be nothing to expect except a virtuous version of Napoleon.[42] He disagreed with the assumption of inerrancy not only on theoretical grounds but also for practical reasons. For it was a brittle thing that could not stand informed attack and therefore put a powerful tool in the hands of the skeptics. "Is not this supposed inspiration of the Bible the handle which every infidel and railer at religion invariably takes up? . . . What a mass of gratuitous difficulties—shall I not say, horrible blasphemies does the Church create and as it were appropriate by this strange doctrine!"[43] The "verbal inspiration doctrine," said Coleridge, was unknown in the early church and has served to make infidels of many inquirers.[44]

Coleridge's critique of the Evangelical use of Scripture is suggestive of his apologetic. For if he found proof texts unpersuasive, so he found equally useless the use of proofs from nature, which had captivated the Church intellectuals. He was particularly incensed at William Paley's *Natural Theology* (1802), which was widely used to "prove" the truth of Christian faith. In *Aids to Reflection* (1825), Coleridge produced an apologetic based on internal evidence, on the effect of a doctrine on the soul, so that the inquirer was invited to consider not so much the miracles of Christ but the way the accounts of those miracles speak to his innermost being. The kind of rationalism that had captivated the Church since the late eighteenth century he believed was bankrupt, and if Paleyism were not jettisoned, it would continue to plague the faith. *"Evidences* of Christianity! I am weary of the Word. Make a man feel the want of it—rouse him, if you can, to the self-knowledge of his need of it, and you may safely trust it to his own Evidence."[45]

CARLYLE'S RELIGION AND ETHICS

Carlyle's interest in German language and philosophy is usually considered central to his intellectual formation. But first place ought to go to his family heritage. Although he threw off the strict Calvinist evangelicalism of his parents (and indeed the Christianity of which it was an expression), he kept much of what flowed from it. He had a high estimate of his father's intellect, artisan and farmer though he was, comparing it with that of Robert Burns. His ideas on truth and justice as inflexible values, and even his manner of speech, came from his father.[46] With good reason did Louis Cazamian say that he remained "impregnated with the Hebraic Christianity of his family" in spite of the self-invented origin of his religious beliefs. Carlyle's study of Kant persuaded him of the categorical imperative as a necessary element in an ethic, but he was already convinced by his upbringing that human action had to be governed by inflexible ethical imperatives beyond personal desires.[47] Carlyle later recalled that among the main influences on him in what he called his "lawless" country was John Johnston, a "simple evangelist" who taught him Latin and was in effect the pastor of the district. Pastor and church together "were the blessing and the saving of many. On me too their pious heaven-sent influences still rest and live."[48]

The religiosity in which he was reared never left him, even after the specific doctrines that informed it did. The incoherence of his ideas made it difficult to pin down what he actually believed, but everything he wrote on the subject of morals was suffused with religiosity. If he was a "Calvinist without the theology"—James Anthony Froude's term—then it was the kind of Calvinism that manifested itself in moral strictures, denunciations, manifestos, warnings. The softer side of Carlyle's personality, which could break through in a time of sorrow, kept the religious sensibilities that he was never able to shake off. "It is God that has done it," he wrote to his mother at the death of his father in 1832, "and our part is reverent submission to His Will, and trustful prayer to Him for strength to bear us through every trial. . . . We shall meet no more, till we meet in that *other* Sphere, where God's Presence more immediately is."[49] Words such as these could come easily to the lips of a Methodist preacher, Evangelical parson, Tractarian academic, Dissenting minister, or Thomas Arnold, being little more than an expression of Christian hope. But what is the meaning of Christian hope that lacks the doctrinal base without which it seems to be pious twaddle? Yet pious twaddle is one of the vices that Carlyle always thundered against.[50]

The religiosity that was always evident in Carlyle's writings seemed to intensify in his late works, which apparently diminished his reputation among some readers. This later work is sometimes described as Calvinist or (paradoxically) Arminian.[51] His father's death brought out much of the latent religiosity that never left him:

> He "had finished the work that was given him to do" and finished it (very greatly more than the most) as became a man. He was summoned too before he had ceased to be interesting—to be loveable. (He was to the last the pleasantest man I had to speak with in Scotland.) For many years too he had the end ever in his eye, and was studying to make all preparation for what in his strong way he called often "that last, that awful change." Even at every new parting of late years I have noticed him wring my hand with a tenderer pressure, as if he felt that one other of our few meetings here was over. Mercifully also has he been spared me till I am abler to bear his loss; till by manifold struggles I too, as he did, feel my feet on the Everlasting rock, and through time with its death, can in some degree see into eternity with its life. So that I have repeated, not with unwet eyes, let me hope likewise not with unsoftened heart, those old and for ever true words, "Blessed are the dead that die in the Lord; they do rest from their labours, and their works follow them."[52]

Perhaps my father, all that essentially was my father, is even now near me, with me. Both he and I are with God. Perhaps, if it so please God, we shall in some higher state of being meet one another, recognise one another. As it is written, We shall be for ever with God. The possibility, nay (in some way) the certainty of perennial existence daily grows plainer to me. "The essence of whatever was, is, or shall be, even now is." God is great. God is good. His will be done, for it will be right.[53]

Carlyle's religious maundering was frequently expressed in what had become common phrases, but the meanings were likely to be very different than in ordinary usage. Recalling the time in 1825 he was at Hoddam Hill, he spoke of his experience there in terms of "what the old Christian people meant by their 'Conversion.'" After dismissing in contemptuous terms the religious movements of the day—"Puseyisms," "ritualisms," "cobwebberies," "Nigger emancipations," "protection societies"—he described his "pious joy and gratitude," for his achievement, which was that he "had become independent of the world." Gratitude to whom? To Goethe, whom he felt had led the way in that kind of experience.[54]

Carlyle's character more than his doctrines came from his parents' convictions. When early in his career he was refused a professorship in the University of Edinburgh and his mother responded, upon learning of the disappointment, "He canna hinder thee of God's providence," Carlyle called this a "glorious truth." Moreover, the defeat was good for him. "It is wholesome to have my vanity humbled from time to time. Would it were rooted out of me for ever and a day."[55] He was an apostle of the value of work, another indication of his Calvinist upbringing, and his own labors over manuscripts at Cheyne Row were prodigious, having bad effects on his health and his relations with his wife. When Ford Maddox Brown painted his famous *Work* (1852), it was fitting that Carlyle occupied an important place on the right edge, glaring at the viewer while standing next to a milder mannered observer, the theologian F. D. Maurice. Some have argued that for Carlyle work was not so much an aspect of religion as the religion itself and that this notion was carried to the general culture by novelists like Dickens.[56]

Willey associates Carlyle with those of Puritan bent who rejected church, creed, and sacrament—which the Scot called "Hebrew Old-Clothes"—while retaining "the deep intuitions of his Calvinistic peasant-childhood." From those intuitions came "the unquestioned moral certainties of Puritanism" and "both his satiric animus and his prophetic energy."[57] This is why Froude referred to him as a Calvinist without the theology. For similar reasons another scholar believes that Carlyle's philosophy of history came right out of the Old Testament: a good king is necessary for a happy people, and when the king is not good, a hero must appear to rescue them.[58]

REFORMING THE INSTITUTIONS OF ENGLAND

There seems to be little or nothing prescriptive in Carlyle's writings. He made it clear that he believed that to be inevitable in the circumstances. There could be no quick remedy for society's problems. "Brothers, I am sorry I have got no Morrison's Pill for curing the maladies of Society." The politicians are the fools' gold of remedies, since they obscure the only way to a solution, which is to obey God's laws, which are the governing laws of the universe. "If we walk according to the Law, the Law-Maker will befriend us; if not, not." The cure must come by "descending into thy inner man" and discovering whether there is a soul there. On the same pages it becomes apparent that the orthodox language is deceptive and that he was not referring to the Christian conception that most of his contemporaries would have meant with those same words. For he identified the "Laws of God" as identical to both "nature's Laws" and the "laws of Fact."[59] They are used, more or less, just to signify the way things are.

He could denounce what seemed wrong to him, and he could gain a following by doing so. But his style alone would appear to preclude a measured, rational argument for the amelioration of the conditions that troubled him. If his failure to suggest concrete measures seems to reveal a certain detachment from life, that is a quality he saw in himself. In the passage about his "conversion," quoted above, he said that since that time he had lived "looking down upon the welterings of my poor fellow-creatures . . . and [had] had no concern" for their various controversies and preoccupations, apart from pity for them.[60]

Coleridge's prescriptions for the reformation of English institutions were like the historical assumptions of Carlyle in that both had biblical antecedents. Coleridge commonly used a typological approach to biblical interpretation, in particular to its historical aspects. The facts of history in biblical accounts were on one level but could be understood only in relation to their broader spiritual context. So they were not merely facts but grist for an understanding of history as a redemptive drama. During the period from 1825 to 1827 in letters and notebook entries, he sketched plans—never brought to fruition—for a universal history in which this understanding would be realized. That is why for Coleridge the Church had to be central to an understanding of society and to any attempt to reform its institutions. The Church was not just a human institution, nor even just a religious institution in the narrowest sense; it was also the medium by which the divine will was to be exercised, a kind of incarnation of the eschatological vision.[61]

If the society's health and welfare is dependent upon its conformity to the will of God, then statesmanship is a theological skill. That is why Coleridge

called the Bible the statesman's manual. For it contains "rules and assis-
tances for all conditions of men under all circumstances; and therefore for
communities no less than for individuals." [62] And this is in keeping with his
broader point about the relationship between the metaphysical and the
social and political: "All the epoch-forming Revolutions of the Christian
world, the revolutions of religion and with them the civil, social, and domestic habits of the nations concerned, have coincided with the rise and fall
of metaphysical systems." [63] This mode of thinking seems perhaps to establish Coleridge as a hopeless conservative standing in the way of progress,
especially when one considers that he opposed the Reform Bill of 1832. But
so insistent a champion of liberty as John Stuart Mill was not so sure of that.
In fact, he thought Coleridge was a better reformer than the Whig cham-
pions of the Reform Bill because he saw what Mill later on took to be
obvious—that the Reform Bill would be at one and the same time a revolutionary change that would not remove the major defects of the political
system. [64] Carlyle's moral preoccupations kept him from seeing much good
in the democratic aspirations that were gradually carrying the day. A decade
after the Reform Bill of 1832, he was telling the public that elections would
avail them nothing if they lacked the moral backbone to do the right thing
with the franchise. "A heroic people chooses heroes, and is happy; a valet or
flunky people chooses sham-heroes, what are called quacks, thinking them
heroes, and is not happy." [65]

Coleridge's solution for the problems of society has been described in opposition to that of his contemporary William Godwin. This is important
because of the well-known idea of the "clerisy," which Coleridge adduced
as the means of rejuvenating society in accordance with a true understanding of its relationship to religion and morality. Godwin's elevation of the
chosen few from whose writings the truth would eventually descend to the
masses Coleridge rejected as a "proud philosophy, which affects to inculcate
philanthropy while it denounces every home-born feeling, by which it is
produced and nurtured." To that hierarchical bifurcation between classes,
Coleridge opposed a biblical understanding: "Go, preach the GOSPEL to
the poor." [66]

The clerisy for Coleridge was the educated elite of the nation, whose role
was to formulate and transmit the best values of the national tradition.
They would be separate from the National Church, which would be understood in a wider sense than the current Church of England, but which
must be Trinitarian. [67] The National Church was not exactly to be a church;
it has been described as "in effect a great national guild of the learned professions." It was separate from the Church of England. Coleridge seemed

to be dividing the capital of England into two segments: the "Propriety" was that portion placed under the state, and the "Nationalty" was to maintain the National Church. He had little faith in the Church of England of his day, but he believed its weaknesses were due to its domination by the state. It had to be freed from the meddling of politicians, and its wealth protected from the same danger. The king would remain the titular head of the church, but its governance would have to be under the control of its own convocation.[68]

These ideas had echoes elsewhere. The Tractarians would shortly make similar points about the Erastian tendencies of the day, and Thomas Arnold would elaborate on an expanded role for the Church of England that borrowed from Coleridge's National Church.[69]

Mill evaluated Coleridge's work with the highest praise, though he took it for what it in fact was—the almost complete repudiation of his own father's teaching and that of his father's master, Bentham. What Mill called the "German-Coleridgian school"—he also called it the "reactionary school"—departed from the serious errors of the eighteenth-century philosophers who had denied the importance of history and the moral teachings that come with it. Coleridge and his fellows "were the first (except a solitary thinker here and there) who inquired with any comprehensiveness or depth into the inductive laws of the existence and growth of human society. . . . Thus they produced, not a piece of party advocacy, but a philosophy of society, in the only form in which it is yet possible, that of a philosophy of history." Mill went on to say that he was not speaking of "a defence of particular ethical or religious doctrines," which means he was endorsing not Coleridge's theological ideas but the social ideas that were their consequences.[70]

It is possible that, as one scholar has put it, Coleridge's theology was not up to the task of accomplishing all that he hoped. For in this view Christian theology was to be the bedrock of a reformed and more just and healthy English society. But his apologetic, concerned as it was with transcending the literalism that he anticipated would not be able to withstand the challenges that would be forthcoming from the Continent, was too subjective to serve the creation of a national ethic. Those of the Broad Church who followed him kept his emphasis on the importance of individual religious experience and thereby forfeited a claim to have that experience speak to and for the whole nation.[71] Still, that is not the whole story, for if his theology was not up to the task, it was a self-imposed task, and the many testimonies of his influence suggest that his work was not in vain.

Coleridge was responsible for no great legislative acts and little in the way of great literature, although the *Ancient Mariner* has been very enduring. But there were so many important people whose thinking was affected by him that we can discern his influence by referring to nineteenth-century biographies. The radical essayist Henry Hazlitt, for example, claimed that to Coleridge belonged the credit of awakening his own creative powers.[72] Just before the Tractarian movement began to crumble, Newman reflected on Coleridge's influence, judging that in spite of the poet's errors his critical writings of the age disposed people to consider Catholic doctrine. "It has indeed been only since his death [five years earlier] that these results of Coleridge's writings have fully shown themselves; but they were very evident when they did appear."[73] When Keble began expressing the characteristic Tractarian understanding of the High Church, he used metaphors that have been identified as Coleridgian in origin—the Church as a work of art.[74] That was not the only influence Coleridge had on the Tractarians; some scholars find echoes of Coleridge in Newman's work. Carlyle, as usual, exaggerated in saying that Coleridge created "a spectral Puseyism," but there was some truth there inasmuch as the whole conservative agenda was given renewed credibility by his belief that the ancient institutions of the land could be given new vitality and relevance.

Coleridge also showed that one could be philosophically sophisticated without accepting the Enlightenment and Benthamite dogmas that insisted on empirical justification for every proposition, especially every religious and moral proposition. John Stuart Mill, whose break away from the hold that Benthamism had had on him was facilitated by Coleridge, once said that every thinking man in the decade or two before the middle of the century was either a Benthamite of the school of progress or a Coleridgian, who held to the traditions of the country. And he did not shrink from acknowledging Coleridge's influence on himself. "Few persons have exercised more influence over my thoughts and character than Coleridge has."[75] His ideas on church and state have been influential in the thinking even of twentieth-century people such as T. S. Eliot and William Temple.

Coleridge's greatest influence was in the area of religion. F. D. Maurice, one of the most important theologians of the century, dedicated his book *The Kingdom of Christ* to Coleridge's son Derwent. There he lauded Coleridge principally for showing so clearly that Hume's critique of religion, which had preoccupied so many religious people for the previous century, held no terrors for theology.[76] Basil Willey believed that Coleridge's apologetic ideas on experience rather than the Paleyite concern for "evidences"

that hitherto had been popular prepared the Church of England for the attacks that would later come from biblical criticism and scientific agnosti-
cism, enabling the Church to reject the evidential "pseudo-foundations"
that had gained so much currency in the era.[77] Another scholar believes that
without Coleridge there would not have been a philosophical conservatism
in the early nineteenth century.[78] The Broad Church movement was heavily indebted to him. Maurice's idea of the society as an organism rather than
an agglomeration of individual desires was Coleridgian in origin, transcending the atomistic test of social utility.[79] Stephen Prickett believes that
Coleridge was part of a line of prophets, going back to the Old Testament
and continuing through the history of the Christian Church, who kept the
vision they had been given in spite of opposition. This was sometimes hard
to see because of his personal faults. Prickett concludes that Coleridge gave
the Church of England what it needed, new concepts and a new climate of
thinking and emotions, and thereby saved it.[80] All this "newness" seems
paradoxical in the face of the almost universal judgment of the conservatism of his thinking. But Coleridge's classical emphasis on Scripture as the
source of religious knowledge was new to those whose thinking was shaped
by Humean skepticism and Paleyite "evidence" to counter it. When the
flood of German scholarship and Darwinian philosophy began to run high
after the middle of the century, there were people prepared by Coleridge's
thinking to keep the ship on an even keel. Maurice, Julius Hare, F. J. A.
Hort, and others kept some of the old ways of thinking alive in a time of
skepticism.[81]

Carlyle's influence was less in his ideas than in his personality, in the
vigor with which he held his convictions, and in the fiery nature of his writings. His historical works, laboriously researched and written as they were,
often seemed to be parables illustrating what he had already said in other
parables.[82] The nature of his message was particularly suited to the religious
temper of his times. Although he left the Scottish Calvinism of his parents,
it never left him, and that is why even in his radical utterances he seemed
so conservative. One scholar says that "he retained the impress of a spiritual
puritanism long after he lost his religious faith. He was forever issuing
stormy spiritual directives to his countrymen at the top of his voice."[83]
G. K. Chesterton thought that his sympathies resembled those of the pre-
Christian pagans and so led him to proclaim "a sort of heathen Puritanism:
Protestantism purged of its evidences of Christianity."[84] A younger contemporary of Carlyle's said that he used the name of God (or sometimes
metaphors like "Eternities" or "Immensities") but that his conception of
what that meant was far different from that of the Christians. Though he
decried the materialism that never lost currency throughout his life, he

never could accept the Christian alternative.[85] Instead, he kept a faith in faith, or a faith that materialism was wrong and destructive, without specifying too closely what was to replace it.

James Anthony Froude credited his mentor and hero Carlyle with saving him from atheism, but the sage drew others out of Christianity. William Hale White, author of the deconversion novel *The Autobiography of Mark Rutherford,* was one of these converts. White's son related the effect of Carlyle's *Heroes and Hero-Worship* and *Sartor Resartus:* "There is nothing in these two books directly hostile to either church or dissent, but they laid hold on him as no books had ever held, and the expansion they wrought in him could not possibly tolerate the limitations of orthodoxy."[86]

Some of his later admirers thought that Carlyle's great achievement had been to neutralize what they considered the baneful influence of the libertine Lord Byron with his clarion call to duty and morality. Among these was the radical journalist Harriet Martineau. In 1861 she thought that Carlyle's influence was already at an end among people in literary and political circles.[87] But that is not likely, given what we know of his effect on others. Leslie Stephen, grandson of Clapham and father of two of Bloomsbury's luminaries, Virginia Woolf and Vanessa Bell, was one of the most influential literary figures of the latter part of the century, and he seemed to have no doubt about Carlyle's continuing influence. He reverenced Carlyle, a feeling that was not reciprocated, as Stephen knew, for the prophet regarded him as a mere materialist. "You might return from the strange gloom and splendour of the *French Revolution* or *Sartor Resartus* revolted or fascinated," wrote Stephen, "but to read it with appreciation was to go through an intellectual crisis; and to enter into this spirit was to experience something like a religious conversion. You were not the same man afterwards. No one ever exercised such a potent sway over the inmost being of his disciples."[88]

The reason Harriet Martineau's opinion of the end of Carlyle's influence was premature is suggested by a scholar who describes his work not as a source of doctrines as much as "an influence, an ambience, almost a stain."[89] George Eliot, in a striking essay, described Carlyle as an exemplar of the meaning of true education, which is not to teach knowledge and skills but to turn people into dynamos for the good, to awaken them from indifference, to impel them to seek the truth no matter what stands in the way. Even if all his books were destroyed, she said, it would not erase his influence, for

it would be only like cutting down an oak after its acorns have sown a forest. For there is hardly a superior or active mind of this generation that has not been modified by Carlyle's writings; there has hardly been an English book written for the last ten or twelve years that would not have been different if Carlyle had not lived. . . . The extent of his influence may be best seen in the fact that ideas which were startling novelties when he first wrote them are now become common-places.[90]

One of those in whom an acorn sprouted was Charles Dickens, who wrote to Carlyle in 1863: "I am always reading you faithfully and trying to go your way," something he had been saying for a long time.[91]

Once you got behind the Carlylian fireworks there was surprisingly little there: not much of doctrine, no method, unless bombast can be considered a method, and little to build upon. More than anything else, it was mood and inspiration that Carlyle contributed to English thinking. But that contribution was nevertheless substantial, as multitudes of his followers attested. Still, many of those followers felt as if he had taken them only so far and then abandoned them. When the poet Arthur Hugh Clough bid farewell to Ralph Waldo Emerson, who was returning to America, he said: "What shall we do without you? Think where we are. Carlyle has led us all out into the desert, and he has left us there." Emerson remarked that he had heard this often from promising young intellectuals in England.[92]

In many periods it is clear that this or that figure is predominantly *religious* (Wesley, Shaftesbury) or *secular* (Bentham, Pitt). It is one of the characteristics of this period that it produced important and influential people who seem to occupy both spheres. These were people strongly imbued with religious principles, usually with evangelical or quasi-evangelical leanings or heritage, who either extended those understandings to broader aspects of society (Coleridge) or, having rejected the doctrinal expressions, as Carlyle did, nevertheless retained the ethical aspects of the religion and its rhetorical flavor while speaking to the society. As their age turned increasingly religious, the philosophical, ethical, and political ideas of the prophets, clothed as they were in religious terminology, became more acceptable. And as that happened, their influence increased. A half century earlier or later, neither would have found the receptive audience they enjoyed.

VIII

What Shall Be Done about the Condition of England?

A TRANSFORMED SOCIETY, which is the subject of this book, implies changing economic conditions and relationships. Surprisingly, little consensus has been reached about the basic facts of the pre-Victorian period. As simple a matter as whether the English people were better or worse off economically as a result of industrialization has engendered considerable disagreement. The pace of technological development was very swift. At the start of the nineteenth century, for example, people traveled pretty much as they had a millennium earlier; a generation later they were touring by railroad. Analogous changes took place in industrial life. As the technologies changed, so did social relationships; consequently there was much dislocation and, for many people, serious hardship. Was this hardship the norm or the exception? To what extent were economic hardships the fault of those suffering them, and to what extent were they imposed by societal arrangements over which the sufferers had no control? Were such hardships the inevitable result of technological change or the product of bad men and bad laws? Were ameliorative efforts more effective if made by the state or by others? Such were the issues debated by contemporaries and by students of the period since then.

We are not concerned here with statutory reform efforts, such as the Poor Law Amendments of 1834, except as they reveal the way people viewed issues of wealth, poverty and pauperism, and destitution and its remedies. Rather, we shall need to consider how people of differing perspectives interpreted the hardships suffered and why they favored one type of amelioration rather than another. People had always suffered privation, and English society had always made provision for them in one way or another, but in the early nineteenth century economic hardship was taken to be a serious national matter that could not be allowed to persist. The diversity of responses to the prevailing conditions was largely a function of the various ways of interpreting the human condition, which means that it ultimately was a religious issue. That is not to say that every Evangelical or every Tractarian had the same view on the subject, but rather that the growing religious consciousness changed the general perception of the society about the existence of privation and brought it to the forefront of public discussion.

VALUES, VIRTUES, AND ECONOMIC LIFE

Invariably, people whose religious inspiration comes from the Bible have concerns about seeking ways to help poor people. The Levitical laws prohibited the Israelites from harvesting the fields more than once; the gleanings were to be left for the poor (Lev. 19:10; 23:22). Moses said to the Israelites, "I command you, You shall open wide your hand to your brother, to the needy and to the poor, in the land" (Deut. 15:11). When Jesus defined perfection of character, he used the same idea: "Sell what you have, and give to the poor, and you will have treasure in heaven" (Matt. 19:21). Throughout the centuries, charitable acts have been among the main priorities of the Christian church almost everywhere. In England the doing of charity received a blow in the sixteenth century when the Anglican Church separated from Rome. Vast tracts of lands that had supported the monastic orders and provided the wherewithal for charity were confiscated by the crown and distributed to its supporters. The Elizabethan poor law was intended to fill the void this created in the means for caring for the poor. Thus, when the religious revival affected increasing numbers of people, it was natural that the treatment of the poor was one of the issues that came to the fore.

Disagreements about poverty usually bespoke deeper philosophical differences that might or might not be made explicit. The arguments about poverty and its alleviation in the early nineteenth century were very sharp and in some ways sound similar to those of our own time. In fact, modern analysis of that period often seems to have practical rather than scholarly ends in mind, and the nineteenth century appears to be a stalking-horse for twentieth-century concerns. The same was true of contemporary analysis. A modern study of the history of English housing commends the radical journalist William Cobbett as an accurate observer of the subject.[1] And so he probably was. But Cobbett's descriptions were almost always related to his disgust with his society and desire to change it. One of his strategies was to contrast its horrors to the blissful conditions of a better day. As he relates a conversation with his son on one of his famous "rural rides," the boy asked Cobbett as they left the Winchester Cathedral if it were true that such a magnificent building could no longer be constructed. "No, my dear," Cobbett replied. "That building was made when there were no poor wretches in England, called *paupers;* when there were no *poor-rates;* when every labouring man was clothed in good woollen cloth; and when all had plenty of meat and bread and beer."[2] Cobbett's strategy was to contrast the present miseries with a mythical golden age. Angry novelists, too, assailed the complacency of the period with harsh denunciations and demands that the nation face the problems of the poor. Often they had the facts wrong, sometimes deliberately so.[3] But right or wrong, they had a powerful tool, and they knew it. Dickens once confided to Southwood Smith, a physician and Benthamite government official, that he would be writing a novel with an exposé of inhuman sanitary conditions among laboring classes that would hit with the force of a sledgehammer.[4]

Just as nineteenth-century writers found their economic conceptions colored by their deeper convictions, scholars studying the period have labored under the same handicap. Modern sensibilities of the Industrial Revolution and the Victorian age have been shaped largely by the work of a small number of students of the period who combined a lively sense of indignation with indefatigable labors. Most prominent among them have been two couples whose publications in the late nineteenth and early twentieth centuries affected the thinking of generations of students. Beatrice and Sydney Webb were early leaders in the Fabian Society and founders of the London School of Economics. They exercised prodigious feats of scholarship in support of their vision for a more humane society, one built on democratic socialism. Their studies of English history portrayed a dark and miserable population, struggling under the burdens of a merciless capitalist system and a rapacious ruling class.

Among their admirers were J. L. and Barbara Hammond, who wrote many books on English society in the nineteenth century that seemed to support the dark vision of the Webbs. The Hammonds' strategy was partly that of Cobbett: pleasant descriptions of the old communal life that had preceded the dark night of rampant capitalism. Although their accounts were not quite as idyllic as Cobbett's, the Hammonds nevertheless made the reader hanker for the good life of the past, where people lived in "a society of free and equal men, in which tyranny was impossible." The squire and parson might seek to control the population, but ordinary people still enjoyed "a world in which the villagers lived their own lives and cultivated the soil on a basis of independence." This world was shattered with the empowering of the oligarchy, and the Hammonds contrasted the pleasures of the few who enjoyed life with the travails of the numerous poor—of "the disinherited peasants that are the shadow of its wealth; of the exiled labourers that are the shadow of its pleasures; of the villages sinking in poverty and crime and shame that are the shadow of its power and its pride."[5] (This sort of nostalgia was not limited to radicals but was also found among Tories who harbored a paternal sense of responsibility toward the unfortunate.)

Later, Christian socialists such as R. H. Tawney wrote of (and exaggerated) the physical evils of the period. Tawney seemed to believe that the Church had completely abdicated its responsibilities and adopted the mechanistic view of the universe that the Enlightenment had promulgated.[6] In the second half of the twentieth century, more sophisticated analyses, often based on Marxist views on the relationship between the classes, beat on the same drum as the Hammonds. The names E. P. Thompson and Eric Hobsbawm are prominent among these scholars, who also have not lacked for critics.[7] The old picture of the teeming slums of the industrial towns has been modified; they were not, of course, garden spots, but it appears that only a few were the hellholes that have long been depicted.[8]

The problem for many people has been not only the capitalist system that became entrenched with the Industrial Revolution but the Industrial Revolution itself. That is what makes the tableaux featuring happy peasants, living in picturesque cottages and enjoying the fruit of the land, so compelling a contrast to grimy towns, pale exhausted workers, and noisome atmosphere. The idyllic picture of the earlier period was never more than a dream, and recent scholarship has forced a revision in our understanding of the Industrial Revolution. In the second half of the eighteenth century, the economy was growing and prosperity increasing. By 1800 society in general was sharing in the prosperity, and there was a good deal of optimism. This conclusion is supported by various strands of evidence—testimony of travelers, modern econometric analysis, scrappy information on family earnings, and analyses that have come down from contemporary sources.[9] Some studies suggest that industrialization increased living standards for farm laborers by more than 60 percent, blue-collar workers more than 80 percent, and workers in general more than 140 percent.[10]

The increasing independence of women may suggest that family life suffered in the Industrial Revolution, but the counterindications are stronger. Extended families seem to have come into existence only with industrialization. One study of highly industrialized Lancashire showed a startling increase of adjacent generations living together. Young people could afford for the first time to support their parents, who in turn minded the grandchildren.[11] Child labor had earlier been widely approved, but this was in the form of cottage industry, whereas conditions in the factories were much worse for the children. Eventually, the effects of child labor were mitigated by legislation, and without harm to the economy. The Hammonds pointed out that the new entrepreneurs who made industrialization possible tended to come not from the great merchant or landlord families but from ordinary artisans who were prepared to work like slaves and thereby become more than ordinary.[12] The old licentiousness of the lower classes gradually gave way as they ascended the social and economic ladder. One analyst interprets this as the coming into being of "a new artisan sub-culture," leading to temperance societies, ethical concerns, Sunday family excursions, and other manifestations of what looked like the middle class—in general a reaction against the old carnival sort of laxity.[13]

As industrial workers became better off economically in the second half of the eighteenth century, agricultural workers also did relatively well. English farm workers lived at a much higher level than the Continental peasantry at midcentury, and conditions for them got better as the years went by. The farmers who employed these workers increasingly seemed more like the gentry, with their improving houses and fashions.[14]

Evidence from the London metropolis shows the same pattern: considerable improvement in economic conditions between the mid-eighteenth and mid-nineteenth centuries. Francis Place, the radical tailor, not only was one of those who testified to the improvement but feared that society would lose forever the knowledge that conditions had become so much better. What he knew from his own memory was not documented, and he was disgusted that social reformers of the 1820s thought bad conditions were new and worse than in the earlier period. This was exactly the opposite of the reality he knew at firsthand. In 1835, when asked for his opinion about James Kay-Shuttleworth's statistics on Manchester, he replied that in the main Kay-Shuttleworth was correct,

> but he gives the matter as it now stands, knowing nothing of former times; his picture is a very deplorable one. I am assured that my view of it is correct by many Manchester operatives whom I have seen; they inform me that his narration relates almost wholly to the state of the Irish, but that the condition of a vast number of the people was as bad some years ago, as he described the worst portion of them to be now. Any writer or inquirer will be misled unless he had the means of comparing the present with former times.[15]

Along with the work of late nineteenth- and twentieth-century scholars, public perceptions of social and economic conditions have been strongly conditioned by novelists. There was Benjamin Disraeli's novel *Sybil* (1845), for example, which followed years of debate on the issues. The future prime minister coined a term that entered the public consciousness when he wrote that there were "two nations" in the country, the rich and the poor. But this idea masked the reality of an infinite gradation that was not static but constantly shifting. There were other divisions that had little or nothing to do with money that in some ways could be more significant—that between Church and Dissent, for example.[16] Dickens's novels have worn much better than Disraeli's, and the miseries of industrial England have been impressed in the minds of millions of people who read them. But even he was conscious that his own age was far better off than a generation or two earlier.[17]

Improving conditions in general coexisted with considerable hardship for many. The most prosperous times bring with them grievous conditions for some, especially under conditions of economic fluctuations and war. There was plenty of both in our period. Harvests waxed and waned with the weather, and prices rose or fell due to changes in government policy (corn laws that affected the importation of grain, for example). These changes came on people with varying consequences. Increases in the price of grain could be calamitous for town families living on the edge but at the same time bring prosperity to rural areas. Even among a given type of economic community, say the industrial towns, one locale could prosper while another declined.[18] Military expenditures ate up much of the national wealth during the first fifteen years of the new century until Napoleon was finally defeated and sent into exile. And there were always individuals and families, during good times and bad, who suffered adventitious financial reverses, illness, and death.

FORMS OF POVERTY RELIEF

The English relief system was based on the Anglican parish, which had the authority to levy a tax called the poor rate. The parish also disbursed the funds it raised through the tax; these decisions were made by the parish vestry, which was subject to the justice of the peace. The administration of the system was local, and there were great variations throughout the kingdom. But since the days of Queen Elizabeth, there were statutes that gave general regulation to the system. Along with the parish system of relief, private charity was an important source of help for the destitute. And especially after the late eighteenth century, individual charity was supplemented by a growing network of charitable societies, many of them evangelical in origin.

This network of support underwent a major change in 1795 when the so-called Speenhamland system began in Berkshire. Under this regime, calculations were made of the amount necessary to support a given family, and the poor rate was used to provide the difference between that amount and what a worker actually earned. One effect of the Speenhamland system was to reduce the wages farmers paid for farm labor, the difference being made up by the parish. The system came into general, but not universal, use, mainly in the south of England. Discussions of poor relief in England seemed to center on the advantages and (more commonly) disadvantages of the Speenhamland system. The disadvantage mainly dealt with the impairment of motivation for workers.[19] When the Hammonds wrote that the effect of Speenhamland was "to spread pauperism far and wide" and turn the worker into "a kind of public serf," they were only repeating many contemporary criticisms.[20] Observers as different as Tocqueville and Engels condemned the system, the former on the familiar grounds that poor laws produce pauperism and the latter, similarly, because they degrade the recipient.[21] Thomas Arnold wrote in a newspaper article that the system operated "under the mask of kindness to the poor" but was really "one of the most degrading systems of oppression."[22] The Evangelical *Record* declared the system to be "vicious in principle, intolerable in practice." It destroyed not only the material basis for prosperity but the moral as well, "hastening forward to misery and ruin."[23] "The heavier the poor-rate, the more boldly does poverty stalk through the parish."[24] If conservatives hated the system, radicals also had hard things to say about it. Cobbett rode around the countryside and saw poor wretches digging holes and filling them in for a pittance while the fields languished for lack of needed labor. The problem, he said, was that the farmers were too poor to pay for the labor they needed because their substance was eaten up by the poor rates.[25]

A SOCIETY IN TROUBLE?

Along with numerous criticisms, there were many expressions of satisfaction with the state of English society, especially in comparison with conditions on the Continent. The fright into which large segments of society were thrown by the enormities of the French Revolution reinforced the widespread Tory sentiment that wholesale changes in the constitutional structure could be disastrous. Sometimes even those who were calling for significant change seemed oddly conservative. Carlyle, who coined the phrase that seemed to summarize the issue—the "condition of England"—could still opine that some of the aristocracy still were "very noble" and that despite the worthlessness of many members of the nobility, the aristocracy "is actually yet the best of English classes."[26] Tocqueville's assessment was similar. He thought there was a genuine attachment to liberty among the English nobility, which was distinguished from its Continental counterparts by the opportunity for new wealth to enter its ranks.[27] Modern analyses comparing the English peers with contemporary groups have come to similar conclusions.[28] Thomas Arnold, who denounced Speenhamland, the "excess of aristocracy" in the whole system, and even the differences in *language* between rich and poor, regarded the aristocracy as all that stood between England and the condition of which it was accused by the French, a purely commercial nation obsessed with buying and selling.[29] Arnold tried to induce Carlyle to join him in establishing a society that would do research on poverty, with an end to stimulating efforts to help the poor.[30] Nothing came of this idea.

Yet others were unimpressed by even half-hearted defenses of the status quo. Radicals like Cobbett could find many admirable features in English society, but they all seemed to have expired long before. Both political parties were beyond redemption, according to Cobbett; one might be in and the other out, but there was no essential difference between them.[31] The schools and universities were full of knaves, fools, and dunces.[32] Cobbett assigned the radical friend and protegé of Francis Place, the MP Sir Francis Burdett, to the same purgatory to which he had already condemned Wilberforce.[33] John Bright, Quaker mill owner and MP, was an example of those with a significant stake in the preservation of society who nevertheless fiercely denounced its exploitative aspects, in particular government privileges that penalized the poor. He led the fight against the corn laws for that reason, condemning them as inhuman, immoral, and unchristian, "the most daring outrage upon human rights which has ever been perpetrated under the name of the law." Those arrayed against such a law, according to Bright, were servants of Christ. As if to echo Cobbett, Bright considered the Parliament—Commons hardly less than Lords—as a bastion of privilege and thought it scandalous that the Reform Bill of 1832 had hardly touched the real abuses.[34]

The Dissenting leader Edward Miall focused on the victims of the situation, associating dire physical conditions with the spiritual destitution that he believed inevitably accompanied them.

> There lies at the bottom of society in this country . . . a thick sediment of physical destitution, which it is morally impossible for the light of Christianity to penetrate and purify . . . men exiled by want from the sympathy, and even notice, of the great mass of their fellows—driven to subsist precariously and scantily on garbage—clothed in rags, loathsome both to sight and smell —preyed upon by vermin. . . . And to the shame of philanthropy in our land be it spoken, these festering heaps of misery have gone on until just lately, increasing in bulk, unnoticed by society until they comprehend hundreds of thousands of individuals. . . . Out of this slimy bed of physical destitution rises perpetually a pestiferous moral exhalation dangerous to all other classes of society.[35]

As a call to action Miall's plea may have been effective, but to the extent that it gives the impression that English society did not make a concerted effort to engage the problem until the middle of the century, it is badly misleading.

THE CALL TO FREE MARKETS

The desperate plight of many of the English people made it seem axiomatic to many that only strong central action, government action, could alleviate the suffering. But others were persuaded by the theoretical work from the last quarter of the eighteenth century that this remedy was actually the cause of much of the problem and that the only corrective that could succeed would dismantle the governmental actions that had already been taken.

Adam Smith's influence on economic thinking has become almost legendary. The "invisible hand" as the mover of economic events under a free market is cited by supporters and scoffers alike. But the distortions that associate markets with amorality in economic relationships, with exploitation of the poor and devil-take-the-hindmost individualism, seem to be succumbing to recent reappraisals of Smith's writings and influence. Smith was a professor of moral philosophy, and *The Theory of Moral Sentiments* (1759) is now increasingly judged to have been work more in keeping with his central concerns than the more famous *Wealth of Nations* (1776). For Smith had the unmodern view that economics and morals were related, if not causally then at least in that the free market makes for both good economics and good morals. It makes for good economics because it brings efficiency to the process of investing capital and also because it makes possible the division of labor, which increases productivity. The market makes for good morals by disciplining the propensity people have for doing evil. A rich man could possibly get away with a dissolute life because he is protected by the accumulated capital provided by earlier productivity, his own or that of benefactors. But ordinary people who live dissolutely experience disaster. The market in this way disciplines them and subdues their passions. Thus commerce, far from being heartless and destructive, tends toward the taming of the wayward spirit; it encourages the virtues, even if only the minor ones such as self-control, decency, sobriety, and frugality.[36]

In 1798, Thomas Malthus, a clergyman and teacher at a college run by the East India Company, published his *Essay on Population*, which in subsequent editions over the next quarter century had an immense influence on economic thinking. Stressing the fact of scarcity, Malthus put a damper on the rising optimism of English thinking by purporting to demonstrate empirically that food production inevitably would lag behind population growth. This seemed to call into question attempts to better the lot of the poor. Such efforts would simply serve to increase the growth of population and thereby multiply the mouths to feed beyond the capacity of the nation to feed them. Thus misery would be multiplied along with people.

Malthus had taken aim squarely at the position of William Godwin, a political thinker whose utopianism was based on the notion that human beings were perfectible and required only a rationally ordered set of social institutions to bring about the highest potential that they possessed. But Malthus was equally opposed to a current of thinking that was much more widely accepted, that of utilitarianism. For the social engineering of the Benthamites would be exposed as hollow posturing if Malthus was correct. In fact, all forms of amelioration by government tinkering were rendered nugatory by the Malthusian perspective. The generation after the initial publication of the *Essay on Population* witnessed a storm of controversy over Malthus's ideas. Among the harshest of the critics were Coleridge and, in a somewhat derivative way, Southey. The latter adduced a theological argument against Malthus: to wit, that since God had created a universe in which an increase in population was the normal course of affairs, it would be impious to assert that he would provide for the production of people for whom he could not produce sustenance. Coleridge objected to Malthus's conflation of sexual relations with the necessity of food and drink in such a way as to assume that just as the latter could not be dispensed with, so the former. Rather, both poets held that the passions could be controlled, and Coleridge used words like *silliness* and *wickedness* to refer to Malthus's position.[37] Southey was fiercer: "Do not forget Malthouses [*sic*] rascally metaphysics," he wrote to a friend, near the start of the economist's long run of popularity. "Break him on the wheel. I will see the sentence registered. You ought to set your foot upon such a mischievous reptile and crush him. . . . I wish . . . you would anatomize him alive."[38]

Many evangelicals followed Malthusian ideas, largely because they seemed scientific. Michael Thomas Sadler, however, compared them with the biblical teaching on which he had been raised and devoted his literary efforts to showing why it did not add up for Christians to espouse them. In 1828 he wrote a preliminary work on Ireland in which he attacked the notion that emigration was the solution to the economic problems of that land. Two years later he published his major effort, *The Law of Population . . . in Disproof of the Superfecundity of Human Beings and Developing the Real Principle of Their Increase.* He denied that either Ireland or England was overpopulated and opposed the naturalist assumptions of Malthus with the biblical injunction to trust in the Lord and so allow providence to care for you. A modern who reads in his newspaper that population growth declines when prosperity comes to a land is startled to learn that Sadler wrote that human happiness and prosperity lessen the propensity to reproduce. He objected to Malthus's advocacy for late marriage on the grounds that family life increases the happiness of the poor and that to postpone it is to multiply misery. Sadler objected not only to Malthusianism but to political economy in general, and he called for an expansion of the poor laws, the maintenance of the corn laws, and in fact almost any measure that he thought would help the poor. His was a celebrated attempt to stop the steamroller that was in the process of flattening English mercantilist assumptions, the best the Tories would muster, and it won him the support of the Duke of Newcastle and a seat in the House of Commons in 1829.[39]

But there was another side to Malthus's teaching that the critics did not emphasize. If it was futile to help the poor by rearranging society, it was nevertheless incumbent upon Christians to obey the biblical commands to help the poor. The Church bore the main responsibility for this. Much of the Evangelical leadership, including the influential Scottish minister Thomas Chalmers, came to agree with Malthus on this point, and their early efforts to reform the poor laws petered out in favor of the direct relief of misery. The poor laws increasingly came to be regarded as oppressive and ineffective. They were "the origin of a great proportion of our national distress," according to the *Christian Observer* in the midst of the depression that came in the wake of Napoleon's defeat. The most important evangelical magazine, the *Eclectic Review,* proposed reducing the amount of public funds spent on poor relief by 10 percent each year.[40] As the century wore on, the *Record* took up the same refrain. The poor laws, it said, were "a fertile source of the distress which abounds," and the reason it gave came straight from Malthus—the stimulation of the excess of population.[41] They harm the poor by encouraging them to look for sustenance outside of the only place from which it can come, the efforts of the poor themselves.

It may seem strange to modern observers, but opinions favoring minimal government interference in economic affairs, including the demand for free trade, were progressive, and religious figures who favored them were conscious that they belonged to a minority in advance of the received thinking of the age. The contemporary name commonly given to this set of ideas was "political economy." James Phillips Kay-Shuttleworth, one of the most important government officials working on social policy in the period, argued that restrictions on trade by government necessarily work to the detriment of all segments of the society. "The relations of commerce are those of unlimited reciprocity—not of narrow and bigoted exclusion." Restrictions on trade beggar our neighbors, but also ourselves. The privations of factory workers unable to find work were due chiefly to restraints of trade designed to benefit certain manufacturers at the expense of the rest of the population. The interesting thing about this argument is that it is the mirror image of later critiques of the period, which argued that privation was caused by free trade. Kay-Shuttleworth said it was precisely the opposite that caused so much suffering, and that compassion demanded the freeing of trade from government intervention. "This unjust system [government controls on trade] is not merely accompanied by economical evils affecting the accumulation and distribution of wealth. The moral and physical depression of the people, which we deplore, may be traced to this fruitful source. Commerce fettered with monopolies and restrictions struggles beneath the load of an enormous taxation."[42] Many Unitarian industrialists and various freethinkers, such as Harriet Martineau, favored free trade for much the same reasons. Martineau thought that factory legislation of the sort proposed by the Evangelical Lord Ashley, no matter how disinterested and compassionate the motivation might be, was misguided and damaging.[43]

Evangelical leaders moved cautiously but, as we saw in the case of the *Record*, mostly came down on the laissez-faire side of the debate. In 1800, William Wilberforce wrote in a letter that Adam Smith's doctrine "is right in the main" with respect to the corn laws. But he thought the principle could "be pushed to an extreme" and thereby become harmful.[44] Seventeen years later, he wrote to his son Samuel, this time omitting any qualification: "Being a political economist, I cannot but admit the beneficial effects which always flow from the division of labour."[45] Thomas Chalmers, almost as influential in England as he was north of the Tweed, held the same opinion, although at a much more sophisticated level. Moreover, his views were seasoned by extensive experimentation in substituting parish relief for public assistance. The *Christian Observer* praised highly his very successful book *The Christian and Civic Economy of Large Towns,* thereby placing the blessing of Clapham on political economy before thousands of Evangelical readers.[46]

Boyd Hilton's valuable study of Evangelical economic ideas concludes that Evangelical thinking on political economy was more influential in getting it accepted than were the writings of the classical economists themselves. He believes that the shift toward the acceptance of free markets was given major impetus not so much by theoretical considerations as by moral ones.[47] Hilton terms the opposition to political economy by people like Southey, Coleridge, and Carlyle "romantic, high Tory, and anti-utilitarian." Because of this commitment to political economy, few evangelicals were prepared to follow their leaders who advocated strong state intervention for the protection of factory workers, even for measures designed to protect women

LORD ASHLEY, BETTER KNOWN
BY HIS LATER TITLE,
THE EARL OF SHAFTESBURY.
By courtesy of the National Portrait Gallery, London.

and children.[48] So pervasive was the influence of Malthus, not only among Evangelicals but also among other Churchmen, including Noetics like Copleston and Whately, that a modern scholar has called Malthusian thinking "Christian political economy."[49]

Much of the support for and opposition to Malthus came from people who were united at least in their rejection of the materialistic premise. On this, Southey and Chalmers would agree. But there was a countercurrent, the materialism of the utilitarians. Sir James Graham, the home secretary, wrote to the prime minister in 1843 about Kay-Shuttleworth's "nostrum" of moral training and went on to laud his own, the "pacifying effect" of cheap bread and other food stuffs.[50] Peter Gaskell's contemporary study of factory workers had much of the same environmentalist leaning. He thought the individual worker under the former system would go home to his cottage and pursue his leisure hours in the company of his family. This freed him from the "bad example" of his coworkers and the attractions of the beer shop. If he frequented a public house, it was likely to be under the proprietorship of a neighbor who might look out for him. But the same man inserted into a manufacturing town, especially after passage of the Beer Act, fell under the spell of dissolute fellows and went bad morally, and from thence it was a short run to physical degradation. Thus the physical surroundings were determinant of the moral and physical outcomes.[51] From the start of Gaskell's book, it was evident that this was the way he would proceed. Men "circumstanced" in conditions of poverty, he wrote in the preface, "become reckless and dispirited" and therefore engage in behavior "far beyond their control."[52]

MORALITY AND POVERTY

The one-sided material determinism that powered the ideas of utilitarians and others was countered strongly, especially by opponents whose thinking had been influenced by the religious revival. These persons thought the moral elements of the situation much more compelling than the material, and for them it became almost axiomatic that economic circumstances were largely the result of nonmaterial antecedents. Sometimes the analysts contradicted themselves on this issue, evidently without realizing it. A modern literary scholar describes the internal difficulties of reformers and novelists alike in a way that accurately captures the conundrum faced by some of our characters: "Most industrial reformers were torn between the conflicting elements in their own propaganda: on one hand they wished to assert their belief in human free will and a benign Providence, and on the other to illustrate the helplessness of individuals caught in the industrial system. Similarly working class radicals maintained on one hand that workers were enslaved and degraded by industrial capitalism, and on the other that workers were ready for the franchise."[53] Thus Peter Gaskell, whom we saw affirm the supremacy of circumstance over freedom to choose, wrote on the same pages that workers, despite the bad conditions in the factories (conditions whose severity he said had been exaggerated), had established in some mills "an admirable system of physical and moral discipline."[54] He was surprised that a generation so full of material advantages, compared to its forbears, should be so full of discontent and immorality.[55] He came to believe that the finest education in the arts and sciences was of no avail if moral instruction did not accompany it and wholesome example was not held up before young children.[56] The family was to provide something no other institution could do: raise children to be civilized, moral, productive, and happy citizens. "The greatest misfortune" that Gaskell thought the factory system had brought about was "the breaking up of these family ties."[57] He pointed to a fact that was in astonishing contrast to much of the thinking about poverty of that period and since: many well-paid workers were living in terrible conditions through their own faults, conditions that would have been more understandable if war, famine, and pestilence had been sweeping over the land. He even described how bad habits were making people physically ugly while ruining their health.[58] His general conclusion was that their separation from religion had coarsened their thinking and their lives. He thus came around to what any sensible position must finally do, achieve some way of capturing the relationship between material and moral factors in the analysis of what was happening in society.

Edwin Chadwick, probably the foremost civil servant of the period, architect of the new poor law and much else besides, was similarly of two minds on the material-moral issue. He was a disciple of Bentham's and did as much as anyone to translate utilitarian principle into public policy. In his famous report on *The Sanitary Conditions of the Labouring Population* (1842), he noted the opinion of physicians and surgeons that although the manufacturing processes were bad for the health of the workers, "intemperance" was a more important cause of distress. "The improvidence of this class of persons arises in many instances from the indulgence of vicious propensities." Chadwick emphasized this point by arranging in columnar form parallel case studies that were intended to show, and indeed *did* show, that material circumstances counted for less than moral factors in the prosperity and happiness of the workers.

John Salt, of Carr Bank (labourer), wages 12s. per week; a wife and one child aged 15; he is a drunken, disorderly fellow, and very much in debt.

George Hall, of Carr Bank (labourer), wages 10s. per week; has reared ten children; he is in comfortable circumstances.

George Locket, of Kingsley (boatman), wages 18s. per week, with a wife and seven children; his family are in a miserable condition.

George Mosley, of Kingsley (collier), wages 18s. per week; he has a wife and seven children; he is saving money.

Thomas Johnson, of Tean (blacksmith), wages 18s. per week; his wife earns 7s. per week; five children; he is very much in debt; home neglected.

William Box, of Tean (tapeweaver), wages 18s. or 20s. per week; supports his wife in bad health, and five children.

Chadwick also gave evidence showing that some industries tended to encourage bad living. "Although the colliers have large wages, they are, from their want of economy and their dissolute habits, uniformly in poverty."[59] Chadwick faithfully reported his findings in this work, but when it came time to evaluate them, ignored the empirical research that had informed him and reverted to his Benthamite roots and their environmental bias. "These adverse circumstances tend to produce an adult population short-lived, improvident, reckless, and intemperate, and with habitual avidity for sensual gratification."[60]

The various reports of the 1840s, whatever their faults, had a great effect on public opinion. Information contained in them was picked up by private groups, such as the Health of Towns Association, that added to the pressures on Parliament to attack the problems described in the reports. One modern interpreter has called the parliamentary reports "invaluable agencies of civic education" and has compared them with the novels of Dickens and Disraeli in their effects on public opinion.[61]

Analysts like Gaskell and Chadwick, whatever their predilections, could hardly help but assign morality or its absence as an important causal factor in the assessment of the health of the society. Morality was in the air, so to speak, as a constant subject of discussion and concern. Whatever Chadwick may have absorbed from Bentham about the materialist basis for human action, he would have lost his credibility and his influence had he implied that people lived well or ill without respect to their morality. Thomas Chalmers, not only a minister in the Church of Scotland but also a noted writer on economics and practitioner in poor relief through church ministry, tied his Malthusian perspective to the general opinion of the centrality of morality. In view of the fact that resources are inherently limited, the "moral and religious education" of the people "is the first and greatest object of national policy." Where this is neglected, the result will be an aimless floundering from one expedient to another. State policies that tinker with the symptom rather than the cause are bound to fail. Logically, then, Chalmers called pauperism "moral leprosy."[62] Kay-Shuttleworth, with his evangelical leanings, showed that same combination of Malthusian and moralist ideas in his denunciation of Irish immigration as a cause of English waywardness because of the bad example the Irish provided to their hosts. This he considered the genesis, in effect, of the problems uncovered in Chadwick's report. The widespread cultivation of the potato in Ireland, he said, encouraged greater population growth than the land could support and forced many of the Irish to emigrate. Meanwhile, the cotton cloth industry in England welcomed the Irish immigration in order to satisfy its demand for cheap labor. The influx of brutish Irish, in turn, infected the English with bad morals. "Debased alike by ignorance and pauperism, [the Irish] have discovered, with the savage, what is the minimum of the means of life. . . . They have taught this fatal secret to the population of this country." He thus contrasted the nature-living of the Irish to the civilization of the English.[63] He was trained as a physician, and much of his thinking was shaped by experiences during his medical ministrations to poor working families.

The repeated concerns about pauperism need to be understood in light of the distinction between that lamentable state and the condition of ordinary poor people who worked for a living. Poverty was considered a normal and even honorable state, especially by Tories who regarded social and economic states as part of the God-given order. Poor people were expected to care for themselves and their families and in fact ordinarily did so. They even created their own institutions to help them do it, such as "friendly societies," which functioned as what might be called mutual insurance companies, pooling premiums and disbursing funds in case of family disaster.[64]

It was the universal opinion that one of the main moral failings that led to poverty was drink. Gaskell thought the beer shops were especially at fault here, having none of the built-in social controls that public houses often employed, although others blamed gin more. He noted that drunkenness led to various immoralities, mainly sexual. Many of the beer shops were illegal because unlicensed, and various stratagems were used to circumvent the law. Gaskell described one in which straw was sold to the customer, with "free" beer thrown into the bargain.[65] Nor was it only the conservatives who railed against drink. Cobbett saw clearly that many of the ills of the country could be attributed to the habit so many Englishmen had of drinking themselves into insensibility. "I look upon drunkenness as the root of much more than half the mischief, misery, and crimes with which society is afflicted."[66]

At times the call for moral renewal seemed to mean simply that the poor were immoral and others were not, but that was far from being the whole story. Some of the most strident moralists thought the rich needed a kind of moral awakening so that they might comprehend the sufferings of the poor and be constrained to do something about them. In particular, after seeing the blundering of those who administered the new poor law, these "paternalists,"—including Richard Oastler, Michael Thomas Sadler, Southey, and Carlyle—considered the problems of poverty to be spiritual, not primarily material, and they wanted men of substance to show a change of heart as an alternative to the maladministration of government relief.[67] The Evangelical Oastler's view was founded squarely on theological principles. He was as caustic as any radical about the tendencies of the age, especially what he called "conservatism," meaning political economy. He said he was not a conservative but an old Tory, which meant that he favored all the supporting institutions for the poor that had been part of the old practices.[68] Sadler's view was similar, but he put the struggle in the context of two great parties that had always struggled for control in England, one the Paternal (which he also called the Progressive), and the other Selfish, made up of those who "fear change." He believed that the Paternal side was the one faithful to the teachings of the Bible, especially to the Mosaic writings. He felt it necessary to justify interference in the market, probably because of the ubiquity of political economy, and he did so by referring to market inefficiencies.[69]

RELIGION AND THE LIFE OF THE POOR

Historians as different as Halévy on the one hand and Marxists like E. P. Thompson (following Marx himself) on the other assessed the influence of religion on poor people in similar ways. Both sides said that it channeled their efforts away from revolution—to the benefit of the country in the first case and to their own detriment in the second. The paradox is that most observers, contemporary as well as later ones, concluded that working people had shown little loyalty toward and small participation in the churches and chapels.[70] Recently, further studies have modified that contention, although the sources are spotty and susceptible to misinterpretation. It now appears that lower class alienation from religious bodies was a reality of the eighteenth and nineteenth centuries, but only one reality, and that it has often been exaggerated, sometimes for partisan purposes.[71]

The parochial system, even apart from the general weakness of the Church of England, was not well suited to reach the lower classes. Often badly located in rural districts, with population growth occurring in newly industrialized regions, the parishes were served by university graduates lacking the training and interest required to serve uneducated people. The early Methodists partially filled the vacuum caused by this dereliction on the part of the Established Church. They gave special attention to evangelism and organization among the poor, whom Wesley considered to be his special calling. "The Gospel of Christ knows of no religion but social," he wrote in the preface to his hymnal of 1739, the year the movement started, "no holiness, but social holiness."[72] We do not have the sources to resolve uncertainties about the number of workers participating in organized religious activity, but scattered studies show that it was far from negligible. For example, mining communities in the nineteenth century almost invariably had chapels of one of the various Methodist persuasions—Wesleyan, Primitive Methodist, or Wesleyan New Connexion. These were paid for by the mining families themselves, usually with the wives doing the fund-raising by holding sewing parties and selling the goods at chapel bazaars.[73]

The Primitive Methodist group began its existence in 1811 and was closely identified with ordinary workers until it was absorbed into the United Methodist movement in 1932. Along with its strictly religious purpose, it functioned as a community of refuge; indeed, some of the names given to them were the biblical names of refuge cities. They were run by self-educated people, selected from among their own numbers. This community association aspect of the chapels may not have been part of the formal reason for their being but nevertheless played that role in the lives of ordinary working people and should not be overlooked in assessing what it was like to live in working-class districts. The chapels mitigated the ordinary indiscipline of the working class, since they were concerned with the gospel implications of every area of life. The chapel community insisted on honesty, chastity, sobriety, and moderation, and expulsion was the remedy reluctantly taken for those who would not conform. Expulsion was serious; the chapel contained one's fellow worshipers but also companions with very similar values. This was extremely important in a period when social change was so rapid, with the attendant dislocations and social anomie.[74]

These communities tended to develop their own leadership from within. We lack good statistics for much of the pre-Victorian period in which we are interested, but a study done on the period beginning in 1831 and continuing to 1874 shows that in various towns in the south Lindsey region of Lincoln the preachers formed anywhere between 10 and nearly 15 percent of the Primitive Methodist chapel members.[75] These were no Newmans in the pulpit, and doubtless many sophisticated Anglicans would have been appalled if they had accidentally heard their sermons, but in the absence of the informal training received in the chapel and the opportunity to make use of it, many of these preachers would probably have remained illiterate, and few would have been able to exercise the leadership skills that had been imparted to them. Later on, people such as they were able to supply much of the leadership in the labor unions. The Methodists taught the seriousness of life and frowned on a frivolous spirit, which set their people apart from many of their neighbors. This trait, combined with good work habits and abstemious living (and therefore capital formation), made them both good employees and eventually good businessmen. They also abstained from the abuse of alcohol that was so common in their class. Joseph Priestley, the scientist and Unitarian leader who had little appreciation for the theology that formed the Methodists, nevertheless prepared an address to them in which he said: "To you is the civilization, the industry and sobriety of great numbers of the labouring part of the community owing."[76] For such reasons, the author of a study of mining villages concludes that the Methodist movement "performed a liberating function" in the nineteenth century.[77]

Some of the motivation for literature distribution was related to the belief that religious conviction would so change moral life that destructive habits would be cast aside and the penitent would contribute to the economic life of society rather than draining it. One participant in the Bible Society described the distribution of cheap Bibles as "a *moral sinking fund* . . . which operates powerfully toward the liquidation of [pauperism]."[78]

Sunday schools were another non-Church agency that provided a few of the same services as the Methodist chapels. They produced literacy in people who otherwise would have never learned to read, and they provided an outlet for service and leadership training in the lower classes. Given the connection between religion and behavior, it was not fanciful for people to attribute social malfunction to the absence of religion.

TOWARD SOCIAL RENEWAL

When Peter Gaskell examined what he believed to be the decline in the "social and physical condition" of artisans, he concluded that the causes had been badly misunderstood. He did not believe that poverty accounted for the condition, or the lack of education. No, "it has arisen from the separation of families, the breaking up of households, the disruption of all those ties which link man's heart to the better portion of his nature."[79] Gaskell believed that the factory commission that had been investigating the condition of the working classes had done its work poorly due to "party spirit" and to its ignorance. "Hence, though many valuable facts have been elicited by these inquiries, they are in such a crude form as to be nearly valueless."[80] He deplored what he evidently considered a concomitant of the degeneration of the household—the failure to bring up children properly. Neither the parents nor older siblings teach good behavior to children, so bad traits are perpetuated to the next generation.[81] But his view of the problem was very different from that of most condition-of-England analysts. He believed the situation was anomalous because *poverty* was not the problem; rather, people behaved badly in spite of the fact that the "great bulk of the population" possessed "many advantages never known or dreamt of by their forefathers." He named these advantages—education, medical treatment, religion, employment opportunities, political privileges.[82] Francis Place had adopted Bentham's materialist philosophy and was a political radical, but his understanding of the value of morality was similar to Gaskell's. Perhaps because he had been desperately poor himself, he lacked the squeamishness about respectability that would later be fashionable among middle-class intellectuals. He regarded self-respect to be the only way a working man could better himself. Place said he had been sustained in his own privation by the hope that he would "be able to maintain my family respectably."[83] Place also agreed with Gaskell's opinion about working people being much better off in the early nineteenth century than they had been in his childhood, but he put much more stress on the moral improvement than on the material.[84]

Perhaps because materialist philosophy was becoming more prominent, the period saw many denunciations of materialism. Coleridge's disciples followed him in this. F. D. Maurice, the leader of the early (and misleadingly named) Christian socialist movement, thought that both conservatives and radicals were infected by the error of assuming that material possessions were the basis of society. Maurice advised both parties that "true radical reform and radical conservation" must go deeper and recognize "human relations" as the real bedrock of the community.[85] Thus the morality of the relationships, or its lack, would tell the tale about the condition of England. Sometimes the recognition of this factor would influence industrial policy. In Shropshire, where the ironmasters were particularly hostile toward Methodism, the Old Park Ironworks in 1801 informed the Methodists that they would be turned out of their cottages and discharged if they did not stop preaching. The threat was withdrawn when the company was made to realize that the Methodists were the best workers they had and that the works could not operate without them.[86]

MOTIVATION FOR HELPING THE POOR

Much of the scholarship on poverty and its alleviation in the eighteenth and nineteenth centuries tells us a great deal about the misery of nineteenth-century industrial life, sometimes leaving us to infer that conditions were much better in the previous century. But that was not the case. We know so much about the miseries of the nineteenth century because the people alive then were unwilling to allow them to persist and worked assiduously with committees, investigations, and surveys to ferret out the evils and to do something about them.[87] A good deal of the impulse for this came from evangelicalism. Dickens could invent a Mrs. Jellyby who swooned with compassion for the natives of Borrioboola-Gha while neglecting her own family, but that was an unfair parody of the evangelicals. For while they were laboring to end black slavery, they were spearheading much of the effort to alleviate suffering in England. The revived interest in Bible reading brought to the fore the immense body of material in both testaments that made care for the poor a religious obligation. This reemphasis of an old practice goes back at least to Wesley, whose calling was not only to preach to the poor but to alleviate their sufferings. "I found some in their cells underground," he wrote in 1753 of a day he spent in London, "others in their garrets, but I found not one of the unemployed who was able to crawl about the room. So wickedly, devilishly false is the common objection, they are poor only because they are idle."[88] The well-known antipathy of evangelical Dissent toward the novel was partly broken down by social novels that exposed the evils of the day, some of them written by Dissenters.[89]

In general the various religious groups resisted charitable actions that were isolated from moral and spiritual matters. This is especially true of the evangelicals, a fact that some have mistakenly supposed meant a disdain for the worldliness of mere material help.[90] There is a basis in fact for the view, whatever inferences have been drawn from it. The evangelical mainstream avoided the unidimensional approaches of both materialist and spiritualist orders. They regarded people as both matter and spirit and believed that their ministry was to be to both dimensions. Reporting in 1811 on the formation of a new benevolent society in Spitalfields, the *Christian Observer* warned against the materialist fallacy and advocated that the society members use the occasion of providing needed supplies "to instruct the ignorant, and to warn and counsel those who neglect God."[91] Similarly, William Wilberforce, who spread his money around with a generosity that approached abandon, wrote that it was "time to have done with that senseless cant of charity, which insults the understanding, and trifles with the feelings of those who are really concerned for the happiness of their fellow-creatures."[92] Arnold would have agreed with him. He preached to the boys at Rugby that only the application of the principles of the gospel could effectively deal with the problems of the society.[93]

Many people rejected charity not only as ineffective but also as harmful to the people it was supposed to help. Robert Chalmers, who constructed a system of help for the poor based on the Scottish parish, testified to that effect before a parliamentary committee. He thought the English system of mandatory assessment to finance relief had effectively ruined the system of relief in Scotland, where it had spread, as well as in England. Chalmers's testimony came in the context of the hearings on the relief of famine in Ireland, and his beliefs were common for evangelicals of the period: relief had to come from voluntary charity, and it had to be accompanied by the moral

and spiritual teaching that alone could prevent wholesale vice and pauperism. This was not a matter in which the government could play any important role; it was rather the task of the local parish to form a genuine Christian community and so envelop the poor in love and concern. Mandatory
assessment replaced this with poorly motivated and impersonally administered funds that could only degrade the recipients.[94] Malthus once confessed to Chalmers that he was unable to see how poor relief could be cut off
without provoking such hardship that rebellion could be expected, until he
had seen a way out in Chalmers's plan for parish relief.[95] One of the reasons
for the general dissatisfaction with the system among Churchmen was the
common observation that the poor remained wretched and ungrateful no
matter what was done for them; hence the inference that the amount of relief was less important than the means by which it was given and the ministry that accompanied it.[96]

Kay-Shuttleworth, who began his career as a physician among the poor
and for many years was a government poor-law bureaucrat, was adamantly
opposed to indiscriminate official philanthropy because of the harm it did
to poor people. In a paper read before the Statistical Society and published
in 1834, he wrote that "universal interference of an officious benevolence
creates a reliance on assistance, and a craving for support, whose demands
it will ultimately be unable to supply." Typical for evangelicals, the moral
element was dominant in his analysis. "None should be assisted in whom
the relief will not encourage industry and virtue, or who are not, from age
and accident, deprived of all chance of making independent exertions."[97]
Cobbett, too, had no use for the poor rates and thought the old system of
help for the poor from the monasteries was far superior.[98]

POOR RELIEF THROUGH CHURCH AND CHAPEL

Critics of the Church of England in the social sphere have abounded for the
last century and a half. Some of the complaints have arisen from assumptions that socialist solutions to the problems were the only ones fundamental enough to do more than palliate the hardships. Others have considered
only the voting record of the bishops in the House of Lords, as if that
were the sum of Church efforts in the social arena. Much of the criticism—
including much that was least fair—has come from Churchmen themselves. The Lambeth Conference of 1897 reached conclusions that seemed
almost perverse in their ignorance of the century of intense social activism
the Church had just experienced.[99] The trouble with that top-down view
of the Church's role is that it ignores almost everything the Church did.

Our knowledge of what actually happened in the parishes is scrappy, coming from isolated memoirs, newspaper accounts, and diary entries. One account, for example, tells of the rector of Finmere and Mixbury in Oxfordshire taking charge of a cask of cod-liver oil and the responsibility for its administration. He concerned himself with the physical as well as the spiritual well-being of the parishioners. He instructed the children in hygiene, gave them combs and brushes, and held head inspections. With his daughter, he provided a dispensary for the village. As elsewhere in Oxfordshire, women of the parish would band together to provide relief for the poor.[100] This nonsystem of Church relief of the poor varied greatly throughout England, depending on the vitality of the parish and the dedication and skill of the incumbent, but without doubt accomplished many thousands of small acts of compassion. In Scotland, Robert Chalmers's attempt to replace public relief by parish relief at St. John's, Glasgow, was a systematic way of doing what had always been done on a more hit-or-miss basis.[101] For a time Chalmers seemed to be having some success in persuading Anglicans that his system of parish relief could be made to work in England, but in the end it was not accepted even in Scotland.[102]

Even if it had not made any conscious effort at relief, Dissent would have contributed a great deal to the benefit of the lower classes. It challenged the consciences of those with something to share, as it did the capabilities of its own members. Later on, Matthew Arnold would sneer at the "philistines," but Bible reading, experience in administration and in preaching, the teaching of moral principles and family and chapel responsibilities, and all the other activities fostered by participation in the chapel community made for a vastly enriched kind of life. The skeptics missed this entirely. The radical journalist Leigh Hunt professed to believe that the dominating motive of the Methodists was self-preservation; for them "it becomes a very little thing indeed to let a woman lie out in the cold all night, while saints are snoozing away in comfort."[103] Engels repeated all the clergy complaints about miners refusing to attend Church but neglected to say anything about the devotion many of them had to the chapel.[104]

Methodist concerns about alleviating the condition of the poor went back to the founders. The Wesleys always related their responsibilities for poor relief to the Scriptures; it was one more command among all the others that they taught their followers. Moreover, they avoided the fatalism of many contemporaries; *hope* was the scriptural answer to that temptation, along with faith and charity. Wesley exhorted the Methodist societies to organize poor relief, and the societies often established revolving loan funds for the purpose. So pronounced were Wesleyan efforts in this regard that modern socialists have looked back to the founder, if not for inspiration, then at least for justification for modern socialist ideology.[105] As the decades wore on, the Methodists gradually came to be more prosperous, with a healthy sprinkling of managers and businessmen among them. The increasing prosperity seemed to increase the willingness of Methodist groups to give generously, even though it tended to reduce the direct contact with the poor. Numerous Methodist biographies contain words like these: "My business prospered more and more. . . . I now had money to spare for the support of God's cause and for the relief of God's poor."[106] Breakaway groups like the Primitive Methodists took up the slack in reaching the poorest people to whom the Wesleyans had formerly ministered. By the 1820s in London, the Primitives alone among Methodists were actively helping the poorest.[107] In all this there is something of a paradox. The Methodists fostered medieval ideas, such as the just price and the prohibition on usury, while at the same time advancing a characteristically Puritan social ethos with which it was difficult to reconcile. Wesley understood the tension: inculcating moral behavior and seriousness of purpose was likely to increase wealth, which in turn stood to subvert the traits that made it possible.[108]

SOCIETIES FOR THE POOR

Since the seventeenth century, the Church accomplished much of its work through societies rather than through the canonical structures. As we have seen, the Society for Promoting Christian Knowledge (SPCK) functioned in the literature field from just before the turn of the eighteenth century. Early in its life it set up charity schools for the benefit of the poor. The motivation for starting these schools was principally religious, but learning to read the Bible surely had spillover effects. Griffith Jones, the founder of the schools in Wales, said the religious and literacy instruction was to "make them good people, useful members of society."[109] When Robert Raikes published an editorial promoting the Sunday schools, he justified them specifically "for the children of the lower class of the people" largely on the basis of their role in preventing crime; they were to be alternatives to the prisons, which Raikes called "seminaries of every species of villainy and profligacy." He argued that the results fully supported the supposition, as could be seen in the deportment of the pupils.[110] Much later, in the 1840s, even poorer children were taken in and given an education under the auspices of the Ragged School Union, which flourished under the leadership of evangelicals, principally Lord Ashley. He was insistent, against some counterpressure, that only the poorest of the poor must be taken in by these schools. "You must keep your Ragged Schools down to one mark: you must keep them as I have said a hundred times . . . in the mire and gutter, so long as the mire and gutter exist. . . . *I* feel that my business lies in the gutter, and *I* have not the least intention to get out of it."[111]

The heyday of the societies, mainly evangelical, came after Raikes had done his work with the Sunday schools. The importance of this has largely been obscured by contemporary and later charges that the evangelicals were so individualistic they lost sight of the communal aspects of Christian faith.[112] Not only were the evangelicals not "individualistic" in their caring about human suffering, but they were also not individualistic in the way they went about alleviating it. The societies that began late in the previous century were concerned in large measure with missions relating to the spread of the gospel. But there were many that were primarily concerned with the relief of suffering. The number of societies was so immense that it is doubtful that they can ever be identified exhaustively. The evangelicals also published a vast literature not only of books and articles but also of tracts and pamphlets, so that the connection between religion and relief of suffering spread almost everywhere. The percentage of social workers coming from evangelical families remained very high even into the twentieth century for that reason.[113]

In 1796, as the privations increased due to the war with France, Wilberforce circulated a questionnaire among his friends to help him learn about the effects of the fluctuation in wages, diet, prices, poor rates, the effect of enclosures, and the condition and attitude of both farm and factory laborers. One result of this was the formation of the Society for Bettering the Conditions and Increasing the Comforts of the Poor (the "Bettering Society"). As in the case of the antislavery efforts, this work was accomplished with a great deal of research. In keeping with many contemporary relief efforts, they attempted to help the poor while avoiding pauperism, the *bête noir* of relief work in the period. In addition to relief this society aimed at persuasion and agitation to improve the lot of particular groups, such as young chimney sweeps working under frightful and dangerous conditions.[114] The Bettering Society did not limit its work to charity in the narrow sense but attacked the exploitation of chimney sweep boys, investigated the condition of miners, and tried with Wilberforce's leadership to pass the first Factory Act.[115]

In Manchester several years earlier, the Methodists had founded a similar group they called the Strangers' Friend Society. There were about thirty persons, almost all Methodists, directly involved in this organization, but in an interesting twist on the meaning of charity, they would serve the poor of any denomination *except* Methodists. Their motto was, "As we are, so shall the stranger be before the Lord."[116]

A group of young London Evangelicals founded the YMCA in 1844, mainly with the aim of spreading the gospel. In addition to prayer meetings, it offered libraries, debating societies, and lectures, thus illustrating the characteristic Evangelical coupling of the spiritual and the practical.[117]

Kay-Shuttleworth, professionally immersed though he was in government efforts to help the poor, was one of the founders of the Manchester Provident Society. One of its activities was to collect money from the poor that went into a fund to buy clothing, furniture, and fuel. He stressed the virtues of self-help, even if this required that others help the poor to help themselves. He opposed "officious benevolence" but encouraged the more helpful kind, that which provides stimulation and training that makes self-help possible.[118] This quick overview of the societies established to help the poor has been able only to suggest the sort of activities they covered. There were societies established for the help of endless groups of the needy: soldiers, sailors, agricultural workers, laborers, prostitutes, and so on. This was a great age for organizing, and it was hard to find a significant need that did not have its collection of sympathizers forming a society to provide help.

AN ARMY OF INDIVIDUALS

To speak of the societies organized to help the needy runs the risk of obscuring an important reality that lies beyond these organizations: they were not impersonal machines processing resources in the service of needs. Rather, they were channels for the active service of individuals and families, belying much of the criticism that would ensue. Engels wrote that the English middle classes, in their dedication to personal freedom rather than state power, value a society "where everybody can exploit everybody else to their heart's content."[119] Engels was not alone in his criticism. Some of the harsher judgments about Wilberforce contrasted his concern about the welfare of black slaves with his supposed indifference to the plight of fellow Englishmen; Cobbett is the most obvious example of that, and some historians have picked up on the same theme. But, contrary to Engels, it would be truer to say that the English middle classes valued a society in which everybody could make his contribution to the public welfare. Some of the harsher strictures against pauperism include the hope that the poor might be made useful to society, evidently in the way the critics saw their own responsibility. Kay-Shuttleworth wrote of a Society in Liverpool to illustrate the kind of service he was advocating. Its members

> include a great number of the most influential inhabitants. The town is sub-divided into numerous districts, the inspection and care of each of which is committed to one or two members of the association. They visit the people in their houses—sympathize with their distresses, and minister to the wants of the necessitous; but above all, they acquire, by their charity, the right of inquiring into their arrangements—of instructing them in domestic econ-omy—of recommending sobriety, cleanliness, forethought, and method.[120]

Simeon likewise organized parish work through a Visiting Society, which he described in a sermon: "Its design is to find out the modest and industrious poor in a time of sickness, and to administer to them relief for their bodies, and at the same time instruction for their souls." He went about this systematically, with teams of visitors going out and reporting back on what they had been able to accomplish. He also provided generous assistance for the poor out of his own pocket.[121] Richard Oastler, later a re-former in the House of Commons, had been reared by devout Methodist parents (and had been blessed as an infant in 1790 by the aged John Wes-ley). His parents brought their children up to visit the poor and sick and to help in the distribution of food and clothing. His father was both a lay preacher and organizer of philanthropic undertakings. Oastler joined with another Evangelical parliamentary activist, Michael Sadler, and the two of them ministered to the sick at great peril to themselves in the typhus epi-demic of Leeds.[122]

The More sisters engaged in similar activities. They taught the women of Mendip how to budget, cook, and use cooperative efforts to buy cheap food, and Hannah even wrote a cookbook for them, *The Cottage Cook*. Un-der their tutelage people in the village learned how to do things coopera-tively, like build a community oven. A modern observer may detect a pa-tronizing quality in their attitudes, but among poor villagers, such as those in the More neighborhood, conditions really could be quite barbaric.

In Clapham, John Venn and his wife founded the Hereford Society, which helped the poor get their corn ground and provided cheap rents and coal. Henry Thornton's daughter Marianne started, financed, and taught in schools for indigent girls.[123] Babington ran a soup kitchen every winter. Buxton became a shopkeeper in Spitalfields to provide cheap food to the in-habitants. Other Evangelicals set up businesses specifically to employ the poor, which they thought was a much better way to help them than giving them charity.[124] Sometimes they led symbolic crusades that did more to mobilize public opinion than provide practical help. In 1795, when food prices rose sharply, Wilberforce introduced a resolution that the Commons passed calling for an association that would take pledges to reduce consumption of wheat by one-third. When the Irish potato famine began to make itself felt in English consciences in 1846, Lord Ashley decreed that his household would buy no more potatoes.[125]

The leadership of these efforts was largely evangelical, although as the century wore on, it became more generally a middle-class phenomenon. And after the middle of the century, ritualist priests added an important dimension to religious service to the poor in the large cities.[126]

The Sadlers and Ashleys might complain about the refusal of their fellow evangelicals to follow their lead in bringing about legislation that would lift the burden of bad conditions from the labor of women and children, but this should not obscure the fact that ideas were changing on that score. The warm support of the *Record* for Ashley's work suggests that political economy would not forever be considered an absolute bar to any legislative action with respect to working conditions. In December 1846 Oastler traveled to Scotland to gain support for the Ten Hours Bill, which would limit the workday for factory laborers. He was especially concerned to gain Chalmers's support, since the minister's reputation and following were almost without peer. Chalmers at first refused to consider Oastler's arguments. Oastler emphasized that the unity of all members of society was a staple of Christian conviction and that insisting on the kind of individualism assumed by political economy was a denial of the core beliefs that Chalmers elsewhere claimed as his own, especially his ideas of a communal social ideal. Although Chalmers retained his convictions about economic liberalism, he found the main thrust of Oastler's position persuasive, and Oastler was able to announce his adherence to the Ten Hours movement.[127]

Even in the earlier period, when evangelical concern about pauperism combined with confidence in political economy was strong enough to debar reliance on public welfare, evangelicals might easily allow compassion to trump theoretical considerations. It did not take much to supplement personal generosity with calls for public expenditure if the hardship was serious enough. Early in the new century, Wilberforce became concerned about "wretchedness" in Leeds and expressed surprise that the poor rates were as low as they were. He recommended that they be raised and also that "the national purse" be used to relieve suffering.[128]

Moderns have a difficult time with the ethical concerns of their predecessors, even when they find policy views palatable. This is especially true of social scientists who dip into the literature of the earlier period and find it so alien to their own assumptions that they sometimes scarcely seem able to credit their senses. One such scholar, looking at the texts that form the basis for the present chapter, noted the ethical injunctions by which Wesley sought to help his charges turn away from self-destructive behavior and interpreted them as being "a disavowal of the natural." Thus, Wesley's "mythology of sin" was a destructive element "which made a fetish of self-control, discipline, work, 'purity,' resignation, self-abnegation."[129] But Francis Place, who shared the naturalist perspective of the modern scholar, could have told him that without those attributes of "fetish" there would be no hope for anyone to rise to a position of relative comfort.

What Accord Hath Christ with Belial?

CHRISTIANS AND
ATHEISTS TOGETHER

THE TWO SCHOOLS

In the early nineteenth century, two different, mostly contradictory, ways of thinking powered much of the reformist activity: evangelicalism and utilitarianism. Analysts have declared one or the other to have been particularly influential, but there is general agreement that despite the obvious contrasts between them, a kind of symbiotic relationship mutually reinforced their work. The common elements up to a point were able to transcend the differences, and the complex relationship between the two did much to change the society.

George Kitson Clark, one of the better known Victorianists of the mid-twentieth century, described utilitarianism and evangelicalism as "the typical creeds of the early nineteenth century." They were complete opposites in their presuppositions, he said, but in their practical results they were much the same.[1] His contemporary on the other side of the Atlantic, Crane Brinton at Harvard, put it differently but seemed to have approximately the same idea. Brinton thought the Victorian period was marked by a series of moral struggles, the central theme of which was an effort to arrive at compromise between two opposing principles, the Enlightenment and Christianity. Unlike Kitson Clark, who believed that the struggle between the two principles had petered out around midcentury, Brinton thought it carried on through Victoria's reign. In spite of the very different outward appearances of the two ways of thinking, Brinton depicted their ethical ideas as being "in almost identical positions."[2]

It has become common to speak of these two ways of thinking as forming the basis for Victorian culture. This is quite astonishing on the face of it. It is one thing to say that two opposing ideas contended for predominance, but quite another to describe them as engaged in highly controversial public activities and coming down on the same side. How are we to account for that?

JEREMY BENTHAM.
By courtesy of the National Portrait Gallery, London.

THE UTILITARIAN ENTERPRISE

Utilitarianism was the nineteenth-century ethical expression of the Enlightenment thinking so common in the previous century, being self-consciously both naturalistic and empirical. It was in large measure a development of the philosophy of Jeremy Bentham. He had caused something of a stir with his *Introduction to the Principles of Morals and Legislation* (1789), in which he argued that the two great springs of human action were the contrary principles of pleasure and pain; human motivation consists in doing what one can to enhance the first and avoid the second. A society that conducted its affairs wisely would further the greatest happiness for the greatest number of people by increasing pleasure to the maximum and decreasing pain to the minimum. Bentham's naturalism meant that for him religion was at best irrelevant and at worst harmful, being directed at ends that had no basis in reality. Edwin Chadwick, probably the best known and most effective of his disciples, remained in the Church, but his biographer wryly noted that for him "the best things in Scripture had been said by Jeremy Bentham."[3] For the utilitarians, as the name implied, the moral justification of an action depended on its usefulness, which in turn was dependent on the happiness it would provide. And that depended on the degree of pleasure or pain that would result from it. Since the world was self-evidently full of unhappiness, there was abundant scope for improvement; hence the utilitarians tended to be activists, engaged in such projects as prison reform, public health, and education. The Benthamites' empirical bias toward the factual, their preoccupation with materiality and the wholly practical remedies for society's maladies, drew upon them the wrath not only of religious people but also of those who recognized and valued the spiritual side of life. Victorian readers knew the target when Dickens had Gradgrind say, "Teach these boys and girls nothing but Facts. Facts alone are wanted in life. Plant nothing else, and root out everything else."

Radicals of various kinds joined the utilitarians in their hostility to religion. The writings of Thomas Paine, with their combination of political radicalism and rejection of Christianity, became very popular, and more than one bookseller spent time in jail on their account. Working-class radicals liked Paine and, antireligious though they were, borrowed some of the tactics of Methodism to spread his teachings. They sent "missionaries" who conducted weekly "classes" and were rewarded by a good deal of enthusiasm during the second, third, and fourth decades of the nineteenth century.[4] The Romantic poetry of Byron and Keats, as well as these writers' open sexual libertinism, was attractive to many in the middle and upper classes. Some radicals, such as Leigh Hunt, professed to abhor only the outmoded shell of a discredited religion, while prizing its neglected spirit.[5] This friend and colleague of Byron and Keats was especially incensed at the Methodists, who, he said in an early work, were guilty of "shocking blasphemies."[6]

With the publication in 1798 of Malthus's *Essay on Population* and the ensuing debates and refinements of his thesis by himself and others, the intellectual case for the radical restructuring of English society along the lines of the French Revolution had been almost completely discredited. (The enormities committed in France had already destroyed the public's readiness for an English version of the Revolution.) The result of the ferment was a consensus for the efficacy of free markets that much of the broad educated center could embrace, including commonsense theoreticians like Malthus, evangelicals like Chalmers, and liberals like Whately.[7] With Jacobinism thus discredited, and with the mostly working-class followers of Paine marginalized by their own weaknesses as well as the persecution by the Tory government, the utilitarians represented the only radical alternative to the developing consensus that the basis for moral life had to be found in religion.

THE NATURE OF THE DISAGREEMENT

Perhaps the most fundamental article of disagreement between Christian and utilitarian on the policy level was over what they thought they were accomplishing. For the former, acts of mercy and wisdom were in keeping with the divine commandments. Even the best intentioned and wisest could not bring into being the Kingdom of God; their actions could be ameliorative but not redemptive. This was not satisfactory for people who thought it was within their ken to provide the greatest happiness for the greatest number. There was something of the idolatrous in this for the Christians because it seemed to them akin to assuming God's attributes. A modern historian concludes that Bentham's devising of a program such as his scheme for prison reform, one that attempted to remold the whole personality of the prisoner through complete control of his environment, resembled "the illusion of a divine omnipresence."[8] Lord Macaulay was afraid of that same tendency and thought the utilitarians might be repeating the discredited role of the Puritans of the seventeenth century. He called Bentham's followers a "republican sect, as audacious, as paradoxical, as little inclined to respect antiquity, as enthusiastically attached to its ends, as unscrupulous in the choice of its means, as the French Jacobins."[9]

This raised a related theological issue: the utilitarian enterprise took up once again the ancient heresy of Pelagianism, the notion that men were able by the power of their mind and will to overcome the effects of sin and build for themselves a version of the divine kingdom. The political problem this raised for people such as the Tractarians was not so much that this or that measure was enacted by Parliament but that it was done without any recognition of the limits of human actions. For people steeped in biblical imagery, this could look like nothing so much as the Tower of Babel constructed anew.[10] This was the common evangelical view as well. Christianity, said the *Record*, "interferes with the vagaries of the Benthamite; it contradicts his views of human nature; it pours contempt upon his promises of a political millennium."[11]

Coleridge was among the intellectual leaders of England who regarded the utilitarian perspective as destructive of human values, primarily because of its reductionism. If people merely acted to maximize their happiness apart from any other value, how could it be said that they were possessed of any moral superiority to dumb beasts? Coleridge also objected to Bentham's too-easy passage from fact to value, so that once the first (desire for happiness) is established, the second (normative value of whatever makes for happiness) necessarily follows. Thus any notion of transcendent values is trumped without any need to demonstrate its falsity. Coleridge did not believe that facts can be ascertained or their meaning derived without a prior knowledge of what the universe is like.[12] Coleridge argued in a response to a *Morning Chronicle* article in 1831 that the elevation of happiness as ultimate was tautological in one sense and destructive in another:

> How can creatures susceptible of Pleasure and Pain do otherwise than desire happiness? But what happiness? The Indian Savage in scalping his fallen enemy pursues *his* happiness naturally and adequately. An Indian Bentham or O. P. Q. [author of the *Morning Chronicle* article] would necessarily hope for the greatest possible indulgence in scalping for the greatest possible number of Indians. There is no escaping this absurdity, unless you come back to a standard of Reason and Duty, as imperative upon our mere pleasurable sensations.[13]

That transcendent standard, of course, is just what the utilitarians could not grant without destroying their whole edifice.

Since the happiness of the individual is a subject known better to himself than to anyone else, the utilitarians could accept the widely held doctrine of political economy that the state should not interfere in the person's economic and other pursuits. The expansion of individual liberty was a characteristic belief of the nineteenth century that the utilitarians adopted, although not consistently, as being in tune with their philosophy. They could not be consistent in their championing of liberty because the theoretical connection between the individual's wishes and his happiness seemed too often frustrated by the mulish tendency of those individuals to choose in ways not approved by utilitarian intellectuals. The late Victorian historian A. V. Dicey lauded the stand for liberty taken by the utilitarians but then exposed the side that would later blossom into strong state controls: "The patent opposition between the individualistic liberalism of 1830 and the democratic socialism of 1905 [when Dicey was writing] conceals the heavy debt owed by English collectivists to the utilitarian reformers. From Benthamism the socialists of to-day have inherited a legislative dogma, a legislative instrument, and a legislative tendency. . . . The dogma is the celebrated principle of utility."[14]

Mill explained the shift in utilitarian thinking from the exercise of free markets to statist controls as, in effect, a transmutation of the Malthusian doctrine. He and his young friends had not been blind disciples of Bentham, he wrote many years later, but had adapted Bentham's thinking along with that of Malthus. They had been enthralled by Malthus's argument against the infinite improvability of human affairs and took it up "with ardent zeal in the contrary sense, as indicating the sole means of realizing that improvability by securing full employment at high wages to the whole labouring population through a voluntary restriction of the increase of their numbers."[15] Thus the young utilitarians turned the whole Malthusian attack against Godwin's notion of the unbounded potential of humanity against itself. Mill tried to foster birth control in order to forestall the grim outcome that Malthus had predicted, a solution that Malthus considered immoral. The mature Mill, looking back on that period, retained the dualistic pattern that was common in the England of his youth—the Enlightenment in its Benthamite form versus the orthodox, or Christian, or what Mill sometimes called the Germano-Coleridgian outlook. He believed that English history fluctuated in a pendular kind of movement and that the more religious and traditional traits of the nineteenth century should have been expected as a natural reaction against its predecessors. As he explained it in his essay on Coleridge (1840):

> Now the Germano-Coleridgian doctrine is, in our view of the matter, the result of such a reaction. It expresses the revolt of the human mind against the philosophy of the eighteenth century. It is ontological, because that was experimental; conservative, because that was innovative; religious, because so much of that was infidel; concrete and historical, because that was abstract and metaphysical; poetical, because that was matter-of-fact and prosaic.[16]

THE UTILITARIAN ANTHROPOLOGY

From the start, Bentham presupposed what amounted to a moral revolution, based on a peculiar understanding of humanity. The economist Nassau Senior, one of his disciples, was quite frank about this, admitting that the philosophy was based upon "an arbitrary definition of man, as a being who invariably does that by which he may obtain the greatest amount of necessaries, conveniences and luxuries, with the smallest amount of labour."[17] It is one of the ironies of the age that that utterly hedonistic assumption came to be increasingly believed at a time of startlingly expanded philanthropy. Just when many were becoming convinced that disinterested generosity was an unscientific idea, Henry Thornton at Clapham was giving away more than half his income, and the benevolent societies were being flooded with contributions from many thousands of people who, in the utilitarian universe, were supposed to be busily maximizing their own comfort.

If the happiness ethic were based on reality, there would be logical connections between it and personal behavior. Everyone should have been adding to his comfort regardless of the censure that unscientific ethical systems might offer. Carlyle wrote in a letter to his brother John that the happiness principle had to lead to personal moral failure, since the philosophy provided no way to transcend one's own selfishness. "Most of these people are obliged to divorce their own wives, or be divorced; for though this world is already blooming (or is one day to do it) in everlasting 'happiness of the greatest number,' these people's own *houses* (I always find) are little hells of improvidence, discord, and unreason."[18]

In later life, Mill professed admiration for Bentham's grasp of practical affairs but distress at the master's weaknesses: "his want of imagination, small experience of human feelings, and ignorance of the filiation and connections of feelings with one another."[19] Utility is the touchstone of Bentham's philosophy, but it may be wondered how useful an ethic can be that is based on so faulty an understanding of humanity. Leslie Stephen, a grandson of Clapham, was himself a freethinker and utilitarian but came to wonder about the shallowness of the philosophy, its valuing of comfort above all, its producing "a quiet ignoble littleness of character and spirit." "Society is the work of law in some proportion," he wrote, "but in a much greater proportion it is the work of very different agents—love of companionship, curiosity, the desire of all sorts of advantages which are to be derived from mutual assistance founded on mutual good will"[20]—in other words, the very things Mill had said were blind spots in Bentham's personality. It was also a blind spot in some of Bentham's followers, most spectacularly in the ideology's main agent in government policy, Edwin Chadwick.

SIMILARITIES BETWEEN EVANGELICALISM AND UTILITARIANISM

It has become almost a commonplace to conflate the influence of these two movements, which were fundamentally antithetical. Dicey recognized the obvious differences between the evangelicals and utilitarians but believed there was a powerful bond between them: they were both individualistic. He thought the contempt for tradition and precedent that marked Bentham and his followers had its logical counterpart in the evangelical indifference to the authority of the Church and in the responsibility of each individual to find salvation in a personal relationship with God.[21] Paradoxically, Dicey also believed there was an inherent conservatism in the utilitarians that harmonized with a similar trait in the majority of Englishmen. They owed much to the ancient tradition of English liberties and the rev-

erence for common law upon which that liberty rests, and they even borrowed from the Puritans. Dicey thought it a point of particular power for
the utilitarians that they could combine the freshness of their radicalism
with the level of comfort that only the familiar could afford.[22]

The increasing religious influence in the culture of early nineteenth-
century England perforce affected the language of even those who lamented
it by making their own language more religious. Theological arguments
were sometimes given by people from whom they sounded incongruous.
There is no ambiguity in Bentham's antireligious position, but he was not
above engaging in the polemical wars by judging his antagonists on the religious side as being insufficiently religious. He was doubtless sincere in his
detestation of religion—he called the Church of England the "Juggernaut"
(shortened to "Jug") at a time when reports from India showed this to be a
huge idol on wheels under which devotees threw themselves to be crushed—
but he nevertheless charged the Church with following the teachings of a
fake Christian, the ancient Apostle Paul. The burden of his book *Not Paul
but Jesus* is conveyed sufficiently by the title. This tactic made good sense
during the evangelical ascendancy when he was writing because of the well-
known evangelical preference for the Pauline epistles that contained the
clearest teaching on justification by faith. In 1831 the *Record*, which had pil-
loried what it considered the godlessness in the *Edinburgh Review*, noted
a change in the publication, particularly in matters of religion. This witty
vehicle for Whig politics had long been antievangelical but of late had
evinced a more respectful attitude toward the movement. The recent issue
surprised the Recordites by publishing a forty-page article on the "Evangelical School." The article made a number of factual errors, according to
the *Record*, but still spoke with "admiration and respect" of the Evangelical
leaders. The editorial showed a good deal of perspicuity in assessing the
meaning of the change. It considered that the *Review* had not gotten a dose
of true religion but that it was following the fashion of the times.[23]

And yet there is at least one sense in which the fashion of the times had
not changed as much as we have been accustomed to thinking. A generation or two ago, several historians repudiated the picture that the Enlightenment had of itself and that was adopted too uncritically by its enemies.
The cold, passionless, rationalism, opposed not only to religion but to all
enthusiasms not scientifically grounded, is partly mythical. Crane Brinton
examined this in his *History of Western Morals* and concluded that these
Enlightenment people "were in word and deed religious enthusiasts, youthful, daring, full of gusto, founders of a faith men still seek to live by."[24] Carl
Becker, a president of the American Historical Association, had earlier

written something similar about the *philosophes*, seemingly so far above the struggles of the world in their solitary quest for truth but in reality on a battlefield, "where they are so fully engaged in a life-and-death struggle with Christian philosophy and the infamous things that support it—superstition, intolerance, tyranny."[25] To be sure, both historians were writing about figures of the French Enlightenment, but the same was true of the utilitarians. When John Stuart Mill described the band of young radicals to which he belonged, composed of those who followed the teachings of Hartley, Malthus, and Bentham, he spoke of the "creed" that they held in common, the spirit of "ardent zeal" with which they followed its dictates, and the "unbounded confidence" that they had in their political convictions. "These various opinions were seized on with youthful fanaticism by the little knot of young men of whom I was one: and we put into them a sectarian spirit."[26] A bystander might be forgiven if he were to observe the utilitarian Edwin Chadwick and the Evangelical James Kay-Shuttleworth toiling away on schemes to improve society and conclude that they were members of the same sect advancing the Kingdom of God through their labors. In fact, both men came from Dissenting families in Lancashire, and modern scholars sometimes point to the Dissenting tradition, Methodism in particular, as the seedbed of modern radicalism.[27] Chadwick's researches often turned up the mutual dependence between moral depravity and bad physical conditions, and at least part of his motive seemed to be to improve the former by alleviating the latter.[28]

Among the various actors on the scene, many were not inveterate Christians or atheists from start to finish. There were always conversions to and from. Later on in the century, when Darwinian ideas and German biblical scholarship became the rage, deconversion novels such as William Hale White's *Autobiography of Mark Rutherford* and Mrs. Humphry Ward's *Robert Elsmere* mirrored the general skepticism that was becoming more common among the educated. But even in our period, there were changes in both directions. James Mill was a churchgoer before meeting Bentham, although there is considerable doubt about the depth of his faith. John Stuart Mill evidently moved in the opposite direction and probably could be considered a theist at the time of his death, although not a Christian.[29] Sir Francis Burdett, protegé of Francis Place in the House of Commons, became progressively more conservative, to the dismay of his erstwhile friends, and won the praise of the *Record*.[30]

But that did not start with Mill. Even before the turn of the century, it was becoming clear that English radicalism had another face besides the pleasure-pain motive presented by Bentham. Francis Place had provided the leadership for the London Corresponding Society, what was for the period a radical group demanding political reforms—annual Parliaments and universal suffrage. (This society went out of existence under the impact of Treason and Sedition Bills of 1795, which outlawed organizations engaged in political agitation and suspended habeas corpus.) In retrospect, Place concluded that the "moral effects" of the society had been salutary:

> It induced men to read books, instead of wasting their time in public houses, it taught them to respect themselves, and to desire to educate their children. It elevated them in their own opinions. It taught them the great moral lesson "to bear and forbear." The discussions in the divisions, in the Sunday evening readings, and in the small debating meetings, opened to them views which they had never before taken. . . . It gave a new stimulus to an immense number of men who had been but in too many instances incapable of any but the grossest pursuits, and seeking nothing beyond mere sensual enjoyments. It elevated them in society.[31]

Such a description could have been made of a Methodist class, newly established in a mining village.[32]

When Tocqueville visited England he found the native radicals very different from their French counterparts. They did not think property was illegitimate, and they were much more favorably disposed to religion, including Dissent. Even among those Englishmen who followed French philosophy, many "are firmly convinced of the political necessity for religion and have a real respect for it."[33] He was not speaking of those at the center of the utilitarian leadership, of course—the circle directly engaged with Bentham—but of the middle and lower ranks.

If the utilitarians had elements friendly toward traditional religion, there was something on the religious side that seemed amenable to utilitarian thinking. We saw in an earlier chapter how the religious renewal in the eighteenth century owed something to the Lockean reliance on experience and made "experimental religion" a touchstone of the evangelical revival. This empirical temper lent a pragmatic tone to the evangelical ethic that resembled that of the utilitarians.[34] Empiricism and pragmatism combine into something less than a disinterested search for the truth. This devaluing of the truth was a common criticism of utilitarianism, but thoughtful evangelical leaders noted that their movement was also susceptible to the charge.[35]

The pragmatism of both parties led naturally to a kind of cultural insensitivity; they encouraged learning conducive to reaching the practical ends they favored but often had little interest in broader cultural affairs. In the case of the evangelicals, the proscription against "worldliness" exacerbated this tendency.[36] A recent study of Victorian sexual attitudes concludes that the antisensual element owed much to both parties.[37]

SIMILARITIES IN POLICY

One of the themes of Boyd Hilton's *Age of Atonement* is the paradox that evangelical emphases on sin and retribution could lead to the same policy recommendations as utilitarian assumptions on incentives and productivity determined by a rational calculus. Each followed its own rationale in urging the elimination of slavery.[38] There was no doubt in the utilitarian mind whose program they were enlisting in. "If to be an anti-slavist is to be a Saint," Bentham exclaimed, "saintship for me."[39] Christopher Dawson chose to deal with the paradox using what was more of a verbal coup than a real solution. They were all humanitarians, in his view; those like Ashley were religious humanitarians, and the Chadwicks of the land were scientific humanitarians. But both used the same fact-gathering commissions and papers, and neither kept his philosophy and assumptions apart from his conclusions and recommendations.[40]

John Stuart Mill argued that radicals and liberals on the one hand and conservatives on the other were wrong to believe themselves enemies; they were "in reality allies," being "opposite poles of one great force of progression." They both react against the "contemptible" conditions that preceded them, each striving in their own way to improve them. The radical or liberal who really knew what he was about would rejoice at a conservative (he mentioned Coleridge in particular as having a political theory that was more coherent and analytical than Bentham's) because in upholding the constitution and the Church of England they were not condoning nonsense and fraud, as so many thought, but setting the stage for improving the status quo. What improvements had been made in English life would have been impossible were it not for those institutions defended so assiduously by conservatives. "Reformers ought to hail the man as a brother Reformer who points out what this good is; what it is which we have a right to expect from things established—which they are bound to do for us, as the justification of their being established: so that they may be recalled to it and compelled to do it, or the impossibility of their any longer doing it may be conclusively manifested. What is any case for reform good for, until it has passed this test?"[41] Just as the radical or liberal can accept the conservative as a brother, said Mill, so he ought to regard the Whig as something less—supposedly on the side of liberty, but really in league with the landed interest.[42]

Mill's idea that the two sides might be something more than enemies was preceded late in the eighteenth century by Bentham's demonstration of that principle. When the government reneged on its promise to back a demonstration of his radically new prison system, the Panopticon, he appealed to Wilberforce to intercede on his behalf with the solicitor-general.[43] Wilberforce made a genuine effort to help. Their friendship was such that the Evangelical used to attend parties at Bentham's house. He was full of compassion for the difficulties Bentham was going through:

> Never was any one worse used than Bentham. I have seen the tears run down the cheeks of that strong-minded man through vexation at the pressing importunity of creditors and the insolence of official underlings, when day after day he was begging at the Treasury for what was indeed a mere matter of right. How indignant did I often feel, when I saw him thus treated by men infinitely his inferiors! I could extinguish them. He was quite soured by it; and I have no doubt that many of his harsh opinions afterwards were the fruit of this ill treatment.[44]

In the House of Commons Wilberforce did not confine his cooperative efforts to his fellow Evangelicals but worked together with all who would support the measures he favored, including radicals. They parted company over such issues as sabbatarianism and antivivisectionism, which were Evangelical issues, but found much on which they could work together.[45] Wilberforce's friend and fellow Claphamite, Zachary Macaulay, editor of the *Christian Observer,* was a close friend of James Mill.[46] It was not only the Evangelical conservatives who had an appreciation for the radicals. William George Ward, the Oxford Tractarian, lauded John Stuart Mill to the skies in *The Ideal of a Christian Church,* written just before Ward became a Roman Catholic, praise that drew Gladstone's ire.[47]

Bentham's thinking on prison reform was similar in some respects to that of the great reformer of a previous generation, the evangelical Dissenter John Howard. Although the Christian and materialist psychologies were antithetical, both men believed that moral behavior could be altered by external stimuli and that prison regimens therefore could be efficacious in reforming prisoners.[48] Similarly, both movements worked in tandem in reforming the treatment of lunatics, denouncing the old methods that relied on the whip and the straitjacket and demanding a more humane practice.[49] Lord Ashley teamed up with such utilitarians as Edwin Chadwick and Southwood Smith to bring about relief from terrible conditions in factories and mines, especially for children, and in various public health measures. Even in the far-flung empire, the two sides might be found working toward the same ends. In India they both sought to turn Indians into Westerners, believing that was the only solution to the pathologies of the subcontinent.[50]

If the utilitarians saw themselves as the vanguard of the reform movement, so did the evangelicals. The former carried out their program largely through the agency of government and the evangelicals through other means, but both were borne up by the conviction that many things were rotten in the kingdom and needed to be fixed. Thus Hannah More, derided as an antediluvian by many moderns, might better be remembered as a radical educational reformer, particularly with respect to the education of women.[51]

Church and Dissenting support for some utilitarian programs and persons was consistent with the fact that some religious backing could be found for almost any reform movement. Chartism, for example, enjoyed the support of numerous Churchmen and Dissenters and sometimes held meetings in houses of worship, however dangerous it appeared to many religious people. There were even Chartist churches formed, with much resentment over charges that Chartism was godless.[52] Feargus O'Connor, the Irish Chartist leader, averred that the Charter ought to promote Christianity. "I am anxious to see every Chartist a good Christian."[53] The program of this movement seems quite tame to twentieth-century sensibilities, but in the 1840s, when it flourished, demands such as universal suffrage without property qualifications, annual Parliaments, and paid parliamentarians elected from equal districts sounded revolutionary to many people.

If the age was such that evangelical language and thinking crept into nonevangelical circles, the reverse was also true. John Keble's review of Gladstone's book *The State in Its Relations with the Church* revealed the Tractarian's favorable view of the future prime minister but complained that he "has not been quite able to keep his language clear of a certain utilitarian tone."[54] Kay-Shuttleworth's biographer described the reformer's support of Lord John Russell's policy as "the expression of modified Benthamism."[55] The hostility to the ecclesiastical establishment, a characteristic of the utilitarians, had numerous echoes elsewhere. The Dissenters of course beat the same drum, but so did the occasional Churchmen, such as Richard Whately, who wrote a treatise arguing the point entitled *Letters on the Church by an Episcopalian* (1826).

The economic depression of 1836 to 1842 apparently marked the highwater mark of the utilitarians. Such social reformers as Carlyle and Dickens, like most of the Christians, believed that moral reform had to be the driving force of meaningful change in the social and economic areas that were the heart of the concerns. F. D. Maurice and the Christian socialist movement were among others sounding the same theme, which became dominant among reformers at least until the 1860s.[56] This was not an ideal environment for the flowering of utilitarianism.

Despite the congruence of many of their activities, it was too much to expect people of such divergent understandings of human life to be more than allies of convenience. The hostilities between evangelicals and radicals were due partly to the support of some of the former for Tory acts that compromised the liberties of Englishmen. Radicals quoted liberally from the Evangelical use of biblical texts to the effect that Christians must obey rulers submissively, and they were especially incensed that the Claphamites in Parliament should favor suspension of habeas corpus. In all this, however, their hostility seemed to be directed more at Wilberforce than at the party for which he provided leadership.[57]

It was inevitable that the underlying hostility of the utilitarians toward the Christians should lead to policy conflict. John Stuart Mill confided in his autobiography that the young men grouped around his father had a "sectarian spirit" (from which he said James Mill was free, at least in intention) directed toward the establishment of a "school" modeled on the example of the French *philosophes* of the preceding century and that they "hoped to accomplish no less results." This desire to lead the country into a revolutionary paroxysm (for that was the outcome of the *philosophe* influence) Mill said had no more ardent proponent than himself as a youth.[58] The utilitarian spirit, in the minds of its adherents, meant science over sentiment, which is why Chadwick lauded the Poor Law Amendment of 1834 as the prime example of scientific policy. The discounting of sentiment and the charity that resulted from it coincided with demands for justice as the alternative. "We are weary of this cuckoo-cry," declared the Benthamite *Westminster Review*, "always *charity, never justice*, always the *open purse*, never the equal measure."[59]

John Stuart Mill's belief that Bentham had no appreciation for the depths of human experience, the "blank" in the utilitarian anthropology, received its confirmation in the character of Bentham's protegé and one-time secretary Edwin Chadwick. Tactless and impetuous, he had the knack of alienating not only those who disagreed with him but also those who were prepared to be his allies. The Benthamite *blank* led him to mistakes that made him one of the most hated men in the kingdom. When he forced local poor law officials to withhold payment for the rites of Christian burial for their charges, he condemned poor people to a fate that horrified them, the pauper's burial. This and other characteristics of the system, especially the separation of pauper family members from each other, caused the workhouses that were its central feature to be known popularly as "bastilles." As the Hammonds said, it was Chadwick's inability to appreciate how human emotions moved people that caused his inability to anticipate the general hostility he was inciting.[60] But this was a failure that was likely based on more than a personal flaw; it was the outworking of the Benthamite anthropology that reproduced Bentham's mark in his disciple.

As if to underline the opposition of their position to that of the Christians, a group of radicals and Whigs, including James Mill, began a counterpart of the SPCK in 1825 which they called the Society for the Promotion of Useful Knowledge. It lasted about twenty years before folding and existed mainly to publish philosophical and scientific material in a publication called the *Library of Useful Knowledge* and a serial called *Penny Magazine*. A similar group was responsible for the founding of London University as a counterweight to the Establishment universities.

Education was bound to be a point of conflict because it cannot function except within the domain of one worldview or another, and the Christian and utilitarian worldviews could not easily coexist. The British and Foreign School Society was funded mainly by wealthy Quakers and led by one of their number, Joseph Lancaster. Among the Quaker supporters the leadership was mainly evangelical, but Francis Place and James Mill managed to insinuate themselves into positions of influence, and the content of the education gradually changed. The first significant change was to drop the requirement that all reading instruction be given only from the Bible, followed by the abrogation of the rule that all the children must be taken to a place of worship on Sundays. Gradually many of the features that had motivated the original founding of these schools disappeared from them. But Place, who could not attain Chadwick's high level of obnoxiousness, still managed to offend people gratuitously, and he was forced off the committee in 1815.[61]

CONCLUSIONS

"But this is one of the peculiarities of the English mind; the Puritan and the Benthamite have an immense part of their nature in common; and thus the Christianity of the Puritan is coarse and fanatical;—he cannot relish what there is in it of beautiful or delicate or ideal." Thus wrote Thomas Arnold to his favorite pupil and future biographer.[62] On the narrowly aesthetic front, there was something in Arnold's notion, but it conveyed a slanted view of the evangelicals that Arnold's son Matthew would broadcast much more widely. Later on, Christopher Dawson puzzled over the relationship and concluded that these two dominant voices in the early nineteenth century, these two "mutually inconsistent orthodoxies," were like flint and steel to each other. "From their contact there sprang the spirit of moral idealism and the passion for reform" that characterized the age.[63] Dawson's metaphor is not quite consistent with Arnold's conclusion, but the confusions in the period were such that the two captured different aspects of the reality. Neither side was noted for its aesthetic sensibilities or contributions, and both contributed mightily to the reform movements, though not necessarily in equal measure or out of the same motivations. The evangelicals made the antislavery issue their own, and later on Lord Ashley and his supporters would do the same for factory reform. The utilitarians were more interested in the scientific applications they believed would increase the store of happiness in the world, and they found a fruitful field of endeavor in conducting investigations and advocating legislation relating to the improvement of public health and the alleviation of poverty. There were also common fields of interest, such as education, and persons, such as James Kay-Shuttleworth, who fit to some extent in both camps.

A definitional problem clouds the issue to some extent. The utilitarians were radicals but represented only one species in the genus. Radicalism had different faces, and there were non- and antiutilitarian versions. There were radical strains in Methodism, for example, particularly the breakaway groups from the dominant Wesleyan Methodists after 1810, so many Methodists were found providing leadership in such movements as Chartism.[64] Many utilitarian leaders also had significant religious backgrounds. We may say without fear of contradiction that Chadwick cannot be understood without considering Bentham's influence on him, but it is at least possible that he cannot be understood without knowing something of his grandfather's influence on him. Andrew Chadwick was a friend of John Wesley who founded the first Methodist Sunday schools in Lancashire. Edwin Chadwick described his grandfather as "a pious unostentatious promoter of measures for the improvement of the condition of the population."[65]

If the radicals differed by species, they also seemed to differ in time. The new poor law was largely the result of utilitarian influence, and its failure to bring to fruition the high hopes with which it was enacted tended to discredit the scientific rationalism that had brought it into existence. One interpretation of the early Dickens novels regarded them as exemplifying the radical faith in progress, dislike for privilege, and neglect of historical heritage common to the radicals but as departing from the Benthamite notion of progress through the application of scientific principles. Thus for some contemporaries, like Dickens, sentimental radicalism was to be preferred to scientific radicalism.[66]

How could the evangelicals, who saw everything in redemptive terms, not only agree to work on common projects with radicals who differed on the basic spiritual issues but even praise them? Some, at least, found in the creation doctrine of the Bible justification for accepting as coworkers on particular projects those who did not accept their core beliefs. Lord Ashley considered Dickens, who shared his dismay at conditions in the factories and whose novels persuaded many on the point, as God's special creation, raised up for that specific purpose. He thought of Dickens as a modern version of Naaman, the general of ancient Syria whom God had delivered from leprosy through the prophet Elisha (2 Kings 5).[67] Newman regarded the utilitarian philosophy in much the same way, because it was based on the realities of the creation. "There was truth in Benthamism. . . . Legislation and political economy were new sciences; they involved *facts;* Christianity might claim and rule them, but it could not annihilate them."[68]

Whatever the younger Mill's religious beliefs, his ethic resembled that of the evangelicals more than it did Bentham's. He described Bentham's ethical thinking—the famous *blank*—as hopeless for the points of behavior that reflected the deeper portions of the human character. Mill believed that only "spiritual development" could answer for the necessity of training the national character, something that Bentham was in no position to consider.[69] This was essentially the animating motive of Wilberforce's *Practical View.* True, they did not mean the same thing when they discussed matters "spiritual." But by Mill's generation, the utilitarian ethic was acquiring some of the same features that the evangelical movement had brought into the mainstream of English thinking. The objection might follow that this was only a surface resemblance, with the essence of the two positions being as far apart as ever. That is true enough, but the partial correspondence helps account for the fact that the religious and irreligious features of the society appeared to be effecting a convergence of sorts.

Evidently the modifications that John Stuart Mill brought to the ideology made it more acceptable to a society that had been infused with religious thinking. His personal crisis, which took him to a bleak despair, was transcended through the help of writers, especially Wordsworth, who taught him to value his feelings as well as his reason and to recognize the legitimacy of a morality that went beyond the requirements of happiness. He even came to appreciate evangelicalism and once said to a friend that if he were not what he was, he might have liked to be a Methodist. He also thought highly of William Wilberforce.[70] This enlarging of the mind of Mill (and through him the thought of utilitarianism) may have stemmed in part from Mill's critique of Bentham, who he thought was exceedingly narrow in having almost no knowledge of, or interest in learning anything about, any philosophy having an ethic based on anything but the standard of utility. Bentham dismissed all of them, including such worthies as Socrates and Plato, with his standard phrase: "vague generalities."[71]

For their part, many of the radicals were willing to swallow the differences between them and the evangelicals because of admiration for some of their practical efforts. Robert Owen dedicated an essay to William Wilberforce in 1812 "as a duty which your benevolent exertions and disinterested conduct demand," namely his work to end the slave trade.[72]

To some extent we are misled about the utilitarians when we take their self-proclaimed method at face value: scientific, dispassionate analysis in the service of utility, without the irrationalities that excite lesser men. Lord Macaulay's review of James Mill's treatise on government, published in the Whig *Edinburgh Review,* complained that Mill completely ignored such realities as real governments in drawing his argument and rested everything on assumptions concerning human nature. "We can scarcely persuade ourselves that we are not reading a book written before the time of Bacon and Galileo."[73] In other words, the whole rationalist venture is unscientific!

The spread of utilitarian thinking is puzzling in a way. It appealed to the general respect for science and reason, despite its willingness to accept unexamined assumptions about them, but it did not speak to the soul of the human being in the way that the contemporary religious movements, or the Lake Poets, or the popular novelists did. The acerbic Hazlitt noted the technical nature of Bentham's writings and their "unintelligible" style, which rendered them of little interest to the educated public. "His works have been translated into French—they ought to be translated into English."[74] In 1825, Hazlitt considered Bentham "little known in England."[75] Recent historians have questioned whether the reputedly far-reaching influence of Bentham's ideas has not been greatly exaggerated; among these analysts there is a tendency to view the evangelicals as much more influential. Some believe that most of the reforms associated with utilitarianism, such as the reform of the poor laws, would have taken place without utilitarian interventions.[76]

Vague terms like *climate of opinion* or *atmosphere* can count for more than easily traced lines of influence. People often have strongly held beliefs, the source of which they may not be able to name. The ameliorative impulse lay heavily on the minds of people in nineteenth-century England, including many whose sympathies were more with the utilitarians than with their religious counterparts. If the sympathies and even the ideas of the utilitarians were to some extent influenced by the spread of the evangelical ethos that increasingly captured the English imagination during the first half of the century, that only shows the intractability of human motivation and action that will not be confined to the boxes that analysts create to contain them.

X

The Conversion of English Culture

THE TEST OF WHETHER a true revolution has taken place is the extent to which the culture has changed. At issue is not the form of governance or the identity of the rulers but rather how people think, feel, and act. What values are important to them? How do they react to questions of public policy that perplex their society? What do they wish their children to believe, and how do they expect them to behave? To be sure, over the course of a number of decades there will always be changes in the ways such questions are answered, but the England of 1850 was so different from a century earlier in these respects that it is not extravagant to say that a cultural revolution had taken place.

Since we are testing the proposition that the effects of the pre-Victorian period lasted well into the reign of Victoria, in this chapter and the next we shall have to seek the evidence somewhat beyond the chronological limits hitherto followed in this book.

THE EDUCATION OF THE ENGLISH

We saw earlier that the religious revival of the eighteenth century had an important educational component. The charity schools organized by the Society for Promoting Christian Knowledge early in the century were intended not only to teach basic literacy but also to inculcate the moral and religious principles that animated the members of the society. In fact, alarm at a curriculum that had become too "literary" for poor children forced the schools to concentrate wholly on reading and manual skills, at the expense of a more advanced education.[1] A generation later, the Wesley brothers insisted not only on basic literacy but also on advanced reading of a moral, theological, and philosophical nature. This body of literature was composed of works written by Methodist leaders but also included reprints of many other authors, often in abstracted form. *The Christian Library* (1749–1755) consisted of fifty volumes of edited material from a variety of sources. This was a kind of *Reader's Digest* two centuries before its time, and it was one reason that even a humble Methodist home was likely to possess a small collection of books.[2] A lively periodical literature also developed, and the Wesley hymns alone provided a fairly comprehensive theological education. Wesley's followers were not in general well educated or sophisticated, but the leadership gave them university-level books to read; the works of Jonathan Edwards, for example (even with the Calvinism excised), provided an intellectual regimen that would have required close attention from almost anyone.

As important as the Sunday school movement was in the spread of both literacy and religion, there was considerable opposition to it on religious grounds in both England and America. Opponents feared that the Sabbath was being desecrated by the secular task of teaching reading, especially when it was done in houses of worship. Some thought that the primacy of the family in teaching religion would be compromised by having it done by others.[3]

Notwithstanding those fears, the Sunday schools were still teaching religion in 1867, when a national survey was taken of Sunday schools operated by the Church of England. This and later surveys—and also biographies—tell of the important role these schools played. In one collection of Lancashire biographies, eleven out of fifty-eight of the subjects born before 1830 were educated exclusively in Sunday schools, with an additional twenty-three receiving some of their schooling there. Of another 107 people, nine were educated at least predominantly in the Sunday schools and thirteen others partially. An 1842 survey of boys in mining towns showed that twenty-seven had no schooling except what they received in the Sunday schools. There was a negative correlation between the distribution of Sunday schools and day schools through the first half of the century, suggesting that the former to some extent served as a substitute for the latter. The day and evening schools should not be thought of as secular in comparison with the Sunday schools, since many of them were Church of England institutions. By 1867, slightly more than 7 percent of the population of England and Wales was enrolled in Church of England day schools, up from 5.6 percent in 1847.[4] During the first half of the nineteenth century, the number of Sunday schools grew from 2,290 (in 1801) to 23,135 (in 1851). Of these, 56 percent were owned by the Establishment at the beginning of the period; by midcentury that number had fallen to 45 percent. During that interval the number of pupils grew from 206,100 (more than a threefold increase from 1788) to 2,099,611.[5] These numbers give some indication of the powerful motivation that religious people brought to the movement and the effect they had on the children of the land. A modern study emphasizes the close connection between the Protestant *word* orientation and the consequent desire to teach reading—especially religious reading. The preponderance of Sunday school teachers "were working men or women who were earnest Christians and who gave up their only free day to help their neighbours' children. In many places, especially the industrial towns of the north of England, the Sunday schools became centres of working-class life and the focus of the powerful Victorian drive for self-help and improvement."[6]

The motivation behind these schools was the moral and spiritual welfare of the students. Robert Raikes, who originated the Sunday school movement, made that clear in a letter he wrote to a local magistrate. The idea for the schools came to him, he said, "entirely owing to accident," the accident being his confrontation with misbehaving poor children in a suburban area. A local woman informed him that on Sundays the streets were full of these children, released from their weekday employment. Such children were totally without restraint, either internal or external, and without the means to learn any better. Raikes concluded that only some kind of educational provision could rescue these children from being permanent blights on society.[7] In addition to moral and religious instruction, the Sunday schools taught reading, manners, sanitation, order, punctuality—in short, the virtues that made it possible for people to have decent lives and the kind of respectability that some in later generations would affect to despise.

As religious schooling emerged from a purely volunteer society to a more professional one, it was increasingly influenced by two rival societies that had similar goals and methods. Joseph Lancaster, born in 1778 to a Calvinist family, had traveled to Jamaica while still in his early teens in order to teach slaves to read. He had been inspired by a Claphamite book, Thomas Clarkson's *Essay on the Slave Trade.* His evangelical piety found expression in the Quaker denomination, and he combined it with his discovery of the monitorial system, which made use of pupils to instruct younger contemporaries. Along with a small group of friends and supporters, he founded the British and Foreign School Society in January 1808. A need for increased funding led them to expand the group two years later, and a number of prominent Evangelicals came in, including William Wilberforce, Thomas Clarkson, and Fowell Buxton. But already the expansion was in ideology as well as numbers, for the enlarged group included William Smith, an ally of Wilberforce's in the House of Commons, and John Martineau, both Unitarians. In 1813, the number was increased once again, and the radical leader Joseph Hume entered along with Francis Place and also several Catholic peers. Lord Byron became one of the vice presidents. This diversity of membership caused serious strains among the leadership and resulted in the dropping of rules requiring reading instruction from the Bible and attendance at Sunday worship services in some of the schools.[8]

Meanwhile Andrew Bell started his version of the monitorial system. He had come to the method in 1789 while in India, at the orphanage in Madras. On his return to England he published a pamphlet describing the system, *An Experiment in Education at the Asylum at Madras* (1797), and began several schools that used the method. He founded the National School Society in 1811 with strong Church backing, especially from members of the High Church group known as the Hackney Phalanx.

The British and Foreign School Society and Bell's National School Society both claimed pride of place in pioneering the monitorial system, and there came to be considerable personal animosity between Lancaster and Bell. Actually, Robert Raikes had devised a version of the system before either of them, having used it at Gloucester Gaol to teach prisoners to read, and later employed it in some of his Sunday schools. Given the nature of the two organizations—Dissent and radicalism on the one hand and Establishment (predominantly High Church) on the other—it was no surprise that politics entered into the dispute. Spencer Perceval, the Evangelical prime minister who was assassinated in 1812, favored Bell and prevailed upon the Prince Regent to withdraw his support from Lancaster.[9]

For several decades the main influence on the direction of teacher training was exerted by the Evangelical physician and bureaucrat James Kay-Shuttleworth. He established the Battersea Training School, which was the prototype for some forty similar institutions. Kay-Shuttleworth understood what he was doing when he founded Battersea in 1842: he intended to set the pattern for the whole English educational system. He regarded the teaching of children as a drudgery that could not be done well except by raising up a corps of dedicated people who would accomplish the task with a sense of calling, rather than merely as a job, and he believed that this sense could be transmitted to the teachers only by combining intellectual and religious training. Kay-Shuttleworth was completely aboveboard about the religious foundation of his system of training teachers and the reason for it. As he wrote later on, "The main object of a normal school is the *formation of the character of the schoolmaster,* as an intelligent Christian man entering on the instruction of the poor, with religious devotion to his work."[10] He believed the right spirit could be inculcated into the prospective teachers by the example and instruction of the principal, by religious services held in the school, by attendance at church services, and by "acts of charity and self-denial," as a prelude to a lifelong habit of such behavior.[11]

WHAT THE ENGLISH READ

The fact that many more English people could read in the early nineteenth century than before had to have made an enormous difference in how they thought and acted. For one thing, this fresh market pulled from the pens of willing writers a flood of hastily crafted work of lower quality than would hitherto have seen the light of day—a much-derided proletarianization of letters. A scholar who has explored this issue concludes that these many thousands of new readers amounted to a "a far-reaching revolution in English culture." New readers tended to be among the upper levels of working people—not the mass of unskilled laborers, but rather shopkeepers and the higher grade of domestic servants, to many of whom the reading material of their betters filtered down.[12] Such people did not rely solely on hand-me-downs, however; many became good customers of the booksellers. A survey taken of a lower-class London neighborhood in 1848 revealed that the average family possessed eleven books; that did not include the serial literature that was the original venue of such estimable works as Dickens's novels.[13] Other surveys in the late 1830s and early 1840s showed that in both countryside and town at least three-quarters of the homes of working poor people contained books.[14] Even many who did not know how to read were affected by the growth of literacy. Workers were often read to at their benches by semiliterate colleagues, one way in which radical thinking spread among the workers.[15] For the better trained there were church and school libraries, and sometimes the workers were reinforced in their reading habits by banding together informally in discussion groups.

Within a few years of Hannah More's death, surveys showed that her *Cheap Repository Tracts* were a mainstay of the English cottager's meager library. The *First Report of the Commissioners of Education in Ireland* revealed the Irish peasants to be assiduous readers of these tracts, and in 1821 the New Edinburgh Tract Society was overwhelmed with demand for them, begging for permission to reprint.[16] Evangelical tracts were usually simple fictional stories intended to illustrate religious principles and enjoin people to come to faith in Christ. John Wesley had established the Society for the Distribution of Religious Tracts Among the Poor, and five years later Wilberforce's Society for the Reformation of Manners began to distribute tracts promoting its agenda. By the middle of the nineteenth century, the Religious Tract Society had 4,363 titles on its list and was distributing them in a total of 110 languages. Some of the tract writers, such as the Dissenting minister George Burder and the clergyman Legh Richmond, had a million or more pieces in circulation, although, of course, vast quantities were given gratis and as quickly discarded.[17] As we saw earlier, Hannah More's *Cheap*

Repository Tracts took the country by storm with enormous press runs, including a special edition on better paper to be sold in bookstores. These little publications were designed to resemble the popular and often ribald chapbooks, including the woodcuts that characterized them. More stopped their production in 1798 because the strain of writing and organizing the effort was proving too much for her. With or without her, the tracts were turned out by the millions and were found everywhere, on into the next century.[18]

To understand better what difference all this made, we have to consider just what all these new readers were reading. In the first place, the Bible was sold and read more than any other book, which was just the end sought by many of the schools when they opened their doors. The Bible also proved to be the catalyst for the creation and maintenance of the most successful of the pan-evangelical organizations. Such groups as the London Missionary Society and the Tract Society suffered internal conflict due to the differing views of Dissenters and Churchmen, but the determination of the British and Foreign Bible Society, founded in 1804, to do only one thing—publish and distribute Bibles without comment, which became the society's "fundamental principle"—saved it from all that. By 1814, the society had more than 100,000 subscribers and numbered auxiliaries in almost every English county. A decade later, by one estimate, there were more than 850 auxiliaries and 500 ladies' groups.[19] England became drenched with biblical knowledge. John Henry Newman, born as the century began, recalled being "brought up from a child to take great delight in reading the Bible."[20] The Quaker MP John Bright described in his memoirs the vivid impression that the family Bible readings made upon his mind: "I fancied I could see the discontented brother of the Prodigal Son returning from the field down the short lane which led from the house to the neighbouring cornfield. These imaginings of my boyhood have remained with me ever since."[21]

Autobiographical writings from the period suggest that after the Bible the two books having the most formative effect on Englishmen were *Pilgrim's Progress* and *Paradise Lost,* themselves both based on the Bible. Bunyan's allegory was taken by many as a historical account of real people, and Milton seems to be the author who created a taste for poetry among the youth. According to Newman's brother-in-law, also a Tractarian leader, people frequently said these two writers did more to influence English religion than even the Bible.[22] Robert Southey undertook a *Life* of Bunyan, even though the task could not pay him for his time. He marveled that so fine a work could be produced by one "whose intellect ever looks thro so thick and coarse a crust of ignorance."[23] The *Christian Observer* cited the *Edinburgh Review*'s favorable notice of Southey's book and took it as a sign that the times were much improved compared with a half century earlier, when one dared not name Bunyan "for fear of a sneer."[24] This sort of literature had the same effect on many people as the Bible did: it either enthralled them or left them completely cold and uncomprehending. Leigh Hunt confessed that he had read *Paradise Lost* as a kind of duty and had found that it was "heathen Greek" to him.[25] Yet to others it seemed almost holy Scripture. Many assiduous students of the Bible were astonished to learn their knowledge of Genesis came from Milton rather than Scripture.[26] Some of the characters in nineteenth-century novels seem to have been patterned after biblical figures; King David was an especially popular choice because of the dramatic episodes of his life and the autobiographical gloss that people took to be his in the Psalms.[27]

One of the most influential pieces of literature during the whole of the century was a grammar textbook written by Lindley Murray of York. He was asked to write a book that would assist instruction in a York school for young women and as a result published *English Grammar* in 1795, a book that was reissued many times over the decades. Murray was a devout Evangelical, and the book was larded with appropriate examples and illustrative precepts that provided the meat for the grammatical bones. It met with the praise not only of evangelicals but of almost everyone interested in the task of instructing people on the intricacies of the English language. But the grammar incorporated a heavy dose of the religious teaching that was already influencing England from so many other sources. Murray closed his book with an address to the pupils on the proper application of their learning in the course of a pious and virtuous life. As with Murray's grammar, so it was with almost all children's literature, a fact that was obvious from reading almost any of the books in the genre. The didactic material for children from the eighteenth century began to be invested with religious meaning and with mystery, principally through the work of the Scot George MacDonald, who began his adult life as a Dissenting minister.[28]

Much of the evangelical literature was designed to be given away or, like the *Cheap Repository Tracts*, sold at heavily subsidized prices, but there was also a thriving market-driven trade in religious literature. The interdenominational Christian Colportage Association stepped in to supply the burgeoning demand for Christian books by recruiting and training evangelicals who saw this task as a calling fully as worthy to be followed as preaching and teaching. The association, which began its work in 1774, trained its traveling salesmen in barrackslike settings and set about to flood the country with evangelical books and pamphlets intended to inspire and inform the public.[29]

Free and subsidized tracts and colportage distribution still left an enormous unserved market—those who could not or would not pay for expensive books but who demanded more than tracts. The common but costly three-volume format of novels priced these products out of the market for many readers, and the lending libraries filled the vacuum. Circulating libraries had existed from the latter half of the eighteenth century, but with a greatly expanded reading public they became much more important in the next century. Hannah More wrote *Cœlebs in Search of a Wife,* which went to thirty editions by the time of her death in 1834, explicitly for them.[30]

C. E. Mudie (from 1842) and W. H. Smith (1858) became the largest buyers of books in the kingdom and in effect were the arbiters of what the reading public would have available. Both were evangelicals. Mudie was a Dissenter who occasionally preached and wrote hymns, and Smith considered becoming a clergyman. They judged books not only from a business perspective but also from the standpoint of their religious faith, avoiding what they considered indecency or blasphemy. Mudie affected the book purchasers' reading habits, as well as the borrowers', because of his influence over the decisions of publishers. Considering whether to publish a new novel, the publishing offices would resound with the crucial question: "What will Mudie say?"[31]

Recent scholarship has questioned the long-standing conclusion that the evangelicals were culturally illiterate.[32] During the Wilberforce generation, which may have been the high-water mark of the evangelical movement in its specifically religious role, many of the evangelicals were far more attuned to the culture of educated Englishmen than their predecessors and successors were. Charles Simeon had little taste for secular amusements, but he went out of his way to avoid turning his personal predilections into a new law for Christians.[33] The earlier Evangelical clergymen—people like Walker of Truro—isolated from men of like mind, had been more defensive, having little appreciation for a culture that appreciated them so little. But as the movement grew, so did its social and intellectual maturity.[34]

Some of the evangelical publications were far from being narrow, strictly religious organs. From the start, the *Christian Observer* dealt with matters beyond the theological and ecclesiastical. In the issue of February 1802, for example, the section entitled "Literary and Philosophical Intelligence" included items on natural philosophy, medicine and surgery, history, poetry, veterinary medicine, landscape gardening, exploration, geography, anatomy, zoology, chemistry, astronomy, archeology, agriculture, and paleontology. There were news items from Britain, France, Prussia, America, Turkey, Russia, and Italy. Each issue had a long section entitled "A View of Public Affairs." The *Observer* claimed a theological basis for its interest in cultural matters, inasmuch as it recognized "no hostility between serious

Religion and Elegant Literature." "Philosophy and genius rejoice to take up their cross and follow Christ."[35] It reviewed Lord Byron's *Childe Harold* more favorably than many would expect, favorably enough in fact to elicit Byron's letter of appreciation.[36] Even the *Record* was surprisingly catholic in its scope, publishing articles from a range of fields almost as broad as the *Observer*'s. Many of the Dissenters were current with the contemporary culture. One of their ministers wrote that he admired the *Christian Observer* and had read it from its inception. But he also took what he called "those Cyclopes of literature—the Edinburgh and Quarterly Reviews."[37]

Evangelical hermeneutics is often described as being literalist, but that is a serious misstatement of the matter. Rather, the evangelicals commonly read the Bible in a typological fashion, and the main "type" was the finding of Jesus Christ in the Old Testament. The striking thing about this, for our purpose here, is that it was not confined to the evangelicals but spread to some of the most influential writers of the age. Ruskin and Carlyle—sons of evangelical families—owed some of the power of their work to this ability to use events in unexpected ways as emblems of the point they wished to make.[38] The pre-Raphaelite painter William Holman Hunt revealed in his diaries that he understood the Dead Sea as an emblem of sin, possessing a kind of beauty when first seen but ultimately leading to death. His paintings were full of small symbolic details of theological significance that he expected the viewer to understand gradually by careful study and meditation.[39] Much of the richness of nineteenth-century literature, as well as the shared experiences and commonality of understanding that made the literature as universally accepted as it was, came from the fact that so many people understood the biblical metaphors.

Yet to speak only of biblical metaphors understates what was happening. A modern literary critic, trying to understand the hold of the Bible on succeeding generations, uses the common terminology of *myth*, but in a way that undercuts its usual meaning. Biblical stories became myths in a sense that is "the opposite of 'not really true': it means being charged with a special seriousness and importance."[40] This special status of the stories triggers the imagination through the centuries by means of a process he calls *resonance*. Thus the image of a winepress in Isaiah, written to celebrate a coming military victory, becomes associated with the day of judgment, and then a powerfully evocative symbol in a marching song like *The Battle Hymn of the Republic* and a book title like *The Grapes of Wrath*.[41] This process was one that governed not only much of the literature of the day but all sorts of communication, and inevitably much of the everyday thinking of the people.

A number of modern interpreters believe that the mainstream literary canon of the period owes much to the evangelical milieu. Consider the

Brontë sisters, for example.[42] Emily Brontë presents a problem because of the dark menace brooding over *Wuthering Heights,* and one solution is to portray her as a rebel against evangelicalism who presents a mirror image that substitutes evil for good, mocking God and the godly community.[43] But whether true or inverted, the biblical images are pervasive. When Jane Eyre learns that Rochester has a wife, Charlotte Brontë has her describe her woe with reference to the Exodus: "My hopes were all dead—struck with a subtle doom, as, in one night, fell on all the first-born in the land of Egypt."[44] The Brontë sisters were the products of an Evangelical vicarage, but later in the century it was common even for writers with a profound distaste for all that the evangelicals stood for, such as Swinburne, to use the same sort of symbology.[45]

Nineteenth-century novels were to some extent morality tales, many of them showing the evangelical influence, whatever the convictions of their authors. Evangelical writers like Hannah More and Legh Richmond, although they are associated with the theology of a religious movement, appeared to many in their audiences as mainstream novelists, and the standards they followed were those by which the novelists in much of the century came to be judged.[46] Before she began writing evangelical books, More made her mark in the broader literature of the eighteenth century, and her close friend Samuel Johnson is reported to have regarded her as the best woman poet writing in the English language.[47] Some of her contemporaries thought she had only one rival in changing for the better the sentiments of the times, and that was Robert Raikes's Sunday schools. The unprecedented success of the *Cheap Repository Tracts* should not make us think that her influence was confined to the poor. Works such as the *Manners of the Great* and *Hints for the Education of a Princess* were read avidly by the highest reaches of the society, including the court.[48]

Many writers who were not part of the evangelical movement nevertheless contributed to the religiosity that gradually came to prevail, even in ways that could not easily be distinguished from those of the evangelicals. Jane Austen's attitude toward the evangelicals was ambivalent but gradually seemed to swing in their favor. More recent scholarship stresses her regular attendance in Church, her conventional piety, the growing acceptance of evangelicalism evident in some of her correspondence, her favorable impression of the writing of the friend of Clapham, Thomas Gisborne, and her views on moral issues.[49]

Sir Walter Scott's influence on the century's sentiments is undisputed. Less widely known is his early criticism of novels of "the fashionable world" that, typical of the Enlightenment century, offended the morality associated with religious devotion. He thus threw himself into public controversy and helped usher in the new day in literary appreciation that would welcome his *Waverly* novels.[50] Scott's novels depicted a medieval Europe, struggling to create a Christian civilization, that was at least analogous to his own age, and this probably had something to do with his popularity. His effect was described by a historian who himself was a descendent of Clapham. G. O. Trevelyan contrasted Scott's sense of history with that of the Enlightenment figure Edward Gibbon. Gibbon, he said, showed us something of the truth of ancient Rome but only a narrow sliver of the truth, with the people of one age quite similar to those of every other age and possessing the cold classicality of a procession on a Parthenon frieze. Scott's characters, by contrast, were suffused with color and life, like what we see in a stained glass window.[51]

But already, Scott seemed to presage what would become common much later in the century: the religious point of view expressed as an effect, without much comprehension of the cause. This was the criticism of such diverse critics as Carlyle and the theologian Frederick Denison Maurice.[52] Some observers think that this impulse was a natural result of the changing society influencing the literature: people demanded books that were friendly to a religious, moral perspective, and novelists responded by providing them, regardless of the shallowness of their commitment and understanding.[53]

Wordsworth is no longer regarded as a pantheist but rather as a Christian—some even say an Evangelical. We have already seen his influence on the Tractarians through Keble, his unabashed admirer. Aubrey de Vere, who knew him well, believed him to be an orthodox Christian, increasingly so as he grew older.[54] He was evidently introduced to evangelical writings through his sister Dorothy and had what he called a "bond of connection" with Wilberforce because of his liking for the *Practical View*. Richard Brantley's view of the poet, which can be seen in his title *Wordsworth's Natural Methodism*, had also been Charles Lamb's view of Wordsworth. Hannah More, who had been disgusted by the young Wordsworth's radicalism, was overcome by the revelation of a very different man in *The Excursion*. Thomas De Quincey informed Dorothy of Wordsworth's visit to Hannah More and announced that her brother "has made a conquest of Holy Hannah."[55]

Religious observers of the nineteenth century commonly regarded the life of George Eliot with sadness, sometimes regarding her as a religious thinker—even a theologian—who lost her way, partly through the sinister influence of George Henry Lewes.[56] Her early letters were full of the Methodist mode of discourse that she had absorbed from her family, loaded with biblical texts, exhortations, spiritual introspections, and the like.[57] But even modern scholars, writing in their characteristically secular perspective, have recognized that although her published works reflect the loss of her faith, they also reflect more than a residue of religious sensibility. "What she brought from her Evangelical background was a radically reverent attitude towards life, a profound seriousness of the kind that is a first condition of any real intelligence, and an interest in human nature that made her a great psychologist."[58] Although there is no doubt of the sincerity of her expressions of unbelief, she retained the imprint of her former adherence, particularly the doctrine of sin, and her depictions of Methodists could be so favorable as to open her to charges of overidealizing them.[59] Perhaps unconsciously, she never lost the apocalyptic mode of historical reasoning that was common to all forms of biblical religion but was especially notable in its evangelical form. This practice related historical events to both the creation and some kind of final culmination and by so doing avoided treating events as merely a series of activities without coherence and without meaning beyond themselves.[60] Much of this tendency probably lay beneath the surface of her consciousness as an ingrained mode of reasoning that could not help but emerge in her fiction and even showed up in philosophical works informed by contradictory ideas, such as Comteanism, with its new Religion of Humanity. One analyst describes the source of that tendency as "that 'remotest past' in which her imagination moved with most ease," which is to say, her evangelical past.[61] It was this quality, perhaps more than any other, that saved her work from the description she had used (before writing her first novel) of "silly novels by lady novelists."[62]

Dickens differed from George Eliot partly in that he never had an evangelical past from which to withdraw. He was a sort of natural Pelagian: the notion of grace was foreign to him, and he was emphatic about the importance of works toward whatever kind of salvation awaited. Virtue is a state arrived at naturally, for Dickens rejected the idea of original sin.[63] Yet the novels are full of the virtues that people had long called Christian virtues. In Christians they were performed out of a sense of duty or out of a responsibility to love one's fellows that was not chiefly an emotion but an inclination of the will. Fitzjames Stephen, a grandson of Clapham who no longer followed the faith, might have been speaking of Dickens in describing those who came after his grandfather's time as subject to a "kind of vapid philanthropic sentiment . . . a creed of maudlin benevolence from which all the deeper and sterner elements of religious belief have been carefully pushed away."[64] In books written from that perspective, the traits of personal character that the New Testament called the "fruit of the spirit" were attained in the fiction while the roots were ignored. There is another perspective that sees Dickens as a more or less orthodox Anglican. The evidence for it lies in such matters as pious wording in his will, his provision for the religious teaching of his children,[65] and the absence in his writings of explicit anti-Christian passages of the sort that one sees in apostate clergymen like Leslie Stephen.[66] There are ambiguous passages in his correspondence: in a letter to his good friend Wilkie Collins, he admonished the novelist to recognize that plots must be constructed in "*the ways of Providence, of which ways all art is but a little imitation.*"[67]

These attempts to discern the state of Dickens's faith are less important for our present purpose than placing his body of work in the context of the religious revival. "The Bible," as one commentator says, "was in Dickens's blood." His themes were usually biblical, centering on such sins as selfishness, pride, indiscipline, and greed. The language and ideas of both the Bible and the prayer book come again and again, and one sees characters acting out the idea of Christian love or personifying the Prodigal Son or the Good Samaritan.[68] He has one scene early in *Great Expectations* that is reminiscent of the painting by William Holman Hunt called *The Awakening Conscience*. In the book young Pip, having just stolen food from his sister's larder to give to the criminal on the moors, spies a black ox with a white spot that reminds him of a clerical collar, and immediately his conscience is awakened. Further on, Dickens puts a statement in Pip's mouth that is almost a paraphrase of the New Testament doctrine of imputed righteousness: "It was not because I was faithful, but because Joe was faithful, that I never ran away and went for a soldier or a sailor. It was not because I had a strong sense of the virtue of industry, but because Joe had a strong sense of the virtue of industry, that I worked with tolerable zeal against the grain." The *Tale of Two Cities* begins with a section called "Recalled to Life." Dickens speaks of the "resurrection" of Dr. Manette, and at the end Sidney Carton, an innocent man, voluntarily gives up his life as a sacrifice of love. There were probably few readers of the book who were unable to see that Dickens was calling attention to the New Testament scene of the crucifixion of Christ. Dickens also seldom wandered from the biblical perspective that concludes that what one sows he also reaps, a kind of inevitability of the punishment of evil. Anyone familiar with his work who reads *Nicholas Nickleby* for the first time will be morally certain that before the story ends, Ralph Nickleby will have either repented or suffered horribly for the evil he did.

Although Dickens could not resist limning a scene that lampooned the foibles of evangelicals—consider, for example, the Dissenting preacher Stiggins who made old Mr. Wellman's life miserable in *The Pickwick Papers*, or the ludicrous Mrs. Jellyby of *Bleak House*—that was not the whole story. He was at one with those evangelicals, Shaftesbury more than any, who were hard at work alleviating suffering. For Dickens was a great humanitarian in an age that found intolerable the level of hardship that formerly had been accepted as one of the givens of life. Moreover, and more profoundly, his ridicule was motivated by the same ethos that directed the evangelicals; they, too, thundered against hypocrisy, which is one of the great sins warned against in the Bible. Both testaments assaulted the pretensions of an outward show of religion that covered a heart of stone, and the evangelicals preaching the Bible followed suit. Like many evangelicals, Dickens hated blood sports and preached against gambling, drunkenness, and public executions. He favored the same family-centered activities as they, notwithstanding the later irregularity of his own family life, and he detested the worldliness of profligacy in the same way the evangelicals did.[69]

Religious cant in Dickens's novels received the same treatment that many evangelical preachers gave it, and if the evangelicals merited confrontation with their own sermons, they could hardly blame Dickens for administering the therapy.[70] That being said, parody is parody, and in this arena as in many others Dickens has to be regarded as a storyteller and as neither an objective reporter nor a propagandist. When he described Nicholas Nickleby as something other than a high-spirited gentleman, it was because his hero "lacked that peculiar excess of coolness and great-minded selfishness, which invariably distinguished gentlemen of high spirit."[71] It was the excess or the hypocrisy that exercised Dickens, not the fact that his target was a gentleman or an evangelical.

To some, Dickens was essentially a preacher. Carlyle, himself as much a moralizer as anything else, thought him a universal preacher, declaiming "to all men in all times and places."[72] In some astonishing way, his novels came to be regarded as a sort of sub-Scripture. Arthur Stanley, preaching in Westminster Abbey the Sunday after Dickens's funeral there, spoke of the parable as a means of instruction in the New Testament, drawing the parallel with Dickens's stories as conveying spiritual truth. The message might have been more convincing coming from another sort of preacher, but it was a faithful reflection of the way the novelist had come to be regarded not only in England but in much of the English-speaking world. By this time the biblical message had become diffuse because it was communicated through minds that were filled with other images and other principles, sometimes contradictory ones—but contradictory in ways that were not apparent to many people who held opposite convictions in their minds at the same time. For this reason what was paramount not only for Dickens but for many of his contemporaries was not the code of the Scripture but what one scholar calls the "fractured code," which is the code broken and reset for other purposes than the original ones.[73]

Novels were especially important in our consideration of the effects of the religious revival on the culture of England because the novelists were not only trying to tell an engrossing tale but consciously teaching the society what to believe and how to behave. When Trollope called himself "a preacher of sermons," he was identifying himself with what had become a dominant feature in nineteenth-century fiction. The novelist, he said, "must teach, whether he wishes to teach or not . . . if he can make virtue alluring and vice ugly." [74]

High Church views were prominent in many novels of the period. Newman, while still at Oxford, opined that during the first quarter of the century, Scott, for all his faults, prepared people "for some closer and more practical approximation to Catholic truth." [75] Charlotte Yonge, as we saw earlier, adopted as the watchword of her novels *Pro Ecclesia Dei* and frankly acknowledged that her purpose had always been to popularize High Church views. [76] Evangelicals did the same for their views, and it has been suggested that evangelicalism's emphasis on the individual made it an especially fertile source of ideas for the novel. [77] *Cœlebs in Search of a Wife* was Hannah More's sermon to evangelical readers on the nature of sexual relations for the young bachelor. A widow sends her twenty-four-year-old son on his quest by warning him not to be captivated by a charming exterior that causes him to overlook deficiencies of intellect or conduct and to avoid "romantic ideas of super-human excellence" but on the other hand not to have low standards. [78] There follow a series of adventures, full of amusing and instructive encounters with various kinds of people, a moving tableau that illustrates Hannah More's theology in action and fully justifies her subtitle: "Observations on Domestic Habits and Manners, Religion and Morals." To the High Church and evangelical examples we can add one from the Broad Church, albeit with the dose of evangelicalism that was common to the period. Thomas Hughes wrote in the preface to the sixth edition of his phenomenally successful novel *Tom Brown's Schooldays* a reply to all those who had objected to his "preaching" in the book and urged him to refrain from the practice in future writings. "Now this I most distinctly decline to do," he wrote. "Why my whole object in writing at all, was to get the chance of preaching. . . . I can't see that a man has any business to write at all, unless he has something which he thoroughly believes and wants to preach about." [79] Some people became tired of all the preaching in the novels, and an exasperated reviewer wrote in the *Athenæum* in 1847, "We are weary of pro- and anti-Pusey novels." [80]

Yet the explicit preaching of religion through novels was not the only or the most effective way Christianity was taught to the public. Often what is assumed rather than what is taught is most likely to engage itself in the inner mesh of the mind because it slips in without engaging the critical faculties of the reader. Thus ideas such as a *providence* that the writers assumed without even thinking about it were inserted into the readers' thinking unobserved, to be reinforced in a thousand other unconscious ways and so fasten themselves on the thinking of the age. This process was especially effective in that it might be part of the mental baggage of the various polemical writers who on the surface were at dagger points with each other.[81] This subconscious means for the transmission of ideas was for obvious reasons of more relevance for the ranks of the newly literate readers of novels than for the well educated. The oft-reviled Bowdler, simplifier and unofficial censor of great authors, it has been suggested, ought to be considered not so much a censor as a popularizer, one who gave Shakespeare to a public that might otherwise never have made his acquaintance. That was the surprising view of the sensual Victorian poet Swinburne, who derided as "nauseous and . . . foolish cant" criticisms by those who assailed Bowdler.[82]

The Christian classics that were increasingly coming to dominate the reading desks of believers and quasi-believers left their mark also on the unlikely audience of unbelievers and antibelievers. The antinomian poets of the early part of the century might damn the Christians, but they almost invariably treated Jesus Christ with the greatest respect; Keats even linked him with Socrates. With an argument that became common in the nineteenth century (popularized by Bentham among others), Shelley called him an "extraordinary person" whose teachings unfortunately were distorted by the church. Byron averred that he had read *Paradise Lost* so often that it was indelibly stamped on his work, which would not have otherwise been possible. Shelley wrote of "the sacred Milton," and however hostile to the entire biblical tradition such men were, they seemed to have accepted a doctrine something like the fallen or imperfect state of humanity. Byron became a serious student of Genesis and dwelt much on Creation and the Fall.[83] Leigh Hunt was a close colleague of Shelley's and recalled that the poet had a great admiration for the Bible, albeit a "peculiar" one. In common with unbelieving Bible lovers, his was a very selective admiration, favoring Job, the Sermon on the Mount, and the epistle of James (probably because of its seeming devaluation of faith in favor of works) and strongly disliking St. Paul, as Bentham did in *Not Paul but Jesus* (which Hunt mentions here). Hunt put the best face on Shelley's peculiarity by saying that he valued the spirit, though not the letter, of Christianity.[84] The age esteemed poetry, and the Evangelical Cowper had a strong following among those whose religious convictions were very different. The youthful Edward Fitz-Gerald, future translator of *The Rubáiyát*, was happy that Thackeray had taken to Cowper and wrote to the novelist of his own affection for the poet: "Some of his little poems are affecting beyond anything in the English language: not heroic, but they make me cry."[85]

Autobiographical writing fits into our story because of the evangelical emphasis on personal testimony as a means of evangelism. Sometimes this was disguised or fictionalized, as in the case of Carlyle's *Sartor Resartus,* or was turned into an anticonversion story like William Hale White's later *Autobiography of Mark Rutherford.* The forms of the anti- or deconversion autobiographies were surprisingly similar to the evangelical ones—the central role of sermons or lectures, the perusing of key literary texts, the intellectual difficulties encountered in one's passage to or away from faith, the moral crisis and its final resolution. The form remained the same while the evangelical content was reversed.[86]

The popularity of reprints of seventeenth- and eighteenth-century Puritan literature acquainted nineteenth-century people with the spiritual autobiographies of the earlier period, literature that was consciously molded by the example of biblical characters. The Puritans revered figures like David, Job, and the apostle Paul and emphasized features of their own lives that seemed to be pertinent to the ancient examples. Paul's Damascus road experience formed the identifying pattern for many a life—and many a *Life*—centuries in the future. In addition to the great apostle, the Exodus account in the Old Testament was a very common source. Bunyan explicitly referred to this in his own autobiography, *Grace Abounding to the Chief of Sinners,* viewing himself as an Israelite in the spiritual sense often adopted by the Puritans, and his own trek through life as a modern Exodus.[87] Such disparate figures as Newman and Mill wrote autobiographies that contained similar features. When Ruskin, traveling in his youthful exuberance, found a copy of Bunyan's *Grace Abounding* in his satchel, he berated his mother for having slipped it in despite her knowledge of his dislike for that sort of literature, full as it was of what he considered morbid introspection. Forty years later, writing his own autobiography, he determined to produce something very different, a hop and skip through his past that would speak of his pleasures and avoid the rest; but in the event he turned out a book that bore a strange resemblance to Bunyan's. Evidently, the Puritan sensibility had so impressed itself on the mind of the nineteenth century that its way of approaching this form of literature could not be avoided without the kind of wrench that offended both the writer, regardless of his intentions, and his audience. As with Ruskin, so with his generation.[88]

None of the old Puritan writings came close to equaling the popularity of the *Pilgrim's Progress,* but there was still a fair amount of reprinting for the edification of the early nineteenth century. The work of the Massachusetts Puritan Cotton Mather (d. 1728) enjoyed a revival when his *Bonifacius* appeared in England in 1807 under the title *Essays to Do Good.* The editor was the Congregationalist minister George Burder, who was the secretary of the London Missionary Society and editor of the *Evangelical Magazine.* This was the first republication since Mather's lifetime, and sixteen editions followed on both sides of the Atlantic.[89]

ART TRANSFORMED

The artistic imagination strikes so closely to the inner convictions of the soul that it is almost inconceivable that the religious revival should not have changed artistic appreciations. Most painting since the Renaissance—since Raphael in particular—had been secular in orientation, in contrast to medieval art. In an age that welcomed the gothic in architecture, what could be more natural than to turn toward religious themes in other arts?[90] Apart from style, there was a certain didactic quality to much of the painting that was apparently closely related to the spread of evangelical thinking. Painters alarmed by the spurning of respectability and the dissolution of the family depicted the sad result of the mania for gambling, promiscuity, or drunkenness—destitution, homelessness, suicide.[91]

Although John Ruskin as an adult shed his evangelical heritage, it is not likely that he shed its subconscious influence. Raised on daily Bible readings, he astonished his pious mother by his understanding of the Scriptures. His recent biographer concludes that this background influenced all his later writing.[92] His usual "prophetic" method of declamation evidently derived from the same source and in fact intensified as he grew older.[93] With a prodigious talent and an appetite for work that matched it, Ruskin attracted the attention of other talented people and exercised a profound influence over their lives and their work. William Holman Hunt, one of the most important painters of the innovative and influential school of art, the Pre-Raphaelite Brotherhood, told Ruskin in a letter that he had been a "contemptuous unbeliever" in any principle but the development of talent, a follower of Shelley, Byron, and Keats, when a fellow student loaned him a copy of Ruskin's anonymously published *Modern Painters,* a work that turned him around completely. Moreover, the whole Pre-Raphaelite school absorbed Ruskin's influence from Hunt's reading, the others in the Brotherhood being too absorbed in other concerns and activities. It was the influence of Ruskin, operating through his disciple Hunt, that gave the Brotherhood its intense preoccupation with religious typological symbolism that was one of its identifying marks.[94]

Later on, Ruskin and Hunt had intense discussions in which Ruskin attempted to induce his old disciple to renounce religion and turn to the master's atheism. As Hunt recalled one of these conversations, Ruskin accused him of doing "a deal of harm by your works in sanctifying blind beliefs."[95] Hunt did not bother denying Ruskin's assertion that his art reflected his religious beliefs because he knew it was true and indeed might have argued that it was inevitably true. He believed that without religious faith, art reflects a materialistic view of reality that must render it lifeless. In a letter to a colleague, he contended that "trying to limit speculation within the bounds of sense only must produce poor sculpture, feeble painting, dilettante poetry."[96]

It took time for Hunt to put his vision into practice. His early *Light of the World* depicted Christ in an etherealized, unworldly way that attracted both praise and criticism. But later paintings were much more earthy without losing their religious message; indeed, their earthiness made it much easier for Hunt to get his point across to the viewer. In *The Awakening Conscience*, for example, a kept woman arises from the lap of her lover, her face contorted with shame and guilt at the sudden realization of the meaning of her status. The distress in her expression contrasts with that of the man, who does not yet realize what is going through her mind. Hunt wrote in a letter of 1854 that the painting was intended "to show how the still small voice speaks to a human soul in the turmoil of life." Such details as the hymnbook on the piano and the bird escaping from the cat portray the possibility of redemption, a road on which the woman has just begun to embark. The painting can be taken as symbolic of the course run by English society in the previous half-century.[97] In *The Hireling Shepherd*, Hunt depicted the gospel parable in striking detail and striking beauty, making clear to all how the temptations of life draw the man from his real duties.[98] Most of the Brotherhood members had no evident religious convictions, but Hunt's faith to some extent as well as the mood of the times affected their work almost as much as if they did. Dante Gabriel Rossetti's *Ecce Ancilla Domini* showed a Virgin much more human than most in the genre of annunciation paintings. John Everett Millais's striking *Christ in the Carpenter's Shop* shows a family with all the verisimilitude we would expect of someone who believed the Gospels really spoke of flesh-and-blood people. The realism of these pictures reinforces the message, which otherwise might be lost in a romanticized haze. But by this time (1850) the earthiness was beginning to be an embarrassment to some, and the *Times* objected to Millais's depiction of "the meanest details of a carpenter's shop."[99] The overly sensitive religious feeling was shading in some quarters into sentimentality and a squeamishness about human flesh and blood that was not too dissimilar from the old Monophysite heresy.[100]

The new art of photography was nearly as capable of reflecting religious presuppositions as a painting. Julia Mary Cameron was a mid-Victorian

THE AWAKENING CONSCIENCE,
BY WILLIAM HOLMAN HUNT.
Photograph © Tate Gallery, London, 1999.

disciple of John Keble who saw her art in the same way that Charlotte Yonge approached her novel writing, as a way to broadcast "Church principles." For her the photograph was "almost the embodiment of a prayer," and making pictures was a religious duty for her. The most common subjects in her pictures were representations of New Testament characters, particularly women.[101]

MUSIC

England did not have the classical musical heritage of some of the Continental countries. But the Wesleys, especially Charles, were poets and musicians. They disagreed with the common Calvinist conviction that only the

Psalms should be sung, and the religious revival was filled with the sound of hymns. From the Methodists, vigorous congregational singing spread to the Evangelicals and thence elsewhere. In the eighteenth century there was little congregational singing in the Church of England and not much more in most of the Dissenting congregations. For Churchmen, hymn singing was a mark of both Dissent and "enthusiasm," neither of which was reputable in the age. Samuel Johnson once remarked that he put a coin in the hand of a little girl "though I saw Hart's hymns in her hand." [102] This close friend of the Wesley brothers did his little act of charity in spite of the impediment of the hymnbook's presence. The changing concerns of the congregations had expression in the music, and one can follow in the lyrics the shifting emphases in public interests and anxieties. Evangelical hymns became popular even in High Church parishes. Tractarian poetry, Dissenting hymns like those of Watts, Wesleyan hymns, and Evangelical poetry such as Cowper's all became mixed together in various types of congregations so that there sometimes appeared to be little connection between the music and the doctrinal formulations it was supposed to reflect. Or perhaps it might be truer to say there was much more in common between the various expressions of Christian faith than the polemics of the period permitted one to see very easily. Still, as late as 1830, Coleridge was complaining there was insufficient congregational singing in Establishment worship, comparing the English unfavorably in this respect to the Germans, among whom "the hymns are known by heart by every peasant." [103]

More important than congregational singing was the increasing popularity of hymn singing in other venues. This reflected the real interests of the mass of people rather than the professional preoccupations of the liturgists. Dickens recalled being lulled to sleep, crying, as a servant girl hummed an evening hymn. [104] In a poetry-loving age, the public loved hymns even more, and the mass audience for hymnody was much larger than for verse, especially later in the century. The journalist W. T. Stead mentioned a string of cab drivers waiting for the next train at a railroad station in the north, sitting on a fence singing hymns. [105] Visiting from France, Hippolyte Taine observed two men in top hats singing hymns on a village green forty miles from London and was told it was common. [106] We cannot measure the effect of hymn singing on the people who sung or heard it, but it must have been enormous. Much later, the literary critic Edmund Gosse (b. 1849) recalled one of Toplady's hymns that he had learned as a child: "To this day I cannot repeat this hymn without a sense of poignant emotion." [107]

The religious revival also stimulated the taste for classical music based on biblical sources. Mendelssohn's genius found an especially warm welcome in England, by some accounts the warmest of the welcomes for Continental composers in the nineteenth century. He made ten trips to the island before his death at the age of thirty-eight, and his influence there was second only to that of Handel two generations earlier. His great triumph was the performance of his oratorio *Elijah* at Birmingham in 1846, one of the few oratorios of the period that is still performed.

SEPARATION FROM THE WORLD

But the effect of the evangelical cultural shift carried with it a countercurrent. For people steeped in the Bible, as the evangelicals were, there is no getting around the issue of the sin of worldliness and its opposite virtue, separation from the world. This comes up in different ways in both Testaments—the prohibition against the Israelites marrying into the surrounding pagan culture, for example, the New Testament call to "come out from among them and be separate" (2 Cor. 6:17), and numerous permutations on the same theme. Now, there are many interpretations of the meaning of these injunctions, and in our period as in other times there were many disagreements about them. Worldliness can be interpreted in a purely religious or inner sense, as a failing to remain faithful to God in the midst of an impious people, or at the other extreme can be thought to require an eremite existence physically separated from other people, or at least other people thought to be ungodly. The evangelicals differed among themselves about the precise meaning of the conception for them, but they generally were near the first of these positions. They had no use for the monastic tradition, and most of them were closely involved in the ordinary affairs of life as farmers, artisans, laborers, and politicians.

The term *Puritan* is often used to describe the evangelicals, and by it is meant (at least in one account) "a distrust both of open-minded speculation and sensuous pleasure."[108] That is not a bad description, but it is incomplete. It is truer to say that what the evangelicals opposed was a frivolous approach to life. That is one reason why they and such people as the satirical canon of St. Paul's, Sydney Smith, stared at each other across a gulf of incomprehension. Most of them lacked a light touch because they were so impressed by the *seriousness* of life. This has been well caught by the title of Ian Bradley's book *The Call to Seriousness*. These were not great jokers, although you would not know that by observing William Wilberforce. (One observer, however, attributes the evangelical preoccupation with seriousness to the influence of Wilberforce's *Practical View*.[109]) Nor were the towns they created temples of delight, according to some visitors: *triste,* warned one Frenchman, writing home—little to do that was not connected with religion.[110] Wesley gloried in the Methodist abstention from "fashionable diversions," light literature, alcoholic spirits, and frivolity and in their satisfaction with plain clothing, diligent behavior, and cleanliness.

W. J. Conybeare, in his famous anonymous article in the *Edinburgh Review,* caught the essence of that aspect of the issue: "The Evangelical party has been too much devoted to practical work to think much of Literature."[111] It was all right to enjoy literature, but its purpose had to be not enjoyment but profit through instruction. When Walter Scott died in 1832, the *Record* took the occasion to explain its main objection to the novelist's work. Acknowledging Scott's great popularity, the paper considered his body of work "in the highest degree injurious" because it was "calculated to lead away the mind from God, and cause men to set their affections upon the things of earth."[112] There was too much important work to be done to allow diversions or fripperies to tug at the imagination and waste the precious hours. For that reason, dances, theater, and races were without distinction all considered "scenes of dissipation."[113] Music too fell under the ban.[114] Even religious music was not spared when unbelievers were encouraged to sing it, as in the case of a performance of *The Messiah* at Exeter Hall. The affair for the Recordites was an "astounding impiety," largely because it was conducted as an "amusement."[115]

The *Christian Observer* published material with a point of view on the novel that was not very different from that of the *Record,* although the editorial policy of the journal was not necessarily the same. Scott was the target of an attack in 1817 in which the author opposed the reading of light literature on the grounds that it detracted from spiritual concerns. In this view, Scott had squandered his considerable gifts for serious philosophical work by pandering to the desire for novelty. If people were sufficiently mature, they could read such work without being misled and distracted from honorable pursuits, but they are not. This article lamented that Christians were descending from the higher standards of the preceding generation.[116]

Fiction was an example of the frivolity that the evangelicals found so objectionable, and it was not until the 1830s that the Religious Tract Society would incorporate the medium into their publications. Taking the lead from Bunyan, however, they admitted allegory. By midcentury the society was using fiction in its products, largely because they were finding that imaginative literature was useful in teaching moral precepts.[117] In a sense, the evangelical critics of fiction were giving the medium its due to a greater degree than were its devotees. For they recognized that one is changed inwardly when identifying and sympathizing with characters in a book and that this change may not be salutary. George Eliot, no philistine, made this point and was critical of Scott for creating characters that exaggerated the tendency. She thought that this powerful trait of the novel form had ruined Scott himself by encouraging him to act out his fantasies, living the life of the Scottish laird as he had portrayed it. When she was asked late in life what influence had first shaken her attachment to evangelical religion, she replied without hesitation, "Oh, Sir Walter Scott's."[118]

The evangelicals gave the theater even lower marks than the novel. Enamored of it before his conversion, as a preacher Whitefield did his best to close the playhouses down wherever he preached. One of the reasons for this was the hostility theaters showed toward religion, and toward Methodism in particular, going so far as to ridicule ministers by name.[119] When contemplating the almost solid evangelical denunciations of the theater in the first half of the nineteenth century, it should be considered that the theater was going through a very bad period. The educated public had largely abandoned it, and in order to draw crowds, the impresarios broadened and debased the performances. The new audiences were rowdy, often illiterate, and to appeal to them the staging was very long and the acting bathetic.[120] It was not only evangelicals who sniffed at theatrical performances.

In 1805, the *Christian Observer* devoted a long review to a thirty-eight-page sermon on lawful amusements by the Dissenting minister George Burder. Since only one of its pages was devoted to permissible pursuits, the reviewer said the sermon might better have been entitled "Unlawful Amusements." Yet the review essentially agreed with Burder's point of view, especially his argument against the legitimacy of attending the theater. Burder said that the players tended to be ungodly and the stories blasphemous or indecent—he even objected to the scenery. A contrary view appeared in the publication, but the *Observer*'s editor was more on Burder's side. Apparently the clinching argument for the editor was the typical evangelical position that there was serious work to be done and that time was fleeing: he who quietly directs a single sinner out of the delusion of his ways will accomplish more than the man who provides intellectual pleasure to ten thousand others.[121] In the next issue the magazine continued the subject, this time cautioning against pharasaism as well as libertinism. "Those who preach against amusements should be careful to shew . . . they are no enemies to cheerfulness and rational enjoyment."[122] Later on, the *Record* was even less favorable. Theaters, opined the editor in 1833, were "pest-houses of vice."[123] Wilberforce, who was as cheerful and generous a man as England could produce, had similar views. In a response to his sister, who evidently had asked his opinion on the subject, he wrote, "I think the tendency of the theatre most pernicious." He did not here give a reason for opposing the theater but said only that his sister would give a bad example to others if she indulged in this form of amusement.[124] To his adult son Samuel he advised that a young friend should resist his parents' urging that he go to plays and operas. "They are quite hotbeds of vice no one, I think, can deny." [125]

It usually remained only tacit, but the goal of the antiworldly emphasis sometimes seemed to be to separate the evangelicals not so much from worldly pursuits as from worldly people. Jabez Bunting, who was to the Wesleyan Methodists of the early nineteenth century almost as authoritative as John Wesley had been in the preceding period, warned one of them away from participation in a fraternal group called the Odd Fellows. Even if they were not a secret cabal and therefore unlawful, Bunting explained, it was still "*highly* improper and unscriptural that religious persons should join themselves with carnal and careless persons in such associations." He cited the usual New Testament passage for this assertion, 2 Cor. 6:7, which was the command to "come out from among them and be separate." [126] The *Record* disagreed strongly with Evangelical politicians who fraternized with political enemies, a practice that "is morally impossible, and when done involves deep guilt." [127] When the paper opposed the use of church buildings in the afternoon or evening for professional concerts, it was at least partly because the musicians might not be believers. [128] Separation in thinking joined with separation from other people, and still the evangelicals considered it their duty to influence the society, which they in fact accomplished. Gladstone noted that the rigid codes of behavior, which he termed "superficial," made it difficult for the evangelicals to play their proper role in public life. Yet he thought the Evangelical clergy somehow made a difference in the lives of their fellows and contributed to the general improvement in clerical standards that took place early in the century. They did this by means of their much higher personal standards, he concluded, which served as both a rebuke and an example for the laxity by which they were surrounded. [129] The evangelicals' reading habits and their tastes gradually diverged from those of their neighbors, and thus mutual comprehension became more difficult. [130] When Granville Sharp, the Clapham self-taught Greek and Hebrew scholar, warned Charles James Fox that Napoleon was a manifestation of the little horn foretold in the Apocalypse, the incredulous politician exclaimed, "The little horn Mr. Sharp, the little horn? And what in the name of thunder is the little horn?" [131]

If the mind and heart of the English people changed as much as the forgoing material leads one to believe, there must have been some corresponding change in their behavior. How true that was is the next thing we shall have to consider.

XI

The Conversion
of English Morality
and Mode of Life

CHANGING MORALITY IN ENGLISH CULTURE

As we saw in an earlier chapter, the moral condition of both upper and lower classes in eighteenth-century England was bad enough to alarm many thoughtful observers. In the early years of the new century, it seemed in some quarters as if little had been accomplished in the task of improving the moral sensibilities of the country. In 1804, the Society for the Suppression of Vice reported the widespread distribution of pornographic materials. Numerous salesmen, and women as well, hawked them on the streets and even entered schools for the purpose. "Who will presume to compute the debaucheries, the adulteries, the domestic wretchedness, &c. involved in the consequences of so insidious and systematic an attack on the morals of the community?" the society wanted to know.[1] At almost the same moment, Robert Southey was objecting to the *Essay on Population* (1798) on the grounds that Malthus had assumed that sexual lust represented a human need that had to be assuaged, in the way that hunger was, and thus made impossible the "moral restraint and the practical virtue of chastity."[2] Such criticisms were becoming more common now, and in his new edition Malthus found it prudent to acknowledge that "moral restraint" could be brought to bear when sexual temptation loomed.[3] As late as 1817, much of the countryside had shown no improvement, and the Newcastle Religious Tract Society lamented the masses "in the neighbouring collieries yet enwrapt in moral darkness, as profound and opake [*sic*], as if they had been reared in a heathen or pagan country." Yet by the early part of the twentieth century, the situation had been more or less completely reversed, and a clergyman reported that the pitman, "as a rule, is a quiet living, religious, and godly man, who enters with the greatest heartiness into all exercises of the communion, which is generally one of the many Methodist bodies."[4] Much of the change occurred in the 1830s and 1840s, and it was accompanied and abetted by the growth of the teetotal movement, which moderated greatly the scourge of drunkenness.[5] By then it was apparent to many that materialist assumptions about the amelioration of social conditions could not avail. The conviction grew that the spiritual and material both had to be considered, and James Kay-Shuttleworth entitled his treatise on the subject *The Moral and Physical Condition of the Working Classes* (1832).

MORALITY AND CLASS

Francis Place recalled his lower class beginnings and in particular the easy availability when he was in his early teens of both sexual books and sexual conversation, which were "much more within the reach of boys and girls than they are now."[6] The streets of London in the 1770s and 1780s were very different than in his old age:

> The manners of the heads of families were coarse and vulgar and frequently indecent to an extent scarcely to be credited[;] their language was inaccurate and mean, their habits in respect to cleanliness very inferior to what they are now, and their sense of delicacy remarkably gross, as a reference to the songs sung in their domestic parties will shew. Their children were permitted to run about their filthy streets, to hear all sorts of bad language and to mix with whomsoever they pleased. Pilfering and Thieving especiall[y] were not then as now almost wholly confined to the very lowest of the people, but were practiced by tradesmens sons, by youths and young men who would now no more commit such act than would the sons of well bred gentlemen. . . .
>
> Want of chastity in girls was common. The songs which were ordinarily sung by their relatives and by young men and women and the lewd plays and interludes they occasionally saw were all calculated to produce mischief in this direction.[7]

"In nothing has the change for the better been greater than in the moral conduct . . . amongst this [lower] class of persons."[8] Place testified to this effect before the House of Commons and put before it evidence for the prevalence of pornography during his boyhood.[9] That such an assessment should come from a leader of the radical atheist faction is suggestive of what the society was becoming.

Some have taken studies based on parish registers as indications that sexual licentiousness was not affected by the religious revival, but closer attention to the studies themselves suggests that such a conclusion is unwarranted. In all of England, only ninety-eight parish registers were deemed complete enough to draw conclusions from. The principal investigator of the registers thinks it a "very shaky" assumption that one can draw conclusions about the prevalence of sexual activity outside of marriage from the il-legitimacy figures.[10] Much of the difficulty lies in the fact that definitions change over time, so that we cannot even use a definition of marriage and assume it always held true. A birth could be held as legitimate at one time and place and illegitimate at another. What appears at first to be hard infor-mation dissolves into subjectivity.[11] Even at that, the parish registers (which ended in 1831, to be replaced by a central government registration system) show the rate of illegitimacy peaking around the end of the eighteenth cen-tury. When the civil registration figures begin, it is at a noticeably higher level, but this is obviously based on a difference in the reporting systems.[12]

Families living on the edge economically had a special stake in the moral condition of husbands, whose status as providers was dependent upon a reasonable degree of regularity. Drunkenness and gambling could turn a marginal existence into absolute penury, and women were known to weep for joy at the conversion of their husbands in the local chapel, for it afforded some hope that the family provider would be able to provide. The oft-told and possibly apocryphal story of the recent convert in a Durham mining village illustrates what happened untold times: the miner, being questioned by his chums, asked them if they remembered what his home was like a few months ago compared with now. If Jesus could turn beer into clothing for his children and furniture for his house, why should he not be able to turn water into wine? These villages were sometimes divided into two separate cultures, the pub culture and the chapel culture. The occasional secularist teetotal would belong nowhere.[13]

For those living in the fifty years before Victoria came to the throne, to be able to exit from a life of drunkenness and debauchery was a kind of lib-eration. The miner did not consider himself oppressed by the ethos of the chapel but rather delivered from the destruction toward which he was head-ing, along with his family. The miner's wife (or the fisherman's or the weav-er's) had bread and meat on the table after payday, and his children had shoes on their feet. A leading Congregationalist minister in Manchester declared in 1843 that commerce "is constantly teaching men that thought and labour, during the years immediately before them, present the only path to repose and enjoyment during the years in the distance. Men are thus taught, that in relation to the affairs of the world, no less than to the affairs of religion, the man who would be successful 'must take up his cross and deny himself.'"[14] Yet that did not quite get it right. It was not "commerce" that did the teaching so much as the minister and his colleagues.

One analyst has called the nineteenth-century version of respectability a democratization of the concept. Prior to that, to be "respectable" re-quired holding title to a certain amount of property. By the new century, respectability was merited by persons of any degree of wealth who had the requisite character to be so regarded.[15] That is very close to the view of those who were saying that true respectability comes from virtue and not position or wealth. When Hannah More urged the upper classes to reform their morals, she meant the cultivation of "those secret habits of self-control, those interior and unobtrusive virtues."[16] Whatever use these virtues are in producing true respectability, they are helpless in attaining the version of respectability lampooned by Lytton Strachey and similar critics, which is to say a merely outward conformity to the prevailing practice. By the time Hannah More wrote those words, a similar vision of what was respectable had begun filtering down to the lower classes, at least in principle, whatever the failures of execution. Francis Place reported that his father (a publican who appears in his son's account as little more than a drunken, brutal lout) "intended that his children, should be honest, sober, industrious and in every sense of the word respectable."[17] It was only well into the Victorian period that the exaggerated public horror at sensuality, and the hypocrisy that turned respectability into a fetish, began having widespread basis in fact.[18]

An American evangelical who studied in Cambridge in the 1840s found the place of mixed report in the moral sphere, having a laxity in sexual matters compared to his home college but being of very high standards in other respects. "A young man who enters there and is disposed to find a truly 'good set' can find one, or indeed have his choice among several sets of really virtuous and religious men." He found the right sort of high moral principle among a small number of students at the university, whom he identified as pupils of Arnold from Rugby, Evangelicals, Dissenters, followers of F. D. Maurice, and High Churchmen.[19]

The religious revival in the Church of England, and to a large extent in Dissent, was primarily a middle-class event. The organizational skills to build the great voluntary societies, the increasing fortunes that men were willing to put to use for the purpose, the widespread literacy that enabled them to learn the principles of their faith and to teach them to others, all combined to make the middle class the great engine of the religious revival. Many of the main features of the Victorian social scene were products of middle-class religious practices. It was evangelical family life, with its family devotions, its father at home and its well-behaved children, its attendance at Sunday worship, its sense of responsibility for its own members and its neighbors, its participation in the societies intended to do good, that became middle-class Victorian family life.

The upper classes were not immune from the religious revival. Whitefield had worked with the Countess of Huntingdon for the conversion of her noble friends, and the effort had not been entirely fruitless. Hannah

More had preached that the reformation of English morals was dependent upon the high-born to show the example to the rest of society: the message was in her title, *Thoughts on the Importance of the Manners of the Great to General Society*. "Reformation must begin with the GREAT, or it will never be effectual. *Their* example is the fountain whence the vulgar draw their habits, actions, and characters."[20] Wilberforce's title showed he had a similar idea: *A Practical View of the Prevailing Religious System of Professed Christians in the Higher and Middle Classes in this Country Contrasted with Real Christianity*. And so also his friend Thomas Gisborne's title *An Enquiry into the Duties of Men in the Higher and Middle Classes of Society* (1794).

By the time Hippolyte Taine visited England after midcentury, he discovered not only that novels were free of explicit sexual material but that it was almost impossible to induce Englishmen to speak of their "illicit *amours;* for many of them this is a closed book the mere mention of which is shocking."[21] He also noted that drunkenness among the upper classes was rare, a very different condition than had obtained a half century earlier.[22] Taine was speaking of the upper classes, but throughout the society the same was true wherever the evangelical ethos had advanced. There seemed to be few Englishmen who believed that the health of the society could be preserved in the absence of personal moral rectitude by the bulk of the population.

Some of the noble families affected by the religious revival were later on ignorant of the real roots of their family ethos. Lord Percy, around the turn of the twentieth century, rebuked a historian for mistaking his family background. He asserted that his family belonged more to the 1870s than the 1890s, inasmuch as it was characterized by hard work, seriousness of purpose, and strong parental discipline. But he recoiled at the suggestion that evangelicalism had anything to do with these characteristics. He said they were rather a product of an inherited code of conduct.[23] But of what origin was the code? And inherited from whom? Through what means? Lord Percy evidently did not know, nor did he think to ask. If his family had exhibited the traits of the 1770s rather than the 1870s, it would likely have had little to do with hard work or seriousness of purpose.

MORALITY AND RELIGION

The late-Victorian biographer John Morley disliked the evangelicals intensely, complaining about "this dull and cramped" religion. But he credited them with "impressing a kind of moral organization on the mass of barbarism which surged chaotically into the factory towns."[24] Even this was not exactly so, since it suggested, as skeptics of the late nineteenth century were wont to do, that this result was achieved by compulsion. Halévy was much closer to the truth in speaking of the evangelicals' moral *influence.* They opposed cruelty to animals on religious grounds, and it fell into desuetude before becoming illegal. In such ways, said Halévy, evangelical religion became the "moral cement of English society."[25] This was a thesis far more defensible than the speculation for which he became famous (and notorious)—the cause-and-effect relationship between Methodism and the lack of revolution in England.

The moral advance of the individual was perhaps most strongly encouraged among the Methodists because of the Wesleyan doctrine of perfectionism. The Wesleys did not deny the continuation of temptation and the giving in to it, but they were much more hopeful of the soul's progress toward something approaching perfection—and in this life. People thus persuaded are less likely to accept the open manifestation of immoral behavior, either their own or their neighbors'. Studies of local Methodist societies reveal social discipline for a host of transgressions, including sexual sins, alcoholic intemperance, failing to keep appointments, and reneging on financial obligations. An engraver noted in the 1820s that in his district (Tyneside) the Methodists "greatly civilized a numerous host of semi-barbarians, the pitmen and others employed in the pit-works. These seemed like Cherokees and Mohawks, but they were more wicked."[26]

Other denominations also opposed immorality, even if not always with the same rigor.[27] Indeed, so ingrained were moral principles in the evangelical ethos that gradually pervaded most of the Protestant groups that Max Weber concluded that the old saw "Honesty is the best policy" was at its heart Protestant in origin and in propagation.[28] The intense self-examination advocated and practiced by the evangelicals, a reprise of the Puritan practice, reinforced the external scrutiny that was a natural consequence of the shared community existence. People keeping watch over their souls in the recommended way are less likely to commit overt transgressions and so offend the public sensibility. Tom Mozley, Newman's brother-in-law, marveled at the honesty of the Wilberforce brothers when they arrived at Oxford, so odd in an environment dominated by the practiced liars from the public schools.[29]

As moral issues came increasingly to the forefront of public attention, fueled by the religious revival, they paradoxically provided an argument for the defenders of atheism. The scientific arguments against religion had more or less dimmed since the heyday of the Enlightenment thinkers (to be revived in the 1860s after Darwin published his *Origin of Species*) and were replaced by the moral argument that became common for much of the nineteenth century. Already in 1797, Southey noted in a letter that the atheists and skeptics he was meeting were not the vulgar egocentrics one might expect but were led to their conviction by a sense of "the existence of moral and physical evil," which they could not reconcile with the existence of a benevolent and powerful deity.[30]

MORALITY AND RESPECTABILITY

Lytton Strachey's smirking remark that Thomas Arnold had taught the public schools the virtues of respectability impressed the Edwardian generation as having struck just the right note. It served the Stracheys of England well to conflate morality with respectability because such a strategy denigrated both; their battle was against both the ordinary virtues and the bourgeois ("respectable") citizens who still valued them. Many historians have written from such a perspective, but not all. George Kitson Clark put it well:

> It is very unfortunate that the whole subject of Victorian respectability, particularly of Victorian prudery, has been considered more as the subject of satire, or humour, or indignation, rather than as a matter for serious historical analysis. . . . [It] is essentially part of the history of the battle for refinement and civilization, and above all the better protection of women, against the promiscuity, animalism, brutality and grossness which had been common even in the eighteenth century.[31]

The moral strictures of serious people increasingly were evangelical ones, and they went far beyond the keeping of the Commandments. Since morality was taken to be a function of religious commitment, it demanded much higher standards than merely refraining from obvious sins. Also required was the cultivation of a spirit of service and selflessness. Gladstone found such virtue when he met the woman he would later marry. Elated, he confided to his diary: "In her . . . I saw what I desired, as I think distinctly developed: the admiration of sacrifice made for great object—and a gentle not unwomanly contempt for the luxurious pleasures of the world."[32]

THE MORALITY OF ART

Inasmuch as morality had come to be for many people one of the main preoccupations of the period, it was natural that they should have become concerned about the means by which moral teachings were conveyed. Among the reasons that evangelicals were suspicious of the novel was the philosophy they saw lurking beneath the agreeable melange of characters and scenes. They were later to be condemned for excessive sentimentality, but it was sentimentality that drew their ire when they judged the novels of the late eighteenth century. This was particularly true when the Rousseau-ean mode of writing became popular, accompanied by tears but noticeably deficient in the requirement to do one's duty. Hannah More was especially critical of characters who seemed to be kind and generous but who typically ignored "obvious and commanded duties." Everything was based on feeling, and law and religion for Rousseau and his imitators were "unjust restraints."[33] She was not alone in this. What seemed like a blatant rejection of culture in the evangelicals was often nothing more than an aversion for what they took to be advocacy for the spread of antinomianism. This was not an abhorrence of the thought that people might be enjoying themselves, as critics later alleged, but a recognition that the powerful emotional response to artistic works can induce the unwary into destructive behavior, including self-destructive behavior.

The minor novelists of the early nineteenth century are seldom thought of today, except by literary scholars, let alone read, but in their own day enjoyed great popularity. Most of them had departed from the novelistic mode of the previous century, the mere time killer, written for and read in the boudoir. Many of their works were religious in nature and were far more serious than the cheap thrillers or erotic novels. One analyst says of these writers that they were serious thinkers who presented serious ideas to their readers. "Their work had an ethical backbone. . . . They wrote not to titillate milady's fancy in her idleness, but to advocate principles upon which men should act."[34] The *ethical* part of that description is the operative one, describing in the field of art what Peter Gaskell argued in the social policy sphere when he declared it useless to teach the child the usual academic disciplines without teaching the moral duties that would determine the shape of its future.[35] When a novelist lacked the moral impulse, he was likely to be the target of serious criticism. Even Scott, who towered above every novelist of his generation, did not escape such critics. As we have seen, both F. D. Maurice and Carlyle protested that beyond the subtleties of plot and character there was very little to Scott's novels. These critics wanted moral lessons to go along with the surface interest of the stories.

As with the novel, so with other forms of artistic expression. Near the end of his autobiography, the painter William Holman Hunt declared that the purpose of art is "to lead man to distinguish between that which being clean in spirit, is productive of virtue, and that which is flaunting and meretricious and productive of ruin to a Nation."[36] Hunt believed that Whistler's personal immoralities necessarily infected his art with superficiality, "the kind which amuses for the moment, like a conjurer's trick confusing common sense." [37] But this was the philosophy of Hunt's youth, shared by that generation, and by expressing it at the end of the Victorian period he spoke in a way that appeared antediluvian.

To say that art should show moral sensibilities is not to say that it must inculcate shallow moralisms. George Eliot explained why moralistic art is enervating rather than efficacious by inviting attention to the reaction of children being told a tale. As long as you stick to the narrative you have their rapt attention, but when you begin to draw moral conclusions you lose them. This, she said, is what the moralizing novelist does.[38] Holman Hunt would have agreed entirely because, while insisting on the moral basis of art, he hated the superficiality that detracted from the artistic integrity of the work. The lesson without the depth that signified truth was "maudlin." In the same passage, he recounts an early conversation with Millais in which he told of his reaction to a book by an anonymous author (actually Ruskin's *Modern Painters*): "You feel the men [of the Venetian school] who did them had been appointed by God, like old prophets, to bear a sacred message, and they delivered themselves like Elijah of old." [39]

MORALITY AFTER RELIGION

The end of our period saw the continuation of a phenomenon that had always been present to some degree—the departure of religious believers to some form of unbelief. But now the fruit of religious faith, in some astonishing way, seemed to persist after the root had withered. The religious revival had ushered in a renewed conviction of the centrality of morality for living a good life, and logically those who came to reject the religion should also have rejected the ethic that was dependent upon it. But that seldom happened. As ripples in a pond keep emanating after the stone that launched them has disappeared, so the moral elements of the faith persisted. They receded from their source and gradually lost their force, but they impress the observer nevertheless with the fact that the pond was not still. By the second generation after Clapham, the stone had long disappeared for some of those families, but the ripples remained. Leslie Stephen rejected the faith of his fathers but retained their sense of moral purpose and devotion to duty.[40] The Methodist William Lovett came to reject his religious convictions and involved himself in radical politics, but he continued to conduct himself morally like a Methodist.[41] This phenomenon is part of what one scholar calls the "evangelical inheritance," [42] and it seemed to be fastened on the heirs in much the same way as an actual legacy—whether the recipient wanted it or not. That was true, notoriously, of George Eliot. As one observer remarks from a study of her letters, "Her rejection of Christian religious doctrine was undertaken in a militantly religious spirit, as a quest for truths worthy of God."[43] In attacking evangelicalism, she argued that if some benevolent act is done because someone else desires it, "the deed ceases to be one of benevolence, and becomes one of deference, of obedience, of self-interest, or vanity."[44] In other words, conventional morality with its common basis in religious belief is less than worthy because it is not moral enough, being undertaken for egocentric reasons. Hers is a higher morality, being selfless. She may not have understood how much of her moral system was dependent upon the doctrines she had rejected.

The increasing ubiquity of these moral values after the late eighteenth century is surprising to people who construe "Victorian" morality too narrowly, both chronologically and ideologically. The modern editor of Francis Place's autobiography was startled to discover that "this working-class radical possessed and extolled some of the Victorian virtues we have come to scorn or to patronize."[45] John Stuart Mill revealed that in his radical coterie he was almost alone in not having discarded religious belief because only he had never had it, so widespread had it become by the middle third of the nineteenth century.[46]

THE LIFE OF THE NEW FAMILY

The evangelical family in the nineteenth century has had a bad press, partly because many of the children who found it most disagreeable grew up and wrote books describing how miserable they had been. But there may have been many happy families for each dissatisfied memoirist. Leslie Stephen turned against the faith of Clapham when he was at Cambridge, but it was not because of the woes of his childhood. Sir James Stephen had headed a household marked by moderation and kindliness. Punctilious in moral duties and abstemious in personal habits, he avoided any hint of priggishness or spiritual pride in rearing his children.[47] The High Churchman G. W. E. Russell described an Evangelical upbringing in the midst of "an abiding sense of religious responsibility, a self-sacrificing energy in works of mercy, an evangelistic zeal, an aloofness from the world, and a level of saintliness in daily life, such as I do not expect again to see realized on earth."[48] Not every portion of that description will strike the typical modern reader as happy, but they evidently all were for Russell. The childhood recollections from Clapham that we possess almost uniformly reflect memories of great joy, despite the usual heartaches in the presence of illness and death.

From the late eighteenth century, the evangelicals, particularly at first the Methodists, emphasized domesticity, the home as a "place apart," with women elevated to a special status in the culture of the household. John Wesley (despite the disorders of his own marriage) compared the ideal religious community to a family, and the spinster Hannah More taught poor women how to care for their husbands and children. For many of the Methodists, in particular, the family occupied the position expressed in the title of a modern book—a "haven in a heartless world." [49] We have evidence of the much greater comfort and health in poor villages where the chapel was a well-established part of the community than in others where it was absent. Sometimes a particularly clean and prosperous village would be found full of children with Old Testament names, abounding with Abrahams, Sarahs, Isaiahs, and so forth. [50]

Recent studies suggest that the stereotype of the bored middle-class Victorian family, where children were saddled with a dreadful Sunday on which there was nothing interesting to do, was a concoction of a later period. Many of these houses were full of music and singing, as well as domestic arts like embroidery, and charitable visiting and caring service took up a good deal of time for many families. [51] Many evenings were taken up by family readings, often of novels. The much derided bowdlerism and the sexual reticence of novels in general were due to the fact that the entire family practiced reading them aloud together. What we think of now as adult literature was there to be enjoyed by children. In fact, some critics believe that many Victorian novels have features that can be understood only on the presumption that the novels were written to be read aloud. [52]

The Clapham example of family worship spread everywhere in the kingdom among middle- and upper class evangelicals and set the tone for much of the nation's culture. Taine, who did not care for this practice, was nevertheless impressed by its cultural power, which he believed enabled the father of the family to exercise "moral leadership." [53]

AN ARMY OF UNOFFICIAL SOCIAL WORKERS

John Morley noted that the 1830s were marked by "a great wave of humanity, of benevolence, of desire for improvement—a great wave of social sentiment, in short—[that] poured itself among all who had the faculty of large and disinterested thinking." Morley cited a number of people of very different convictions who were part of this movement, including Pusey and Newman, Thomas Arnold, F. D. Maurice, and Richard Cobden, and, on the far end of the spectrum, John Stuart Mill. The various schools all wanted the same thing, according to Morley, and that was "social renovation."[54] A freethinker, Morley could not bring himself to draw the logical conclusion from the insight—*the religious revival had so permeated the core of English thinking that those from differing parts of it, and even those completely outside its sphere, had adopted its social ethic.*

But we must not allow the big names to distract us from the more important underlying truth that a veritable army was marching through England doing good, or at least trying to do good. The church visitors were the unofficial and unpaid social workers of the nation. Many of the Evangelical clergymen had what amounted to relief agencies in the parishes, with (mainly) women taking turns visiting the sick and needy. The big national societies had local chapters making a difference in the condition of neighborhoods, towns, and hamlets. Food, clothing, and medical care, training for productive work, rescue from prostitution, and education in the ragged schools were among the wares carried in the volunteer's kit. As in the case of the national societies, most of this activity was conducted by evangelicals, but their example was taken up by others as well. Even after the young men at Clapham married and began raising families in the late 1790s, they continued to give away large sums of money for these purposes. Evangelicals of all economic classes emphasized the obligation to provide generously for the needy, and when the Tractarian movement metamorphosed into Ritualism, it took root mainly in poor parishes desperate for material as well as spiritual help. One angry woman, writing to the American Unitarian leader William Ellery Channing, complained that Hannah More, by writing *Cœlebs in Search of a Wife*, had made devoting two evenings a week to visit the poor "a fashion and a rage." *Cœlebs* was published in 1809, and the first ladies' auxiliary of the British and Foreign Bible Society appeared two years later, swelling the ranks of the visitors.[55] This activity lasted decades and took innumerable forms. The Manchester Town Mission had fifty-two full-time workers visiting houses, urging attendance at public worship, and telling parents of the importance of securing an education for their children. Much of their operating funds came from voluntary donations from working-class districts.[56] Ellen Ranyard, an Evangelical born in 1810, trained a corps of women to help poor women manage their household, teaching them to cook, clean, and do needlework. She enrolled a group of poor women to train as itinerant nurses and so increase the effectiveness of the other women making their rounds. She called these women "Bible nurses." Workers like Mrs. Ranyard became an example to others, and similar efforts were made by Quakers, Jews, Catholics, and others.[57]

Even animals benefited from all this activism. The evangelical campaign against blood sports led to the founding in 1824 of the Royal Society for the

Prevention of Cruelty to Animals by Arthur Broome, an Evangelical clergy-man, and the inaugural meeting had Thomas Fowell Buxton in the chair, with William Wilberforce present. Queen Victoria gave her patronage to the organization in 1840.

THE SPREAD OF THE RELIGIOUS STYLE

It has been said that in the early nineteenth century, Methodism was "in the air."[58] That is a true statement if Methodism is taken to include (as it often was in the period) the Evangelicalism of the Establishment. It was meant in the highbrow sense that the Romantic poets, Christian and otherwise, combined the empiricism of Locke and his followers with the spiritual applications emphasized by Wesley. But the same was also true of almost every other sphere of English life, humble as well as exalted, and this revolutionary fact is the substance of what we have to consider here.

However much we may wish to avoid inchoate words like *style* in favor of solid and verifiable statements, it is not always wise to try to do so. We observe that patterns of behavior are different: family life, sexual life, crime, manners, religious observances, the arts, and attitudes toward drunkenness all change. We observe further that these changes appear to be not fortuitous but connected; therefore, especially in the absence of the statistical evidence that would only later be collected by governments and scholars, it seems meaningful to speak of the style of the society. Mark Pattison, the rector of Lincoln College, who lived through the tumultuous 1830s and 1840s at Oxford, a man of surpassing bitterness, wrote in his old age that the evangelical movement (which he hated) had penetrated far beyond the domain of the Methodists and Evangelicals that had been its original home. He thought that it had profoundly affected both the ideas and the practices of the nation.[59]

Nearly every local study of Methodism shows the pattern of increasing acceptance at the lower levels of society. In the mining communities of Cornwall, for example, the Methodists went from being outcasts in a lawless society (Wesley visited in 1743 and 1766 and was disgusted by the crudity of the population) to being leaders of the temperance and teetotal movements. There was plenty of conflict along the way, and contests between revelers and psalm singers, but by 1840 the Wesleyan minister was leading services on the fairground.[60] An account from a Cornish mining village in the 1840s showed some of the "enthusiasm" so hated by the previous century, but it also makes us wonder about the alleged gloominess of the evangelicals: "They had given up the public-house—they had now something better to cheer them than dreams of smuggled spirits—they felt no need and had no thought of theatre or dancing room. All the relief, the refreshment, the congenial excitement of their underground life they found in the preaching house or in the classroom. There they let themselves go; they shouted, they wept, they groaned, they not seldom laughed aloud, with a laugh of intense excitement, a wonderful laugh."[61] In the north of England (Lincoln County), the wildness of the county fairs was considerably tamed after midcentury where the Methodists were strong. The scholar who reports this finds it "remarkable" that the "rapid transformation in the behavior" of the fairgoers extended to those without any active religious participation.[62] Toward the end of the century, only about one-sixth of the population living in the Deerness Valley in central Durham were members of either the Wesleyan or the Primitive Methodists, yet because their general influence extended far beyond formal membership, it was generally accepted that about 40 percent of the people were Methodists.[63] In a Yorkshire fishing village a struggle between the two cultures—here the scholar calls them the "popular" and the "sacred"—took place, with the latter winning out in the sense of defining the quality of life followed by the village. But here, too, there was nothing like a clear-cut victory, with the eradication of one side; rather the tension more or less remained, with "cross-fertilisation" preventing a final demarcation or showdown.[64]

Few confrontations symbolized the two points of view better than that between the church or chapel and the public house. They had long coexisted more or less peacefully, with the vestry meeting and the Sunday school sometimes being held in the pub. Teetotalers were eccentrics and easily ignored before the 1830s. But with the increasing seriousness of people affected by the religious revival, the devastation of habitual drunkenness became less acceptable. Temperance associations spread far and wide and eventually paved the way for a movement in favor of complete abstinence from alcoholic beverages. There ensued a struggle for predominance, with the pub appealing to customers with some of the trappings of the religious societies—organs, hymn singing and nonalcoholic drinks—and the temperance societies hiring professional entertainers.[65] The alcoholic temperance movement, which turned into an abstinence movement, was another evangelical effort to improve the society. One result of this was the replacement of many public houses with coffeehouses featuring serious reading material and discussion as well as refreshments. By the 1840s, there were almost two thousand such coffeehouses in London alone. One of the most successful of them subscribed to fifty-six newspapers (London, country, and foreign), twenty-four monthly magazines, four quarterlies, and eleven weeklies.[66]

If the religious revival turned ordinary people toward what seemed to be an older, or traditional notion of moral behavior, it also affected the radicals who wished to overturn some of the basic institutions of the society. The Chartist leaders included among their number preachers and legions of Bible readers, and Chartist chapels dotted the English countryside during the height of the movement. Tocqueville became acquainted with many of the radical leaders and noted how different they were from their French counterparts—much more respectful of property and of religion as well, including a great number of what he called "enthusiastic sectarians," which is to say evangelical Dissenters.[67] The radical writer Harriet Martineau was more affected by the religious revival than she ever acknowledged. Her modern biographer believes that she did not realize how indebted her thinking was to the religious doctrines that she consciously rejected. Her intense interest in the Bible as a child developed into theological pursuits, and although they did not persist, the residue of the beliefs never left her, and her criticisms of the Church of England seem little different from the standard Dissenting line.[68] An old history of socialism says that in order to understand the radical William Godwin (d. 1836), "It must always be borne in mind that he was essentially a Calvinist preacher. His materialism is inverted Calvinist theology."[69] That is to say, the radical content was transmitted with the moral intensity of the evangelical environment. Robert Taylor, a notorious former clergyman, delivered spellbinding radical sermons at the Blackfriars Rotunda in London, a center of militant causes. Professing himself to be an unbeliever, he preached his gospel with all the zest and emotional power of the most fervid evangelical preacher in the kingdom. He was not alone.[70]

The rhetorical influence was so pervasive it is impossible to separate it absolutely from the content. As G. M. Young put it,

> If we consider the effect, beginning in childhood, of all the preachers on all the congregations, of men loud or unctuous, authoritative or persuasive, speaking out of a body of acknowledged truth to the respectful audience below them we shall see why the homiletic cadence, more briefly Cant, is so persistent in Victorian oratory and literature. It sufficed to persuade . . . the upper middle classes that Emerson was a philosopher. Mr. Gladstone formed his style by reading sermons aloud and his diaries are full of self-delivered homilies. Old Sir Robert Peel trained his son to repeat every Sunday the discourse he had just heard. . . . The sermon was the standard vehicle of serious truth, and to the expositions and injunctions of their writers and statesmen the Victorian public brought the same hopeful determination to be instructed,

and to be elevated, which held them attentive to the pleadings, the denunciations and the commonplaces of their preachers.[71]

Even James Mills's single-minded training of his son in the utilitarian model, some believe, was a copy of what the evangelicals were doing in the tenets of their beliefs.[72]

Although we can follow the influences that spread religious faith in the period, we cannot follow them exhaustively. We know about church and chapel services, itinerant preachers, missionary societies, Bible readings, and tract distribution, but we cannot know much below the surface, where myriad personal contacts spread the revival from person to person and from town to town. This was true on every level. All evangelical groups advocated personal "witnessing," which is to say, preaching conversationally to one's friends and acquaintances. This was true in the coal mine and on the fishing vessel, but it was true at the highest levels as well. Wilberforce used to tell of his ploys to turn the dinner conversation to religion so that he could explain the gospel to friends and political associates. Personal influence counted for much with all the religious groups. Newman explained in his memoirs what was true almost everywhere:

> As is the custom of a University, I had lived with . . . the junior fellows of my College, without form or distance, on a footing of equality. Thus it was through friends, younger, for the most part, than myself, that my principles were spreading. They heard what I said in conversation, and told it to others. Under-graduates in due time took their degree, and became private tutors themselves. In their new status, they in turn preached the opinions, with which they had already become acquainted. Others went down to the country, and became curates of parishes. Then they had down from London parcels of the Tracts, and other publications. They placed them in the shops of local booksellers, got them into newspapers, introduced them to clerical meetings, and converted more or less their Rectors and their brother curates. Thus the Movement, viewed with relation to myself, was but a floating opinion; it was not a power.[73]

W. C. Lake, who became dean of Durham, remembered similarly the influence in the late 1830s at Oxford of W. G. Ward, who preceded Newman to Rome. Ward's conversations "left their traces upon many of us for life."[74] Ward himself was strongly influenced as a child by an evangelical governess, whose piety so affected him that his mother used to say that he was in love with her.[75] This was a common pattern; we have seen that Dickens as a child was crooned to sleep by a hymn-singing evangelical servant, and Ashley always attributed his accession to Christian faith as a boy to his pious governess.

THE LANGUAGE OF BELIEF

During the first quarter of the nineteenth century, the ordinary language of the English increasingly took on a biblical sound. This was a natural result of their familiarity with the Book of Common Prayer and the popularity of sermons, sermon books, Bible reading, hymn singing, Sunday schools, religious publications, and every other manifestation of the religious revival. When Lord Ashley wanted to show his determination to the House of Commons on a piece of legislation he considered a matter of simple justice, he said that if he should be silent, "the very stones would immediately cry out."[76] It is likely that everyone in the House knew he was quoting from the New Testament. That is an unnatural tone to most people in a later generation, sounding falsely pious and full of cant, but the biblical sound of the language became natural to those who used it and then to those who heard it. It even became natural to those who meant something entirely different by it or almost nothing at all. Radicals of various kinds, including those without any interest in religion, often used the same kind of words. Writing to her recently bereaved sister-in-law, a young woman includes this pious hope: "May He whose hand is the only sure guidance we have in this vale of tears, be a lamp to your feet and a light to your path: and may He guide your feet into the way of Peace." Not a Claphamite, not a Methodist, nor a parishioner of Keble, but Harriet Martineau![77] Engels, venting his spleen at the English middle classes, whom he accuses of grinding the workers into the earth, calls them "pharisees."[78] Carlyle, referring to the coming impoverishment of St. Edmundsbury Monastery, writes that "the Convent will be as one of Pharaoh's lean kine."[79] Mill exclaims to Carlyle over an article the Scot had written, "It is a glorious piece of work, and will be a blessed gospel to many if they read it and lay it to heart."[80] A working man cries out in protest at an address by a High Churchman: "Atheist as I am, no man shall stand between my soul and my God!"[81]

It is the particular nature of unbelief in an age of belief that it takes on the coloration of its believing adversaries. Leslie Stephen's modern biographer notes that this unbeliever seemed to have "a double portion of the Clapham spirit" of his grandfather. He had the sense of belonging to a group apart, and his campaign for the northern side of the American Civil War took on aspects of the Clapham war on slavery.[82] The atheists of the nineteenth century sound nothing like Voltaire or the early English deists but not altogether dissimilar from their Methodist neighbors.[83] Numerous secular prophets of the late eighteenth and early nineteenth centuries adopted the language and beliefs of millennial eschatology and adapted them to their own rationalist or unbelieving philosophies, so that to some extent Priestley and Owen could sound like Irving and Newman.[84] These characteristics were still alive in the late Victorian period. A socialist observer, elaborating on his predecessors in the early meetings of the founders of the Fabian Society, writes: "They began to meet every Friday to perfect themselves, to subordinate the material to the spiritual, and to be single-minded, sincere and strenuous—these were words with hands and feet for the Victorian of true Faith."[85]

THE NEW LANGUAGE IN PRINT

As we have seen, a flood of publications accompanied the religious revival: Bibles, tracts, books of argumentation, sermons, novels, newspapers, and magazines. These were Evangelical, High Church, Dissent, and more. Some of the serial publications were community debating organs as well as purveyors of information and argument. The *Christian Observer* appears to the modern reader like nothing so much as an early version of an Internet forum, with continuing triangular debates between the editor and the readership. The publication was Evangelical but admitted of conflicting views on a great variety of issues. Although each of these journals was published by a particular faction, all tended during this period to be rather open-minded on whom or what they would publish.[86] The *Record* had articles by Newman at the height of the Tractarian controversy. Coleridge wrote to a friend that he hoped to have an article appear in the *Eclectic Review* or the *Christian Observer*.[87]

At the same time that the number of religious serials was increasing rapidly, some of the other types of publications were becoming more religious—following the lead of the increasingly religious readership, as it were. We have seen this shift in the Whig journal the *Edinburgh Review*, with its passage noted by the *Record*.

The evangelical publications not only were peculiar expressions of a quasi-sectarian group but entered the mainstream of English life. Few novels were as widely reviewed and praised as Hannah More's *Cœlebs*. The *Evangelical Magazine* did not have the broadness of that appeal but was of the same order in some ways. Published by both Dissenters and Establishment people, it had been founded in 1793 and became the most widely published religious periodical in the land, claiming 100,000 readers in 1813. In 1808, the High Church Robert Southey called it "offal and hog's wash" and thought it "presumptuous," but he conceded that it was "a powerful engine—the most powerful in this country." In 1835, he acknowledged that he had subscribed to it for many years in order to gauge the state of opinion of those to whom it catered.[88]

THE DOMINANCE OF EVANGELICALISM
IN ENGLISH MORAL LIFE

Taine believed that the dominating characteristic of the English was "the primacy of the moral being," by which he meant that they thought of everything in the light of its moral implications. He considered the root of that tendency to be their religion, and since his examples were mostly evangelical ones, we may say that he saw evangelicalism as the complex of ideas that ruled English culture.[89] Although this domination was never official, and although it was resisted at every turn, it was still there, and it showed up in the work and life of its opponents as well as in its supporters. In both Britain and America, the reformed style of Protestantism replaced the quietist, which meant that those with strong religious sensibilities were not content to confine them to the home and the church (or chapel) but displayed them openly and saw them in some sense as normative even for those who did not agree with them. The society had to conform because these religious convictions were privileged not by virtue of the fact that they were *theirs* but by virtue of the fact they were true. God expected not only believers to live in accordance with the divine commandments but the whole society, which could legitimately enforce compliance through the political organs. Gladstone did not think the Evangelical movement ever became dominant politically in the sense that the Established Church in Scotland had but felt it had achieved the kind of dominance that came from moral and cultural influence. By a process of "infusion," he said, it had changed the tone of the clergy, so that the "vessels of zeal and fervour . . . far outweighed the heroes of the ball-room and the hunting-field."[90] This clerical shift had propelled the whole society in a similar direction. Conybeare concluded that by the middle of the century the Evangelicals had become the most influential party in the Establishment.[91] Lecky thought the great increase in the preaching of the gospel in the church, even by clergymen who were not of the Evangelical party, came because of the pressure by the Evangelical clergy to replace the old moralizing sermons with the Christian gospel.[92] Boyd Hilton's conclusion, reached after years of immersion in the subject, was of a piece with those more contemporary views: the evangelical impact on the nation came about "by establishing a moral hegemony over public life."[93]

The sort of influence the evangelicals exercised may be seen in the practice of Sunday observance, which Halévy took to be emblematic of the difference between English and Continental Christianity, although he acknowledged its superficiality. In the upper classes people would eat cold meals on Sundays so that their servants could observe the Sabbath just as the masters were doing. They might refrain from all secular activities or at least restrict them to reading and walking. And this was done, if not universally, then generally, without benefit of legislation requiring it. (The lower classes tended to be much less observant, just as they were much less punctilious about attending Sunday services.) The Evangelicals handled this issue as they did almost everything else: they started a society, in this case the Lord's Day Observance Society (LDOS) in 1831. Later on, Dissenters formed their counterpart to the LDOS.[94]

In general the societies were the most effective means of promoting particular points of view and also relieving the needs of the destitute. There was an air of self-congratulation in the *Record*'s assessment of the societies, but it was on the mark nevertheless. People did not participate in them for love, wealth, fame, or power, according to the paper. "It is not from such considerations the cell of the prisoner, or the chambers of the sick and dying are visited, the widow, the orphan, and the destitute are relieved. . . . Nothing but Christian principle" accounts for such activities.[95] That captured the same point that Gladstone had made in congratulating himself on his future wife's character: morality was not only a matter of the evils to be avoided but of the good that one did not leave undone.

One effect of the spread of evangelicalism was the binding together of people who otherwise would seem to have little in common. The societies had members from all strata of society but the lowest. The churches held landlord, farmer, and worker; the chapels welcomed artisan, laborer, miner, and factory worker. There is even a sense in which the evangelical ethos bound together the English and the colonial populations.[96]

As the renewal went on, the religious underpinnings of the society were more openly acknowledged and more commonly figured in parliamentary debates, even on the "wrong" side. When, for example, the Sabbatarians in 1837 attempted to impose their position on the country by legislative means, an opponent of the measure argued against it using Scripture.[97] Apart from any formal lines of authority, the politicians were as susceptible as any other occupation to the religious currents of the time. Wilberforce noted in his diary that when he went to the Scottish church to hear Robert Chalmers preach in 1817, a number of prominent politicians were also there, including the free trade advocate William Huskisson and the future prime minister, George Canning. "I was surprised to see how greatly Canning was affected," he wrote. "At times he quite melted into tears. I should have thought he had been too much hardened in debate to show such signs of feeling."[98] The Claphamites and their allies in Parliament, reformers like Sadler and Ashley and a great many little-remembered parliamentarians, were most basically motivated by the principles of the religious revival. Not all of their activities were unambiguously beneficial. In particular, their concern for the eradication of blasphemy and atheism caused them to favor the imposition of strict laws, punishing violators with prison sentences.[99]

Even in the Parliament the Evangelicals had brought about a marked improvement in the honesty with which the public business was conducted. One colleague said to Wilberforce, "It must be a satisfaction to you to have observed that the moral tone of the House of Commons, as well as of the nation at large, is much higher than when you first entered upon public life; and there can be no doubt that God has made you the honoured instrument of contributing much to this great improvement."[100] This association of public policy with moral principle was characteristic of the Evangelicals and increasingly of the entire national ethos. When the Claphamites railed against slavery, it was because the institution was both an injustice and a defiance of the sovereignty of God.[101] By the middle of the century, as the historian Lecky put it, moral thought was "all in one direction—toward the identification of the Bible and conscience," a development that he disliked intensely.[102]

THE NEW CENTRAL PARADIGM OF ENGLISH LIFE

An American historian once remarked that nineteenth-century Englishmen were all "building the new Jerusalems."[103] This new City on the Hill, such as the Puritan settlers of the New England coast and the followers of Oliver Cromwell set out to build, was also the obsession of a host of Englishmen of the pre-Victorian period. And no wonder; those phrases come from the Bible, and thus does the idea come to a people who discover or rediscover the Bible, for it provides the images of not only righteous people but also a righteous nation. The example, or at least the ideal, of Israel transfers in the minds of those who study it to their own societies. Such was the condition not only of England in the early nineteenth century but of much of the English-speaking world. Perry Miller observed that at that time in

America, the Old Testament was "so omnipresent . . . that historians have as much difficulty taking cognizance of it as of the air the people breathed."[104] Another historian says that "the study of American civilization is in no small part the study of the Bible." His reason is that for Americans "the Judeo-Christian scriptures have provided a vast reservoir of themes, phrases, meanings, and habits of thought."[105] In Scotland, evangelicalism from the 1780s began to dominate the culture of all classes and continued thus for a century, at least in the case of the middle class.[106] And, as we have seen in this chapter, the same was true in England. The Hammonds, who were not in sympathy with this development, nevertheless believed that England during the period enjoyed "a general civilising movement," without specifying what had caused it. In keeping with their preoccupations, they credited this movement with a decline in class hostilities toward the middle of the nineteenth century.[107]

What caused that civilizing movement was on the surface a rediscovery of the insights of the Protestant Reformation, but more basically it was a rebirth of the traditions and standards that had characterized the Christian culture of Europe many centuries earlier, traditions that had been eroded by neglect and by the acceptance of other beliefs, other sentiments, other symbols. The system of ethics taught in this renewal tended to be based on the Bible: the sermons were increasingly biblical sermons, the novels were full of biblical symbolism, and the art treated biblical subjects. The ethic that said love must overcome power was taken to be normative, and if it was ignored or ridiculed in many quarters, it nevertheless was taken more seriously in England than it had been in many decades, and it made a difference in ways that so impressed the Hammonds. It made a difference in that the sons of drunken and neglectful fathers were themselves sober and loving husbands and fathers; that those who grew up in filthy hovels raised their children in decent little cottages; that a brawling, rude generation was succeeded by one that valued courtesy and kindness; that people who reveled in low and disreputable living saw their children growing up to be respectable; that a generation that found it acceptable that their country should supply slaves to the colonies while their own countrymen lived in squalor and misery should be followed by one that wanted something better for others and determined to make it possible. This was no small change. A much less thoroughgoing transformation was enough to give a change in French governance the name *revolution;* what we have seen take place in England surely deserves that strong a word.

The Conversion of English Institutions

THE CONTEXT OF REFORM

The transformation of consciousness and morality being as widespread and as deeply ingrained in the people of England as it was, it is hardly conceivable that it should not have had some effect on English institutions. If the connection between spirit and matter sometimes seems tenuous and the evidence indirect, that is in the nature of this kind of investigation. Still, we are not limited to conjecture, since many of the actors in the drama make clear to us in books and correspondence that their work in social and political institutions was closely related to their spiritual quest.

A number of religious streams went into making the early Victorian period what it was, but the main ethos operating was the evangelical one. That immediately poses a problem for any analysis seeking the connection between the cultural spirit of nineteenth-century England and the shaping of its institutions. After all, the common understanding is that the prevailing mind-set of evangelicalism centered on the individual at the expense of the society. One of the most prominent Dissenting ministers later in the century, the Congregationalist R. W. Dale, charged his fellow evangelicals with the kind of individualism that focused almost exclusively on the individual spiritual condition and failed to relate the precepts of the faith to the concerns of the larger society.[1] This contention became almost commonplace in later discussions of the issue (and it may reflect more faithfully conditions as they were later on in the century), but it exaggerates the case for the pre-Victorian period. It is more true to the situation to say that the moral revolution set the stage for a social and political revolution.

THE CHANGING FACE OF ENGLISH POLITICAL LIFE

Whatever progress might have been made toward reforming the political system in the late eighteenth century was cut short by the horrified reaction of most influential Englishmen to reports of the French Revolution. Even radicals who were initially favorably disposed toward the events following 1789, like the young men who would later be known as the Lake Poets, found themselves unable to accept the massive bloodshed of the Terror. The reaction against both religion and monarchy had led to the most unspeakable crimes within France, and then the wars of conquest threatened all of Europe and would likely have swept away England's liberties had not its island status protected it. Thus the natural tendency to preserve English institutions was supplemented by an aversion to anything smacking of the ideology that had taken over France. The fear of suffering a repetition of the French experience explains the willingness of Wilberforce and many like-minded people, who in other circumstances would have been led by their habitual kindness, to support harsh measures against the publishers and distributors of such literature as the works of Thomas Paine and thereby to incur the hatred of the radicals. As late as 1835, when the danger of Bonapartism was long past, the *Record* was still warning about the perils of revolution in England—and about the Whig party, which it claimed was the chosen instrument of the radicals seeking to establish the democracy that would surely end in tyranny.[2] These fears did much to explain the solid wall of opposition to the Chartist movement, the main demands of which would be enacted a few decades later, when the fear of revolution had largely disappeared.

R. W. Dale was perhaps too close to the cultural revolution of the century to see just how the evangelical campaign was conducted. The evangelicals associated the material and political health of the nation with its moral and spiritual condition. Thus curing the ills of the nation was thought to require not so much this or that set of policies as the moral reconstitution of the people, the repentance from their sins and follies and their determination to do better. There was nothing new about this—it was a familiar theme of the Bible, especially the Old Testament, and had been part of the thinking of the Puritan Revolution—but it had largely gone out of public view after the Restoration of 1660. When the Evangelicals persuaded George III to issue the proclamation against vice in 1787, a start was made in the long process of bringing the consciousness of sin back into the center of public consciousness. The constant harping on private morality was not only for the sake of the individual making decisions that had moral implications but for the sake of the whole society, which could not withstand the internal disorders inflicted on it by an immoral people.

This idea was not embraced only by evangelicals. By the early part of the nineteenth century, it was taught by some of the most influential intellectuals of the day. For Coleridge, the "Statesman's Manual" was the Bible, whose morality was not only for individuals but for communities as well.

"The Bible," he argued, "has been the main lever by which the moral and intellectual character of Europe has been raised to its present comparative height."[3] The terrible cholera epidemic of 1832 was widely believed to be the result of God's judgment on the nation, and, at the urging of the Evangelicals, Parliament declared a national day of fasting, prayer, and humiliation on March 21. Bishop Blomfield, preaching in the royal chapel from the prophet Isaiah, urged the king to consider that the moral failures of the English might have been the cause of the plague and that the catastrophe ought to lead to national repentance.[4]

THE EVANGELICALS AND PARLIAMENT

Some of the Evangelical politicians believed that to give full consideration to the moral aspects of policy it was necessary to assign less importance to the party considerations that ordinarily trumped almost everything. The Clapham Evangelicals in Parliament, numbering about thirty and derisively called "the Saints" by their detractors, did not find the choice ambiguous: "I am decidedly convinced," Wilberforce wrote in a letter, "that PARTY is one of the chief evils which in politics we now have reason to regret."[5] Apart from the issue of slavery, their most consistent legislative activity was directed at economic and administrative issues. They were invariably proponents of reforms that would make the government more honest and efficient, and they and their allies made significant contributions in reforming the navy, chancery law, the East India Company, and abuses such as bribery and purchase of governmental offices. They found offensive the corruption that was endemic in the government and had long been tolerated, and they did what they could to bring the problem to the forefront of debate.[6] Similar concerns led them to champion the reform of the currency, in particular the evils caused by debasement through the indiscriminate use of paper money. They had solid intellectual preparation for this task in Henry Thornton's study published in 1802, *Enquiry into the Nature and Effects of the Paper Credit of Great Britain.* Thornton, a banker who knew the effects of currency debasement better than most parliamentarians, was part of the Bullion Committee's efforts to restore a sound currency in 1810, a measure strongly backed by the *Christian Observer.*[7] (His book has been considered sufficiently seminal to have been republished at least twice in the twentieth century, with an introduction by F. A. Hayek, who would later be awarded the Nobel prize in economics.)

The techniques used by Clapham to carry legislation it favored seem surprisingly modern. They divided up responsibilities for the various tasks at "cabinet" meetings, usually in Thornton's library at Battersea Rise. Wilberforce, for example, took charge of the parliamentary campaign to authorize missionary activity in the East India Charter Act of 1813. Charles Grant was responsible for activities within the company and for providing information to others. Zachary Macaulay prepared circulars to send around the country, and Thomas Babington organized the mass petitioning that followed up on the circulars. In April 1812, the Evangelical brain trust met to set up special committees for coordinating the campaign outside of Parliament.[8] This debate showed the power of the Clapham technique, since the subject did not have the inherently wide interest of, say, the slavery issue. Nevertheless, there were 837 petitions circulated, which brought back an unprecedented half-million signatures. Many people were horrified by the implications of this technique, but Wilberforce attributed the victory to it.[9]

The heyday of Clapham's influence ended with Wilberforce's retirement from politics in 1825 and the emergence of a harder edged group of Evangelicals coalescing around the *Record*, which began publication in January 1828. This latter group departed from Clapham by opposing the repeal of the Test and Corporation Acts, which had withheld political rights from Dissenters, as well as the ending of official discrimination against Roman Catholics. Recordites also had a dimmer view of cooperation with Dissent, especially Unitarian Dissenters. As the *Record* warmed to its task, it became increasingly critical of what it took to be the lack of commitment of the Clapham Evangelicals and contrasted their state with the glory days when Wilberforce was still active. The successors of the Clapham generation, and in particular the *Christian Observer*, were, in the Recordite view, too inclined toward compromise with secular ideas and people. Any softening around the edges in Clapham's successors may have been more a function of changing times than anything else. As evangelical influences spread, it seemed to be something of a contrivance to continue to fulminate about public evil in the way the *Record* did. Wilberforce's chosen successor, Thomas Fowell Buxton, showed the same personal commitments as his predecessor: evangelical piety and compassion for the poor. In addition to the antislavery campaign, Buxton expended efforts on behalf of prisoners and prison reform and for the rescue of shipwrecked sailors.[10]

There were many Evangelicals who had convictions little different from Wilberforce's but who had a different sense of how to carry on their responsibilities as Christians. Spencer Perceval, the prime minister who was assassinated in 1812, was fully Evangelical not only in his private life but also in the way his religious convictions influenced the execution of his duties.[11] There was also strong Evangelical influence in the Liverpool, Canning, and

Peel ministries.[12] The Scottish evangelical Thomas Chalmers made his mark in personal ways that would have later policy results. Many English politicians had high respect for him, and Peel and Gladstone in particular were influenced by him.[13]

There have been varying views on exactly what constituted the nature of the Evangelical influence on English parliamentary life. The historian G. M. Trevelyan was apparently impressed most by the techniques they introduced or perfected: the agitation aimed at influencing and mobilizing public opinion; the use of argument and evidence; the wide dissemination of information and propaganda; the harnessing of the power of a myriad of independent societies and other assemblages of influential people.[14] Others lay greater stress on the moral influences of the Evangelicals on the actions of the Parliament. Ian Bradley avers that although their influence in the Commons had declined significantly by the 1830s,

> Their work of redeeming the nation was done. . . . They had acted in parliament as a leaven in the lump. . . . On a whole range of issues from the game laws to the lottery parliament had shown itself more sensitive to moral considerations than it had been a generation or so earlier. The Saints could not, of course, claim sole credit for this. . . . But they had certainly played a significant part in bringing about this development in parliament both by their introduction of specifically moral issues for debate and by their steady witness to the Christian position on all matters which came up there.[15]

That was a rosier view than some of the parliamentary Evangelicals might have accepted. Perhaps because of the monumental flaws in the electoral system, which the Reform Bill of 1832 barely made a start in remedying, the religious temper of the country was only dimly reflected in Parliament. The Claphamites considered several measures of a directly religious nature, such as the appointment of a national fast day, but abandoned them. With a number of very important issues to fight for, they could not afford to be quixotic and waste their political capital by expending it where there was no chance of success. For to do so, as Wilberforce put it, "It would be necessary to argue on grounds which were never considered by the generality of members." This gap between the convictions of the country and those of the MPs was the reason for the massive petitioning campaigns. There had to be a way to translate popular support into political action.[16] The *Record* was especially bitter about what it believed was the hostility of the ruling class to the Christian faith. Parliament would tolerate the opinion of almost anyone, it said in 1830, a wise man or a fool, "but to speak as a Christian is to speak in a tongue unknown in these high places of the earth, or known only to excite contempt, scorn, and aversion."[17] At the time of the Reform Bill, the paper was demanding equal rights. "Why may not we Christians, as public men, act according to our principle, as well as you infidels according to your principle?"[18] Only to be expected from those extremists, we might think, but early in the new reign the *Christian Observer* was saying something similar: "The general policy of the Queen's government has very much tended to check the growth of religion. . . . The theatre finds more favour than the church."[19]

This was an age when democracy and policies relating to it came to the fore and, like almost all serious matters, were debated in the religious context. The Chartist movement of the 1840s demanded the parliamentary framework that would later be standard in the liberal democracies, a development too advanced for that period to accept. The radicals pressed for far-reaching changes in a society that they believed was fundamentally unjust. Even so, a few of the older ones, in reflective moments, could see that things were not really so bad. Francis Place, whom we have seen depicting the England of the 1830s as a far more humane and moral place than it had been a half century earlier, also acknowledged—in an autobiography that would remain unpublished for more than a century—that the political institutions had made similar progress. "Indiscriminating, sanguinary and cruel as our Statutes are, they . . . were much more so fifty years ago, and they were administered in a much more unfeeling and barbarous manner."[20] The improvements Place and others wanted had to do with putting power in the hands of the people, or at least the representatives chosen by the people—in the shorthand of the era, *vox populi vox dei*. Apart from the politics of the idea, this formula was theologically repugnant to all of an orthodox frame of mind because it justified the replacement of a traditional morality recognizing a higher authority with one that was self-justifying and therefore idolatrous. The *Record* charged that the reform movements championed especially by the Whigs, having their natural consequence in such a result, would end up with the extreme transformations called for openly by the radicals.[21] If the voice of the people really were the voice of God, there would be no brake on the reign of the self. "It [democracy] will dig the grave of every Government that shall attempt to rest upon it."[22] Coleridge's version of this line of criticism was less fevered but no less alarmed: "I never said that the Vox Populi was of course Vox Dei; it may be—I put it may, and with equal probability a priori, be Vox Diaboli. That the voice of 100 million of men calling for the same thing is a Spirit, I believe; but whether that be spirit of Heaven or Hell, I can only know by trying the thing called for by the prescript of Reason and God's Will."[23]

REFORMING PARLIAMENT

Even before the Reform Act of 1832 broadened the electorate and eliminated the rotten boroughs, the Parliament was improving, though still far short of the standards that later generations would demand. Soon after it began publication in 1828, the *Record,* not given to praise of Parliament, allowed that it was an "admitted fact, that the state of the House of Commons has of late years materially changed. It is now no longer asked, who proposed or who recommended a measure; but what is the measure itself, and by what arguments is it supported?"[24] But for many Englishmen that was not good enough, and the next few years saw increasing pressure for political reform, in particular of the flawed system of representation, in which voting was closed to all but the wealthy and in which much of the representation bore no relation to any significant body of constituents. By 1832, Edward Bickersteth, secretary of the Church Missionary Society, thought that there was a "craving" for reform in both spiritual and political matters, "a resolution to sift every human institution to its very foundations."[25] The Recordite wing of the Evangelicals, both in and out of Parliament, opposed the coming Reform Bill, evidently out of a general fear of the triumph of radicalism and democracy. The *Record* said it favored reform, "but not of the sort that elevates the people into a mob."[26] The Claphamites thought otherwise, on religious as well as political grounds, because such reform was "just and necessary." The strength of the country was in the middle classes, and those were the people who would be enfranchised by the Reform Bill. Still, the *Observer* did not hold that the position of the Recordites was foolish and in fact acknowledged the "chief danger" to be something similar to the anarchy and destruction against which the *Record* warned.[27]

To the evident surprise of the *Record,* the reform Parliament turned out to be an improvement. The paper opined that Wilberforce's oft-repeated fears that the Parliament was too anti-Christian to listen to the counsel of Scripture had proved to be too pessimistic. The paper now hoped that the good beginning of the reform Parliament would serve as a pattern for the months to come and that the private religious convictions of many of the members would be matched by their public actions.[28]

By the 1840s, it was becoming more difficult to associate the religious revival with particular policies. The anti–corn law agitation saw religious arguments on both sides of the issue, even by those of the same nominal affiliation. The Evangelicals in particular were divided. The *Record* opposed the Anti–Corn Law League, partly because of the Dissenters connected with it.[29] The more moderate Evangelicals were on the other side from the

1820s, on the grounds that the corn laws raised the price of bread to the needy. The league decorated its envelopes with Bible verses and publicized widely the famous Manchester conference of August 1841, in which seven hundred ministers of the gospel met to proclaim the idea that free trade in grain benefits the poor.[30]

Apart from the international slave trade, few foreign policy issues drew the concerted attention of the religious parties. But that did not mean religion was held to be irrelevant to the international affairs. Wilberforce opposed his intimate friend, Prime Minister Pitt, on the war policy with France in 1795, and the breach while it lasted was a grievous matter for both. Wilberforce was openly snubbed by the king as a result of this position. He did not follow through on his initial idea of rousing the middle classes to the peace cause, as he had done on slavery, because he doubted he could succeed; his stand made him, as he put it, "an object of popular odium."[31]

If the abortive peace initiative failed, the Evangelicals did better in the campaign to end the de facto exemption of Indian colonial policy from the religious revival in the homeland. Cynics had long said that when colonial officials undertook the long voyage from England to India they became unbaptized on the way. By the early part of the nineteenth century, officials of the East India Company were participating in temple offerings on behalf of the company. Even where there was no particular religious reason for the policy, company officers resisted the effort to bring the gospel to India because they feared their political and economic interests might suffer from religious conflict.

The change in company policy was due largely to two Scottish officials who experienced evangelical conversions after beginning their service in India, Charles Grant and John Shore (afterwards Lord Teignmouth), who both later became closely associated with Wilberforce and his friends. Grant became interested in the conversion of the Indian people in 1784 as a result of a letter he received from an associate of Wesley. The evangelicals were motivated, as usual, by their desire to spread the gospel, but they were also determined to put an end to horrible Indian practices, such as suttee (the immolation of widows on the funeral pyres of their husbands), that they associated with Hinduism. Wilberforce spoke of the pagan deities as "absolute monsters of lust, injustice, wickedness, and cruelty; in short their religious system is one grand abomination."[32] To a large extent the English public were made aware of the abhorrent practices of India through a treatise written by Grant in 1793, *Observations on the State of Society among the Asiatic Subjects of Great Britain, Particularly with Respect to Morals, and on the Means of Improving It.*[33]

The effort got underway in earnest in 1812, with Wilberforce providing much of the leadership. He called into question the very right of the East India Company to continue if it persisted in blocking the spread of Christianity among the native Indians. There followed the usual Clapham agenda: petitions, manifestos, studies, circulars, and deputations to the prime minister, the Evangelical Spencer Percival. Their immediate goal was the establishment of a bishopric in India, which they attained the next year, along with a grant for Indian education. Not content with overcoming the political influence of the company, the Evangelicals infiltrated it at the highest level. For most of the first thirty years of the century, either the chairman or the deputy chairman of the board of directors was an Evangelical. The Evangelical Lord William Bentinck, second son of the Duke of Portland and close associate of Charles Grant, became governor-general of India in 1827, and among his achievements was the abolition of suttee.[34]

If Protestant Christianity was the motivating power behind the opening of India to Christian mission, the moderate Evangelical wing took a different position toward the religious disputes with Ireland. Their view of Christian faith was not compatible with force, and they could not easily swallow the use of compulsion to bring about the Protestant hegemony over a Roman Catholic population. Sir George Grey, speaking in the House of Commons in 1845, described British religious policy in Ireland as "an act of arbitrary and unjustifiable force," and he thought it a serious error to speak of this "iniquitous proceeding" as Protestantism.[35] This fairly represented the position of the successors of Clapham, although other Evangelicals preferred an Irish policy that combined anti-Catholicism with evangelism.

THE NEW SHAPE OF ENGLISH EDUCATION

If politics could not be separated from religion in the early nineteenth century, education was even more entangled with it. Two motives, sometimes interrelated, quickened the interest in education from the late eighteenth century: the practical and the religious. The period may have begun the modern habit of perceiving education as the solution to any malady afflicting society. The organizers of the early charity schools and Sunday schools were chiefly motivated by religious considerations, although they expected practical benefits in moral behavior. After 1789 some supporters of expanded educational opportunities thought that the right kind of teaching had the potential to dispel the temptations toward revolution that might entice the lower classes; occasionally these considerations were openly avowed.[36] Each rumble of the revolutionary forces on the Continent seemed to produce an echo in England that called for the provision of schooling to prevent the contagion from crossing the channel. In 1839 R. A. Slaney warned the House of Commons that if it did not provide educational opportunities for the lower classes, the result would be such social unruliness as could not be contained by either party in the House. That seemed to be a consensus opinion in the wake of disturbances roiling the English countryside following the 1830 revolution in France.[37] Yet this should not be taken to mean that education was to be exclusively a means controlling seditious forces; rather, it was a tool to affect all behavior. The common assumption seems to have been that antisocial behavior could be eradicated from society by teaching children the basis for right conduct.

Common assumption though it may have been, it was in general only religious groups that believed it firmly enough (or backed it with sufficient motivation) to put it into effect.[38] Some analysts have noticed that contemporary writings commonly speak of education's role in two different ways—as a tool for social control and for the improvement of morality—and therefore conclude that there was some ambivalence in the writers.[39] But this supposed ambivalence separates the moral and spiritual from the material and social, a dichotomy that religious educational theorists and practitioners of the age would have thought absurd. Except for the Benthamites and other radicals, almost all educational thinking was bound up with religious issues. Religious efforts in education went back at least to the work of the Society for Promoting Christian Knowledge early in the eighteenth century and were later supplemented by the Methodists, the Sunday schools, scattered individual labors, and the rival schemes of Lancaster and Bell that we examined in previous chapters. Of the radical education innovations of the nineteenth century, a considerable number came from those of Methodist upbringing. That educational reformers like Hannah More, whose ideas were close in some respects to those of radicals like Mary Wollstonecraft, should have been slighted by historians of education may be explained largely by the fact that her party is viewed by the educational establishment as among the losers of the past, and therefore irrelevant.[40] One reason religiously based education was so pervasive was the conviction among traditionalists of all sorts that "secular education" was a contradiction in terms. Carlyle deprecated the struggle between Church and Dissent over the control of education, but he ridiculed the notion that there could be anything like education without religion. In this he seemed to speak for almost all thoughtful people of the age who were not numbered among the radicals or indifferents: "For, in very truth, how can Religion be divorced from Education? An irreverent knowledge is no knowledge . . . no culture of the soul of a man. A knowledge that ends in barren self-worship, comparative indifference or contempt for all God's Universe except one insignificant item thereof, what is it?"[41] In the midst of the brouhaha surrounding the founding of the University of London, the *Record* reminded its readers: "We have frequently protested, and always shall do, against any scheme of education either for rich or poor, which excludes religious instruction."[42]

Much, but not all, of the early educational energy of the Establishment was channeled into the efforts of the High Churchmen who supported the National Society for the Education of the Poor in the Principles of the Church of England. Day schools—often called "infant schools"—were opened by parishes beginning in 1819, and the movement gained enough momentum that Evangelicals cooperated with Dissenters to open in 1836 the Home and Colonial School Society with an associated teacher training college.[43] The National Society aimed to have a school in each parish, an ideal that was never realized, even when boards made up of local clergymen of all parties were established for the purpose.[44] The parish-centered nature of the schools ensured that the effort would be uneven until the Educational Reform Act of 1870. But where schools were not begun in the parishes, it was more often because of a lack of resources than because of a lack of commitment. Clergymen who were unable to start schools often suffered from a sense of failure as a result. In 1854 the vicar of Blackbourton in Oxfordshire lamented to his bishop that he had been unable to establish a day school. "I am short of my strength entirely for want of one. I could make use of the school for giving lectures at night and otherwise instructing my poor ignorant congregation."[45] Some of the Clapham Evangelicals, particularly Wilberforce, Thornton, and John Venn, actively supported the establishment of parish schools; Macaulay in Sierra Leone and Grant in India did the same in the colonies. Henry Venn the younger led the Church Missionary Society to carry on Macaulay's efforts in West Africa, advocating that Africans be instructed in English, geography, history, mathematics, native African languages, music, art, Bible and church history, preaching, pedagogics, mechanical arts, and agriculture.[46] He assured one of the missionary teachers that education was "one of the chief branches of missionary work" and refused to speculate whether it or preaching was of superior importance.[47] After 1840 Establishment interest in education broadened from its eleemosynary orientation to devote more attention to the education of Anglican middle-class children in boarding schools.[48]

It is impossible to state with any certainty how widespread Anglican education had become in the period. A survey conducted in 1832 found that of 8,588 returns, 6,730 parishes conducted some form of church school.[49] This is not an insignificant achievement, especially when it is considered that we have no way of knowing how many additional schools were present in parishes that did not respond to the survey.

The role of Dissent in education was different from that of the Establishment. The Methodists during Wesley's lifetime were not numbered among the Dissenters, yet their educational enterprises were not typically Anglican. Poor people were encouraged to learn to read and then to read at a level far in advance of their peers. The Methodists also were among the leaders in the setting up of Sunday schools and then day schools. In 1841, the Wesleyan Conference established a committee on education, partly to define the education of what by then had become a denomination. Standards were set, which included the use of the authorized version of the Bible, the Wesleyan catechism and hymnbook, and the Psalmody. The schools were to admit all children, Methodist or otherwise, but each teacher had to be a Wesleyan recommended by a minister. In 1844, the conference appropriated a fund of £20,000 for educational purposes, and after this the number of day schools was expanded rapidly. In 1857 the conference reported 434 day schools enrolling 52,630 pupils, compared with 31 schools in 1837. At the same time there were more than 400,000 children in the Wesleyan Sunday schools.[50]

Even before the evangelical revival, Dissent had been more effectively engaged in educational enterprises than the Establishment. The English universities were in deplorable condition in the eighteenth century, having become more like finishing schools than places of serious scholarship. Barred from them, the Dissenters educated their youth in academies, some of which attained high standards of learning. Perhaps because of their religious ties abroad, they remained in closer touch with intellectual life on the Continent than did Cambridge and especially Oxford. Still, for most of these academies, the preparation of ministers was foremost, so the study of religion occupied a central position in the curriculum.[51]

In the middle years of the nineteenth century, the single most important voice on educational issues was that of the experienced physician and government official we have seen a number of times before in this study, James Kay-Shuttleworth, the secretary of the Committee of Council on Education. The son of Dissenting evangelicals, Kay-Shuttleworth was a member of the Church of England. Although he was not associated with a party of the Church, there were many indications that he was at heart an Evangelical. His son's recollection makes clear that the pattern of his existence resembled almost a textbook description of evangelical life:

> Deep religious faith, a thorough knowledge of the Bible, and extensive reading in biblical literature were common to both my parents, and constituted a strong bond between them. Daily family prayers—my mother's beautiful Bible-lessons to her children—my father's love of having the Psalms read

to him, especially when he was ill—his occasional expositions to children and servants at family prayers—his earnest sermons . . . these were outward and noticeable signs of my parents' religious life. . . . He used to visit sick neighbours of all classes. With his old skill as a physician, he would sometimes advise and prescribe for them; at other times he would read a chapter of the Bible to a friend—for instance, an old miner who had risen to be a colliery manager.[52]

As we would expect from such a man, Kay-Shuttleworth agreed with the generally prevailing opinion that religious teaching should be the foundation for all education. But he departed from many of his contemporaries in his insistence that this could be accomplished within the framework of a publicly funded system of schools. He held this view even though it was almost impossible to arrive at a working reconciliation between the Establishment and Dissent on how religious instruction should be accomplished. He was afraid that failure of the parties to reach agreement would jeopardize the religious character of education by raising, as he put it in a letter to the parliamentary committee studying the matter, the issue of "whether they shall not prefer a system of secular education to one which violates the conscience of all classes." His warning was not heeded, and Church and Dissent continued their controversy.[53] Yet it may be wondered if the differences were bridgeable by a compromise formulation such as Kay-Shuttleworth desired; he may have been attempting to square the circle of disagreement within English religion. He had to accommodate secular education, religious education, and public financing and control, and he had to do it with the consent of all segments of the population. As he put it in an address to a local Sunday school, the day school, which he regarded as a natural extension of the Sunday school, would "always retain the object of bringing up our youth religiously, but it will also be adapted to the political wants of the State, and to the civil rights of the minority." Perhaps he thought this improbable scheme feasible because he did not see it as happening at a stroke but, in typical English fashion, as an organic movement. "We do not make revolutions in England, but our institutions grow and spread like our oaks. So this school system, which has had a congregational origin, will grow, change and spread until it is national."[54] If the system were not to be solely private in control and funding, neither could it become purely secular. "All efforts to promote a secular, or purely civil system, supported by rate-payers, outside the pale of religious organization, failed," wrote Kay-Shuttleworth as late as 1868, and presumably they could be expected to continue to fail. Here again he reiterated the necessity of combining state control with religious education and the preservation of civil rights that did not injure the conscience.[55] (Two years later, the government enacted the landmark Elementary Education Act, which was brought by Thomas Arnold's son-in-law, William Forster.)

There were important reasons to reform the serious deficiencies in the prevailing patchwork system of English education, but there was little agreement on what they were. Many observers agreed with the Methodist minister who maintained that "too much has been expected of the Sabbath schools. . . . It is absurd to suppose that a few hours on one day in seven should be sufficient for the moral and religious training of children."[56] From the other side of the spectrum, a (Benthamite) report of the Poor Law Commissioners on the training of pauper Children (1841) complained that the Bible was "in almost all the schools the only class-book, and the schools are deficient in the necessary elementary works on education, and corporal punishments are still in use; no system of rewards has hitherto been found practicable."[57]

Along with being subject to the civil authorities, the teacher of even the "secular" school was to inculcate religious principles as well as other subjects. There were not to be separate teachers of religion as there were of mathematics; rather, ordinary teachers were to be men of religious principles that would penetrate all their teaching. Their training had to inculcate these principles if they were to be expected to fulfill their role. Hence Kay-Shuttleworth demanded that the training institution (of which he was the primary designer) be constructed with a strong religious component at the center. The training college's principal aim was not to impart a body of knowledge but to produce a future teacher whose character had been prepared for this calling by the inculcation of religious principles.[58] The normal school was to become something like a monastery and a testing ground for a lifetime of devoted service: "This religious life is to be nurtured by the example, for the public instruction of the Principal, and by his private counsel and admonition; by the religious services of the household; by the personal intercourse of the students, and the habits of private meditation and devotion which they are led to form; by the public worship of the church, and by the acts of charity and self-denial which belong to their future calling."[59]

That was the mission intended when Kay-Shuttleworth founded the normal school at Battersea. He used some of the Swiss schools as his model, with their reliance on hard work, a common religious calling, and a sense of idealism. The school opened in February 1840 with eight aspiring teachers, all of them living with the family in the manor house. Kay-Shuttleworth's approach was both spiritual and environmental. He insisted both on the primary responsibility of each individual to make the best of his environment—that is, to behave morally—and also on the need for improving the environment so as to make life better for others. This typically evangelical analysis of the problem of social dysfunction does not sit well with modern analysis, which regards it as ambivalent or even contradictory.[60] Kay-Shuttleworth would have replied to this criticism that only one without the other is bound to fail. Many of the normal schools that were established after Battersea followed his approach to training teachers. There can be little doubt of his influence in the training of teachers for several decades. He even assisted the Colonial Office in 1847 in the design of a system of education that was intended eventually to produce a native middle class.[61] But he suffered many disappointments in the execution of his plan. The main problem was that the class of students willing to give their lives in poorly remunerated service was deficient in every way. "There is . . . no opportunity for selection; and unless other sources be developed, even this imperfect supply is precarious, and liable soon to fail. Too often the students were physically defective, and they were almost all deplorably ignorant."[62]

Kay-Shuttleworth had many critics, especially since he lived into a period when the evangelical moral hegemony began waning. Matthew Arnold did not think him cultivated enough—"not smooth and genial" was one of his comments. But, Arnold went on, "the faith in popular education which animated him was no intriguer's passion. It was heroic."[63] Kay-Shuttleworth's vision for a unified, state-ordered, religiously based educational system was bound to founder eventually on the intractable problem of religious disunity. As early as 1843, the government had to withdraw a bill for the state support of education because, as Prime Minister Peel put in a letter to Queen Victoria, "as success depended upon general concord and goodwill, [the bill] must be ultimately unavailing, and the progress of [it] must infallibly embitter religious animosity and strife."[64] Gradually ways were found to funnel taxpayer money to the schools, and the Church received the bulk of it. Many clergymen resolved the religious issue by excusing Dissenting children from religious instruction.[65] Among Churchmen, the Tractarians were most adamantly opposed to state funding of education if the control were to be placed anywhere but in the hands of the Anglican clergy.[66]

Richard Cobden, friend of radical causes, proposed a solution that would teach religious subjects in a nonsectarian way but found himself under attack mainly by Churchmen, though he was one himself.[67] Cobden avowed an attachment to the religious system of education but saw no way to bring it about in the face of the mutually exclusive convictions of the parties. "I have found," he wrote in 1851, ". . . such insuperable difficulties in consequence of the religious discordances of this country,—that I have taken refuge in this, which has been called the remote haven of refuge for the Educationalists,—the secular system,—in sheer despair of carrying out any system in connection with religion."[68] Six years later, Lord Macaulay attended a Church in which he heard a "detestable" sermon advocating government control of education under complete control of the Church. "If the maxims of this fool, and of others like him, are followed," he commented, "we shall soon have, not the mutiny of an army, but the rebellion of a whole nation, to deal with."[69] Much of the leadership of the Roman Catholic Church, which was not very potent politically, had similar objections to the use of state funds for providing the kind of religious instruction they had reason to believe would be inimical to Catholic convictions.[70] The Education Act of 1870 would provide a fig leaf to cover the state involvement and allow for the protection of the conscience of Dissenters. Rejecting both denominationalism and secularism, it contributed state funding toward what amounted to a generic Protestantism. But the compromise could not have satisfied Kay-Shuttleworth's desire for the content of deeply religious education such as he sought to instill at Battersea.

By the middle third of the nineteenth century, the English universities had come a long way since their nadir in the previous century. Serious learning was again possible, and the level of research and writing was much higher than previously. But there were still serious deficiencies. Many clergy of the Church of England were prepared for the ministry at Oxford and Cambridge, but there was no professional-level training for them or for many other professions. The universities were located in rural areas that were not convenient for much of the population of the country. And the fact that Dissenters could not graduate from either one, or even matriculate at Oxford, raised serious political difficulties. The idea for a new university that overcame these problems is said to have originated with the poet Thomas Campbell. He was influenced by the superior level of the Scottish and Prussian universities and also by the example of the University of Virginia. But ideology was also responsible for the start of the University of London. Two of Bentham's followers, Henry Brougham and Joseph Hume, were active in the drive to start the institution. Because of the disabilities against them in the traditional universities, Dissenters joined the radicals in establishing the institution. The university opened its doors in 1828, and the instruction included engineering, medicine, law, and economics, as well as the traditional subjects. Stung by the innovation, the Anglicans opened King's College in 1831 with a similar course of studies. In 1836, the University of London (now University College) lost that designation, and the new University of London became the body managing and awarding degrees at both colleges.[71]

Excluded from the traditional universities, Dissenters gave substantial support to the University of London, even though the influence of unbelievers was strong there and theological study was not part of the curriculum. They were persuaded to agree to that stipulation by the argument that it would be impossible to teach theology in a way that would be acceptable to all the religious bodies. Staunch Anglicans detested the institution for its toleration of Dissent, but especially for its radical bent. As we saw earlier, Thomas Arnold felt compelled to withdraw from the board of the new university when it became clear that it would not be a hospitable place for religion. The *Record* crowed prematurely over some financial and enrollment difficulties the university had in 1833, with its collection of "Infidel, Radical, Jewish, Independent, Socinian, Arian, and Baptist" people.[72] Earlier, the paper had called for the creation of King's College on the grounds that it would stimulate the Church to meet its responsibilities for the diffusion of knowledge.[73]

The public schools of England were changed largely by the example of Thomas Arnold's Rugby, although some have suggested that accounts of Arnold's reign were more influential than the reign itself.[74] People who say that have in mind principally Thomas Hughes's immensely popular novel *Tom Brown's Schooldays,* with a secondary position given to Arthur Stanley's biography of the schoolmaster. The fact that these were both Old Boys writing out of immense respect for Arnold gave added authority to the narratives.

Through the whole of our period, practically all education was paid for, administered, and taught by people who believed that education should be religious, and for most of whom religion was the motivating force that impelled them to give, to start schools, and to teach. Many of them were volunteers, and there were countless English people who could read and even write because the religious revival impelled their benefactors to these charitable efforts. Up to the end of the period and beyond, the rivalries between Church and Dissent were not definitively solved, and if this prevented the formation of a monolithic educational establishment that controlled all of English education, it was not self-evidently detrimental to the country. Some specialists regard it as a boon, inasmuch as competitive energies were multiplied and a type of despotism of the mind (which John Stuart Mill had warned against) was averted.[75] For those who advocated that education in a Christian country should be Christian, to a large extent that ideal was realized until the Education Act of 1870, when denominational rivalry combined with a lessening of religious fervor to bring about something closer to the modern ideal of secular education.[76]

PENAL REFORM

John Howard's evangelical conversion, by his own report, was the defining event that made possible his life as a prison reformer, and prison reform remained a staple of evangelical concern for many decades. There are elements in the very notion of prison that seem to account for this. Some of the heroes of the Bible were prisoners: Joseph, Jeremiah, Paul, Peter—Jesus himself. That the worst sinners could be redeemed made it seem worthwhile to try reformation rather than writing off as hopeless a soul for whom Christ had suffered. Compassion was to be the ruling motivation for a Christian social ethic, and Jesus had defined his disciples as those of whom he could say: "I was naked and you clothed me, I was sick and you visited me, I was in prison and you came to me" (Matt. 25:36).

Howard was born to a wealthy family in 1726 and died in 1790, having contracted a fever while visiting a military hospital in Russia after years of appearing in prisons full of pestilence. Appointment to the post of high sheriff in Bedfordshire in 1773 brought him in contact with the local jail and acquainted him for the first time with the appalling conditions under which prisoners were kept. He devoted the remainder of his life to visiting prisons, writing about conditions in them, and urging legislative remedies for their deficiencies. Wesley and others had denounced the conditions of places of incarceration and had for their pains been denounced as fanatics, but it was harder to dismiss Howard, with his status as a financially independent country squire. His basic message was that prisoners should be treated as human beings, and those who were susceptible to such an argument could not easily resist his entreaties. Such treatment included a decent bill of fare and above all the opportunity to reform the prisoners by ministering to their spiritual needs.

> The hours of rising, of reading a chapter in the Bible, of prayers, of meals, of work, etc. should all be fixed by the magistrates, and notice of them given by a bell. A Chaplain is necessary here in every view. To reform prisoners, or to make them better as to their morals, should always be the leading view in every house of correction. . . . As rational and immortal beings we owe this to them; nor can any criminality of theirs justify our neglect in this particular. . . . and I am no less persuaded, that it is religion alone which can effectually accomplish so great and so desirable a work.[77]

When much later the *Record*, in its second month of publication, attributed crime to the absence of religion, it was squarely in the tradition of the great prison reformer.[78]

Howard was a Congregationalist, but one with a remarkable ability to appreciate the strengths of other traditions. Married to a member of the Establishment, he would attend worship with her and then go on to his own chapel. In 1795, this Dissenter's likeness was the one statue at St. Paul's Cathedral in London.[79] He had considerable sympathy for the Quakers, his own piety being similar to their quiet introspection, and his plain clothing was like theirs. Some of his ideas on the spiritual reformation work in prison, such as the isolation of prisoners in cells and in chapel compartments, borrowed from that form of piety, which he believed would facilitate the necessary process of introspection, followed by repentance and faith. All this was to be the heart of the work of the "penitentiary house." The Quakers were much taken with Howard's work for these reasons, in addition to their own heritage of imprisonment as a consequence of religious persecution.[80] He was encouraged by his only meeting with John Wesley, who wrote in his diary that Howard was "one of the greatest men in Europe.[81]

Howard's work was carried on by others, including those who had no sympathy with his religious convictions. Samuel Romilly, who led the struggle against the death penalty for a wide spectrum of offenses, wrote of Howard's *State of the Prisons* that it was not great literature but that it was "one of those works which have been rare in all ages of the world—being written with a view only to the good of mankind."[82] Bentham's Panopticon was inspired in part by Howard's work, although there is little chance that Howard would have approved the inhuman efficiency of that typically utilitarian solution to the problem.[83]

But the evangelicals also carried on Howard's work. As early as 1787, Wilberforce railed against "the barbarous system of hanging." He supported Romilly's efforts and those of others, including the Evangelical MP Thomas Fowell Buxton. He was on the Select Committee on Criminal Laws and was an active member of the Society for the Improvement of Prison Discipline and for the Reformation of Juvenile Offenders. The whole Clapham group in the House of Commons lined up behind Wilberforce on this issue, and Buxton made it a special matter of effort.[84] Buxton's interest was probably sparked by his long association with the Quakers, although he was a member of the Establishment. His mother and wife were both Quakers, and his sister-in-law, Elizabeth Fry, is probably the one who should be regarded as having succeeded to John Howard's mantle. Mrs. Fry began to visit Newgate prison in 1812, her purpose apparently being the usual evangelical effort to teach prisoners the gospel. Her example proved infectious, and others began doing similar work. William Allen, a wealthy Quaker, had first introduced Mrs. Fry to Newgate. Having been very active from the 1780s in the antislavery crusade and various evangelical charities, especially the Society for Bettering the Condition of the Poor, he was the editor of the *Philanthropist,* the leading charity journal. In 1817, to support her work, he founded the Prison Discipline Society, which became the main lobby for prison reform. Also active in this society were Buxton and another of Mrs. Fry's brothers-in-law, Samuel Hoare. The society publicized conditions in the prisons, causing a great scandal with the public. This provoked several parliamentary actions in the 1820s and 1830s that instituted reforms: justices were required to submit plans for prison reform and to inspect the prisons regularly, with quarterly reports to be sent to the home secretary; jailors were to receive salaries, rather than living by extorting fees from the prisoners; there were to be regular visits by surgeons and chaplains; prisoners were to be instructed in basic literacy and in religion; and women prisoners were to be in the charge of warders of the same sex.[85]

INDUSTRIAL REFORM

Proponents of legislation for the amelioration of harsh conditions in the factories had the advantage of an evangelical fervor that was increasingly intolerant of harsh conditions in any circumstance that could be moderated by legislative activity. The choice was not to be dictated by prudential considerations—still less by political expediency. Rather, the argument went, it was a matter of good and evil. As early as 1794, Wilberforce's friend Thomas Gisborne called for legislation providing relief for children working in factories. At the turn of the century, the Bettering Society demanded that Parliament act on the matter, a demand that received the powerful support of Sir Robert Peel (the elder), who was reputed to be the wealthiest industrialist in the country. With the strong backing of the evangelicals, Peel successfully introduced a bill in 1802 that was the first legislative interference with the factory system on the grounds of compassion. One historian remarked that it looked as if Hannah More had drafted it. Peel said that its main end was "to promote the religious and moral education of the children." Wilberforce and Spencer Perceval wanted the scope of the bill increased even further.[86] In a speech in 1816, Peel justified factory legislation on the basis of the Old Testament passage that read, "Thou shalt not oppress an hired servant that is poor and needy."[87] The clergyman G. S. Bull, one of the most prominent proponents of the Ten Hours Bill of 1846 (which limited the hours that might be worked by children), remonstrated with a parliamentary commission studying factory conditions that allowing present conditions to persist was a violation of the divine commandments to provide equal justice without consideration of class or financial status.

"*I protest as a Christian Man, and as a Minister of the Church of England.* The God whom I desire to serve is 'no respecter of persons.'"[88]

The landmark Ten Hours Bill, proposed after years of relatively ineffectual factory acts, exemplified the Manichaean excesses to which the debate could be carried. When Richard Oastler traveled through York on his tour to promote the passage of the bill, signs that greeted him proclaimed, "For God and our Children."[89] One participant in the campaign evidently thought such expostulations were too tame: "It is the question of law or no law—order or anarchy—religion or infidelity—heaven-sprung truth and peace and love; or hell-born, withering atheism. It is the working of the mystery mentioned in the Holy Scripture—the mystery of ungodliness. . . . It is the battle between God and Mammon—between Christ and Beelzebub, the prince of devils."[90]

As was common among the evangelicals, Richard Oastler's leadership in the movement for the Ten Hour maximum workday for children was initiated by a dramatic religious experience that illustrates the impact that serious Bible reading had on innumerable people of the day. On September 29, 1830, the forty-year-old Oastler, a Methodist turned Evangelical, was called into the room occupied by his friend, the wealthy industrialist and Evangelical Tory John Wood, where he found Wood reading the Bible by candlelight:

On my advancing towards the side of his bed, he turned toward me, reached out his hand and in the most impressive manner pressing my hand in his he said: "I have had no sleep tonight. I have been reading this Book and in every page I have read my own condemnation. I cannot allow you to leave me without a pledge that you will use all your influence in trying to remove from our factory system the cruelties which are practised in our mills." I promised him I would do what I could . . . I felt that we were each of us in the presence of the Highest and I knew that that vow was recorded in Heaven.[91]

That same day Oastler wrote his famous "Yorkshire slavery" letter, in which he compared the mills of Yorkshire with the plantations on which Negro slaves languished. "Thousands of our fellow-creatures . . . are this very moment existing in a state of slavery *more horrid* than are the victims of that hellish system, '*colonial slavery.*'"[92]

Oastler's tour through Yorkshire and into Scotland to promote the bill was a series of triumphs, with enthusiastic crowds greeting him everywhere. The Scottish Presbyterians were as enthusiastic as the English evangelicals. It was on this trip that Oastler accepted Robert Chalmers's invitation to breakfast, after which Oastler convinced the Malthusian clergyman that his profession of Christ was incompatible with his opposition to the Ten Hours Bill, and Chalmers switched sides.[93] Despite manifestations such as these, historians have often concluded that the reform movement proceeded without much religious support. This is partly due to misleading statements in Lord Ashley's memoirs.[94] But Ashley was notoriously morose, and setbacks habitually caused him to lament extravagantly. Although the participation of evangelicals in the factory movement was considerable, it is often denigrated, partly because the Clapham group opposed much of the early legislation. But that view ignores too much of the movement's leadership.[95] Halévy was not far off the mark: "The historian of the movement which produced the factory acts must not forget the many tributaries which swelled the stream. But the source of the river was the piety and Christian sentiment of the Evangelicals."[96] In the 1840s similar religious appeals availed. In 1842, when Ashley campaigned for legislation to improve the lot of miners, he used the same kind of language in the Parliament. He pleaded to the members "to break off our sins by righteousness, and our iniquities by showing mercy to the poor." Not even the mining lobby, though it opposed the legislation, questioned publicly the religious presuppositions.[97]

THE AMBIGUITIES OF SOCIAL REFORM
IN THE CONTEXT OF POLITICAL ECONOMY

Analyses of the factory movement and its analogues in other fields are often too quick to assign moral values to one side or another. If hardness of heart was responsible for the opposition of some people to reforms, others were motivated by sincere doubts about the proposed course of action, had convictions that suggested different remedies, or in some cases were put off by a certain wackiness in the supporters of the reforms. When the Rev. T. Nunn, clergyman of St. Paul's, Leeds, came out in support of the Ten Hours Bill, it was not only because it would benefit the poor but also because it would benefit the rich. It would do so by making the mill owners more humane, less avaricious. It would, in the words of a contemporary observer, "make men love each other" and abjure the idolatry of pursuing filthy lucre.[98] This almost mystical veneration of the power of legislation could not make friends for the legislation out of doubtful Christians of orthodox views. It ran counter not only to the beliefs of evangelicals and many High Churchmen but also to some of the larger intellectual currents of the day—for example, to Southey's belief that there "is no other means whereby nations can be reformed than by that which alone individuals can be regenerated."[99] There seemed to be a contradiction between the notion of an organic society and the demand for the mutual support of the classes in such an act as the Ten Hours Bill. One might as justly insist that such a society would be subverted by a legislative *requirement* that its institutions be supported; that would introduce an artificiality belying the claim of organic relationship and also create mutual resentments.

There were sometimes overpowering reasons for people to submerge important religious differences and cooperate on various activities that they thought were inferences from their deepest beliefs. Thus Edwin Chadwick and James Kay-Shuttleworth labored together on the poor law administration. Ashley worked with Chadwick and Southwood Smith on public health issues, later joining with Smith to form the Health of Towns Association, a group with surprising breadth of membership. Oastler's concern about the ethics of slavery led him to abjure his Whig background and campaign for Wilberforce in the 1807 election. For years he boasted about the injury he suffered when he was struck by a brickbat intended for the candidate. Later on, he reveled in his Toryism and with his characteristic pugnacity defended it against its challengers as the outlook that guaranteed the rights of the poor:

> A Tory is one who, believing that the institutions of this country are calculated, as they were intended, to secure the prosperity and happiness of every class of society, wishes to maintain them in their original beauty, simplicity and integrity. He is tenacious of the rights of all, but most of all the poor and needy, because they require the shelter of the constitution and the laws more than the other classes. A Tory is a staunch friend of Order, for the sake of Liberty; and, knowing that all our institutions are founded upon Christianity, he is of course a Christian, believing with S. Paul that each order of society is mutually dependent upon the others for peace and prosperity. . . . I never changed my name, I never saw any charm in the word "Conservative". I am still an old-fashioned ultra-Tory.[100]

Since the organic view of society made the classes mutually dependent, Oastler and many like him opposed the New Poor Law of 1834. Most of them were not insensible to the evils of the Speenhamland system of poor relief, but to loosen traditional societal bonds was to them akin to sacrilege, and they predicted dire consequences to its enforcement. As Oastler put it in one of a series of letters to the Prime Minister, Lord John Russell, if the prime minister enforced the New Poor Law, "you will throw down the glorious fabric of the British Empire, you will untie the knot which binds society together."[101]

The Tories more or less adopted Oastler's version of the party's heritage of ameliorating the condition of the lower classes. Triumphant in the election of 1841, they began to make good on their acceptance of the reform package that dated from midway through the previous decade. In 1835, Peel had advanced his Tamworth Manifesto, in which he not only accepted the Reform Act of 1832 but promised to redress the grievances of the working class. Even Disraeli, who generally opposed Peel on these issues, declared in his campaign of 1841 that the condition of the working class was his main interest. The party followed Ashley's lead in enacting reform acts with regard to lunatics and the employment of women and children in the mines.[102]

An organic view of society, with responsibility of the upper classes for the lower, inevitably carried with it a paternalist connotation. This paternalism the evangelical practitioners of social help avowed unashamedly. During the 1827 debate on the condition of workers in the silk trade, Michael Sadler, who brought Ashley into the movement after Sadler lost his seat in the House of Commons, called for government intervention "to exhibit itself in the attitude of a kind parent who, while exulting in the strength and vigour of his elder born, still extends his fostering care to the young and helpless branches of his family." Even so strong a reformer as Charles Dickens hated this attitude and published articles in the press denouncing the ragged schools because they treated people like children, condemning them to perpetual dependency with their patronizing. The philanthropists were even accused of fostering helplessness by their constant catering to it.[103]

The contradictions between free markets and the organic nature of society requiring mutual care were only apparent contradictions, according to some contemporaries. That is why Wilberforce could call himself a political economist and yet expend vast sums in helping the poor. It also explains why Thomas Chalmers could be a follower of Malthus and yet teach what his modern biographer calls "a communal social idea, based upon a shared Christian purpose." When the individual submitted to a compassionate God, he voluntarily subordinated his interests to those of the larger community. In this way the "godly commonwealth" would come into being.[104] But how was the natural selfishness of men to be overcome so as to bring this about? Chalmers's answer came in his treatise on political economy: even if a society cared nothing about morality and everything about procuring wealth, still "moral and religious education is the first and greatest object of national policy" because in the absence of a general public morality governmental measures can avail nothing.[105] It made no sense to Chalmers that some men advocated measures to increase prosperity or to overcome the effects of poverty without considering the moral state of those who were to be helped. In this, he was at one with the English evangelicals, and increasingly with much of English society.

THE REFORM OF THE CHURCH OF ENGLAND

A religious renewal, if it really is that, is bound to have some effect on the institutions through which it is mediated. The Church of England was called the Establishment because it was the official religion of the nation. This was both its strength and its weakness. It had come into existence at a time when it was considered normal throughout Europe that the sovereign should establish the religion of the people, and numerous sixteenth-century Englishmen lost their lives challenging that proposition. This privileged position continued until a time when large and increasing numbers of Englishmen had no allegiance to this Church—a time, too, when a nascent democracy found it increasingly difficult to accept this anomaly. Hence the term *Establishment,* while retaining its formal status, increasingly had the meaning drained from it. This Establishment had functions not only at the national level but even more pervasively in the innumerable localities in the kingdom, so that the local vestry had both religious and civic functions. It established policy for the local church, and it set church rates (taxes) and administered the poor law, thereby increasingly coming into conflict with Dissenters. Clergymen were increasingly taken into service as local magistrates. Some accounts have it that by early in the nineteenth century more than half the magistrates were in holy orders. This political dominance at all levels was challenged not only by Dissent but also by radicals who portrayed the Church as part of the mingled institutional oppression of the lower classes. "The Saviour lived and died for man," went the doggerel, "To live *upon* him is the Bishops' plan."[106] The young Southey might accept an establishment, but only one that formed a big tent, not much different from that which Thomas Arnold would later champion. It would teach that there is one God and that Christ is the savior but not require subscription to other articles. As far as the current arrangement was concerned, "I am an enemy to the establishment. Church and state produce but a mulish kind of barren religion."[107] Decades later, Coleridge said that "the fatal error" that the Church had fallen into from the time of the Reformation was its "clinging to Court and State instead of cultivating the People."[108] Coleridge's scheme did not call for a disestablishment but rather for a reformulation, with the Church emphasizing its spiritual mission rather than its political role.

This was also Gladstone's early view. He thought it fallacious to suppose that religion is secularized by contact with the state. Rather, a national church could elevate and purify personal religion by bringing moral suasion to bear on the openly ungodly, and this was true despite the imperfections of the Church.[109] Yet Gladstone was evidently reconsidering this position even while his book was in the press, and though he remained High Church throughout his life, he did not apply the doctrine when he had the power to do so, or at least the power to persuade others through his high office. He became the designer of the disestablishment of the Church of Ireland in 1869.[110]

The major evangelical organs had the same conception. Even the Recordites, who did not have the optimistic postmillennial expectations of Clapham, disavowed the idea that religion should stand alone, "separate and distinct from other things." Rather, it was a driving force in a society, and a society that acknowledged it would flourish.[111]

One reason the Church was able to survive the onslaught of Dissenters, radicals, and friendly but disgusted critics was that it provided a service that was not easy to duplicate. To say that it was a complete social service agency may be too idealized a view, but granting the spottiness of their distribution, the parishes nevertheless provided a pastoral presence and source of help that most English families could reach either regularly or in times of special need. This function appealed to many people, probably an increasing number in our period; if they did not have any grand expectations for the transformative effects of the institution, they could still appreciate its help in ordinary needs and personal tragedies of the localities.

Of the major influences on the society, religious or secular, the only one that seems to have ignored the ideal of societal improvement was the Tractarian. There was a certain pessimism at Oxford, even as Newman and his friends turned out tracts and other writings with great energy and argued forcefully for the vision of the Church that animated them. That vision was dualistic, with matter and spirit differentiated in such a way as to make it difficult to see the societal implications of elevating the Church to what they considered its proper place. Sin was so endemic to humanity that it would continue to affect its institutions profoundly, and that a culture could be Christianized was too much to expect.[112] (These observations do not apply to the Ritualists who took up the High Church mantle after the Tractarians disappeared as a major party in the Church of England.)

The census taken on March 30, 1851, proved beyond a doubt what had been widely suspected: that the right of the Church of England to be taken as the official ecclesiastical body of the realm rested on exceedingly shaky grounds. Of more than seven-and-a-quarter million people who attended religious services that day, only slightly more than half entered an Anglican Church. This was highly disconcerting to the Establishment, and no similar survey was taken for the remainder of the century.

There were various reasons for the declining importance of the Church in an age that was undergoing a religious revival. One of them was that it had not completely purged itself of the abuses that had fastened themselves on it in the eighteenth century. Tocqueville compared it in 1831 with the Catholic Church in France on the eve of the revolution; both, he said, were beset by the "three great causes of ruin of spiritual powers"—great wealth, bad organization, and abuses.[113] Tom Mozley, like most of the Tractarian leaders jealous for the good name of the Church, absolved the great mass of the clergy from the criticisms being leveled at it from what seemed like all quarters but in his zeal to do so revealed the institution's darker side. "It was not the fault of the clergy generally that bishops and dignitaries made fortunes, and used their patronage for private purposes. There was a broad line between the rich and the poor clergy in those days; but in truth the poor clergy represented the Church, the rich clergy her oppressors and plunderers."[114] Earlier, we saw Prime Minister Peel's disgust with venality among the clergy.

The inequalities of the Church brought trouble to it in another way. There were great disparities from one diocese to another in the income that bishops received, leading bishops to regard an appointment to, say, Bristol, Oxford, or Llandaff (at something like £500 a year) as a stepping-stone to a more lucrative post and preventing long-term efforts to reform the diocese. Also, given that the bishop expected to pay the expenses accruing to the post—hospitality, a house in London, charitable generosity, personal secretary and other employees—he was faced with the necessity of holding other preferments, thus contributing to the pluralism that was one of the banes of the Church.[115] The great inequalities of clerical pay were as prevalent at the parish level as in the bishops' houses. The *Christian Observer* noted that this was why so many clergymen (especially Evangelicals) took on private pupils. They had to do it to avoid starvation, but that reduced their effectiveness as parish priests.[116]

More serious for the Church's ministry than the pay of the ordinands was their questionable quality. Mostly Oxford and Cambridge graduates, the new parsons lacked specialized training for their work until after mid-century. It was not until 1854 that Parliament passed an act that led to the creation of special training colleges, such as that established in Cuddesdon by Samuel Wilberforce, bishop of Oxford. Early in his episcopal career, Bishop Blomfield—later the reforming bishop of London—interviewed new ordinands before ordaining them only under pressure, preferring not "to put them to so much trouble."[117] Clergymen were disliked because of a general perception that they were standing in the way of reforming the abuses out of the Church. The *Record* remarked that whereas the clergy were of different minds on the subject, they had not met a single layman who did not believe it was necessary.[118]

Defenders of the Church against such critics have at least one point in their favor—the Church had so little power of independent action that it was a wonder it could find the strength to reform at all. The convocation of bishops had not met since 1730, and it came to be taken for granted that the prelates were responsible to the Parliament. (Even before convocation had breathed its last, it had become politicized to the point that it had little independence.)[119] The High Churchmen at Oxford came to lament the Church's lack of a central authority, and their enemies at the *Record* did the same, saying that the institution seemed to observers to have become "a feeble adjunct of the State, and appears to be viewed by the State chiefly as an instrument for accomplishing its views."[120] As the Parliament became the de facto pope of the Church of England, the Church's authority was being eaten away at the bottom. Patronage, the right to appoint incumbents of parishes, was a form of property and was no more likely to be given away than was the manor. These advowsons were bought and sold, and although a clergyman might not buy one for himself, he could act through a middleman. The House of Lords proved to be a roadblock in the path of reform in this respect, being especially sensitive on the matter of property rights. Even where the bishops retained the right of appointment, they sometimes misused it. Well past the middle of the century, this type of abuse still persisted, with even the archbishop of Canterbury appointing relatives to choice positions.[121]

In the half-decade beginning with 1828, the Church was rocked by successive blows to its prestige. The repeal of the Test and Corporation Acts followed by the Roman Catholic Relief Act marked the beginning of the end of its privileged position, as first Dissenters and then Roman Catholics received their full political rights. At this point the *Record,* than which no publication more loyal to the Church existed, announced that never in the history of the world had a church stood in greater need of reform than the Church of England at that moment, and it confessed that it, in common with everyone else, had no idea how the task could be done.[122] The Reform Bill of 1832 increased the suffrage, and many more middle-class Dissenters had the right to vote, making it likely that the interests of the Church would not be protected as heretofore. Moreover, the opposition of the bishops voting in the House of Lords to the second attempt to pass the Political Reform Bill in 1831 raised the hostility to the Church to a fever pitch. The motion lost by a vote of 199 to 158; two bishops voted in favor of the bill, six abstained, and twenty-one voted no. Sydney Smith, the sardonic canon of St. Paul's, noted that after that happened, "It was not safe for a clergyman to appear in the streets."[123] Nine years later, Smith recalled the occasion in more colorful terms in a letter to Bishop Blomfield: "The Bishops never re-

mained unpelted; they were pelted going, coming, riding, walking, conse-
crating, and carousing; the Archbishop of Canterbury, in the town of Canterbury, at the period of his visitation, was only saved from the mob by the
dexterity of his coachman."[124] In 1833, the government announced its intention to suppress ten of the Irish bishoprics, an act that so outraged the
High Churchmen of Oxford that they were stimulated to launch the Tractarian movement. The preponderance of evidence suggests that in this period the Church was undergoing a crisis of public confidence and that the
alarm in Oxford was not mistaken.[125] The Hammonds adverted to the
hatred that ordinary workers had for the parsons, probably exaggerating it
greatly. But they did point to something that had the ring of truth: a great
many clergymen were also magistrates, and it was in this capacity that they
carried out the rigorous demands of a legal system that still had far to go before it shook off the harsher penalties of previous ages.[126]

Meanwhile Thomas Arnold, whose every other thought seemed to be
connected with Church reform, was saying that many of those who piously
called for the reform of the Church were frauds, seeking rather the destruction of the Church. They cared nothing about the Church, he contended,
but much about money.[127] At almost the same moment, the *Record* was saying that the High Church was the side that was resisting reformation; they
wanted to keep the "fat livings" and all the other practices that had forced
two million people into Dissent. The guilty ones were "the slumbering pluralists, who are now alarmed because their craft is in danger," and the
heroes were "the working Clergy, whose numbers God increases more and
more."[128] Thus the haters of the Church and all it stood for were joined in
the attack not only by Dissenters tired of their inferior status but also by
some of its most fervent admirers and supporters. Thirteen years later, the
Christian Observer was still lamenting the "triple union of High-churchism
with Popery and Evangelical Dissent, against the Church of England as a
National Institution."[129] The Church, then, assailed by its enemies and its
friends, under the domination of political authorities in Westminster, its
ministers chosen largely by lay property holders over whom it had no control, seemed more like a weakling unable to control its circumstances than
like a tyrant grinding the poor under its heel. And if its most glaring abuses
remained unreformed, its intellectual ramparts unmanned except by this or
that faction, that may be what one must expect from an Establishment that
in principle had no competitors and had dwelled close to the center of power
in the government and the universities. Its flaccid response to the attacks
upon it was almost foreordained by the long decades of monopoly power
and the complacency that it bred.[130] It was against this background that
people like Gladstone saw the Tractarian movement arise out of the swamp

and thought it would be the salvation of the Church of England, something to complement the Evangelical revival and correct its weaknesses.[131]

What finally brought the Church of England, despised from almost every quarter, out of its low state? W. J. Conybeare, in his *Edinburgh Review* article of 1853, described as harshly as anybody the depths to which the Church and its clergy had sunk in the eighteenth century—"The spirit was expelled, and the dregs remained." He thought much of the credit for the renewal of the Church was due the Evangelicals, and he found it necessary to "deny . . . that the Old Evangelical party is effete." It had been hurt by its lack of learning (a fault of the whole Establishment, he thought) and by the emergence of the Recordite party, which he did not even believe should be called Evangelical, so far had it departed from the Clapham tradition.[132] Among the most important factors in the renewal of the Church was the increase in the quantity and the quality of its workers. Studies of the clergy show that the numbers doubled between 1835 and the end of the century. Moreover, something was done about the mischief caused by nonresidence. After 1810 the number of beneficed clergy not performing parish duties fell slowly until it reached about 31 percent in 1835. Then it fell rapidly in the next fifteen years. By 1850 it stood at only 9.5 percent. Combining the rapid growth in numbers of clergy with the significant decline in those who were not actively serving shows an important increase in the provision of pastoral services. This was augmented even further because the number of curates assisting incumbent clergymen also increased greatly, doubling between 1835 and 1841, when there were 2,032. Twelve years later, the Church boasted 3,437 assistant curates.[133]

More important than the increase in the number of clergy was the improvement in the quality. This may have been due partly to the fact that the notion of absolute rights of property with respect to clerical appointments was also undergoing some modification. By the 1820s, there was some agreement that the parson's right to his appointment was not the same as other property but was in a sense a kind of trust; the right to enjoy it was conditioned on the fulfillment of the purposes for which it existed.[134] In the words of a modern scholar, "Evangelicalism and Tractarianism struck from opposite directions at the unregenerate heart, adding to the general voice their own affectionate insistence that the English clergy must be beyond reproach."[135] Moreover, much of the improvement of the parsons was not their improvement in a narrow technical sense but their increasing general acceptance by the people.[136]

In addition, some of the prime ministers of the early nineteenth century were taking their responsibilities for ecclesiastical matters more seriously, and Perceval and Liverpool were thought to be especially good in this respect.[137] Charles Blomfield, bishop of Chester, was translated to London in 1828 and became a reforming prelate who did much to break himself and then the Church out of a position of comfort in order to serve the multitudes of the capital city. He insisted that the Church must turn from self-regard to selfless service. He regarded it as not only immoral to keep to the old ways but also politically stupid; the Church must recognize its changed environment and change with it, or it would die. His younger colleague, Samuel Wilberforce of Oxford (William Wilberforce's favorite son), was energetic and determined enough to become one of the most effective bishops of the century. One historian regards the work of these two "political bishops," as he calls them, as having done much "to save the Church of England and its temporal wealth from radical spoliation."[138] The acerbic High-Church historian Sabine Baring-Gould, who met Wilberforce several times, concluded that he had "recast the whole idea of the Episcopate, and . . . successfully raised the tone of clerical life."[139]

The major institutional change of the Church during the period came out of Peel's conviction that something had to be done to rescue the Church from its reputation and from its past. In early 1835, after consulting with Archbishop Howley and Bishop Blomfield, Peel established a commission composed of laymen chosen by himself and clergymen chosen by the archbishop of Canterbury. There were institutional changes in the original makeup of the commission, and the next year the work went on under Melbourne's second ministry, but it was widely recognized that Peel deserved the credit (or blame, in the case of both radicals who thought the Church would be strengthened by it and conservative Churchmen who thought it would be seriously damaged) for having set the process in motion. High Churchmen were especially troubled by the fact that the Parliament, which now was composed partly of Dissenters, was reasserting its right to rule the Church, which seemed to them impious and destructive. In the words of an eminent Church historian, Peel's short ministry (only three months between taking office and resigning) "changed the history of the church. He showed that even Tories wanted reform and so made reform possible."[140] In a series of measures between 1836 and 1840, Parliament enacted the recommendations of the Ecclesiastical Commission into law. By these actions livings could no longer be held at the same time as sees, the great disparities between bishops' incomes were reduced, two sees were created and two were merged with others, the Ecclesiastical Commission was made a permanent body, strict limits were placed on the holding of more than one benefice, the power of the bishops over the parishes was strengthened, and the administration of cathedrals was reformed. Money saved by reducing the administrative structure of the cathedrals was used to create new parishes in the previously neglected cities. Notwithstanding the initial dismay of radicals and Dissenters, the effect of these reforms on the Church was so pronounced that few historians would think it more than an excusable overstatement to say that "if any two men could be said to have saved the church from its enemies, they were Peel and Blomfield."[141]

Physical proximity to the church building was extremely important at the time because of the primitive transport available, especially for poor people without horses. A parliamentary commission reporting in 1853 concluded that if the roads and weather were decent, people would walk a mile to go to church services, but not much further. Therefore, the maldistribution of church buildings, because of internal migrations associated with industrialization, was a very serious matter for the health of the Church and the allegiance of people to it.[142] Of the enormous capital possessed by the Church of England, much consisted of buildings, the stock of which had been greatly augmented in our period. The spotty placement of these physical assets was worsened by the sad state of neglect that afflicted many of them, some of them being almost beyond saving. In the first half of the nineteenth century, 2,500 were erected at a cost of £9 million, of which £7 million was donated privately. In the fourteen years after 1851, the Establishment built another 1,000 churches and reconstructed an additional 300.[143]

The old High Church was responsible for much of the church-building activity. A good deal of the energy and the funds for the extensive period of church building came from the Church Building Commission, established by legislation in 1818. The prime force in that event was the work of the High Churchmen known as the Hackney Phalanx, who began lobbying for an extensive program in new church building in 1810. The preamble of the 1818 legislation mentioned the need to provide free seating for the poor in the churches, and the act provided £1 million for the enterprise, which the commissioners could draw on. Six years later another half-million was placed in the fund. It was one of the unfortunate happenstances of the building program that no sooner had it done its work than the style of worship changed. Built for the gospel- and sermon-centered approach to worship that the evangelical revival had ushered in, these churches were much less suited to the more liturgical approach that the resurgent High Church had instituted from its Oxford beginnings; consequently, these "commissioners' churches" have had a bad reputation for both practicality and esthetic beauty.[144] The new aesthetic in church buildings was led by a group of Cambridge undergraduates that formed in 1837 under the leadership of John Mason Neale, who came from an evangelical clerical family.

The Cambridge group called itself the Cambridge Camden Society. The Roman Catholic architect Augustus Pugin added intellectual ferment and technical skill to this movement, whose essence was a love for medieval church architecture and a corresponding disdain for the churches of the nineteenth century. This movement was extraordinarily successful in that many of its ideas were taken over and translated into bricks and mortar by people who had no use for the theology that animated it.[145]

George Bernard Shaw's famous *mot* had it that "religion is coming back upon men—even clergymen—with such power that the Church of England itself cannot stop it." Shaw would have been more to the point had he made the joke a century earlier (and in any case, one suspects he heard it from his friend Chesterton). It is hard for people almost two centuries later to imagine the fervor that went into what now seems the arcane subject of church reform, but in that time there were few subjects of greater importance to vast numbers of people. For religion was still thought to be not only belonging to a private realm but a force with powerful implications for how the society conducted itself. And even for those of another sort of thinking, the fact that there was an Establishment, and the further fact that as many people worshiped Sunday after Sunday in other houses of worship, perforce made such matters a vital subject of the day.

P. T. Marsh has described the Church of England in this period using the metaphor of the alpine climber, one of the stock figures in the craze for physical fitness that was a feature of the nineteenth century. The five-year period beginning with the repeal of the Test and Corporation Acts in 1828 he likens to a situation in which the ground under the climber's feet is falling away, threatening to hurl him over the precipice. "But with resourceful determination [the Church] lifted itself safely up to a stretch of high terrain. The walking here was never secure, there were always crevices in sight; but for a while they served only to challenge the exhilarated walker to further efforts."[146] Another historian says that the Church was not merely made more efficient after 1830 and did not merely experience a revival. "It was metamorphosed."[147] These assessments agree with many contemporary ones. In his *Charge to the Clergy of His Diocese . . . On the Occasion of His Sixth Visitation* in 1850, Bishop Blomfield exulted in the thousands of churches and schools that had been built in recent years. He lamented over the wretchedness of the Establishment in his youth but said that although it had been asleep it was not dead and that now it had awakened from its long slumber.[148] The successors of Clapham had the same idea. In the preface to the 1846 edition of the *Christian Observer*, the annual assessment of the state of the nation rejoiced "in the continued and increased prosperity of our National Zion" (this language used for the nation is instructive) but also in the state of the established Church: "The statistics of our Anglican schools, churches, and religious and charitable institutions, evince a striking advance of zeal and efficiency," especially in comparison with Dissent, although the advance of popery, both within and without the Church, was a continuing worry for these Evangelicals.[149]

The Recordite wing of the Evangelicals began seeing the fruit of Church renewal about the same time as others. In early 1833, they believed that the Church "is now beginning really to flourish."[150] A few years later, they took the long view and interpreted the preceding half century as a time when the preaching of the Church of England turned away from "heathen ethics" to the true gospel.[151]

The most intensive study we have of the Evangelicals in Parliament in the early nineteenth century concludes that there was no concerted movement among them to reform the Church. Rather, there were spectacularly effective efforts by a few of them that belied the general record. The reason for that evident lassitude in comparison with prodigious efforts in other fields was apparently the lack of regard in which the Church was held by so many Evangelicals. This was partly because of the low state into which the Church had descended but was also a function of Evangelical theology, which posited a direct connection between the individual and God without the necessary intervention of a third party or an institution.[152] On the other hand, there were other ways to reform the Church than through legislation. Gladstone, although he did not agree with the Evangelical ecclesiology, believed that "the juice and sap of the Evangelical teaching has in a very remarkable manner coursed through" the Anglican Church. He made clear what he meant by the "juice and sap" when, in the same passage, he reminisced about his childhood, when morality was "taught without direct derivation from, or reference to, the Person of Christ." Gladstone's view of the Evangelicals was like their own: "The Evangelical preachers of the English Church were not innovators, but restorers," and their reintroduction of Christ into the Church "has now penetrated and possessed it on a scale so general that it may be considered as pervading the whole mass."[153] The dyspeptic and antievangelical Mark Pattison, rector of Lincoln College, had something similar to say. He thought that the Evangelicals, as a party, had no future but that their influence had "penetrated far beyond those party limits."[154]

Central to the convictions of almost all the parties of the religious revival was the conjoining of spirit and matter, of religious beliefs and their incarnation in the institutions of the society. Even those of a more quietist sort, like the Quakers, came over to this reformed point of view. That was always Wesley's belief, and it was one of the things that united him with his Calvinist colleagues and adversaries. When true religious revival should break forth in the land, it would have to affect the way people behaved as individuals *and* the institutions that made up the society. In that respect, at least, they found their expectations borne out in the first half of the nineteenth century.

There were important gaps in the visible march of the evangelical spirit through the institutions of England. Few references to evangelicals crop up in accounts of the great political Reform Bill of 1832 or the reform of the poor law two years later. Much of the hard work of Church reform came from other sources—there was an older, more traditional sort of piety animating Peel and Blomfield. There was, moreover, enough truth in R. W. Dale's characterization, reported at the beginning of this chapter, to suggest that many evangelicals thought that if the underlying spiritual sickness were dealt with, solutions to the institutional problems would follow without the need for institutional fixes. Given the way evangelical thinking and culture migrated from the party to much of the nation, there may be more truth to that contention than is generally recognized. In that case we might say that even where the evangelicals did not actively involve themselves, their demand for public righteousness still prepared the way for others.

XIII

A New Nation for a New Queen

BY THE TIME THE VAGARIES of the genetic process and the final call for William IV handed the throne to the young Victoria in 1837, the transition this book chronicles was largely complete. In some ways the reforming movements had become overripe and begun to spoil, and, as usual, we are hard pressed to say just when one trend terminated and the next began; they shade into each other imperceptibly. Features we are pleased to associate with the eighteenth century—radical unbelief, for example—persisted into the nineteenth century and through the long Victorian years. Others characteristic of the later Victorian period, such as Christian socialism, made their first appearance in the early years of the reign. Still, notwithstanding the inevitable messiness of the process, it is possible to make generalizations about the generation before Victoria came to the throne, not the least of which is the fact that its central feature was what the Hammonds referred to, not without distaste, as "a great public baptism," which is to say the evangelicalization of the culture.[1]

RETURNING TO THE ROOTS

John Stuart Mill interpreted the origin of the religious environment in which he lived as part of the ongoing historical process through which one "excess" is corrected by a swing in the opposite direction, leading to the other excess and a decreasing oscillation until the society finally settles down into a kind of equilibrium. Within this framework it made sense for him to say that the reaction against a sterile scientism of the eighteenth century was succeeded by what he called (somewhat obtusely) the "Germano-Coleridgian doctrine," which reacted against it.[2] But this simple reactive understanding was little more than a restatement of the kind of naturalism from which the culture was departing.

Boyd Hilton, entitling his study *The Age of Atonement*, stood on more solid ground by interpreting the period in terms of one of its dominant ideas, which   f what Mill had called a reaction. *Atonement,* in Hilton's treatmen   t a mere abstraction for people living then but stood at the heart o   the thinking, the literature, and the debates and was the spring of   millions. Gladstone, like many intellectuals, believed that the reem   atonement was to a large extent the restoration of the ancient doctrine of the Church that the Establishment had neglected and that this restoration was largely the achievement of the Evangelicals. He suggested that the Tractarians, whose leaders he counted among his friends, were unconsciously completing the work of the Evangelicals. The Evangelicals' "great gift" of reintroducing the preaching of Christ "has now penetrated and possessed [the Church] on a scale so general that it may be considered as pervading the whole mass."[3] Gladstone was speaking of the diffusion of the doctrinal framework of the Atonement throughout the Church, but there was a further diffusion throughout the nation; at the margins it was less theological and conscious than cultural and implicit, but still it was there.

The famous census of 1851, which is sometimes interpreted as evidence that religion was on the wane, in fact shows its strength, despite the lamentations of contemporaries. (The real surprise was that Dissent had virtually drawn even with the Church of England in the loyalties of the populace.) For on census Sunday about 61 percent of the population in England and Wales attended worship service.[4] If we consider absences due to emergencies, the continuing maldistribution of Establishment places of worship, the difficulty of canvassing little chapels in isolated hamlets, and the people whose piety did not take institutional form, it is probable that a substantial majority of the population had a measure of commitment to some form of English Christianity, notwithstanding the inevitable admixture of hypocrisy. Moreover, it is likely that the attendance at worship increased after the census.[5] It sometimes seems extraordinary that even those who rejected the dominant religious ethos could not imagine how to carry on without it. Leslie Stephen, who had none of the religious convictions that animated his Clapham grandparents, nevertheless was unable to see any way outside of religion to buttress the moral certainties that he still held.[6]

THE MAKING OF ENGLISH DECENCY

But the numbers mean little unless they reflect the way people lived. Character makes all the difference. We lose sight too easily of what Francis Place knew looking back from his old age to his childhood: that the rough, uncouth, brutal society in which he had come to adulthood had been replaced by a kinder, more decent one. These changes took place on all levels of the society and were nowhere more evident than in the characters of the people who led the renewal. The influence the leaders of the religious revival had on others was as much due to their character as to the force of their intellects. Stanley said of Arnold, "I have never felt such reverence for any one since," even as he acknowledged that this feeling went beyond the pull of Arnold's ideas. In his old age, one of Stanley's classmates said of Arnold's example that "the lapse of years has only served to deepen in me the conviction that no gift can be more valuable than the recollection and the inspiration of a great character working on our own."[7] That is one of the main reasons people so freely gave their allegiance to the persons and the principles of innumerable leaders of the moral revolution.[8] Wesley, Wilberforce, Newman, and Keble exerted the same sort of magnetism on people.

Beyond the attraction of the major leaders, the interests, values, and virtues of the masses have an independent influence of their own. Gerhard Lenski, a sociologist of religion who has studied this issue, concludes that it is a mistake to measure the influence of religious associations on society exclusively by their success or failure in bringing about the institutional changes they advocate. He thinks that far more important than those organized campaigns are the "daily actions of thousands (or millions) of group members whose personalities have been influenced by their lifelong exposure" to the religious impulses.[9] That insight is the one that is most useful for understanding the effect of the cultural revolution of the early nineteenth century. The Cambridge historian Herbert Butterfield once remarked that the importance of Christianity in the history of the West cannot really be understood very well by the historian who draws his information exclusively from documents. It lies rather in the constant preaching to the multitudes— often illiterate multitudes— of love and humility week after week in such a way that how people feel, think, and behave is vastly different than it otherwise would have been, a phenomenon that has tended "greatly to alter the quality of life and the very texture of human history."[10] Only when the changes in this preaching and its effects take place as rapidly as they did in England in this period of rapidly expanding literacy can we easily appreciate their importance. This is very difficult to see when we are considering "English" life; it is when we get down to localities and see what people do in everyday relationships that it becomes apparent. Thus a study of Ulster speaks of the "quiet spirituality and daily charities of generations of Ulster evangelicals" and advocates attending to them as much as to the great events that make it into the newspapers.[11] These cultural traits have powerful effects on the direction and force of a society. Who, for example, could calculate the magnitude of the effects of the replacement of *honor* as an ideal in England by *humility?* A slight that might be taken as sufficient to require a duel can be brushed off by a man who newly thinks such affronts are best met by love and humility. There is also a strong cultural force in *repentance* as a theologically sanctioned and socially accepted requirement because it permits the turning away from destructive behavior to a new beginning.[12] When such acts are multiplied by the million, it cannot help but bring about large-scale change, the sort that the historian can only despair of trying to track and quantify with anything approaching precision.

Chesterton, with his customary hyperbole, wrote that the early nineteenth century produced great men because it taught that men were great. "It made strong men by encouraging weak men."[13] He could reach this conclusion because he saw that in that age Negro slaves, against theory and practice, were considered human beings. Illiterate and ill-behaved ragamuffins were worthy of being taught how to read. People had come to believe that these various outcasts had souls, a fact that the religious revival recognized and taught but for which eighteenth-century rationalism and its utilitarian counterpart could find little warrant within their own set of assumptions.

Hippolyte Taine, an unbeliever observing the kinds of changes that we are considering, was struck by the benefits that Victorian England enjoyed over his native France. He included among its advantages England's political constitution and its wealth, but the third category was English religion, the main effect of which was its ethical sway over the nation. "The young man starting out in life, the mature man in full career, are, up to a certain point, restrained and guided by a body of traditional, popular and fortifying beliefs which provide them with a rule of conduct and a noble idea of the world." He described the French, in contrast, as starting out with a kind of moral *tabula rasa* that they fill in more or less arbitrarily or fail to fill in at all.[14] When Lord Brougham urged the House of Lords to approve the Reform Bill of 1832 that would enfranchise several hundred thousand of the English middle classes, he did so by characterizing the future new voters as "sober, rational, intelligent, and honest" and therefore able to exercise the franchise responsibly.[15]

The much-vaunted and much-ridiculed moral sensibility of the nineteenth century was not the source of rigidity its critics have claimed but rather the source of its opposite—tremendous vitality and mobility. From the understanding of human nature that led to self-discipline, combined with the sense of calling introduced by the revived Protestant ethic, came the channeling of energies into socially beneficial activities. Drunken wastrels became sober family men, working through the day, studying in the evening, and sending their children to school. Those children grew up, saved their money, built businesses that employed their neighbors, and sent *their* children to the universities and to the House of Commons.

There is another way in which the religious revival facilitated dynamic change. Although none of the religious reform movements as such were associated with the Reform Bill of 1832, some analysts contend that the tradition of English Dissent made the movement toward democracy possible by legitimizing opposition to the official positions taken by the state. Since it presupposed and institutionalized the legitimacy of withholding assent from the religious Establishment, it made it seem acceptable that one might also dissent from the politics of the state and that such dissent could legitimately have formal legislative expression. The German social theorist Ernst Troeltsch argued that the multiplicity of churches made political liberalism possible, especially in the English-speaking countries.[16]

THE SPIRIT OF THE AGE AND THE WANING OF THE RATIONALIST ENTERPRISE

John Stuart Mill published an essay in 1831 that he entitled "The Spirit of the Age," an idea that he did not think had ever been used prior to a half century earlier. This concept belonged to a time of transition, Mill said, and its purpose was to draw a line between those who were of the old thinking and those who belonged to the future.[17] The exact nature of the transition may be fruitfully argued, and Mill's generalization may be true on several different levels, some of which Mill may not have realized or agreed with. At least one aspect of the transition was that the rationalist project of the eighteenth century, the one that had nurtured and formed Mill himself, was in the process of unraveling. Its showiest triumphs (the new poor law, for example) may have come in the 1830s, but thereafter its progress was thwarted not only by the growing influence of the religious revival but also by the historical consciousness that accompanied it.

One of the vulnerabilities of rationalism lay in its dependence on ideological considerations from which supposedly it was ridding the world. We have seen that Lord Macaulay, reviewing James Mill's treatise on government, savaged it for its reliance on airy theories without regard to the facts of how governments actually work. He was saying, in effect, that the rationalist structure, which trumpeted so proudly the cause of science, was itself unscientific and irrational. One of the skeptics of the age, William Hazlitt, lamented in his own work *The Spirit of the Age* (1825) that the world was growing old. Apparently overcome by his own skepticism, he interpreted the vast technological achievements of the nation as portending future fail-ure, since there was nothing new to learn, nothing more to achieve.[18]

Harriet Martineau's modern biographer suggests that Martineau's scien-tism stemmed from her belief in mesmerism, which she took as a presage of the discovery of new laws of nature. But this was the sort of scientism that led the playwright and journalist Douglas Jerrold to represent her creed as "There is no God, and Harriet is his prophet."[19] Turn over the rock of skepticism or atheism, in other words, and you find it to be supported by a faith. Tocqueville's interpretation of the French Revolution was similar. He thought the upper classes had turned to skepticism while the common people had remained religious. But that skepticism was a thwarted sort of religion, turning into the channel of revolution, which then became a reli-gion of its own and "created an atmosphere of missionary fervor and, in-deed, assumed all the aspects of a religious revival." He believed that this revolutionary religion paralleled the Christian in that it claimed to be pro-ducing "nothing short of a regeneration of the whole human race."[20]

Mill's pendular notion entailed the more or less mechanical replacement of the scientistic with the Christian worldview, but this does not mean that all those who rejected Paine and Bentham and their followers were Chris-tians in any sense that Wilberforce, Newman, and Arnold would recognize. Rather, their worldviews were compatible with English Christianity in a way that they were not with radicalism. The Russian Orthodox theologian Alexander Schmemann explained this distinction with nicety in conclud-ing that Alexander Solzhenitsyn should be regarded as a Christian writer. He was not speaking about whether Solzhenitsyn was a believer in Chris-tian dogma or ritual or the church but rather had in mind "a deep and all-embracing, although possibly unconscious perception of the world, man, and life, which, historically, was born and grew from Biblical and Christian revelation, and only from it."[21] It was such very basic ways of perceiving reality that separated the Enlightenment and Christian worldviews in the early nineteenth century. Differences of that sort did not prevent Christians and utilitarians from cooperating on projects, but they explain why Ben-tham's plan for the housing of prisoners was radically different from John Howard's and why utilitarian views on preparing teachers for service could not remotely resemble Kay-Shuttleworth's.

Although the differences between the rival worldviews were a bright line, the same might not be true of the influences upon the people holding them, which often were diverse. Wilberforce may have considered all things new with his conversion, but he did not thereby forget everything he ever learned in Yorkshire and Cambridge. Chadwick was much taken with the charismatic leadership of Bentham, but that did not erase from his mind everything his Methodist grandfather had passed on to him.

There is another explanation for the cohabitation of the two spirits of the age in relative peace: that the "secularity" of scientism is a development of biblical thinking. There is a common argument to the effect that modern science could grow only in a world that had been desacralized and that this could only happen within a view that a transcendent God had created it. Once people lost the belief that trees and rocks had souls or that spirits resided in mountains, it became possible to study them objectively.[22] Keith Thomas's magisterial account of the history of magic concludes that belief in magic declined under the weight of conviction that the world was under the care of "a single all-directing providence," a particular emphasis of the Reformation.[23] This was the conviction that made the development of modern science possible. When Prince Albert cast about for an inscription with which to decorate the title page of the official catalogue of that great paean to science and technology, the Crystal Palace exhibition of 1851, he used this one:

> Say not the discoveries we make are our own—
> The germs of every art are implanted within us,
> And God our instructor, out of that which is concealed,
> Develops the faculties of invention[24]

On this showing, the partisans of the "secular" were dependent on the religious ideas against which they were rebelling, which suggests the limitations of the common religious-secular dualism.

UNITIES BEYOND THE RELIGIOUS DISUNITY

One of the tragedies of the period was the hostility that poisoned the atmosphere between persons and parties whose basic worldview and concerns about the society were similar. We cannot know what might have happened if these hostilities had been subsumed under an overriding unity of purpose and if the energies devoted to religious polemics had been given more productive outlet. The ending of the hostility between Calvinists and Arminians and the fruitful cooperation between the adherents (or former adherents) of both in the innumerable projects and societies in which evangelicals engaged themselves suggest that much might have been accomplished. In previous chapters we have devoted a good deal of attention to the strife, but here it is time to consider the underlying unities that so often escape the attention of observers. In a judgment that recalls Gladstone's view, the Cambridge historian Owen Chadwick believes that evangelicalism considered as a spirit rather than a party suffused nearly the whole of English Christianity, with a "left wing" in primitive Methodism and a "right wing" in Tractarianism and even in the Ultramontanism of the Roman Catholic Church. "The evangelical revival was a mighty movement of religious spirit" that was contained by no party, in this view.[25]

Sometimes contemporaries described the unity behind the religious reform movements as a spirit that somehow was in the air, even if they had a hard time specifying just what it was. Newman wrote a letter explaining his disastrous Tract #90 in terms of a vague *something* that lay behind all the dominant movements of the period. It had been attested to, said Newman, by the belles-lettrists Scott, Coleridge, and Wordsworth. Even Edward Irving was a "witness" to it. Unhappily, he went on, only the Roman Catholic Church, despite its "errors and evils . . . has given free scope" to it. And what was *it?* For Newman it was a sense of the numinous in the midst of the mundane: "feelings of awe, mystery, tenderness, reverence, devotedness, and other feelings which may be especially called Catholic."[26] Newman and all segments of the religious revival saw themselves as doing battle with the prevailing skeptical and materialist spirit characteristic of the eighteenth century, which persisted in the thinking of the utilitarians and the Churchmen he called "liberals."

Surprisingly, even the Recordites, as divisive and protective as they were of their version of Evangelicalism, recognized the dangers of sectarianism. They seldom used the word *Evangelical* in describing their position, preferring to be "on the Lord's side," regardless of what it was called. Early in its tenure the *Record* said that it would neither "disclaim nor appropriate" the title of Evangelical. It even denied being the organ of a party within the Church.[27] There may have been something disingenuous about this stance, but it reflected a consciousness hiding behind the scenes in all the parties that there was something untoward about the sectarianism that had sundered the unity of the Church of England. On the first anniversary of its existence, the paper avowed that its purpose was "to blunt the edge of party spirit" in both religious and secular matters and to "take a position on the broad basis of our common Christianity, whence to endeavour to heal, not to irritate" the injuries caused by controversy.[28] Yet within a year or two the *Record,* by then under the control of the hard-line Scot Alexander Haldane, was involved in feuds even with the *Christian Observer,* which, it claimed, had "slid into the evil temper of the age."[29]

Among the disparate parties, the High Church and the Evangelicals seem to have had the most potential for fruitful cooperation. There has been in modern Anglicanism a tendency to consider Catholic and Evangelical strains of the Church as necessary parts of the Anglican heritage, denying that there is a contradiction between them. In 1936, the archbishop of York wrote that they are "not two separate things which the Church of England must hold together by a great feat of compromise," but complementarities.[30] An Evangelical of that generation opined that the original Tractarian leaders were more or less on the mark.[31] These later views were not far different from some expressed by the main actors of our period. Even the common view of Evangelicalism as antisacramental needs to be qualified. The practice of communion had atrophied in the eighteenth-century Church and received renewed attention from the Evangelicals. When John Venn began his ministry at Clapham, he brought with him the revival of the celebration of Holy Communion, which took place monthly. Between the start of the century and 1813, the number of communicants increased 50 percent.[32]

Pusey said that he affirmed everything the Evangelicals affirmed, departing from them only when they began denying. He took the argument to a scion of the Clapham Evangelicals: "I challenged my friend Henry Venn Elliott to frame his belief in words which I could not accept."[33] That was more or less Newman's position in his early Tract #11, *The Visible Church*, written in the first year of the Tractarian movement. He told his readers that he was in no sense trying to dissuade them on any subject but rather was asking them to consider adding to their beliefs what he took to be the scriptural teaching on the Church. To dispel any doubt about whether his audience was the Evangelicals, he supported his case by alluding to an unnamed person who "was both a Calvinist and a strenuous High-Churchman."[34] A modern study entitled "The Evangelical Sources of Newman's Power" emphasizes the common elements of the two parties.[35] Toward the end of his life Wilberforce himself recognized the propensity toward the High Church of his three clerical sons and accepted it with equanimity.[36] After Samuel Wilberforce became bishop of Oxford, it became difficult to assign him a place in the party scheme. Identified with the High Church in some respects, he never lost his Evangelical convictions. The *Christian Observer* published a long extract from an 1846 sermon to new ordinands that might have come from Simeon, Newton, or one of the Venns:

> Your one work is to win souls with Christ: not to produce a certain general decency and amendment in the fact of society round you, but as God's instrument, and through the power of Christ's name, to work in living souls the mighty marvel of their true conversion. . . . Go out to visit in your parish not because you ought to spend so much time in visiting your people, but because

they have souls; and you have committed to you (feeble as you are) the task of saving them, in Christ's strength, from everlasting burnings. . . . We must *show* them in our risen lives, that Christ indeed is risen.[37]

The High Church historian and theologian Sabine Baring-Gould could be scathing in his analysis of Evangelicalism, yet he believed that the movement offered the High Church some relief from the dangers of formalism while in turn profiting from an appreciation of the worth of the Church as an institution.[38]

If there was considerable acceptance of High Church principles among Evangelicals, the converse was also true. Newman never abjured his Evangelical conversion, and he affirmed its reality in the *Apologia*. Some modern observers see in his thinking, including his later thinking as a Roman Catholic, numerous evidences of that Evangelical heritage. And this was true not only of Newman but of the whole movement that he led. Pusey's essay on *Justification* (1853), written long after the demise of the movement at Oxford, was at pains to insist (perhaps beyond plausibility) that all Christians had essentially the same beliefs on that subject, and he expressed those beliefs in terms that Evangelicals would be likely to accept. "And yet all believe that this justifying faith does not justify us by any quality of its own, but simply brings us to God, Who, of His own free bounty and love, justifies those who believe in Him, and who, being drawn by Him, hold not back from Him, but come unto Him by Whom they have been called and drawn."[39] Gladstone, who was excellently placed to understand both the Evangelicals and the Tractarians, believed that more than the Tractarians said or even knew, they were "pupils and continuators of the Evangelical work," in addition to everything else they were.[40] Some of Newman's sermons from his Tractarian days look hardly different than we would expect Evangelical sermons to read. The inheritors of the Tractarian mantle, the Ritualists, have been described by a German scholar as "evangelical Anglo-Catholics," partly because of their indebtedness to Methodist thinking. Their best known priest, Alexander Mackonochie, described his fellow Ritualists as "the fruits of the labor of Wesley."[41] Even the *Record* acknowledged that some of the Tractarians were converted men and that some of the Evangelicals were not. It also said that under pressure of the Evangelical surge, High Church preaching was changing, becoming more evangelical in substance.[42]

The Arnoldian relations with the Tractarians and Evangelicals were in some ways analogous to those between the other two bodies. What the three shared was the unbending centering of their religious thinking on Christ, Thomas Arnold perhaps more single-mindedly than the other two.

For Arnold believed that the Evangelicals had a doctrine of Scripture that sometimes obscured the Christ-centered emphasis he favored, and he detested what he thought was the High Church's obsession with itself, overemphasizing the hierarchy, the splendor, the episcopal palaces, and so on. That made it easy for him to undervalue the humble piety of a Newman or even of his own friend Keble, which was focused on Christ.[43] His vision for conversion was not noticeably different from that of the Evangelicals. "It is not improvement that is required," he preached to the boys, "but a change of heart and life; a change of principles, of hopes, of fears, of masters; a change from death unto life; from Satan to God."[44] James Stephen of Clapham said of Arnold: "I like him hugely. I have seldom met a man more to my taste."[45] On the publication of Stanley's *Life of Arnold,* three years after the headmaster's death, the *Christian Observer* had many favorable things to say of him. They acknowledged errors in Arnold's theology but added that "many passages, and especially the references to our blessed Lord, are so beautiful and touching, that it may seem as unjust as it is painful to imagine anything of latent doctrinal error in the opinions of the writer." Arnold's last days the *Observer* called "a beautiful exhibition of piety and resignation."[46] More surprising was the similarly favorable opinion toward Arnold of the *Record,* which had critical remarks to make of his theology but which lauded his personal qualities, his love of family, his passion for service to his society, his conviction that Christian faith should animate all areas of life, his independence of mind, his attempt to make Rugby a Christian school, his loyalty to Christ, and the firmness of his faith as his death drew near.[47] Even apart from their view of Arnold, the Evangelicals could regard as friends and allies the Noetics, or those Newman would excoriate as "liberals." In 1831 the *Christian Observer* had given high praise to one of them, Richard Whately of Oriel College.[48]

With all the hostilities between Arnold and Newman and their respective followers, there was an undercurrent of respect. We have already seen that Newman viewed Arnold's pupils as having brought to the growing liberal party in Oxford "an elevation of character" that their opponents were bound to respect. In the same passage, Newman went on to say that as far as outside observers could tell from their actions, these Arnoldians became more conservative (which is to say, in Newman's lexicon, more responsible and praiseworthy) as they grew older. Moreover, they did so not by rejecting Arnold's influence but "from the mere circumstance of remaining firm to their original professions."[49] This was an extraordinary statement, given the nature of the hostilities between the two men, and indeed the two camps. Newman was saying that no matter how much he disliked this or that opinion of Arnold's (mainly Arnold on "priestcraft" and the other issues that the Tractarians called "Church principles"), the headmaster's teaching still bore fruit that the Tractarians looked upon with favor. W. G. Ward, whose conception of the Church was so high that he preceded Newman to Rome, never lost his admiration for Arnold. Ward's son believed that his father was attracted mainly by Arnold's dislike of worldliness, his treatment of Scripture, and his sense of equality between Christians of different stations of life. The younger Ward wrote that Arnold's pupils at Oxford were a revelation to his father, "a sort of flesh and blood argument for the powerful living force of Arnold's religion." [50] Yet his attachment to Arnold did not prevent him from becoming a disciple of Newman, nor did the relationship with Newman turn him away from Arnold. When Arthur Stanley left Rugby for Oxford, he went to hear Newman preach and found himself reminded of none other than Arnold—the Arnold whose sermons he praised to the skies in his biography of the headmaster. As Stanley put it, "There was the same overpowering conviction conveyed that he was a thorough Christian." [51] Long after the heat of battle had cooled (and Arnold was in his tomb in the Rugby chapel), the Tractarian Tom Mozley numbered the headmaster among those who were "good and great." [52] All this is not to say that Arnold and Newman were equivalent but rather that serious disagreements and bad personal relations between the various leaders do not exhaust the universe of evidence to consider.

THE DECLINING INFLUENCE OF ORTHODOX RELIGION

Modern analyses of the evangelical movement usually show it peaking some time in the period between the 1820s and the 1840s, although the reasons given vary. By 1834 Richard Cope, a former director of the London Missionary Society, was lamenting about the failures of the evangelical spirit that manifested themselves in declining willingness to cooperate between denominations on the basis of a shared faith in the same gospel. Since the halcyon days of the LMS, "the zeal of Christians has generally declined; ordinary and extraordinary Prayer Meetings have no longer an attractive influence." [53] Evangelical practicality, with its relative lack of interest in theology or in theoretical meditation of any kind, made it difficult to react productively to changing circumstances. An understanding of *church* that associated it almost entirely with the universal, invisible church made it difficult to give the kind of attention to reforming the Church of England as an institution that it was getting from other quarters. Being too impatient to reform the institution they had inherited, they went around it to create their own institutions. The Methodists were also by then suffering from ennui. Jabez Bunting's disciple, F. A. West, put it this way in 1842: "We are . . . much in a crisis respecting our own home-work . . . in numbers, finances & spiritual state . . . The spirit of the times, our commercial depression, & our notorious neglect of pastoral work (I say it of myself & the bulk of our preachers) & alienating the minds of our people just so much as to make them ready to be querulous and offensive."[54]

In the mid-1840s, the *Record* lauded the achievement of the Evangelicals in rescuing the Church of England from the torpor and unbelief into which it had descended but was bitter about their failings, the chief of which, the paper thought, was their timidity, by which it meant their unwillingness to confront the evils of the age, the chief evil being popery.[55] Newman thought that what the Evangelicals had lost was the "simplicity and unworldliness" that he so admired in the earlier period.[56] What seems to have happened is what we can expect when any outcast sect gradually enters the mainstream, or even—as seems to be the case here—when the mainstream joins it. Perhaps those two cases cannot be distinguished very sharply. A hot stream and a cold stream run together and sooner or later become one tepid stream. Even the hottest had that happen to them. The Primitive Methodists, for whom the post-Wesley Wesleyans had lost their savor, had themselves abandoned their faith in visions and dreams as arbiters of scriptural interpretation, and their view of worldliness relaxed enough for them to join the mania for sports to which the English nation in general had succumbed.

The number of Evangelicals in the Church of England grew throughout much of the nineteenth century. By some accounts, at the beginning of the century 5 percent of the clergy were Evangelicals; at the two-decade mark, 10 percent; just past the middle of the century, possibly more than one-quarter.[57] But the nature of the beast had changed. It is perhaps true, as one study maintains, that the vigor of evangelicalism remained until long after our period and that the decline did not set in until the 1870s.[58] But if that case can be made, it is only by focusing on leaders like Edward Bickersteth, Fowell Buxton, and Henry Venn the younger. Beneath that level, at the cultural level that is the main preoccupation of the present book, disquieting changes were taking place that would in time come to dominate the movement.

Basil Willey seemed to be suggesting something of the same idea in his analysis of the work of William Hale White, famous principally for his deconversion novel *The Autobiography of Mark Rutherford*. Willey believed that White was a minor version of George Eliot, hardened against the piety of his youth because his acquaintance was with a Puritanism in decline, "a Puritanism petrified and mammonized, clinging to shibboleths without real conviction."[59] White was reacting against an ossified religious shell in much the way the older Puritans (for that we may read "evangelicals") had reacted against the hardened shell of eighteenth-century religion.

EXPERIENCE, SENTIMENT, AND SENTIMENTALITY

An eminent scholar of Victorian England once warned against judging the age by laying too much weight on aesthetic matters as if taste, with its changing vagaries, were the ultimate criterion.[60] This admonition has not been taken much to heart but rather has been followed (as it was preceded) by considerable ridicule over the sentimentality of the period. Critics have been especially hard on the roots of sentimentality in evangelicalism. Newman warned about this problem in his "Lectures on Justification" during his Tractarian phase. "They rather aim at experience within, than at Him that is without. They are led to enlarge on the signs of conversion, the variations of their feelings."[61] Newman was not alone in this opinion, which was often expressed by the gibe "justification by feeling." For the same reason, Carlyle was scornful of the Methodism of his own century, which he thought was a sorry sight compared with when the Wesley brothers were alive. He called it "Methodism with its eye forever turned on its own navel."[62] Emphasizing inner contemplation and the high regard for feeling to which it leads was a temptation to which the entire culture was subject. A twentieth-century scholar writes of the most eminent of the Victorian novelists, "Again and again one feels that Dickens and his readers enjoy their tears."[63]

At its worst this sentimentality approached the grotesque as evangelicals, concerned to understand the tragedies of life as well as the joys through the eyes of faith, sweetened the hard places overmuch. When Henry Venn the elder broke the news of his wife's death in a letter, he began in this way: "I have some of the best news to impart." His reason was that his wife was now in Heaven, and the pious phrases in his report were meant to suggest that it was unseemly for people of faith to mourn.[64] The evangelical argot detracted from the effect of much of the effort to make converts through tracts and other literature because they were written from within the cave, so to speak, and did not use language accessible to those outside. Gladstone, in the midst of his praise for the Evangelical revival of the preaching of the gospel, noted that afterwards *preaching the gospel* became a "cant phrase."[65]

At its outer limit sentimentality is a form of dishonesty, since it is more taken with feeling than with the truth that might call its validity into question. And the next step after the sentimental form of dishonesty is hypocrisy, the sort that allows one to enjoy the feeling while also enjoying the fruits of contravening its source. Clyde Binfield entitled his study of Dissent *So Down to Prayers* from the comment made to him by his great-grandfather, who was both a deacon and a grocer. His fellow grocers, the old man told him, would mix sand into their sugar "and then go down to prayers with their families and assistants."[66] But far short of that sublime hypocrisy was the reduction of the evangelical theology and ethos into a rote incantation, a standard and constantly repeated corpus of Scripture references that encapsulated the evangelical emphases, along with a characteristic phraseology that established the evangelicals as a subcultural unit to which outsiders did not belong and that they might not even understand. This was partly due to the ideas expressed, but perhaps more so to the kind of language used, liberally laced with obsolescent words that came from the Authorized Version of the Bible, which had been translated under the sponsorship of King James I and published in 1611. (Some of these expressions were retained from older translations and had a musty sound even in the early seventeenth century.)

So offensive to many ears was the evangelical terminology that numerous evangelicals became disgusted with it. As early as 1805, the Dissenting evangelical John Foster wrote a book entitled *On Some of the Causes by Which Evangelical Religion Has Been Rendered Unacceptable to Persons of Cultivated Taste.* Foster maintained that more care must be taken in expressing the gospel. Refined persons are repelled by special terminology that does not comport with standard English as it is spoken in ordinary life. Foster kept referring to the imputation of fanaticism and held that it could be averted by changing the language that elicits it. "You may have observed that in attributing fanaticism, they often fix on the phrases, more than on the absolute substance, of evangelical doctrines."[67]

The problem was not only a public relations one; it affected the intellectual processes of the evangelicals, inasmuch as the offending phrases were, as Foster put it, "not so much vehicles of ideas, as the substitutes for them." For those who use such terminology, "the diction is the convenient asylum of ignorance, indolence, and prejudice."[68] The problem became worse after Foster wrote his book because the peculiar language spread along with the movement and became progressively more shallow. In the case of Henry Venn, the mode of speaking may have appeared idiosyncratic, but Venn was a man of spiritual depth. Later on, the lingo came from many who hardly understood what they were saying. In 1850 a prize-winning essay was published that itself was full of evangelical language but that bemoaned the widespread use of evangelical terminology that no longer spoke to the modern ear. "True, the majority of our congregations do not perceive the defect. They have all their lives long been accustomed to the 'evangelical dialect.'"[69]

Although the Clapham group was not generally prone to this vice, Wilberforce's wife, according to some reports, was. Henry Thornton's daughter wrote that Barbara Wilberforce associated with people who used evangelical jargon, some of whom did not have the moral standards called for by their profession of faith. She thought the Wilberforce sons had gone to the High Church because of their disgust with these friends of their mother's.[70] Even the *Record* felt itself forced to reply to the many protests it had received about the "tone and phraseology of many of our advertisements which have reference to religious objects." These complaints are of terminology "which mars all true beauty . . . which offends and disgusts many individuals . . . which, in fact, absolutely revolts their feelings, and induces a belief that what is assumed as the alone *true religion* rather lies in a peculiar vocabulary, in an unmeasurable length of cant phrases, than in a change of heart and of life." The paper defended the use of evangelical terminology as an antidote to worldliness but then went on to acknowledge that the critics had a point, that anything can be "overdone" and taken to "extremes." One almost expects it to defend the Tractarian doctrine of reserve: "There is a modesty of diction, as well as of deportment and of conduct. . . . On the whole we reach the conclusion that not a few of our advertising friends (we shall say nothing of ourselves) might with advantage cut off some of the exuberance of religious terminology which gives offence to many of their brethren."[71]

The "deconversion" of John Ruskin illustrates the problem Foster's "men of taste" had with the aesthetics of the evangelical argot, although in his case he had to go to Italy for the experience. This son of Evangelical parents was still a firm Protestant, he said, until 1858, when, steeped in the power of the art of Roman Catholic Italians, he walked into a Waldensian chapel in Turin, "where a little squeaking idiot was preaching to an audience of seventeen old women and three louts, that they were the only children of God in Turin; and that all the people in the world out of sight of Monte Viso, would be damned. I came out of the chapel, in sum of twenty years of thought, a conclusively un-converted man."[72] Ruskin describes the event in terms of a theological disagreement, but he had just come from viewing Veronese's *Queen of Sheba* and was "under quite [an] overwhelmed sense of his God-given power," as he put it nineteen years later. No simple preacher could have seemed anything but mundane after such an experience, and one is left with the unmistakable impression that Ruskin's disgust was aesthetic as much as anything else. Yet many critics of evangelical language distinguished between the form, which they deplored, and the substance, which they defended vehemently. Even Dickens drew that distinction in the book-length version of his first novel. He stated that the barbarous language so often used was directly counter to the genuine religion that it purported to defend but suggested that if the expression was barbarous, perhaps it was because the speaker was not single-minded. "It is never out of season to protest against that coarse familiarity with sacred things which is busy on the lip and idle in the heart."[73] Dickens was not alone in this. Numerous contemporaries chafed under the assault of emotive phraseology and the constant repetition of a few themes so that what once burst with freshness upon the world of English religion came to have a dreary, tiresome quality. People sometimes reacted as if they were being flailed by evangelical language.

THE DUALISTIC CONUNDRUM

The reformist tendencies of the religious renewal came from a particular vision of the relationship between matter and spirit. This was the conviction that the spiritual and material worlds did not exist separately in watertight compartments, that a profession of religious faith carried with it imperatives that went well beyond private morality, and that the relationship between spirit and matter, if it were genuine, had to include the penetration of the spirit into the society. Love, understood in the biblical sense, required Christians to work actively for the betterment of society, in particular for those in the society who were most needy. That is why evangelical literature harped so incessantly on the need for social activism, and the endless array of societies testified to the fact that action followed words. The same was true of Thomas Arnold's teaching, although it was not until after his death that his followers were able to put those ideas into action. The Tractarians were not like that. They so elevated the status of the Church and the spiritual life that it embodied that they had little regard for the material problems that so exercised their contemporaries. (That was not to be true of their Ritualist successors.) Newman thought the emancipators' Low Church convictions more noteworthy than their work to end slavery, and Pusey grumped about the expenditure of £20 million in compensation to slaveowners. The evangelical reformers of the age, as well as Arnold and his followers, assumed that their religious convictions had to issue forth in good works; hence the societies without number, the endless visiting and provisioning of the poor, and the legislative remedies for harsh conditions in factories and mines that we saw earlier.

But it seemed to become harder as time went on to maintain that understanding, and a certain dualism gradually grew stronger—the loss of the conviction of the interpenetration of the spirit and the world and a consequent withdrawal into the Church (or chapel) and family. That is what lay behind Ashley's exaggerated complaints about the failure of the evangelicals to support factory reform; as time went by, fewer of them saw the connections between the faith they professed and the needs of the society in which they professed it. A modern analyst observes with sadness that they "seemed to make an unconscious division in their thought between matters of religion and matters of this world, even those of social reform."[74] This division between matter and spirit, between the community of faith and the larger social world, made it increasingly difficult to see how the life of faith could possibly influence something of such a radically different order as the society. This was not much of an issue for the Clapham generation, but as the thinking of such influential ministers as Edward Irving and the Church of Ireland priest J. N. Darby spread, and as the *Record* and its supporters gained an increased hearing, it became increasingly more acute. Or perhaps it might be better to say that the earlier generation drew their doctrine of salvation and their inspiration for social and ethical action from the Scriptures without working out the theology that lay behind and lent support to their program. Questions raised from the 1820s that would have cast doubt on the Clapham program came to the fore when that generation was scattered.

According to one modern scholar, "the tragedy of evangelicalism," one that dogged it through the century, was "that it rightly stressed the importance of applying faith to the whole of life while lacking a theology capable of being so applied in any but the most negative fashion." Thus evangelicals condemned the theater out of hand, making it impossible to replace (or at least supplement) the decadent theater of the day with one that reflected the Christian faith and opening themselves to seemingly sanctified forms of pride and self-deceit.[75] The separation between matter and spirit had become so sharp that it was difficult to recommend engaging in the culture in moderation, with good sense or prudence. It had to be all or nothing. People who seek the "golden mean" in such matters, according to the *Christian Observer* in 1840, seem to forget that once they "open the flood gates" to worldliness it is impossible to stop the flow.[76] It is one or the other, the faith or the world, heaven or hell, separation or surrender. All subtlety seemed to have fled as midcentury approached, and without nuance it is very hard to influence those with another point of view.

Although the evangelicals would not be noted for their intellectual life, they were paradoxically sometimes thought to be rationalistic. Leslie Stephen, agnostic son of Evangelicals, thought that this trait led to their decay, inasmuch as they sought answers when there were none to be found; there could be no first principles, rationally conceived, such as the evangelicals demanded. "Protestantism in one aspect is simply rationalism still running about with the shell on its head," he said of the Evangelicals in particular.[77] The preoccupation with truth, a natural consequence of the recovery of doctrines that the previous age had buried with neglect, was one reason the rational faculties were foremost in the attention of the evangelicals. And it was natural that people with aesthetic interests should recoil from them. That may have been one reason there was so much hostility between evangelicals and both the Tractarians and the Cambridge Camden Society. And it was surely one reason that Ruskin turned against them. He was unhappy not only that they paid little attention to aesthetics but that their attempts at beauty were so pitiful in quality. They "ought no longer to render their religion an offence to men of the world by associating it only with the most vulgar forms of art."[78]

Why did the evangelicals, who decried the allurements of "worldliness," increasingly depart from the sobriety and humility they taught as virtues? The analysis that seems to explain it best is the weakness of a theology that placed all its value on the long-neglected doctrine of the Atonement while undervaluing correspondingly the doctrines of creation, incarnation, and sanctification. This was a common criticism of Tractarians and others and necessarily induced the dualism between the spiritual and material that regarded the second as the enemy of the first. The New Testament warnings against sin that used the term for the old nature prone to iniquity, *flesh,* was taken to refer to the body, and the things that the body did became naturally suspect. Thus recreation on a Sunday, catering as it did to the desires of the senses, became forbidden. And so did anything that was pleasurable without having also practical purposes. The theater in the period was indeed deficient and immoral, but that did not impel the evangelicals to improve it, probably because it was considered frivolous at best—frivolous and unimportant inasmuch as it seemed to have no bearing on atonement and all the doctrines and activities that were associated with atonement. Theater and its analogues were, in a word, unspiritual. But a theology that considered fully the implications of creation and incarnation might have been able to convince them that that was not necessarily a telling blow against it, because God was interested not only in spirits but also minds and bodies and in the cultures created by those minds and bodies. The *Christian Observer* thought George Burder's idea about unlawful amusements was too censorious, exaggerating the evil of everyday activities, but it had no alternatives to offer, nothing to redeem, say, the theater, so that it might produce better plays, better performed, more true to life.[79] Gladstone viewed this sort of dualism as the reason the movement was "not, probably, well calculated to fit its agents for exercising social influence at large."[80]

As the evangelicals became involved in their own organizations, their own pastimes, their own increasingly homogenous and therefore idiosyncratic communities, the repression of activities appealing to the senses took forms that may not have been, even by their own standards, improvements over the proscribed activities. Evangelical children, not permitted normal displays of talent, performed their musical and other skills at Sunday school affairs. Since dramatic performances were not countenanced, emotional needs were similarly satisfied by oratorical performances in the pulpit or by the emotional fireworks at an Edward Irving service. These anomalies did not escape the notice of evangelicals of the day. Henry Thornton's daughter, Marianne, ruefully referred to them when speaking of "we good people who do not go to plays" but cavort in worldly ways at Evangelical gatherings.[81]

The physical and emotional separation from the society was accompanied by a falling away from the single-minded dedication of the Wesley-Simeon-Newton-Wilberforce generations as evangelicals entered the mainstream of political and social life and the mainstream of the Church. No longer an embattled minority, this very acceptance led to a lack of wariness, to the lukewarmness and love of comfort that their predecessors had decried. The nodding off may have been a long process, but still it had its effect. Thus the novelistic takeoffs on evangelicals (such as Dickens's Chadband and Charlotte Brontë's Brocklehurst) tend to be, as one student of the period puts it, "caricatures of men who are themselves caricatures of those who had lived at Clapham."[82] Sabine Baring-Gould, with his customary bite, put it this way: "But after the passing away of the early Fathers of Evangelicalism what a falling off was there! When we come to their successors Evangelicalism had become fashionable—it was not the religion of the Gentiles, but of the Genteels."[83] In 1846, Henry Venn the younger, by then secretary of the Church Missionary Society, feared that secularity was invading even that Evangelical stronghold.[84] The Hammonds did not have much sympathy for the Methodist cause, but they were right to note that in the 1840s it "had fallen to some extent under the same shadow as the Church, the shadow of respectability."[85] By this they did not mean the respectability attained by responsible behavior, but the conformity that would be lampooned by later generations. Modern students of the evangelical novel around midcentury notice a softening of the concept of sin, so that it was no longer something to repent of with bitterness, as the Tractarians continued to teach, but rather an emotion that served to sentimentalize the repentance that followed.[86] The Dissenters did not escape the malady. William Jay, by the time his long ministry ended in 1853, found his parishioners too fond of "sentimental comfort" in place of real repentance for sin.[87]

Secularization often borrowed heavily from the dominant evangelical culture. The teetotal movement, for example (including its many evangelical members), used *conversion* as a metaphor to describe the change that taking the pledge could make, and the postmillennial optimism of Clapham had its counterpart here. As the historian of the movement put it, "The teetotalers and prohibitionists directed attention away from an other-worldly paradise towards an earthly utopia, which would be realized after moral suasion or prohibition had teetotalized the world." [88]

This veering between oddball sectarianism and gradual amalgamation into respectability has been explained by modern sociologists of religion as what is to be expected among dissident movements. There is a "cultural editing," a grinding off of the hard edges, and a slide into conformity. [89] Some such analysis may be the best explanation for the split among the Church Evangelicals into those factions represented by the *Christian Observer* and the *Record*. As the conformist tendency grew in the post-Clapham era, the Recordites grew more frantic. "The Church and the world exists now in as full and diametrical opposition to each other as in the days of our Lord." [90] They had lost the old Puritan theology that made societal transformation intelligible, just as the accommodationists had lost that part of it that made it desirable, and were therefore reduced to rhetorical exaggeration and flagellation, making their goal ever more unattainable. This was not because the Recordites were foolish but because they understood that the transformational power of true religion had a double edge, that the covenant offered blessing for those who kept it but destruction for those who flouted it, that the original City on a Hill, Jerusalem, fell because of its apostasy, because it "sinned grievously therefore . . . became filthy," and so went under judgment (Lam. 1:7ff).

Because of their emphasis on the Pauline doctrine of justification by faith apart from works of the law, the evangelicals were periodically revisited by antinomianism. If salvation came without respect to obedience to the law—to hold otherwise would be "legalism," and contrary to the Reformation doctrine—then what was the bar to riotous living? There were answers to that question, and the evangelicals taught them but had always to guard against the temptation. That was true in the late eighteenth century as well as the later period. As one Dissenting minister wrote to another in 1787: "Antinomianism sets aside half the work of Christ . . . and leaves us where it found us, the slaves of sin, utterly unchanged." [91] In 1802, the *Christian Observer* suggested that some Evangelical preachers either were antinomians or at least were unwittingly preparing the way for the heresy. [92] The Dissenting minister R. W. Dale believed this temptation came from an overreaction to the moralistic teachings of the eighteenth century "before the

Revival began." Moral teachings came to be associated with the paganism of the period, inducing many to think that "moral teaching was unnecessary to spiritual people."[93] England was still full of serious evangelicals who regarded themselves as disciples of Christ, and it would be for many decades, but there was also a softness at the heart of the movement. One of the most respected interpreters of the age thought there was a striking contrast between the movement at the middle of the century and what it looked like a generation or two before. The militant movement concerned with the righteousness of the person and of the nation had "grown complacent, fashionable, superior."[94]

If the Evangelicals in the Church of England, along with those in Dissent, were becoming soft at the edges as the new Queen mounted her throne, they were in a different way becoming harder at the same time. In 1844, the editor of the *Christian Observer* adverted to the growing problem of disunity in the ranks. He referred to the period around 1832 when the societies were riven by strife and the Evangelicals "had lost something of that fraternal union" that hitherto had largely prevailed. Now, twelve years later, "differences of opinion" made it difficult to carry on his work as editor.[95] It must have been a function of the lessening of the sense of being an outcast minority that released energies now used for purposes of internal strife. Sometimes it is said that the Evangelicals proceeded from being a movement to being a party, which means that political considerations within the Church (and even within their own ranks) began to rival the ideas for which they had striven. The more inclusive sympathies of the earlier generation, the sort that would allow close relationships between Church and Dissent, for example, were becoming more rare. This tendency toward fragmentation was not a condition peculiar to religious entities but may be better considered a characteristic of the age. Leslie Stephen described the entire intellectual life of the nation in similar terms. He believed Samuel Johnson was the last in a line of English intellectual leaders who practically defined the ideational life of their generations. In the nineteenth century Carlyle and Macaulay could only be leaders of factions, since the literary world had become "multitudinous and chaotic."[96] That also describes the religious situation and perhaps the political as well.

The increasing chaos of ideas, the declining sense of intellectual and cultural cohesion, is the kind of problem that can only be addressed by those with a coherent sense of truth. The Evangelicals had this, yet were unable to deal with the issue successfully or for the most part even know the problem existed. They were, as their theology stressed, experience driven. Beginning with Wesley, they had rebelled against the dull formalism of standardized religion, in both its antinomian and its moralistic forms, and had insisted that the experience of grace in the believing heart, of conversion with its wiping away of the old and the bringing in the new, was the essence of Christian faith. Intent on bringing back this long-neglected facet of religion, they had ignored what they considered to be lesser matters. That is the reason for the Tractarian gibe that the evangelicals put all the emphasis on justification and next to none on sanctification and for the more universal complaint that the evangelicals, who claimed the Bible as their source of religious knowledge, tended to neglect it all except the letters of St. Paul, which had the clearest teachings on the doctrines of salvation that were central to the faith that was transmitted by the Reformation. This constricted view of Christian faith was married to an activism, also biblical in origin, that impelled them both to preach the gospel and to do good to their fellow men. Hence the societies related to mission work, to righting such wrongs as slavery, and to helping the poor. But since the doctrines judged important were few and not hard for a new convert to understand, and since the calls for action were so plain and urgent, the evangelicals did not engage much in serious intellectual effort. This was to prove a serious limitation once the initial flush of zeal gave way to the course of ordinary life. Pusey's disciple and biographer, Henry Liddon, regarded the Tractarian movement as "a completion" of the Evangelical revival, and one of the reasons he believed the latter needed completion was that with all its accomplishments it failed to adumbrate a whole gospel in an intellectually consistent manner.[97]

Even on those matters that the evangelicals thought important, there came to be a quirkiness that revealed the lack of depth to much of their thinking. Apocalyptic speculation became common. One of Wilberforce's friends reported that the master of Magdalen Hall at Oxford told him around 1833 that a local clergyman predicted in a sermon the year Christ would return.[98] The party stressing the Bible as the source of truth was sometimes remarkably feeble in using it. The *Record* identified the Tractarians as the tares among the wheat of the Church,[99] completely missing the point of the parable, which was to show that human ken was not up to the task of distinguishing the tares from the wheat, that such a determination would have to await the final judgment. The *Christian Observer* found it necessary to explain to its readers that the displeasure of God against David when he numbered the people of Israel should not be taken to mean that it was not legitimate for England to have a national census.[100]

When the Evangelicals produced competent people for the various tasks to be done, they found it difficult to back them up with support or replacements. The editor of the *Christian Observer*, Samuel Wilks, lamented in 1846 that he had been laboring at the task for thirty years, and now his pen was "worn to the stump." He would like to have retired but was unable to find anyone to carry on the work. In the December issue recently published, he had written almost every line on his own. This he held to be a sad situation, "but the original phalanx of writers have either gone to their rest, or are now unable to render much aid," and the Evangelical clergy "generally shrink from services of this nature" because they do not sufficiently appreciate their value.[101] As the number of Evangelical clergy climbed through the first half of the century, their intellectual integrity and subtlety seemed to decline. This was at least partly due to the increasingly vociferous nature of the controversies, which made reasoned discourse seem less to the point than vigorous restatements of the party position.[102] A modern analyst surveying the various religious parties of the era concludes that the same failure of leadership was true of all of them—Tractarian, Methodist, Dissent, Arnoldian. "There were no longer giants in the land."[103]

THE CRYSTALLIZATION OF VICTORIAN CULTURE

It might be said in partial explanation for the new scarcity of strong leaders that to some extent they were not necessary. The advanced secularity of the Enlightenment century had been laid to rest, and the new religiosity was firmly in place. This was recognized by the foes as well as the friends of the new order. For that reason, John Stuart Mill disapproved of attempts to weaken the national faith in Christianity. This would only make the society worse, in Mill's view, regardless of the sincerity with which it was done. Knocking the spiritual props out from under the people would deprive them of the only base for moral convictions available to them, while providing them with no substitute. Mill was here dealing with Coleridge's proclamation of a national corps of intellectual leaders, the clerisy who would guide the nation's progress, and arguing that the skeptic should be excluded from it. He was obviously not arguing for the truth of the Christian message but was rather taking into consideration what he seemed to think was more to the point—"the wants and tendencies of [the] age."[104] Even James Mill, a much more consistent secularist than his son, thought the moral training of the society should be in the hands of a church. Not the Church of England, which he considered to be socially harmful, but one whose teachings were in keeping with the Benthamite faith. Each clergyman would have his own district to serve, called a parish; a number of districts would be combined under a bishop or "inspector"; on Sundays there would be a common meal, the preferred drink being tea or coffee.[105] The elder Mill's scheme prefigured Comte's Religion of Humanity that so enthralled George Eliot, also with its version of the Christian sacraments, and may even have influenced

Aldous Huxley's twentieth-century dystopia, *Brave New World*, in which groups of worshipers bowed before "Our Ford," using a version of a communion service.

Although unbelief arose as a powerful force once again to challenge religion not long after midcentury, many of the assumptions of the 1840s remained in place. A royal commission report of 1887, for example, had as its first point of conclusion: "The board attach very great importance to the religious instruction in their schools. Their intention is that it shall be carefully and regularly given, in order that the knowledge imparted to the children about the facts and principles of Holy Scripture may be comprehensive and thorough." The board went on to emphasize the schools must begin their daily work "*invariably*" with a hymn, prayer, and Bible lesson and end it with a hymn and prayer. Numerous additional provisions for a proper religious education followed.[106]

EARLY CRITIQUES OF THE CULTURE

There is scarcely an element of the twentieth-century critiques of Victorianism, just or unjust, that was not anticipated in the literature long before the death of the queen. The strengths of the period almost inevitably bore the impress of the weaknesses. An age that recovers its moral balance breeds hypocrisy. One that vastly increases the proportion of literate citizens finds vulgarity and sentimentality growing apace in its literature. Religious sensibility gives way to pride and exclusivity. Taking one's heritage seriously brings with it party spirit. Growing wealth, more widely spread, breeds materialism and complacency. All these faults were recognized and criticized without pity by endless Victorian social analysts, and, some scholars believe, much more thoroughly at that time than in the twentieth century, when despair accompanies complacency in such a way as to excuse the most flagrant violations.[107]

No consideration of modern interpretations of the era can ignore the widespread condemnations of Victorian "repression" of the sexual urge, which is a typical example of the failure of the historical imagination—the failure, that is, to understand a society in the light of what preceded it rather than what followed it. Hypocrisy is a common addendum to the charge because, as always, many people then were tempted to live short of their principles. But as a recent study of Victorian sexuality notes, it is not the Victorians that were out of step with the broad range of humanity but rather their twentieth-century critics who have regarded sensual pleasure as the something like the be-all of existence. That is why "to suppose that there is anything out of the ordinary about the basic framework of sexual orthodoxy in the Victorian period is a blunder of the crudest sort."[108] One might say it is the failure of the tone-deaf to understand why people should appreciate music.

An additional obstacle to understanding the period today is simple ignorance of the materials that formed the ideas, images, and sensibilities of the period. (There are presently active scholars who are working to redress this deficiency—I have referred earlier to the work of George Landow and Linda Peterson.) Some of what sounds incomprehensible to twentieth-century people would be intelligible if they had any knowledge of the Bible, especially the Old Testament. The frequent assertions, then and now, that the evangelical rise represented a recrudescence of Puritanism should be enough to alert us that the Old Testament, which Puritanism regarded as a document providing social guidance for all ages, furnishes an important clue to understanding the mind and matter of the nineteenth century in England. The great growth in Bible reading among all classes that we earlier saw to have permeated the nation had itself an enormous transformative effect. A Marxist scholar has recently concluded after extensive study that something similar happened in the seventeenth century and had much to do with the revolutionary nature of that period. The Bible provided then a great motivation for the spread of literacy and permeated the culture of the period, not only its private readings and its worship services but such cultural artifacts as wall hangings, almanacs, songs, and so on. It was everywhere, in houses and alehouses alike, and even people who never opened a Bible and could not read it if they did were familiar with its teachings.[109] The same was true in the early nineteenth century—only more true because the literacy level was much higher (itself partly a function of biblically inspired missionary and educational work) and because the organs of cultural activity were more varied and omnipresent: novels and tracts spread the word to every class.

HOLDOUTS TO THE PRE-VICTORIAN RELIGIOUS REVIVAL

Notwithstanding the larger trends of the society, the English countryside was full of backwaters that remained largely immune to change. One writer recalled in 1894 his youth a half century earlier, when witchcraft and magic suffused the thinking of his fellow villagers and the riotous living associated with the past still persisted.[110]

There were always people who disliked the revival of religion in England, and in the second half of the century and into the next their numbers would grow. For the more thoughtful, the problem would become how to preserve what was best in the society when the best was to some extent tied to the religion they had come to disbelieve. A symposium conducted in the first issue (1877) of the *Nineteenth Century* considered "The Influence upon Morality of a Decline in Religious Belief," and only one participant did not predict moral decline, although the symposium also included well-known unbelievers like Fitzjames Stephen and T. H. Huxley.[111] Stephen concluded that without the sanctions posited by Christianity the society ran the risk of descending into barbarism and that the only remedy was to impose external sanctions; hence he called for the hangman's increasing importance for the maintenance of society. Huxley agreed with him. They thought that Mill's emphasis on freedom was a sentimental and dangerous illusion that could not preserve the society in the absence of religious sanctions.[112]

But those fears were to be largely a matter for the future. For the early and mid-Victorian years, the religious revival continued to bear fruit even for those who were not persuaded, or no longer persuaded, of the truth of the doctrines. George Eliot and Leslie Stephen were only among the best known who dropped the doctrine while keeping ever more fanatically to the moral teachings implied by the doctrine. This perhaps accounts best for the preoccupation of later generations with Victorian "hypocrisy." But there may be worse things than hypocrisy; as Nietzsche warned, retaining morality while rejecting the religion on which it was based results in an instability that could only be temporary and then was likely to lead to moral collapse.[113]

The great moralists tried to face this dilemma squarely. George Eliot chose the Comtean Religion of Humanity as the replacement for her evangelical heritage in order to supply the missing moral basis for her life. George Orwell had no use for Christianity and discredited it as he could, but he foresaw the difficulties more clearly than most people who shared his outlook. He wrote in 1940 that people of his persuasion had been sawing at the branch of Christianity for two centuries, and now that it had fallen down they discovered that they had been sitting on the end of it. At the bottom "was not a bed of roses after all, it was a cesspool full of barbed wire. It is as though in the space of ten years we had slid back into the stone age." Orwell's solution was not original but was about all he could devise: he posited a secular faith, based on notions of decency,[114] and not very different from Orwell's own contemporaries in the United States who had issued the Humanist Manifesto of 1932.

The pre-Victorian period we have been considering was a remarkable one because it seemed to belie the oft-repeated historicist admonition that we cannot turn the clock back. We hear this mainly from progressives who decry the resisting of trends that seem to be dominant ones and who wish to continue what has been set in motion. But the impulse behind the remark is a conservative one; it wishes to preserve the trend against those who would change it. People who were setting the new agenda in the eighteenth century ended up creating a very different society in the nineteenth. Wesley and Whitefield, Venn of Huddersfield and Walker of Truro, thought they were recreating in tiny villages or in isolated parishes the promise of a gospel that had atrophied from neglect and self-interest. As the movement spread, it coalesced around academic leaders in Cambridge and then political leaders in Clapham; it spawned publications and societies almost beyond number; it attracted the allegiance of many millions of people who accepted its claims upon them. And then it attracted the attention of people who were critical of its shortcomings, who trained a new generation in Rugby and other public schools, in Oxford, and from there a thousand parishes. It fragmented into competing and often antagonistic schools in both Church and Dissent, but the fragments were sparks, setting fires as they were scattered throughout the land. There were many differences among the fragments, but they were united on a few main principles. They were one in their rejection of the laxity and shallowness that dominated eighteenth-century English religion and society, the Christ-less conjunction of moralism with a deep and pervasive immorality. They all sought the recovery of the gospel that had animated the early church, and they all believed in the seriousness of religious profession and the conduct that flowed from it.

The evangelicals saw that *gospel* in narrow terms, believing that the recovery of the teaching about sin and redemption in Christ would lead to whatever else was necessary. The Tractarians believed that nothing could avail if the vessel in which the gospel was found—the *Church*—was neglected. Coleridge and Arnold and their followers had their focus on the *world* that ought to be transformed by the recovery of the gospel. Gospel, Church, and World. The extent of the change wrought in society by the religious revival was revolutionary in its scope and its depth, and in the staying power of the transformation, but we have not seen in this what might have happened if the three visions had been combined more perfectly into one, mutually compensating for each other's deficiencies.

In the late stages of the revival there were evidences of a certain over-ripeness, the sort that comes when the movement that had freshened a stale society itself becomes stagnant. It reminds one of the Dutch still life paintings so common in the seventeenth century. The ripe fruit looks lush and inviting, but as you examine it more closely you see that in places it has begun to split and ooze. That is how an overripe religious renewal badly in need of refreshening appears to observers; the surface piety remains, but there is a gathering putrescence in the depths of those who have lost the religious vision of their predecessors but are going through the motions as if they had not. At first only a few prophets can perceive that something has gone awry. Eventually the rot becomes evident to others, and a general revulsion ensues. But that is not to say that the fruit was not once good and wholesome, ripe but not overripe.

That decay is mostly in the future as the new society takes its characteristic "Victorian" form. In our period there are only hints of the falling away that is to come. Here, the tincture of vital religion has spread through the society, giving it the coloration of a revived Christianity. This new society, a product of the silent revolution from within its own resources, its own history and traditions, was far from perfect, but it freed the slaves, taught the ignorant, brought spiritual life where there was darkness, turned the drunk and indigent into useful citizens and effective parents, and ameliorated the harsh conditions brought about by industrialization, internal migration, and rapid population growth. It was a revolution that succeeded in making almost all things better. There are not many like that.

Notes

INTRODUCTION

1. W. R. Ward, "The Religion of the People and the Problem of Control, 1790–1830," in *Popular Belief and Practice*, ed. G. J. Cuming and Derek Baker (Cambridge, England: Cambridge Univ. Press, 1972), p. 237.

2. Muriel Jaeger, *Before Victoria* (London: Chatto & Windus, 1956), p. 80.

3. These examples are given in Asa Briggs, *Victorian People: A Reassessment of Persons and Themes, 1851–67* (Chicago: Univ. of Chicago Press, 1955), pp. 6–7.

4. E. C. P. Lacelles, "Charity," in *Early Victorian England 1830–1865*, ed. G. M. Young, 2 vols. (London: Oxford Univ. Press, 1951 [1934]), vol. 2, pp. 337–38.

5. John Bright, *The Diaries of John Bright*, ed. R. A. J. Walling (New York: William Morrow, 1931), p. 471. Bright recorded his conversation with Gladstone on the subject.

6. Lytton Strachey, *Eminent Victorians* (London: Chatto & Windus, 1918); J. M. Robertson, *A History of Freethought in the Nineteenth Century*, 2 vols. (London: Watts, 1929).

7. Norman Dennis and A. H. Halsey, *English Ethical Socialism: Thomas More to R. H. Tawney* (Oxford: Clarendon Press, 1988), pp. vii–viii.

8. James Obelkevich, *Religion and Rural Society: South Lindsey 1825–1875* (Oxford: Clarendon Press, 1976), p. ix.

9. The famous "Middletown" studies of an anonymous American city (Muncie, Indiana) in the 1920s, for example, have been criticized because they adopted unconsciously an evolutionary assumption, amplified by the rationalization theories of Max Weber, and consequently concluded that religion was a vestige of a simpler, more primitive time and would thus disappear as modern institutions developed. Robert S. Lynd and Helen Merrell Lynd, *Middletown: A Study in Contemporary American Culture* (New York: Harcourt, Brace, 1929). Theodore Caplow led a team of investigators that restudied Muncie and concluded that religious belief was *more* pervasive a half century after the Lynds had reached their conclusions. See Theodore Caplow et al., *All Faithful People: Fifty Years of Change and Continuity in Middletown's Religion* (Minneapolis: Univ. of Minnesota Press, 1983).

10. Judith Walkowitz, *Prostitution and Victorian Society: Women, Class, and the State* (Cambridge, England: Cambridge Univ. Press, 1980).

11. Basil Willey, *Nineteenth-Century Studies: Coleridge to Matthew Arnold* (New York: Columbia Univ. Press, 1949), pp. 51–52.

12. Crane Brinton, *A History of Western Morals* (New York: Harcourt, Brace, 1959), p. 350.

13. Jerome H. Buckley, *The Victorian Temper: A Study in Literary Culture* (New York: Vintage Books, 1964 [Cambridge, Mass.: Harvard Univ. Press, 1951]), p. 7.

14. John Holloway, *The Victorian Sage: Studies in Argument* (New York: W. W. Norton, 1965 [1953]), pp. 1–2.

15. G. M. Trevelyan, "Introducing the Ideas and Beliefs of the Victorians," in *Ideas and Beliefs of the Victorians,* no ed. (London: Sylvan Press, 1949), p. 15.

16. Michael Mason, *The Making of Victorian Sexuality* (Oxford: Oxford Univ. Press, 1994), p. 1.

17. Simon Winchester, "A Century after His Death, Everyone Seems to Love RLS," *Smithsonian* 26 (August 1995): 54.

18. Desmond Bowen, review in *Victorian Studies* 33 (1990): 507.

19. Boyd Hilton, *The Age of Atonement: The Influence of Evangelicalism on Social and Economic Thought* (Oxford: Clarendon Press, 1988), p. 373.

20. Élie Halévy, *The Birth of Methodism,* trans. Bernard Semmel (Chicago: Univ. of Chicago Press, 1971); also Élie Halévy, *England in 1815,* vol. 1 of *A History of the English People in the Nineteenth Century,* trans. E. I. Watkin and D. A. Barker (New York: Barnes & Noble, 1961 [1924]). Later materials on the Halévy thesis are collected in Gerald Wayne Olsen, ed., *Religion and Revolution in Early-Industrial England: The Halévy Thesis and Its Critics* (Lanham, Md.: Univ. Press of America, 1990).

21. Paul Hazard, *The European Mind: 1680–1715,* trans. J. Lewis May (New Haven, Conn.: Yale Univ. Press, 1952), p. xv.

22. Alexis de Tocqueville, *Journeys to England and Ireland,* ed. J. P. Mayer, trans. George Lawrence and K. P. Mayer (New Haven, Conn.: Yale Univ. Press, 1958), p. 66.

23. Ibid., p. 82.

24. G. M. Young, "Portrait of an Age," in Young, *Early Victorian England,* vol. 2, p. 415; J. Wesley Bready, *England before and after Wesley: The Evangelical Revival and Social Reform* (New York: Russell & Russell, 1971), p. ii; Gertrude Himmelfarb, *Victorian Minds* (New York: Harper & Row, 1970 [1968]), p. 283; Bernard Semmel, *The Methodist Revolution* (New York: Basic Books, 1973).

25. E. Digby Baltzell, *Puritan Boston and Quaker Philadelphia* (New York: Free Press, 1979), p. 5.

26. S. T. Coleridge, *The Statesman's Manual; Or the Best Guide to Political Skill and Foresight: A Lay Sermon Addressed to the Higher Classes of Society* (London: Gale & Fenner, 1816), p. 16.

27. John Stuart Mill, "The Spirit of the Age," in *The Emergence of Victorian Consciousness: The Spirit of the Age,* ed. George Levine (New York: Free Press, 1967), pp. 70–71. First published in the *Examiner,* January 1831.

28. Clyde Binfield, *So Down to Prayers: Studies in English Nonconformity, 1780–1920* (London: Dent, 1977), pp. 59–60.

29. Jenifer Hart, "Nineteenth-Century Social Reform: A Tory Interpretation of History," *Past and Present*, no. 31 (July 1965): 45.

30. Christopher Dawson, *Progress and Religion* (New York: Sheed & Ward, 1938), p. viii.

31. This is one of the conclusions in T. W. Heyck, *The Transformation of Intellectual Life in Victorian England* (New York: St. Martin's Press, 1982), pp. 9–13.

32. This issue will be taken up in chapter 8.

33. I have adopted the common practice of rendering the Evangelicals in the Church of England with the capital letter and reserving the lowercase *evangelical* for Dissenters or for the movement in general.

34. E. M. Forster, *Marianne Thornton, 1797–1887: A Domestic Biography* (London: Edward Arnold, 1956), pp. 52–53.

35. For example, D. C. Somervell, *English Thought in the Nineteenth Century* (Westport, Conn.: Greenwood Press, 1977 [1962]), p. 3.

36. Robin Furneaux, *William Wilberforce* (London: Hamish Hamilton, 1974), p. 98.

37. Jonathan Mendilow, *The Romantic Tradition in British Political Thought* (London: Croom Helm, 1986), pp. 47–48.

CHAPTER I

1. J. Wesley Bready, *England before and after Wesley: The Evangelical Revival and Social Reform* (New York: Russell & Russell, 1971), pp. 24–25.

2. Horton Davies, *Worship and Theology in England: From Watts and Wesley to Maurice, 1690–1850* (Princeton, N.J.: Princeton Univ. Press, 1961), p. 143.

3. William Thomas Cairns, *The Religion of Dr. Johnson and Other Essays* (Freeport, N.Y.: Books for Libraries Press, 1969 [1946]), p. 3. The Evangelical *Christian Observer* quoted this passage in March 1846 (p. 164) to argue that as bleak as their own period might look, it was still far better than a century earlier.

4. Bready, *England*, p. 19.

5. Kenneth Hylson-Smith, *Evangelicals in the Church of England* (Edinburgh: T. & T. Clark, 1988), p. 5.

6. Elisabeth Jay, ed., *The Evangelical and Oxford Movements* (Cambridge, England: Cambridge Univ. Press, 1983), p. 1.

7. *Christian Observer*, March 1802, p. 180.

8. John S. Harford, *Recollections of William Wilberforce Esq.*, 2nd ed. (London: Longman, Green, 1865), p. 103.

9. Bready, *England*, p. 60.

10. Hugh Evan Hopkins, *Charles Simeon of Cambridge* (Grand Rapids, Mich.: Eerdmans, 1977), p. 14.

11. J. L. Hammond and M. R. D. Foot, *Gladstone and Liberalism*, 2nd ed. (New York: Collier Books, 1966 [1963]), pp. 10–11.

12. Katharine Chorley, *Arthur Hugh Clough, the Uncommitted Mind: A Study of His Life and Poetry* (Oxford: Clarendon Press, 1962), p. 14.

13. Richard Johnson, "Educational Policy and Social Control in Early Victorian England," in *The Victorian Revolution: Government and Society in Victoria's Britain,* ed. Peter Stansky (New York: New Viewpoints, 1973), p. 210.

14. James Obelkevich, *Religion and Rural Society: South Lindsey, 1825–75* (Oxford: Clarendon Press, 1976), chap. 6. Obelkevich has been criticized for not making clear the nature of the relationship between Christians and pagans in South Lindsey. For that discussion see Hugh McLeod, "Recent Studies in Victorian Religious History," *Victorian Studies* 21 (1977): 249–51. For other examples of popular superstition, see David Vincent, *Literacy and Popular Culture, England 1750–1914* (Cambridge, England: Cambridge Univ. Press, 1993 [1989]), pp. 159–60.

15. William Connor Sydney, *England and the English in the Eighteenth Century: Chapters in the Social History of the Times,* 2 vols. (New York: Macmillan, 1891), vol. 1, pp. 264–75; see also W. A. Armstrong, "The Countryside," in *Regions and Communities,* ed. F. M. L. Thompson, vol. 1 of *The Cambridge Social History of Britain, 1750–1950* (Cambridge, England: Cambridge Univ. Press, 1990), pp. 128–29.

16. John Rule, "Methodism, Popular Beliefs and Village Culture in Cornwall, 1800–1850," in *Popular Culture and Custom in Nineteenth-Century England,* ed. Robert D. Storch (London: Croom Helm, 1982), pp. 62–63.

17. Keith Thomas, *Religion and the Decline of Magic* (New York: Charles Scribner's Sons, 1971), pp. 636–37.

18. Ernest Marshall Howse, *Saints in Politics: The "Clapham Sect" and the Growth of Freedom* (Toronto: Univ. of Toronto Press, 1952), p. 67.

19. For an analysis of the morality of modern Britain in relation to the national history, see Gertrude Himmelfarb, *The Demoralization of Society: From Victorian Virtues to Modern Values* (New York: Alfred A. Knopf, 1995).

20. G. V. Cox, *Recollections of Oxford* (London: Macmillan, 1870), p. 5.

21. Thomas Carlyle, *Reminiscences,* ed. James Anthony Froude, 2 vols. (St. Clair Shores, Mich.: Scholarly Press, 1971 [London: Longmans, Green, 1881]), vol. 1, p. 51.

22. Sydney, *England and the English,* vol. 1, p. 62.

23. M. Dorothy George, *London Life in the Eighteenth Century* (Chicago: Academy Chicago, 1984 [1925]), pp. 41–43.

24. J. H. Whitely, *Wesley's England: A Survey of XVIIIth Century Social and Cultural Conditions* (London: Epworth Press, 1938), pp. 76–77.

25. George Otto Trevelyan, *The Early History of Charles James Fox* (London: Longmans, Green, 1899), p. 69.

26. Francis Place, *The Autobiography of Francis Place (1771–1854),* ed. Mary Thale (Cambridge, England: Cambridge Univ. Press, 1972), p. 45.

27. Ibid, p. 14.

28. For representative examples and illuminating commentary, see Herbert M. Atherton, *Political Prints in the Age of Hogarth: A Study of the Ideographic Representation of Politics* (Oxford: Clarendon Press, 1974).

29. Élie Halévy, *The Liberal Awakening 1815–1830*, vol. 2 of *A History of the English People in the Nineteenth Century*, trans. E. I. Watkin (New York: Barnes & Noble, 1961), p. 263.

30. Ivy Pinchbeck, *Women Workers and the Industrial Revolution 1750–1850* (New York: Augustus M. Kelley, 1969 [1930]), pp. 310–11. Some writers in succeeding generations, particularly those of Marxist orientation, have concluded otherwise: that poverty and injustice were the causes of moral misbehavior.

31. Hannah More, *Thoughts on the Importance of the Manners of the Great to General Society and an Estimate of the Religion of the Fashionable World*, new ed. (London: Cadell & Davies, 1809 [1788]), p. 131.

32. Bready, *England*, pp. 126–37.

33. G. C. B. Davies, *The Early Cornish Evangelicals 1735–60: A Study of Walker of Truro and Others* (London: Society for Promoting Christian Knowledge, 1951), pp. 28–29.

34. Brian Harrison, *Drink and the Victorians: The Temperance Question in England, 1815–1872* (Pittsburgh, Pa.: Univ. of Pittsburgh Press, 1971), pp. 37–39.

35. H. L. Short, "Presbyterians under a New Name," in C. Gordon Bolam et al., *The English Presbyterians: From Elizabethan Puritanism to Modern Unitarianism* (Boston: Beacon Press, 1968), p. 222.

36. G. E. Mingay, *English Landed Society in the Eighteenth Century* (London: Routledge & Kegan Paul, 1963), p. 137.

37. Mark Pattison, *Memoirs* (Fontwell, England: Centaur, 1969 [1885]), p. 52.

38. Leslie Stephen, *History of English Thought in the Eighteenth Century*, 3rd ed., 2 vols. (New York: Harcourt, Brace, 1962 [1902]), vol. 1, p. 316.

39. J. M. S. Tompkins, *The Popular Novel in England 1770–1800* (Lincoln: Univ. of Nebraska Press, 1961 [1932]), p. 101.

40. Hoxie Neale Fairchild, *Religious Sentimentalism in the Age of Johnson: 1740–1780*, vol. 2 of *Religious Trends in English Poetry* (New York: Columbia Univ. Press, 1942), pp. 6–8, 191, 280–81.

41. G. R. Balleine, *A History of the Evangelical Party in the Church of England* (London: Longmans Green, 1909), p. 16.

42. R. I. Wilberforce and S. Wilberforce, *The Life of William Wilberforce*, 5 vols. (London: John Murray, 1838), vol. 1, p. 129.

43. Robert Vaughan, *Religious Parties in England: Their Principles, History, and Present Duty*, 2nd ed. (London: Thomas Ward, n.d. [1839]), p. 108.

44. Perry Butler, *Gladstone, Church, State and Tractarianism: A Study of His Religious Ideas and Attitudes, 1809–1859* (Oxford: Clarendon Press, 1982), pp. 142–43.

45. Charles J. Abbey and John H. Overton, *The English Church in the Eighteenth Century*, new rev. ed. (London: Longmans, Green, 1887), p. 300.

46. Leigh Hunt, *Autobiography*, ed. J. E. Morpurgo (London: Cresset Press, 1949 [rev. ed. of 1859]), pp. 62–63.

47. J. A. Froude, "The Oxford Counter Reformation," in Chorley, *Arthur Hugh Clough*, p. 41. First published in J. A. Froude, *Short Studies on Great Subjects* (Longmans, Green, 1905), p. 241.

48. Christopher Dawson, *Progress and Religion* (New York: Sheed & Ward, 1938), p. 213.

49. J. L. Hammond and Barbara Hammond, *The Town Labourer: The New Civilization 1760–1832* (Garden City, N.Y.: Doubleday, 1968 [4th rev. ed. of 1925]), p. 192.

50. W. E. Gladstone, "The Evangelical Movement: Its Parentage, Progress and Issue," *British Quarterly Review* 70 (July 1879): 14.

51. John Walsh, "Origins of the Evangelical Revival," in *Essays in English Church History in Memory of Norman Sykes*, ed. G. V. Bennett and J. D. Walsh (New York: Oxford Univ. Press, 1966), pp. 140–41.

52. Wilberforce and Wilberforce, *Life of William Wilberforce*, vol. 5, p. 339. Wilberforce, who agreed in general with that commentary on the state of the clergy, was not inclined to take this report too seriously, remarking pointedly to Boswell that religious clergymen might not be inclined to lend their confidence to anyone who surrounded himself with men such as Johnson's friends.

53. Gladstone, "Evangelical Movement," p. 13.

54. Stephen Prickett, "The Religious Context," in *The Romantics*, ed. Stephen Prickett (London: Methuen, 1981), pp. 115–16.

55. Frank Booth, *Robert Raikes of Gloucester* (Nutfield, England: National Christian Education Council, 1980), pp. 23–24.

56. *Record*, June 29, 1829. Whenever the *Record* is cited, I omit the page number because the reference is always to the last page of the paper. This is usually p. 4, occasionally p. 6, and once or twice p. 8.

57. E. R. Norman, *Church and Society in England 1770–1970: An Historical Study* (Oxford: Clarendon Press, 1976), p. 51.

58. Eugene L. Williamson, *The Liberalism of Thomas Arnold: A Study of His Religious and Political Writings* (University: Univ. of Alabama Press, 1964), pp. 122–23.

59. For example, Desmond Bowen, *The Idea of the Victorian Church* (Montreal: McGill Univ. Press, 1968), p. 25.

60. For example, Alan D. Gilbert, *Religion and Society in Industrial England: Church, Chapel and Social Change 1740–1914* (London: Longman, 1976), pp. 106–12.

61. Place, *Autobiography*, p. 40.

62. W. O. B. Allen and Edmund McClure, *Two Hundred Years: The History of the Society for Promoting Christian Knowledge, 1698–1898* (London: Society for Promoting Christian Knowledge, 1898).

63. William Jay, *The Autobiography of the Rev. William Jay*, ed. George Redford and John Angell James (London: Hamilton, Adams, 1855), p. 144.

64. Newton to Wilberforce, November 15, 1786, in *The Correspondence of William Wilberforce*, ed. Robert Isaac and Samuel Wilberforce, 2 vols. (London: John Murray, 1840), vol. 1, p. 18.

65. Bolam et al., *The English Presbyterians*, esp. chap. 5 by Jeremy Goring, "The Breakup of the Old Dissent."

66. Arthur Warne, *Church and Society in Eighteenth-Century Devon* (Newton Abbot, England: David & Charles, 1969), p. 98.

67. E. T. Davies, *Religion in the Industrial Revolution in South Wales* (Cardiff: Univ. of Wales Press, 1965), pp. 11–13; W. R. Lambert, *Drink and Sobriety in Victorian Wales, c. 1820–1895* (Cardiff: Univ. of Wales Press, 1983), p. 5.

68. Viscountess Knutsford [M. J. Holland, Macaulay's granddaughter], *Life and Letters of Zachary Macaulay* (London: Edward Arnold, 1900), p. 4; James Stephen, *The Memoirs of James Stephen*, ed. Merle M. Bevington (London: Hogarth Press, 1954), p. 41.

69. James Hunter, *The Making of the Crofting Community* (Edinburgh: John Donald, 1976), pp. 94–96.

70. Élie Halévy, *England in 1815*, vol. 1 of *A History of the English People in the Nineteenth Century*, trans. E. I. Watkin and D. A. Barker (New York: Barnes & Noble, 1961 [1924]), p. 410.

71. Georgina Battiscombe, *John Keble: A Study in Limitations* (New York: Alfred A. Knopf, 1964), p. xiii.

72. William Wilberforce, *A Practical View of the Prevailing Religious System of Professed Christians in the Higher and Middle Classes in This Country Contrasted with Real Christianity*, 2nd ed. (London: Cadell & Davies, 1797), p. 4.

73. Wilberforce and Wilberforce, *Life of William Wilberforce*, vol. 4, p. 391.

74. [W. J. Conybeare], *Church Parties* (London: Longmans, 1854), pp. 2–3. First published as an anonymous article in the *Edinburgh Review*, no. 200 (October 1853).

CHAPTER II

1. For example, Walter E. Houghton, *The Victorian Frame of Mind: 1830–1870* (New Haven, Conn.: Yale Univ. Press, 1959), pp. 359–60.

2. Gordon Rupp, *Religion in England, 1688–1791* (Oxford: Clarendon Press, 1986), pp. 289–92. Historians have identified at least three explanations for the revival. These are summarized by John Walsh (who finds them worthy of consideration, without believing that they have been proven) as (1) a remnant of High Church piety, (2) a reaction against the rationalism of the eighteenth century, and (3) an "eruption" of the old English Puritanism that for a time had lain dormant. See John Walsh, "Origins of the Evangelical Revival," in *Essays in English Church History in Memory of Norman Sykes*, ed. G. V. Bennett and J. D. Walsh (New York: Oxford Univ. Press, 1966), pp. 132–62. R. H. Tawney, the twentieth-century Christian socialist, thought Puritanism marked English Protestantism more than anything else. But he completely misunderstood the theology of the Puritans, turning them in effect into Pelagians who depended on the strength of their own wills for salvation. See R. H. Tawney, *Religion and the Rise of Capitalism: A Historical Study* (New York: Mentor, 1947 [1926]), pp. 165–67.

3. Rupp, *Religion in England*, p. 327.

4. D. W. Bebbington, *Evangelicalism in Modern Britain: A History from the 1730s to the 1980s* (London: Unwin Hyman, 1989), pp. 2–3. Evangelicals of the period, and others as well, used different definitions. The *Christian Observer*, in the context of discussing the enemies of evangelicalism in 1825, identified evangelical

characteristics as a recognition of the fall of mankind into sin, the inability to save oneself by personal effort, the necessity of redemption by God's Holy Spirit, and the obligation not to be conformed to the world but to be renewed according to the divine image. *Christian Observer,* 1825, p. iii.

5. L. E. Elliott-Binns, *The Early Evangelicals: A Religious and Social Study* (Greenwich, Conn.: Seabury Press, 1953), pp. 121–23.

6. Henry Venn, ed., *The Life and a Selection of Letters from the Late Henry Venn,* 6th ed. (London: Hatchard, 1839), p. 18. The first Henry Venn was followed by his son John, who became rector at Clapham during the Wilberforce period. John is the author of the *Life* in this volume. His son Henry, grandson of the subject of the *Life,* is the editor of the volume.

7. John Henry Overton, *The Evangelical Revival in the Eighteenth Century* (New York: Anson D. F. Randolph, n.d. [1886]), pp. 7–8.

8. Walsh, "Origins of the Evangelical Revival," p. 143.

9. Ted Campbell, *The Religion of the Heart: A Study of European Religious Life in the Seventeenth and Eighteenth Centuries* (Columbia: Univ. of South Carolina Press, 1991), pp. 102–3.

10. J. S. Reynolds, *The Evangelicals at Oxford, 1735–1871: A Record of an Unchronicled Movement* (Oxford: Basil Blackwell, 1953), pp. 6–7.

11. Robert Southey, *The Life of Wesley and Rise and Progress of Methodism,* 2nd American ed., 2 vols. (New York: Harper, 1858), vol. 1, pp. 158–60. This conversion experience is often reduced to a naturalistic explanation. See, for example, Christopher Herbert, *Culture and Anomie: Ethnographic Imagination in the Nineteenth Century* (Chicago: Univ. of Chicago Press, 1991), pp. 174–75, which compares the experience with that of the anthropologist going through a period of anomie and then recovery on beginning fieldwork.

12. Elliott-Binns, *Early Evangelicals,* pp. 138–39.

13. Ibid., p. 139. Walpole's statement was not without irony, and he compared the interest of the English ladies with that of the matrons of ancient Rome dallying with goddess worship.

14. T. B. Shepherd, *Methodism and the Literature of the Eighteenth Century* (New York: Haskell House, 1966), pp. 27.

15. Bernard Semmel, *The Methodist Revolution* (New York: Basic Books, 1973), pp. 43–44.

16. S. Baring-Gould, *The Evangelical Revival* (London: Methuen, 1920), p. 2.

17. These statements and others were collected by G. R. Balleine, *A History of the Evangelical Party in the Church of England* (London: Longmans, Green, 1909), pp. 42–43.

18. Wesley also had practical reasons for wishing to remain within the Church: he believed the movement would prosper better there. He thought that Puritanism's failure to achieve a national reformation was due to its neglect of the unity of the Church. For these pragmatic considerations, see John Walsh, "Religious Societies: Methodist and Evangelical (1738–1800)," in *Voluntary Religion,* ed. W. J. Sheils and Diana Wood (Oxford: Basil Blackwell, 1986), p. 292.

19. J. Wesley Bready, *England before and after Wesley: The Evangelical Revival and Social Reform* (New York: Russell & Russell, 1971), p. 206.

20. Alan D. Gilbert, *Religion and Society in Industrial England: Church, Chapel and Social Change 1740–1914* (London: Longman, 1976), p. 78.

21. George Pellew, *The Life and Correspondence of the Right Hon. Henry Addington, First Viscount Sidmouth*, 3 vols. (London: John Murray, 1847), vol. 3, p. 53.

22. See Erik Routley, *The Musical Wesleys* (New York: Oxford Univ. Press, 1968), pp. 23–32 and passim.

23. Robert Southey to Wilberforce, January 3, 1818, in William Wilberforce, *Correspondence,* 2 vols., ed. R. I. Wilberforce and S. Wilberforce (London: John Murray, 1840), vol. 2, p. 389.

24. Richard E. Brantley, *Locke, Wesley, and the Method of English Romanticism* (Gainesville: Univ. of Florida Press, 1984), pp. 1–2, 13.

25. Richard E. Brantley, *Coordinates of Anglo-American Romanticism: Wesley, Edwards, Carlyle and Emerson* (Gainesville: Univ. of Florida Press, 1993), pp. 1–2.

26. Brantley, *Locke, Wesley,* p. 25. It is largely because of his role as the mediator of Locke to contemporaries and followers that Brantley, in effect, endorses Southey's judgment quoted earlier by calling him a "founder of the Religious Enlightenment": "Wesley's intellectual influence surpassed that of all other intellectuals of his century, for he popularized as well as contributed to almost any field that one can name." Ibid., p. 124. Brantley also stresses the influence of the Massachusetts clergyman and theologian Jonathan Edwards as cofounder with Wesley (p. 215). Wesley routinely digested and published the writings of people whose thinking he admired, and he did so with Edwards's work—omitting the Calvinist portions.

27. There is a wealth of information on this in Samuel F. Pickering, Jr., *John Locke and Children's Books in Eighteenth-Century England* (Knoxville: Univ. of Tennessee Press, 1981). For an overview of experiential religion in this period, see Campbell, *Religion of the Heart.*

28. See Jeremy Goring, "The Breakup of the Old Dissent," in C. Gordon Bolam et al., *The English Presbyterians: From Elizabethan Puritanism to Modern Unitarianism* (Boston: Beacon Press, 1968), chap. 5.

29. Shepherd, *Methodism,* p. 229.

30. Bebbington, *Evangelicalism,* pp. 52–53.

31. For the development of these reading groups, see R. K. Webb, *The British Working Class Reader, 1790–1848: Literacy and Social Tension* (London: George Allen & Unwin, 1955), pp. 14–21.

32. Walsh, "Religious Societies," pp. 289–91.

33. Harry S. Stout, *The Divine Dramatist: George Whitefield and the Rise of Modern Evangelicalism* (Grand Rapids, Mich.: Eerdmans, 1991), p. 206.

34. Baring-Gould, *Evangelical Revival,* p. 53. Baring-Gould was guilty of even a worse distortion when he said that Wesley's emphasis on instant conversion amounted to "self-absolution" from sin (p. 77).

35. Balleine, *History of the Evangelical Party,* pp. 94–96.

36. Leonard Elliott-Binns, *The Evangelical Movement in the English Church* (London: Methuen, 1928), pp. 24–25.

37. Handley C. G. Moule, *Charles Simeon* (London: Intervarsity Fellowship, 1965 [1892]), pp. 24–26.

38. William Carus, *Memoirs of the Life of the Rev. Charles Simeon*, 2 vols. (London: Hatchard, 1847), vol. 1, pp. 44–45; Hugh Evan Hopkins, *Charles Simeon of Cambridge* (Grand Rapids, Mich.: Eerdmans, 1977), p. 84.

39. H. L. Short, "Presbyterians under a New Name," in Bolam et al., *English Presbyterians*, pp. 221–22. Other scholars are in general agreement on the Presbyterians and Unitarianism—Bebbington, for example, in *Evangelicalism*, pp. 18, 100.

40. Élie Halévy, *England in 1815*, vol. 1 of *A History of the English People in the Nineteenth Century*, trans. E. I. Watkin and D. A. Barker (New York, Barnes & Noble, 1961 [1924]), p. 433.

41. John Venn of Clapham dealt with this in his biography of Henry Venn. He concluded that his father had been converted without having any connection with the Methodists and that the same was true of other Evangelical leaders as well. Venn, *Life of Venn*, pp. xiv–xv. See also Walsh, "Origins of the Evangelical Revival," pp. 136–37; Elliott-Binns, *Early Evangelicals*, pp. 123–34, has considerable material supporting the same conclusion.

42. Overton in Charles J. Abbey and John H. Overton, *The English Church in the Eighteenth Century*, new rev. ed. (London: Longmans, Green, 1887), pp. 314–15; Walsh, "Origins of the Evangelical Revival," pp. 154–55. Both of these works treat the Evangelicals as more politically passive than I show them to have been in a later chapter.

43. Rupp, *Religion in England*, p. 330.

44. John Walsh, "'Methodism' and the Origins of English-Speaking Evangelicalism," in *Evangelicalism: Comparative Studies of Popular Protestantism in North America, the British Isles, and Beyond, 1700–1990*, ed. Mark A. Noll, David W. Bebbington, and George A. Rawlyk (New York: Oxford Univ. Press, 1994), pp. 26–27. See also Wellman J. Warner, *The Wesleyan Movement in the Industrial Revolution* (London: Longmans, Green, 1930), chap. 6, which argues that the early Methodist movement had strong societal repercussions for the better. Later chapters of the present book deal in some detail with this aspect of the whole religious revival.

45. H. F. Mathews, *Methodism and the Education of the People, 1791–1851* (London: Epworth Press, 1949), pp. 78–79.

46. There are numerous works describing the function of the Methodist societies. In addition to those already cited, I have found the following useful: Anthony Armstrong, *The Church of England, the Methodists and Society 1700–1850* (London: Univ. of London Press, 1973); Richard Carwardine, *Transatlantic Revivalism: Popular Evangelicalism in Britain and America, 1790–1865* (Westport, Conn.: Greenwood Press, 1978); there is a brief explanation of the formation of societies in the eighteenth century, providing some insight as to how Wesley adapted for his purposes what was already widely practiced, in T. S. Ashton, *The Industrial Revolution 1760–1830* (London: Oxford Univ. Press, 1970 [1948]), pp. 88–89.

47. M. G. Jones, *The Charity School Movement: A Study of Eighteenth Century Puritanism in Action* (Hampden, Conn.: Archon Books, 1964 [Cambridge, England: Cambridge Univ. Press, 1938]), pp. 152–53; Michael R. Watts, *The Dissenters: From the Reformation to the French Revolution* (Oxford: Clarendon Press, 1978), pp. 423–24; David Owen, *English Philanthropy, 1660–1960* (Cambridge, Mass.: Harvard Univ. Press, 1964), p. 23; see also Roger H. Martin, *Evangelicals United: Ecumenical Stirrings in Pre-Victorian Britain, 1795–1830* (Metuchin, N.J.: Scarecrow Press, 1983), pp. 25–26.

48. Frank Booth, *Robert Raikes of Gloucester* (Nutfield, England: National Christian Education Council, 1980), p. 114.

49. Ibid., pp. 91–92.

50. W. R. Ward, *Religion and Society in England, 1790–1850* (London: B. T. Batsford, 1972), p. 13.

51. Halévy, *England in 1815*, p. 421.

52. Semmel, *Methodist Revolution*, p. 198. There is a similar interpretation of the influence of evangelical religion in American life in Nathan O. Hatch, *The Democratization of American Christianity* (New Haven, Conn.: Yale Univ. Press, 1989).

53. R. I. Wilberforce and S. Wilberforce, *The Life of William Wilberforce*, 5 vols. (London: John Murray, 1838), vol. 1, p. 5.

54. Baring-Gould, *Evangelical Revival*, pp. 61, 109.

55. Southey, *Life of Wesley*, vol. 2, pp. 198–99.

56. "London Tabernacle Minutes, no date, 1746," in *Two Calvinistic Methodist Chapels, 1743–1811: The London Tabernacle and Spa Fields Chapel*, ed. Edwin Welch (London: London Record Society, 1975), p. 11.

57. N. U. Murray, "The Influence of the French Revolution on the Church of England and Its Rivals, 1789–1802" (D.Phil. dissertation, Oxford Univ., 1975), p. 92.

CHAPTER III

1. Standish Meacham, *Henry Thornton of Clapham, 1760–1815* (Cambridge, Mass.: Harvard Univ. Press, 1964), pp. 24–25.

2. Boyd Hilton, who wrote what is probably the last word on the social and political thought of the Evangelicals, provides considerable evidence for the divisions in the Evangelical ranks. On the "Ten Hours" controversy of factory reform, for example, see *The Age of Atonement: The Influence of Evangelicalism on Social and Economic Thought* (Oxford: Clarendon Press, 1988), pp. 212–13.

3. The Tractarian clergyman Henry Liddon, biographer of Edward Pusey, believed that Evangelicalism could be understood as a reaction against both latitudinarianism and its opposite, moralism. Henry P. Liddon, *Life of Edward Bouverie Pusey*, 4 vols. (London: Longmans Green, 1893–1897), vol. 1, pp. 254–55. Sometimes the definitions are drawn too narrowly, so that such staunch Claphamites as Thomas Clarkson and Granville Sharp are considered outside of the Evangelical pale. For a contrary view, the one taken in the present study, see Horton Davies, *Worship and Theology in England: From Watts and Wesley to Maurice, 1690–1850* (Princeton, N.J.: Princeton Univ. Press, 1961), pp. 538–39. Sharp became a

self-taught biblical scholar and published studies of the Greek and Hebrew texts. He enlisted as a foot soldier in Wilberforce's army of antislavers. On his biblical scholarship, see David Brion Davis, *The Problem of Slavery in the Age of Revolution, 1770–1823* (Ithaca, N.Y.: Cornell Univ. Press, 1975), pp. 389–448. The modern visitor to Clapham will see Sharp's name on the plaque, damaged by World War II bombs, affixed to the wall of the parish church where they all worshiped. The danger here is drawing rigid boundaries that do not correspond to real alliances and correspondences of thought. I much prefer the practice of Hilton in *Age of Atonement*, although he has been criticized on this point. His way of proceeding, for example, enables him to see that Edward Copleston, though he was not an Evangelical, nevertheless exhibited certain influences that could have come only from that source. Copleston was very interested in the evangelical Scottish clergyman Edward Irving (before Irving entered his Adventist phase) and drew the comment from Charles Simeon in 1822 that Copleston was more in accord with his views of Scripture than almost any other person (pp. 29f).

4. For example, L. E. Elliott-Binns, *The Early Evangelicals: A Religious and Social Study* (Greenwich, Conn.: Seabury Press, 1953), p. 384.

5. Richard J. Helmstadter, "The Nonconformist Conscience," in *The Conscience of the Victorian State*, ed. Peter Marsh (Syracuse, N.Y.: Syracuse Univ. Press, 1979), p. 141.

6. Henry Venn, ed., *The Life and a Selection of Letters from the late Henry Venn*, 6th ed. (London: Hatchard, 1839), p. 29.

7. Michael Hennell, *Sons of the Prophets: Evangelical Leaders of the Victorian Church* (London: Society for Promoting Christian Knowledge, 1979), p. 8.

8. James Stephen, *The Memoirs of James Stephen*, ed. Merle M. Bevington (London: Hogarth Press, 1954), p. 110.

9. "I am no predestinarian, and do not believe that the children of God can never fall away." Wilberforce to Lady Waldegrave, April 15, 1805, in William Wilberforce, *Correspondence*, ed. R. I. Wilberforce and S. Wilberforce, 2 vols. (London: John Murray, 1840), vol. 2, p. 23.

10. *Christian Observer*, May 1802, p. 319.

11. *Christian Observer*, July 1804, p. 434.

12. *Christian Observer*, 1810, preface, p. iv.

13. *Christian Observer*, March 1808, p. 170.

14. Mary Milner, *The Life of Isaac Milner*, 2nd ed. (London: Seeley & Burnside, 1844), p. 251.

15. Hugh Evan Hopkins, *Charles Simeon of Cambridge* (Grand Rapids, Mich.: Eerdmans, 1977), pp. 173–75.

16. William Carus, *Memoirs of the Life of the Rev. Charles Simeon*, 2 vols. (London: Hatchard, 1847), vol. 2, p. 600. Another version of Simeon's remark is reported by Joseph Gurney, who was told: "When I come to a text which speaks of election, I delight myself in the doctrine of election. When apostles exhort me to repentance and obedience, and indicate the freedom of the will, I give myself up to that side of the question, and behold I am an Arminian!" Joseph John Gurney, *Reminiscences of*

Chalmers, Simeon, Wilberforce, &c (n.p., n.d. [1835]), p. 121. There are other examples of this attitude toward the issue in D. W. Bebbington, *Evangelicalism in Modern Britain: A History from the 1730s to the 1980s* (London: Unwin Hyman, 1989), p. 63. Bebbington believes there was a renewed interest in Calvinism stemming from contacts made with the renewal in Geneva. The chief influence on England came through the banker Henry Drummond's influence on the Scottish minister Edward Irving, as well as on a younger set at Oxford University (p. 77). But Irving's moment of fame in London, flashy though it was, was a byway in English religious history, interesting chiefly for the opposition it aroused, and whatever the youths of Oxford might think and do in the 1820s was swallowed up in the Tractarian eruption of the next decade.

17. *Christian Observer,* March 1802, pp. 172–74.

18. *Christian Observer,* October 1802, pp. 670–71.

19. *Record,* February 6, 1837.

20. Leigh Hunt, *An Attempt to Shew the Folly and Danger of Methodism* (London: John Hunt, 1809), pp. 12–14.

21. R. I. Wilberforce and S. Wilberforce, *The Life of William Wilberforce,* 5 vols. (London: John Murray, 1838), vol. 3, p. 473.

22. *Christian Observer,* May 1802, p. 318. Donald M. Lewis, in *Lighten Their Darkness: The Evangelical Mission to Working Class London, 1828–1860* (Westport, Conn.: Greenwood Press, 1986), p. 30, has identified a small group of hyper-Calvinists in the 1830s who veered off into antinomianism, to the horror of the Evangelicals.

23. Wilberforce to William Hey, March 17, 1801, in Wilberforce, *Correspondence,* vol. 1, p. 224.

24. Stephen to Wilberforce, July 26, 1811, in Wilberforce, *Correspondence,* vol. 2, p. 209.

25. Robin Furneaux, *William Wilberforce* (London: Hamish Hamilton, 1974), p. 9.

26. Wilberforce and Wilberforce, *Life of William Wilberforce,* vol. 1, p. 54.

27. John S. Harford, *Recollections of William Wilberforce, Esq.,* 2nd ed. (London: Longman, Green, 1865), pp. 56–57.

28. October 18, 1827, John Henry Newman, *Letters and Correspondence of John Henry Newman during His Life in the English Church,* ed. Anne Mozley, with a brief autobiography, 2 vols. (London: Longmans, Green, 1891), vol. 1, p. 169.

29. R. K. Webb, *Harriet Martineau: A Radical Victorian* (New York: Columbia Univ. Press, 1960), p. 135.

30. Furneaux, *William Wilberforce,* p. 283.

31. William Hazlitt, *The Spirit of the Age* (London: Oxford Univ. Press, 1954 [1825]), p. 242.

32. Wilberforce and Wilberforce, *Life of William Wilberforce,* vol. 2, p. 173.

33. February 24, 1791, Furneaux, *William Wilberforce,* p. 99.

34. Newton to Wilberforce, April 21, 1797, in Wilberforce, *Correspondence,* vol. 1, p. 163. Newton also urged him to bring out the book in a smaller, cheaper edition

so more of the middle class would be able to buy it. Newton to Wilberforce, June 3, 1797, in Wilberforce, *Correspondence*, vol. 1, p. 177.

35. Wilberforce and Wilberforce, *Life of William Wilberforce*, vol. 2, p. 199; Ernest Marshall Howse, *Saints in Politics: The "Clapham Sect" and the Growth of Freedom* (Toronto: Univ. of Toronto Press, London, 1952), pp. 100–101.

36. Furneaux, *William Wilberforce*, p. 164.

37. Stewart J. Brown, *Thomas Chalmers and the Godly Commonwealth in Scotland* (Oxford: Oxford Univ. Press, 1982), pp. 55–56.

38. William Wilberforce, *A Practical View of the Prevailing Religious System of Professed Christians in the Higher and Middle Classes in This Country Contrasted with Real Christianity*, 2nd ed. (London: Cadell & Davies, 1797), pp. 8–13.

39. Thomas Gisborne, *An Enquiry into the Duties of Men in the Higher and Middle Classes of Society in Great Britain* (London: White, 1794).

40. Robert Fishman, in his study of suburbia, takes the move to Clapham by Wilberforce and his friends as a rejection of the vices of the city, enabling them to maintain their offices in the city while escaping its vices. He overdoes the escape aspects of the motivation, and in fact Wilberforce and some of the others moved back into the city before their careers were over. See Fishman, *Bourgeois Utopias: The Rise and Fall of Suburbia* (New York: Basic Books, 1987), pp. 53–55.

41. Macaulay to Selina Mills, June 16, 1798, in Meacham, *Henry Thornton*, p. 61.

42. Furneaux, *William Wilberforce*, p. 126.

43. Reginald Coupland, *Wilberforce*, 2nd ed. (London: Collins, 1945), pp. 204–5.

44. E. M. Forster, *Marianne Thornton, 1797–1887* (London: Edward Arnold, 1956), p. 42. Forster was a descendent of the Thornton family, here writing a biography of his relative from the family archive. He was not the only member of the Bloomsbury "immoralists" (John Maynard Keynes's autobiographical term) to be descended from Clapham. See Gertrude Himmelfarb, "A Genealogy of Morals: From Clapham to Bloomsbury," in *Marriage and Morals among the Victorians* (New York: Knopf, 1986), chap. 2.

45. Forster, *Marianne Thornton*, p. 43.

46. See Fishman, *Bourgeois Utopias*, pp. 57–59.

47. David Owen, *English Philanthropy, 1660–1960* (Cambridge, Mass.: Harvard Univ. Press, 1964), pp. 94–95.

48. G. R. Balleine, *A History of the Evangelical Party in the Church of England* (London: Longmans, Green, 1909), p. 149.

49. Christine Bolt, *Victorian Attitudes to Race* (London: Routledge & Kegan Paul, 1971), p. 229.

50. C. J. Shore (Lord Teignmouth), *Reminiscences of Many Years*, 2 vols. (Edinburgh: David Douglas, 1878), vol. 1, p. 2.

51. Viscountess Knutsford, *Life and Letters of Zachary Macaulay* (London: Edward Arnold, 1900), pp. 19–20. This effort was largely a failure.

52. John Pollock, *Wilberforce* (New York: St. Martin's Press, 1977), p. 258.

53. This is the position of one of the most ambitious interpretations of the pre-

Victorian period, that of Ford K. Brown, *Fathers of the Victorians: The Age of Wilberforce* (Cambridge, England: Cambridge Univ. Press, 1961), p. 155 and passim. Brown is almost uniformly hostile to the Evangelicals, sometimes almost irrationally so. For a devastating review of this book, see David Newsome, "Fathers and Sons," *Historical Journal* 6 (1963): 295–310.

54. Wilberforce and Wilberforce, *Life of William Wilberforce*, vol. 1, p. 54.

55. Ian Bradley, "The Politics of Godliness: Evangelicals in Parliament, 1784–1832" (D. Phil. thesis, Oxford Univ., 1974), p. 49.

56. David Spring, "The Clapham Sect: Some Social and Political Aspects," *Victorian Studies* 5 (1961): 36.

57. *Christian Observer*, March 1803, p. 169.

58. Ibid., p. 185.

59. *Christian Observer*, June 1810, pp. 395–96.

60. *Record*, March 7, 1828. The paper made clear it was speaking only about "orthodox" Dissenters; it remained unremittingly hostile to Unitarianism.

61. *Record*, January 1, 1828.

62. Josef L. Altholz, "Alexander Haldane, The *Record*, and Religious Journalism," *Victorian Periodical Review* 20 (Spring 1987): 24. Altholz believes Haldane never lost his Presbyterian convictions, and he finds it ironic that the editor of an Anglican organ "was never, at heart, an Anglican" (p. 25). For evaluations of the whole range of the religious press in nineteenth-century England, see Josef L. Altholz, *The Religious Press in Britain, 1760–1900* (New York: Greenwood Press, 1989).

63. *Record*, September 15, 1831.

64. Bradley, "Politics of Godliness," pp. 234–63.

65. On the unpopularity of the Evangelicals, see Owen Chadwick, *The Victorian Church*, 2nd ed., pt. 1 (London: Adam & Charles Black, 1970), pp. 446–47. Chadwick rests the case partly on such novels as those by the Trollopes, which exaggerate the point, and he acknowledges that much of the criticism is one-sided and unfair.

66. There was an attempt to respond to the Tractarians by using the term *Evangelical High Church* in 1840. This was the creation of Henry Christmas, who took over as editor of the *Church of England Quarterly*. The attempt went nowhere and was lampooned by the *Record* of August 24, 1840: "Evangelical Churchmen we know there are, and many, too, we are glad to say. But of such an heterogeneous race as Evangelical High Churchmen we know nothing: nor can we believe that such do really exist." See Peter Toon, *Evangelical Theology 1833–1856: A Response to Tractarianism* (Atlanta, Ga.: John Knox Press, 1979), pp. 41–42. The *Record* was incorrect in denying categorically the existence of such people.

67. *Christian Observer*, June 1817, p. vi.

68. *Record*, January 1, 1828.

69. G. F. A. Best, *Shaftesbury* (London: B. T. Botsford, 1964), pp. 52–62.

70. Balleine, *History of the Evangelical Party*, p. 181.

71. Carus, *Memoirs of Simeon*, vol. 1, pp. 44–45.

72. Ibid., p. 138. On Simeon's High Churchmanship in the context of voluntary

missions, see John C. Bennett, "Charles Simeon and the Evangelical Missionary Movement: A Study of Voluntaryism and Church-Mission Tensions" (Ph.D. dissertation, Univ. of Edinburgh, 1992).

73. Meacham, *Henry Thornton*, p. 9.

74. Robert S. Dell, "Simeon and the Bible," in *Charles Simeon, 1759–1836*, ed. Arthur Pollard and Michael Hennell (London: Society for Promoting Christian Knowledge, 1959), pp. 30–31.

75. H. C. G. Moule, *Charles Simeon* (London: Intervarsity Fellowship, 1965 [1892]), p. 148. That is more or less the majority opinion. For a contrary modern view, see John Kent, *The Unacceptable Face: The Modern Church in the Eyes of the Historian* (London: SCM Press, 1987), p. 86. I cannot see that Kent makes his case.

76. Hopkins, *Charles Simeon*, pp. 83, 119–20.

77. Charles Smyth, *Simeon and the Church Order: A Study of the Origins of the Evangelical Revival in Cambridge in the Eighteenth Century* (Cambridge, England: Cambridge Univ. Press, 1940), pp. 100–101.

78. Ibid., p. 250.

79. Amy Cruse, *The Englishman and His Books in the Early Nineteenth Century* (New York: Benjamin Blom, 1968 [1930]), pp. 63–64.

80. M. G. Jones, *Hannah More* (New York: Greenwood Press, 1968 [1952]), p. 63.

81. The narrative is given in the memoirs of Martha More, *Mendip Annals or a Narrative of the Charitable Labours of Hannah and Martha More*, ed. Arthur Roberts (London: James Nisbet, 1859), pp. 12–13. The Wilberforce brothers included that account, hitherto unpublished, in their *Life of William Wilberforce*, vol. 1, pp. 238–40.

82. More, *Mendip Annals*, p. 188. On her High Church convictions, see Jones, *Hannah More*, pp. 78, 100–101.

83. [A. C. H. Seymour], *The Life and Times of Selina Countess of Huntingdon*, 2 vols. (London: William Edward Painter, 1844), vol. 1, pp. 293–94. Hannah More to John Bowdler: "The Methodists it has been my avowed object to counteract, inasmuch as their preachers have inveighed against me by name in their pulpits, and they are the avowed enemies of my schools for attracting the people from their meetings to the church." Jones, *Hannah More*, p. 21.

84. More, *Mendip Annals*, p. 78.

85. Wilberforce to More, March 19, 1822, in Wilberforce, *Correspondence*, vol. 2, p. 457.

86. Alan D. Gilbert, *Religion and Society in Industrial England: Church, Chapel and Social Change 1740–1914* (London: Longman, 1976), p. 74.

87. Brown, *Fathers of the Victorians*, p. 400.

88. Hannah More to Thomas Gisborne, Feb. 28, 1827, *Memoirs of the Life and Correspondence of Mrs. Hannah More*, 2nd ed., ed. William Roberts, 4 vols. (London, 1834), vol. 4, pp. 311–12.

89. W. E. Gladstone, "The Evangelical Movement: Its Parentage, Progress and Issue," *British Quarterly Review* 70 (July 1879): 24.

90. Walter Bagehot, *The English Constitution*, 2nd ed. (Garden City, N.Y.: Doubleday, n.d. [1872]), pp. 306–7.

91. John H. Pratt, ed., *The Thought of the Evangelical Leaders: Notes of the Discussions of the Eclectic Society, London during the Years 1798–1814* (Edinburgh: Banner of Truth Trust, 1978 [1856]), p. 1. See also J. S. Reynolds, *The Evangelicals at Oxford, 1735–1871: A Record of an Unchronicled Movement* (Oxford: Basil Blackwell, 1953), pp. 56–57. Reynolds's interest here is to show the influence of Oxford on the movement.

92. Pratt, *Thought of the Evangelical Leaders*, p. 92. Josiah Pratt was the first editor of the *Christian Observer* but was succeeded after three months by Zachary Macaulay, who held the post for many years.

93. Henry Morris, *Charles Grant: The Friend of William Wilberforce and Henry Grant* (London: Society for Promoting Christian Knowledge, 1898), p. 41.

94. Leslie Howsam, *Cheap Bibles* (Cambridge, England: Cambridge Univ. Press, 1991); William Canton, *The Story of the Bible Society* (London: John Murray, 1904), pp. 6–12.

95. Brown, *Fathers of the Victorians*, pp. 246–47.

96. *Christian Observer*, January 1819, p. 58.

97. R. J. Morris, *Class, Sect and Party: The Making of the British Middle Class, Leeds, 1820–1850* (Manchester, England: Manchester Univ. Press, 1990), p. 178. Morris has a good deal of material on the importance of the society as a *form* that would have a great effect on institutions without any relationship to the original religious impulse.

98. Gilbert, *Religion and Society in Industrial England*, pp. 80–81. For an example of the savagery of Cobbett's attacks on the Church, see William Cobbett, *Rural Rides*, ed. George Woodcock (Harmondsworth, England: Penguin Books, 1967 [1830]), pp. 50–51.

99. See, for example, John Garrard's study of northern towns, *Leadership and Power in Victorian Industrial Towns, 1830–1880* (Manchester, England: Manchester Univ. Press, 1983), pp. 110–11.

100. *Record*, March 7, 1828.

101. *Record*, February 29, 1844. But there was in this not a hint of secessionary sentiment, and the paper said in the same passage that the Evangelicals would be less likely to secede from the Church than would others.

102. *Christian Observer*, 1825, preface, p. iii.

103. Warren Roberts, *Jane Austen and the French Revolution* (New York: St. Martin's Press, 1979), p. 124.

104. Howse, *Saints in Politics*, p. 172.

105. Arthur J. Tait, *Charles Simeon and His Trust* (London: Society for Promoting Christian Knowledge, 1936).

106. *Record*, January 1, 1828.

107. Howse, *Saints in Politics*, p. 172.

108. Moule, *Charles Simeon*, p. 55.

109. Wilberforce and Wilberforce, *Life of William Wilberforce*, vol. 1, pp. 134–35.

110. Harford, *Recollections of William Wilberforce*, p. 107.

111. John Henry Newman, *Apologia pro Vita Sua,* ed. A. Dwight Culler (Boston: Houghton Mifflin, 1956 [1864]), pp. 49–50.

112. Gladstone, "Evangelical Movement," p. 14.

113. See, for example, G. F. A. Best, "The Evangelicals and the Established Church in the Early Nineteenth Century," *Journal of Theological Studies* 10, pt. 1 (April 1959): 63–78. Best here describes the Evangelicals as divisive, destructive in their Calvinism, superficial, and pietistic, trying to eat their cake and have it as well. It is surprising to see such a failure of nuance in a capable scholar. Note 53 for this chapter referred to the work of Ford K. Brown and David Newsome's critique of it.

114. Venn, *Life of Venn,* p. xv.

115. W. E. H. Lecky, "The History of the Evangelical Movement," *Nineteenth Century* 6 (1879): 280–81. Lecky drew the distinction explained in the text but muddied it with a bit of careless writing at one point in which he spoke of the "party" when he meant the "movement." Lecky's point was taken up and expanded much later by Charles Smyth, "The Evangelical Movement in Perspective," *Cambridge Historical Journal* 7 (1941–43): 160–74. The cultural effects of the religious revival are the subject of a later chapter of this book, when we take up the story of Hannah More again, this time to examine the literary side of her work.

116. Leonard Elliott-Binns, *The Evangelical Movement in the English Church* (London: Methuen, 1928), p. 43.

117. Raymond Chapman, *Faith and Revolt: Studies in the Literary Influence of the Oxford Movement* (London: Weidenfeld & Nicolson, 1970), p. 27.

118. Thomas Carlyle, *Reminiscences,* ed. James Anthony Froude, 2 vols. (St. Clair Shores, Mich.: Scholarly Press, 1971 [London: Longmans, Green, 1881]), vol. 1, pp. 235–36.

119. Andrew Landale Drummond, *Edward Irving and His Circle* (London: James Clarke, n.d. [1938]), p. 115.

120. *Christian Observer,* August 1823, pp. 490–92. The *Observer* here attributes the coarseness partly to the fact that Irving was not English.

121. *Christian Observer,* August 1829, pp. 510–11.

122. *Record,* April 16, 1837.

123. *Record,* March 21, 1833.

124. Carlyle, *Reminiscences,* vol. 1, pp. 188–89.

125. There is a good treatment of the shift in Lewis, *Lighten Their Darkness,* pp. 14–18.

126. *Record,* August 4, 1841.

127. Chadwick, *Victorian Church,* part 1, p. 446. Chadwick adverts, as I have, to the blurred lines between Evangelicals and others.

128. Gladstone, "Evangelical Movement," p. 7.

129. S. Baring-Gould, *The Church Revival: Thoughts Thereon and Reminiscences* (London: Methuen, 1914), pp. 102–6. The same theme of far greater influence than number is found in David Newsome, *The Wilberforces and Henry Manning: The Parting of Friends* (Cambridge, Mass.: Harvard Univ. Press, 1966), pp. 8–10.

130. Pollock, *Wilberforce,* p. 307.

131. Lecky, "History of the Evangelical Movement," pp. 283–85.

CHAPTER IV

1. There were both similarities and differences between the old High Church and the Tractarians. These are discussed in Peter B. Nockles, *The Oxford Movement in Context: Anglican High Churchmanship, 1760–1857* (Cambridge, England: Cambridge Univ. Press, 1994); I have taken the description of the High Churchmen from p. 26 of this book. John Keble's modern biographer has explained Keble's understanding of his own thinking as a simple continuation of the High Church tradition, which is different from the sharp break with the immediate past that his colleagues saw in their work. Georgina Battiscombe, *John Keble: A Study in Limitations* (New York: Alfred A. Knopf, 1964), pp. 10–11. Nockles shows that Newman and Pusey had more or less given up on the High Church, and by the 1840s the distinction between it and the Tractarians was generally accepted (pp. 35f).

2. Defenses of the High Church can be found in Nockles, *Oxford Movement in Context*, passim, and in Kenneth Hylson-Smith, *High Churchmanship in the Church of England: From the Sixteenth Century to the Late Twentieth Century* (Edinburgh: T. & T. Clark, 1993), pp. 101–2.

3. J. H. Newman, "State of Religious Parties," *British Critic*, April 1839, pp. 399–400. There is a good discussion of this in G. B. Tennyson, *Victorian Devotional Poetry: The Tractarian Mode* (Cambridge, Mass.: Harvard Univ. Press, 1981), pp. 14–17. Tennyson also names Southey and Wordsworth as having been signified in the *British Critic* article, although Newman did not name them.

4. For an example of the huffiness that intimations of this connection could engender, see Isaac Williams, *Autobiography*, 3rd ed., ed. George Prevost (London: Longmans, Green, 1893), pp. 119–20. Williams here plays down the Evangelical connections, not entirely ingenuously.

5. John Henry Newman, *Apologia pro Vita Sua*, ed. A. Dwight Culler (Boston: Houghton Mifflin, 1956 [1864]), p. 24. There is a good exposition of this event and its background in Ian Ker, *John Henry Newman: A Biography* (Oxford: Clarendon Press, 1988), pp. 3–4. Of the exact nature of his conversion there has been some controversy. The Swedish scholar Yngve Brilioth says it was a Calvinist conversion rather than an Evangelical one, a distinction that makes little sense and would not have been recognized by many contemporaries. Yngve Brilioth, *Evangelicalism and the Oxford Movement* (Oxford: Oxford Univ. Press, 1934), p. 24. Newman himself was in his youth privately in some doubt about whether his experience was a genuine evangelical one because of stereotypes about conversion that some Evangelical leaders publicly denied: the necessity for an instantaneous and emotional experience. We have this in some private writings from the 1820s, published in John Henry Newman, *Letters and Correspondence of John Henry Newman during His Life in the English Church*, ed. Anne Mozley, with a brief autobiography, 2 vols. (London: Longmans, Green, 1891), vol. 1, pp. 123–24.

6. David Newsome, *The Wilberforces and Henry Manning: The Parting of Friends* (Cambridge, Mass.: Harvard Univ. Press, 1966), p. 148.

7. Mary C. Church, ed., *The Life and Letters of Dean Church* (London: Macmillan, 1895), pp. 7–8.

8. Desmond Bowen, *The Idea of the Victorian Church* (Montreal: McGill Univ. Press, 1968), p. 352.

9. Henry P. Liddon, *Life of Edward Bouverie Pusey*, 4 vols. (London: Longmans Green, 1893–1897), vol. 1, p. 255.

10. On this see Herbert Leslie Stewart, *A Century of Anglo-Catholicism* (New York: Oxford Univ. Press, 1929), pp. 57–58 and passim.

11. The best expositions of this and related issues I have found are the various works of Stephen Prickett. See his treatment of Keble and Wordsworth in *Romanticism and Religion: The Tradition of Coleridge and Wordsworth in the Victorian Church* (Cambridge, England: Cambridge Univ. Press, 1976), pp. 100–109.

12. Ibid., p. 260.

13. Liddon, *Life of Edward Bouverie Pusey*, vol. 1, p. 254.

14. Thomas Carlyle, *Reminiscences*, ed. James Anthony Froude, 2 vols. (St. Clair Shores, Mich.: Scholarly Press, 1971 [London: Longmans, Green, 1881]), vol. 1, p. 311.

15. Church, *Life of Church*, p. 14.

16. Amy Cruse, *The Victorians and Their Reading* (Boston: Houghton Mifflin, 1935), pp. 34–35.

17. Alice Chandler, *A Dream of Order: The Medieval Ideal in Nineteenth-Century English Literature* (Lincoln: Univ. of Nebraska Press, 1970), p. 23.

18. Ibid., pp. 152–53.

19. Newman, *Apologia*, pp. 38–39.

20. The most forceful recent work arguing this point of view is Nockles, *Oxford Movement in Context*.

21. Newman, *Apologia*, p. 54.

22. Liddon attributed Keble's alarm to these acts, as well as to the great Reform Bill of 1832. *Life of Pusey*, vol. 1, p. 266.

23. Battiscombe, *Keble*, pp. 151–52. According to H. L. Stewart, Keble's sermon was absurd because it confused the political relationships against which he railed with the spiritual state of the English people. But Stewart's objections, typical of 1920s scholarship, were all based on assumptions that made perfect sense to a nonbeliever or a Protestant. He was unable to enter into the thinking of a High Churchman. After making those arguments, he acknowledged that Keble was right to accuse the government of acting on a view of the Church and state that was opposite to the one it professed. He acknowledged it, but it made no difference to his assessment. Stewart, *Century of Anglo-Catholicism*, pp. 75–77.

24. Bowen, *Idea of the Victorian Church*, p. 44.

25. Newman, *Apologia*, p. 65. The principle of dogma was the first of Newman's original three "propositions": the other two were the truth of the visible church and the illegitimacy of Roman Catholicism. The first two beliefs he retained until the writing of the *Apologia* (pp. 65–69).

26. Ibid., p. 74.

27. This argument is found in John Henry Lewis Rowland, *Church, State and Society: The Attitudes of John Keble, Richard Hurrell Froude and John Henry Newman, 1827–1845* (Worthing, England: Churchman Publishing, 1989), p. 220.

28. R. W. Church, *The Oxford Movement: Twelve Years, 1833–1845,* ed. Geoffrey Best (Chicago: Univ. of Chicago Press, 1970 [1891]), p. 261.

29. Ibid., p. 79.

30. Newman, *Apologia,* p. 52.

31. Richard Hurrell Froude, *Remains,* ed. J. H. Newman and John Keble, 4 vols. (London: Rivington, 1838–39), pt. i, vol. i, p. 389.

32. W. H. Oliver, *Prophets and Millennialists: The Uses of Biblical Prophecy in England from the 1790s to the 1840s* (Auckland, New Zealand: Auckland Univ. Press, 1978), pp. 142–43.

33. To cite one example, this was the main complaint of Lord Ashley, later Shaftesbury, in spite of his high personal regard for his relative Pusey. G. F. A. Best, *Shaftesbury* (London: B. T. Botsford, 1964), p. 58.

34. Bernard M. G. Reardon, *From Coleridge to Gore: A Century of Religious Thought in Britain* (London: Longman, 1971), p. 118.

35. Tennyson, *Victorian Devotional Poetry,* p. 9, argues that this was found more plainly in their belles lettres than in their doctrinal or polemical work. Cf. R. J. White, *From Peterloo to the Crystal Palace* (London: Heinemann Educational Books, 1972), p. 100: "It was one of the great attractions of the Oxford Movement that its leaders—when they kept away from poetry—appealed immensely to the aesthetic sense. . . . Indeed the Oxford movement may be said to have brought religion in England back to the great prose tradition which it seemed to have deserted." For the effect of High Church spirituality on the church-building program, in particular the Gothic revival, see James F. White, *The Cambridge Movement: The Ecclesiologists and the Gothic Revival* (Cambridge, England: Cambridge Univ. Press, 1962).

36. Ker, *John Henry Newman,* p. 122. On the same page Ker quotes Newman on the liberals: "The Rationalist makes himself his own centre, not his Maker."

37. Williams, *Autobiography,* pp. 89–91.

38. Samuel F. Pickering, *John Locke and Children's Books in Eighteenth-Century England* (Knoxville: Univ. of Tennessee Press, 1981), p. 17.

39. Elizabeth Jenkins, *Jane Austen* (New York: Farrar, Straus & Cudahy, 1949), p. 394.

40. Church, *Oxford Movement,* p. 26. In the nineteenth century the evangelicals were still in contention with Law, for the same reason that Wesley had been. In its review of Southey's *Life of Wesley,* the *Christian Observer* objected to Law's failure to make the Atonement the center of his theological system. *Christian Observer,* November 1820, p. 747.

41. Prickett, *Romanticism and Religion,* pp. 95–96.

42. Evelyn Banish Greenberger, *Arthur Hugh Clough: The Growth of a Poet's Mind* (Cambridge, Mass.: Harvard Univ. Press, 1970), p. 135.

43. Christopher Dawson, *The Spirit of the Oxford Movement* (New York: AMS Press, 1976 [1934]), pp. 64–68.

44. Froude, "Remarks on Church Discipline," *Remains*, pt. 2, vol. 1, pp. 273–74.

45. Ibid., pt. 1, vol. 1, p. 400. Keble's openness to a breach with the Establishment has been a matter of some dispute. Georgina Battiscombe believes he was willing to countenance a split in order to extricate the Church from an untenable position (*Keble*, pp. 155f). J. H. L. Rowland thinks he was too much in sympathy with the ancient history of the Church, going back at least to Constantine, in which it was allied in some close relationship with the state, to consider disestablishment (*Church, State and Society*, p. 214).

46. Froude, *Remains*, pt. 1, vol. 1, pp. ix–xi.

47. Ibid., pp. 307–8.

48. Ibid., p. 433.

49. Hylson-Smith, *High Churchmanship*, pp. 116–17.

50. Froude, *Remains*, pt. 2, vol. 1, p. iii.

51. Peter Hinchliff, *Benjamin Jowett and the Christian Religion* (Oxford: Clarendon Press, 1987), p. 8. Hinchliff's judgment is based on the contrast between the Noetics and Jowett, the latter representing a later development in which the essentials of Christian faith were called into question in a way that they were not among the Noetics of the 1820s and 1830s.

52. Arthur Penrhyn Stanley, *The Life and Correspondence of Thomas Arnold, D.D.*, 6th ed. (London: Fellowes, 1846), p. 352.

53. Ibid., p. 354. Newman's brother-in-law and disciple Tom Mozley later said that Arnold was ignorant of his subject, having left Oxford before he had a chance to know Newman and the others, but Arnold's acquaintance with the flood of publications from the place made that a thin argument. T. Mozley, *Reminiscences; Chiefly of Oriel College and the Oxford Movement*, 2nd ed., 2 vols. (London: Longmans, Green, 1882), vol. 1, p. 252.

54. *Record*, December 2, 1833.

55. *Record*, December 5, 1833.

56. *Record*, January 9, 1840.

57. *Record*, November 12, 1840.

58. *Record*, October 16, 1845.

59. Newsome, *Wilberforces and Henry Manning*, pp. 173, 179–80.

60. S. Baring-Gould, *The Church Revival: Thoughts Thereon and Reminiscences* (London: Methuen, 1914), p. 311.

61. Halévy called Tract #90 "a Jesuitry frank to the point of stupidity." Élie Halévy, *Victorian Years (1841–1895)*, vol. 4 of *A History of the English People in the Nineteenth Century* (New York: Barnes & Noble, 1961), p. 60.

62. Newman, *Apologia*, p. 100.

63. Nockles, *Oxford Movement in Context*, p. 279.

64. Newman to Rose, December 15, 1833, in Newman, *Letters and Correspondence of Newman*, vol. 2, p. 2.

65. Owen Chadwick, *The Victorian Church*, 2nd ed. (London: Adam & Charles Black, 1970), pt. 1., p. 169.

66. Church, *Oxford Movement*, pp. 92–93.

67. Katharine Chorley, *Arthur Hugh Clough, The Uncommitted Mind: A Study of His Life and Poetry* (Oxford: Clarendon Press, 1962), pp. 44–45.

68. G. V. Cox, *Recollections of Oxford*, 2nd ed. (London: Macmillan, 1870), pp. 237–38.

69. Liddon, *Life of Edward Bouverie Pusey*, vol. 1, pp. 270–71.

70. Battiscombe, *John Keble*, p. xviii. Battiscombe also describes him as lazy, citing the paucity of his published work (p. 235). She was apparently not overly impressed with his workload as a conscientious parish priest. How many priests publish anything at all?

71. Walter Lock, *John Keble: A Biography*, 6th ed. (London: Methuen, 1894), p. 14.

72. Ibid, p. 17.

73. Perry Butler, ed. *Pusey Rediscovered* (London: Society for Promoting Christian Knowledge, 1983), p. ix.

74. Newman, *Apologia*, pp. 76–77.

75. Ibid., p. 77.

76. Battiscombe, *John Keble*, p. 186.

77. Nockles, *Oxford Movement in Context*, p. 6, argues that later opinion of the Church of England of the period was influenced too much by Liddon's *Life of Pusey* and Church's *Oxford Movement*, works of partisanship written by disciples, respectively, of Pusey and Newman. Their writings were thus composed with "hagiographic devotion, in which their respective heroes were cast as innocent victims of intolerance and misunderstanding on the part of the ecclesiastical authorities."

78. Newsome, *Wilberforces and Henry Manning*, p. 69.

79. Mark Pattison, *Memoirs* (Fontwell, England: Centaur, 1969 [1885]), p. 182.

80. Ibid., p. 244.

81. Baring-Gould, *Church Revival*, p. 157.

82. Amy Cruse, *The Victorians and Their Reading* (Boston: Houghton Mifflin, 1935), p. 44.

83. W. E. Gladstone, "The Evangelical Movement: Its Parentage, Progress and Issue," *British Quarterly Review* 70 (July 1879): 6.

84. Battiscombe, *John Keble*, p. 349.

85. Dieter Voll, *Catholic Evangelicalism: The Acceptance of Evangelical Traditions by the Oxford Movement during the Second Half of the Nineteenth Century, A Contribution to the Understanding of Recent Anglicanism*, trans. Veronica Ruffer (London: Faith Press, 1963), pp. 25–26. For arguments that ritualism was a natural outgrowth of Tractarianism, see Nigel Yates, *The Oxford Movement and Anglican Ritualism* (London: Historical Association, 1983).

86. Bowen, *Idea of the Victorian Church*, p. 350. Bowen calls this Pusey's "transition from Tractarianism to . . . missionary churchmanship" (p. 351).

87. Diana McClatchey, *Oxfordshire Clergy, 1777–1869: A Study of the Established Church and of the Role of its Clergy in Local Society* (Oxford: Clarendon Press, 1960), pp. 89, 165–66.

88. Josef L. Altholz, "The Tractarian Moment: The Incidental Origins of the Oxford Movement," *Albion* 26 (1994): 287.

89. This is argued in Edward Norman, *Church and Society in England 1770–1970: An Historical Study* (Oxford: Clarendon Press, 1976), pp. 71–72.

90. Perry Butler, *Gladstone, Church, State and Tractarianism: A Study of His Religious Ideas and Attitudes, 1809–1859* (Oxford: Clarendon Press, 1982), pp. 25–26.

91. *Apologia*, pp. 74–75.

92. Battiscombe, *John Keble*, p. 212.

93. Church to the Warden of Keble College, May 23, 1877, in Church, *Life of Church*, p. 260. Church was making the application to the problem they faced at the time, which was the persecution by the government of the ritualist priests.

94. Bowen, *Idea of the Victorian Church*, pp. 52–53, concluded this from studying the pamphlets of the era.

95. Georgina Battiscombe, *Charlotte Mary Yonge: The Story of an Uneventful Life* (London: Constable, 1943), pp. 13–14.

96. Cruse, *Victorians and Their Reading*, p. 45.

97. Owen Chadwick, ed., *The Mind of the Oxford Movement* (London: Adam & Charles Black, 1963), pp. 58–59. Elsewhere (*Victorian Church*, pt. 1, p. 230), Chadwick put it this way: "The Puseyites weakened the Church of England in politics and popular esteem. They strengthened the Church of England in its soul."

CHAPTER V

1. The term *Broad Church* evidently was first employed by the poet and Rugby Old Boy Arthur Hugh Clough (according to Benjamin Jowett), was used by Arthur Stanley in an *Edinburgh Review* article in July 1850, and then was popularized by an unsigned article written by W. J. Conybeare that appeared in the *Edinburgh Review* in October 1853. Charles Richard Sanders, *Coleridge and the Broad Church Movement: Studies in S. T. Coleridge, Dr. Arnold of Rugby, J. C. Hare, Thomas Carlyle and F. D. Maurice* (New York: Russell & Russell, 1972 [1942]), p. 7.

2. For example, Wilfrid Ward, *William George Ward and the Oxford Movement* (London: Macmillan, 1889), p. 46. Wilfrid Ward here was writing of his father's role in the Tractarian movement. William George Ward was turned from liberalism to the High Church by Newman's sermons and preceded Newman into the Roman Catholic Church by a few weeks. Even a highly knowledgeable modern scholar like Boyd Hilton called Arnold a latitudinarian. Boyd Hilton, *The Age of Atonement: The Influence of Evangelicalism on Social and Economic Thought* (Oxford: Clarendon Press, 1988), p. 28.

3. Arnold to T. S. Pasley, February 16, 1838, in Arthur Penrhyn Stanley, *The Life and Correspondence of Thomas Arnold, D.D.*, 6th ed. (London: Fellowes, 1846), p. 437.

4. Ibid., p. 24. This aspect of Arnold, indispensable as it is in understanding the man, is often missed in modern studies, as it was by many of his contemporaries.

5. Eugene L. Williamson, *The Liberalism of Thomas Arnold: A Study of His Religious and Political Writings* (University: Univ. of Alabama Press, 1964), pp. 92–93.

6. Michael McCrum, *Thomas Arnold Head Master: A Reassessment* (Oxford: Oxford Univ. Press, 1989), p. 13.

7. S. Baring-Gould, *The Church Revival: Thoughts Thereon and Reminiscences* (London: Methuen, 1914), p. 384. Baring-Gould had no use for Stanley, who rose to be dean of Westminster, regarding him as a typical Erastian of vague theological views—possibly Unitarian views—who treated the clergy as "the moral police force of the State" (p. 385).

8. See, for example, Bernard M. G. Reardon, *From Coleridge to Gore: A Century of Religious Thought in Britain* (London: Longman, 1971), pp. 50–51.

9. Thomas Arnold, *Sermons*, 3 vols. (London: Rivington, 1829), vol. 1, p. 2.

10. Ibid., pp. 2–3.

11. Ibid., p. 53.

12. Meriol Trevor, *The Arnolds: Thomas Arnold and his Family* (New York: Charles Scribner's Sons, 1973), p. 31.

13. *Christian Observer*, March 1845, p. 154.

14. Ibid., p. 161.

15. *Record*, January 30, 1845.

16. Élie Halévy, *The Liberal Awakening 1815–1830*, vol. 2 of *A History of the English People in the Nineteenth Century*, trans. E. I. Watkin (New York: Barnes & Noble, 1961), p. 162.

17. J. Wesley Bready, *Lord Shaftesbury and Social-Industrial Progress* (London: George Allen & Unwin, 1926), pp. 15–16.

18. Jeffrey Richards, *Happiest Days: The Public Schools in English Fiction* (Manchester, England: Manchester Univ. Press, 1988), p. 9. Note the irony of Froude's recollection in a book bearing this title.

19. Hugh Evan Hopkins, *Charles Simeon of Cambridge* (Grand Rapids, Mich.: Eerdmans, 1977), p. 14.

20. *Record*, February 22, 1830.

21. Stanley, *Life of Arnold*, p. 144.

22. For example, Sir George Grey, friend of Wilberforce. M. Creighton, *Memoir of Sir George Grey* (London: Longmans, Green, 1901), pp. 12–13.

23. Brian Simon and Ian Bradley, eds., *The Victorian Public School: Studies in the Development of an Educational Institution* (Dublin: Gill & Macmillan, 1975), p. 13.

24. Richards, *Happiest Days*, p. 41.

25. McCrum, *Thomas Arnold*, p. 25.

26. Stanley, *Life of Arnold*, p. 90.

27. Ibid., p. 131.

28. Ibid., p. 118.

29. R. L. Archer, *Secondary Education in the Nineteenth Century* (London: Frank Cass, 1966 [1921]), p. 36.

30. There are several contemporary examples of this collected in E. G. W. Bill, *University Reform in Nineteenth-Century Oxford: A Study of Henry Halford Vaughan, 1811–1885* (Oxford: Clarendon Press, 1973), pp. 8–10.

31. For example, T. W. Bamford, "Thomas Arnold and the Victorian Idea of a Public School," in Simon and Bradley, *Victorian Public School*, p. 67.

32. T. W. Bamford discounts George Moberly's testimony, published by Stanley, quoted above. He points to the irony of Stanley appealing to Arnold's enemies, or at least the friend of his enemies, for testimony and terms Moberly's statement "debatable" but seems to have nothing to say that actually makes one wish to discount Moberly. T. W. Bamford, *Rise of the Public Schools: A Study of Boys' Public Board Schools in England and Wales from 1837 to the Present Day* (London: Thomas Nelson, 1967), p. 45.

33. Ibid., p. 52.

34. Ibid., p. 53. "It is quite awful to watch the strength of evil in such young minds, and how powerless is every effort against it. It would give the vainest man alive a very fair notion of his own insufficiency, to see how little he can do, and how his most earnest addresses are as a cannonball on a bolster; thorough careless unimpressibleness beats me all to pieces." Arnold to George Cornish, August 1830, in McCrum, *Thomas Arnold*, p. 49.

35. T. W. Bamford, *Thomas Arnold* (London: Cresset Press, 1960), p. 179.

36. See Edward C. Mack, *Public Schools and British Opinion, 1780–1860* (Westport, Conn.: Greenwood Press, 1973 [1938]), pp. 296–97.

37. D. C. Somervell, *English Thought in the Nineteenth Century* (Westport, Conn.: Greenwood Press, 1977 [1962]), p. 113.

38. Thomas Hughes, *Tom Brown's Schooldays*, new ed. (London: Methuen, 1904), p. 208.

39. Archer, *Secondary Education*, pp. 53–68.

40. Patrick J. McCarthy, *Matthew Arnold and the Three Classes* (New York: Columbia Univ. Press, 1964), p. 21. Also J. R. de S. Honey, *Tom Brown's Universe: The Development of the Victorian Public School* (London: Millington, 1977), pp. 3–4.

41. Thomas Arnold, *Thirteen Letters on our Social Condition Addressed to the Sheffield Courant* (Sheffield, England: n.p., 1832), p. 9.

42. Williamson, *Liberalism of Thomas Arnold*, p. 35 and passim, has collected a number of quotations to this effect from Arnold's works.

43. Trevor, *Arnolds*, p. 39.

44. Arnold, *Sermons*, vol. 1, p. iv.

45. For arguments on the influence of Coleridge on Arnold, see Williamson, *Liberalism of Thomas Arnold*, pp. 47–52.

46. Ibid., pp. 47–48, 158.

47. Arnold, *Thirteen Letters*, p. 37.

48. Baring-Gould, *Church Revival*, p. 158.

49. Thomas Arnold, "Principles of Church Reform," in *Miscellaneous Works* (London: Fellowes, 1845), p. 259.

50. Ibid., p. 280.

51. Ibid., p. 284.

52. Arnold to the *Hertford Reformer,* January 12, 1839, in *Miscellaneous Works,* p. 441.

53. Arnold, "Principles of Church Reform," p. 269.

54. See the discussion of this issue in Desmond Bowen, *The Idea of the Victorian Church* (Montreal: McGill Univ. Press, 1968), pp. 357–60.

55. Arnold to Archdeacon Hare, March 18, 1842, in Stanley, *Life of Arnold,* p. 601.

56. Arnold, *Sermons,* vol. 1, p. 44.

57. Mack, *Public Schools and British Opinion,* p. 251.

58. *Record,* January 27, 1845.

59. George Granville Bradley, *Recollections of Arthur Penrhyn Stanley* (New York: Charles Scribner's Sons, 1883), p. 37.

60. Asa Briggs, *Victorian People: A Reassessment of Persons and Themes, 1851–67* (Chicago: Univ. of Chicago Press, 1955), p. 147.

61. Hughes, *Tom Brown's Schooldays,* p. 347.

62. Dennis W. Allen, "Young England: Muscular Christianity and the Politics of the Body in 'Tom Brown's Schooldays,'" in *Muscular Christianity: Embodying the Victorian Age,* ed. Donald E. Hall (Cambridge, England: Cambridge Univ. Press, 1994), pp. 114–32.

63. Edward Norman, *The Victorian Christian Socialists* (Cambridge, England: Cambridge Univ. Press, 1987), p. 81.

64. William S. Knickerbocker, *Creative Oxford: Its Influence in Victorian Literature* (Syracuse, N.Y.: Syracuse Univ. Press, 1972 [1925]), p. 79.

65. Stanley, *Life of Arnold,* pp. 144–45.

66. R. W. Church, *The Oxford Movement: Twelve Years, 1833–1845,* ed. Geoffrey Best (Chicago: Univ. of Chicago Press, 1970 [1891]), p. 261.

67. John Henry Newman, *Apologia pro Vita Sua,* ed. A. Dwight Culler (Boston: Houghton Mifflin, 1956 [1864]), p. 273. Newman also said in the same passage that in proportion as these liberals lost their egoism but kept their earnestness, they became increasingly identified with the conservative cause.

68. Christopher Kent, *Brains and Numbers: Elitism, Comtism, and Democracy in Mid-Victorian England* (Toronto: Univ. of Toronto Press, 1978), p. 5.

69. Owen Chadwick, *The Victorian Church,* 2nd ed., pt. 1 (London: Adam & Charles Black, 1970), p. 160.

70. Honey, *Tom Brown's Universe,* p. 27.

71. Bamford, *Thomas Arnold,* p. 170.

CHAPTER VI

1. R. W. Dale, *History of English Congregationalism,* 2nd ed. (London: Hodder & Stoughton, 1907), p. 507.

2. Ibid., pp. 556–57.

3. D. W. Bebbington, *Evangelicalism in Modern Britain: A History from the 1730s to the 1980s* (London: Unwin Hyman, 1989), p. 21.

4. Alan D. Gilbert, *Religion and Society in Industrial England: Church, Chapel and Social Change 1740–1914* (London: Longman, 1976), pp. 36–40.

5. Dale, *History of English Congregationalism*, pp. 580–81. Dale believed that the disparity was even greater, inasmuch as he considered it unlikely that the episcopal management was able to find the smallest meetinghouses. Some of the same ground is covered in Henry W. Clark, *History of English Non-Conformity*, 2 vols. (London: Chapman & Hall, 1911–1913). Clark emphasized more than Dale the debt of Dissent's renewal to events in the Established Church, which he termed the "resurrection of Puritanism" (p. 206).

6. Gilbert, *Religion and Society*, pp. 51–52.

7. Elizabeth Isichei, *Victorian Quakers* (London: Oxford Univ. Press, 1970), chap. 1.

8. Michael Ignatieff, *A Just Measure of Pain: The Penitentiary in the Industrial Revolution, 1750–1850* (London: Penguin Books, 1978), pp. 148–50.

9. W. R. Ward, *Religion and Society in England, 1790–1850* (London: B. T. Batsford, 1972), pp. 67–68. There is a useful discussion of the Quaker split in Owen Chadwick, *The Victorian Church*, 2nd ed. (London: Adam & Charles Black, 1970), pt. 1, pp. 430–32.

10. See Herbert McLachlan, *The Methodist Unitarian Movement* (Manchester, England: Manchester Univ. Press, 1919).

11. Anthony Lincoln, *Some Political and Social Ideas of English Dissent, 1763–1800* (New York: Octagon Books, 1971 [1938]), pp. 172–73. Chadwick has a good explanation of the two types of Unitarianism, which he calls "evangelical biblicism" and "rational deism." See *Victorian Church*, pt. 1, pp. 396–97.

12. Dale, *History of English Congregationalism*, pp. 588–90.

13. Henry Forster Burder, *Memoir of the Rev. George Burder* (London: Westley & Davis, 1833), pp. 148–49.

14. The statistics are in Bebbington, *Evangelicalism in Modern Britain*, p. 21.

15. William Jay, *The Autobiography of the Rev. William Jay*, ed. George Redford and John Angell James (London: Hamilton, Adams, 1855), pp. 40–41.

16. G. V. Cox, *Recollections of Oxford* (London: Macmillan, 1870), p. 223.

17. Newton to Wilberforce, November 15, 1786, in *The Correspondence of William Wilberforce*, ed. Robert Isaac and Samuel Wilberforce, 2 vols. (London: John Murray, 1840), vol. 1, p. 18.

18. J. P. Cobbett, *Selections from Cobbett's Political Works*, vol. 4, pp. 52–53, reprinted in David M. Thompson, ed. *Nonconformity in the Nineteenth Century* (London: Routledge & Kegan Paul, 1972), p. 33. E. P. Thompson made use of Cobbett's antipathies, in particular those against the Methodists. See, for example, *The Making of the English Working Class* (New York: Vintage, 1966 [1963]), pp. 394–95. After quoting extensively from Cobbett on the evils of Methodism, Thompson said that "this was one of his consistent prejudices." But it was also one of Thompson's.

19. Gilbert, *Religion and Society*, pp. 135–36.

20. Peel to Henry Goulburn, Jan. 29, 1835, in Robert Peel, *Sir Robert Peel from*

His Private Papers, ed. Charles Stuart Parker, 3 vols. (New York: Kraus Reprint, 1970 [1899]), vol. 2, p. 283.

21. W. R. Lambert, *Drink and Sobriety in Victorian Wales, c. 1820–1895* (Cardiff: Univ. of Wales Press, 1983), pp. 130–31.

22. Robert Vaughan, *Religious Parties in England: Their Principles, History, and Present Duty,* 2nd ed. (London: Thomas Ward, n.d. [1839]), p. 93.

23. Chadwick, *Victorian Church,* pt. 1, pp. 79–81.

24. See the account in Bernard Lord Manning, *The Protestant Dissenting Deputies,* ed. Ormerod Greenwood (Cambridge, England: Cambridge Univ. Press, 1952), pp. 175–84.

25. David M. Thompson, "The Liberation Society, 1844–1868," in *Pressure from Without in Early Victorian England,* ed. Patricia Hollis (London: Edward Arnold, 1974), pp. 210–38. See also Dale, *History of English Congregationalism,* pp. 634–37. The British Anti-State Church Association changed its name in 1853, when it became the Society for the Liberation of Religion from State Patronage and Control, popularly shortened to the Liberation Society.

26. Edward Miall, "The British Church in Relation to the British People (1849)," in *The Evangelical and Oxford Movements,* ed. Elizabeth Jay (Cambridge, England: Cambridge Univ. Press, 1983), pp. 101–4.

27. Josef L. Altholz, *The Religious Press in Britain, 1760–1900* (New York: Greenwood Press, 1989), pp. 60–61; E. E. Kellett, "The Press," in *Early Victorian England, 1830–1865,* ed. G. M. Young, 2 vols. (London: Oxford Univ. Press, 1951 [1934]), vol. 2, p. 84.

28. E. D. Bebb, *Nonconformity and Social and Economic Life, 1660–1800* (London: Epworth Press, 1935).

29. Gilbert, *Religion and Society,* pp. 62–67. The main source for this conclusion is the information in several thousand nonparochial registers. These were deposited with the registrar-general after the passage of legislation in 1836 that provided for the national registration of births, marriages and deaths.

30. Hippolyte Taine, *Notes on England,* trans. Edward Hyams (Fair Lawn, N.J.: Essential Books, 1958 [1872]), p. 10.

31. Ian R. Christie, *Stress and Stability in Late Eighteenth-Century Britain: Reflections on the British Avoidance of Revolution* (Oxford: Clarendon Press, 1984), pp. 205–6. Christie speculates that the self-respect gained by artisans and lower middle–class people from leadership roles in the chapel helped them cope with the challenges of the Industrial Revolution and so averted the buildup of frustration and discontent (p. 214). The accession of much of Methodism to at least lower middle–class status is supported by statistical analysis in Clive Field, "Methodism in Metropolitan London" (D.Phil. thesis, Oxford Univ., 1974), especially pp. 251–52.

32. Brian Heeney, *Mission to the Middle Classes: The Woodard Schools, 1848–1891* (London: Society for Promoting Christian Knowledge, 1969), pp. 12–13.

33. George Kitson Clark, *The Making of Victorian England* (Cambridge, Mass.: Harvard Univ. Press, 1963 [1962]), p. 176. A similar point is made by John W. Derry, *Reaction and Reform: England in the Early Nineteenth Century, 1793–1868* (London:

Blandford, 1963), pp. 198–99. Derry deals here with the unfairness in Matthew Arnold's famous "Philistine" characterization of the Dissenters and emphasizes the genuine educational advantages gained by them from their work in the chapel and their study of the Authorized Version of the Bible.

34. T. S. Ashton, *The Industrial Revolution, 1760–1830* (London: Oxford Univ. Press, 1948), pp. 14–15.

35. John K. Walton, *Lancashire: A Social History, 1558–1939* (Manchester, England: Manchester Univ. Press, 1987), p. 130.

36. Stanley D. Chapman, *The Early Factory Masters: The Transition to the Factory System in the Midlands Textile Industry* (Newton Abbot, England: David & Charles, 1967), p. 104.

37. Alan Everitt, *The Pattern of Rural Dissent: The Nineteenth Century,* Department of English Local History Occasional Papers, Second Series, no. 4 (Leicester, England: Leicester Univ. Press, 1972), pp. 64–67. Everitt points out that the lack of homogeneity of Dissent makes it dangerous to indulge in facile generalizations (p. 62). The same view is held by Gilbert, *Religion and Society,* pp. 61–62. Gilbert thinks the error is compounded by contemporary denominational leaders emphasizing the uniqueness of their communions.

38. J. H. S. Kent, "The Role of Religion in the Cultural Structure of the Later Victorian City," *Transactions of the Royal Historical Society* 23 (1973): 153–73. Kent's argument deals mainly with the late Victorian period, but he refers to earlier developments as formative.

39. For example, Jacob Viner, *The Role of Providence in the Social Order: An Essay in Intellectual History* (Philadelphia: American Philosophical Society, 1972), p. 51. Viner uses the rural-versus-urban divide to adduce reasons of financial gain for maintaining the hostility between Church and chapel.

40. James Walvin, "Freeing the Slaves: How Important Was Wilberforce?" in *Out of Slavery: Abolition and After,* ed. Jack Hayward (London: Frank Cass, 1985), pp. 39–40.

41. Albert Goodwin, *The Friends of Liberty: The English Democratic Movement in the Age of the French Revolution* (Cambridge, Mass.: Harvard Univ. Press, 1979), pp. 65–67, 151.

42. David Hempton, "Evangelicalism in English and Irish Society, 1780–1840," in *Evangelicalism: Comparative Studies of Popular Protestantism in North America, the British Isles, and Beyond, 1700–1990,* ed. Mark Noll, David Bebbington, and G. A. Rawlyk (New York: Oxford Univ. Press, 1994), pp. 161–62.

43. R. A. Soloway, *Prelates and People: Ecclesiastical Social Thought in England 1783–1852* (London: Routledge & Kegan Paul, 1969), pp. 262–63; for an argument, possibly overdone, for the dependence of the Chartist movement on Dissent, see Raymond G. Cowherd, *The Politics of English Dissent: The Religious Aspects of Liberal and Humanitarian Reform Movements from 1815 to 1848* (New York: New York Univ. Press, 1956).

44. Cecil Driver, *Tory Radical: The Life of Richard Oastler* (New York: Oxford

Univ. Press, 1946), p. 61. Michael Sadler and Lord Ashley had the same complaint about the Evangelicals. *Record,* April 23, 1838.

45. Gladstone was astonished at the spread of Dissent revealed by the 1851 census. High Churchman though he was, he began having increasing contact with the leaders of Dissent and ultimately pronounced a noble triumph the way it had Christianized the English cities, where the Church's record was spotty. See Deryck Schreuder, "Gladstone and the Conscience of the State," in *The Conscience of the Victorian State,* ed. Peter Marsh (Syracuse, N.Y.: Syracuse Univ. Press, 1979), p. 121.

46. George Kitson Clark, *The English Inheritance: An Historical Essay* (London: SCM Press, 1950), p. 129.

47. The standard work on this is Manning, *Protestant Dissenting Deputies.*

48. Élie Halévy, *The Liberal Awakening 1815–1830,* vol. 2 of *A History of the English People in the Nineteenth Century,* trans. E. I. Watkin (New York: Barnes & Noble, 1961), p. 179.

49. John Benson, *British Coalminers in the Nineteenth Century: A Social History* (New York: Holmes & Meier, 1980), p. 88.

50. Barrie Trinder, *The Industrial Revolution in Shropshire,* 2nd ed. (London: Phillimore, 1981), pp. 166–67.

51. Ward, *Religion and Society,* p. 85.

52. Field, "Methodism in Metropolitan London," p. 2.

53. Asa Briggs, *Victorian Cities* (New York: Harper & Row, 1963), pp. 206–7.

54. Ibid., p. 281.

55. Clyde Binfield, *So Down to Prayers: Studies in English Nonconformity, 1780–1920* (London: Dent, 1977), pp. 59–60. There is a bit of ambiguity here. The clergyman was Walter Hook, a High Churchman who sometimes used the word *Methodist* when referring to Dissent.

56. David Roberts, *Victorian Origins of the British Welfare State* (New Haven, Conn.: Yale Univ. Press, 1960), pp. 69–70.

57. J. L. Hammond and Barbara Hammond, *The Town Labourer: The New Civilization, 1760–1832* (Garden City, N.Y.: Doubleday, 1968 [4th rev. ed. of 1925]), p. 233.

CHAPTER VII

1. Lamb to Thomas Manning, April 5, 1809, in *The Letters of Charles Lamb to Which Are Added Those of His Sister Mary Lamb,* ed. E. V. Lucas, 3 vols. (London: J. M. Dent, 1935), vol. 1, p. 179.

2. Stephen Prickett, *Victorian Fantasy* (Hassocks, England: Harvester Press, 1979), p. 2.

3. Coleridge to Rest Fenner, circa September 22, 1816, in *Selected Letters,* ed. Earl Leslie Griggs, 6 vols. (Oxford: Clarendon Press, 1956–1971), vol. 4, pp. 674–75.

4. George P. Landow, *Elegant Jeremiahs: The Sage from Carlyle to Mailer* (Ithaca, N.Y.: Cornell Univ. Press, 1986), pp. 17–18, 59. For a discussion of Carlyle as a "type," raised in a strict biblical environment and then rebelling against it but

retaining its essential shape in spite of the rebellion, see George Allan Cate, ed., *The Correspondence of Thomas Carlyle and John Ruskin* (Stanford, Calif.: Stanford Univ. Press, 1982), p. 8. Cate treats Ruskin as someone of the same type.

5. Leigh Hunt, *Autobiography*, ed. J. E. Morpurgo (London: Cresset Press, 1949 [rev. ed. of 1859]), pp. 426–28.

6. William Holman Hunt, *Pre-Raphaelitism and the Pre-Raphaelite Brotherhood*, 2 vols. (London: Macmillan, 1905), vol. 1, p. 353.

7. Ben Knights, *The Idea of the Clerisy in the Nineteenth Century* (Cambridge, England: Cambridge Univ. Press., 1978), p. 76.

8. Thomas Carlyle, *Reminiscences*, ed. James Anthony Froude, 2 vols. (St. Clair Shores, Mich.: Scholarly Press, 1971 [London: Longmans, Green, 1881]), vol. 2, p. 336.

9. For a roll call of these, see Gertrude Himmelfarb, *The Idea of Poverty: England in the Early Industrial Age* (New York: Random House, 1985 [1983]), pp. 201–2. "Agreeing with almost no one and unsparing in his contempt for almost everyone, Carlyle came as close as anyone to being the intellectual hero of the age."

10. Thomas Carlyle, *Past and Present* (London: Dent, 1960 [1843]), p. 93.

11. See John Holloway, *The Victorian Sage: Studies in Argument* (New York: W. W. Norton, 1965 [1953]), pp. 3–10.

12. Crane Brinton, *English Political Thought in the Nineteenth Century* (London: Ernest Benn, 1933), pp. 167–68.

13. Norma Clarke, "'Strenuous Idleness,' Thomas Carlyle and the Man of Letters as Hero," in *Manful Assertions: Masculinities in Britain since 1800*, ed. Michael Roper and John Tosh (London: Routledge, 1991), p. 29.

14. Graham Hough, "Coleridge and the Victorians," in *The English Mind: Studies in the English Moralists Presented to Basil Willey*, ed. Hugh Sykes Davies and George Watson (Cambridge, England: Cambridge Univ. Press, 1964), p. 176.

15. For discussions of Coleridge's antideterminist views, see Bernard M. G. Reardon, *From Coleridge to Gore: A Century of Religious Thought in Britain* (London: Longman, 1971), pp. 63–65; David Pym, *The Religious Thought of Samuel Coleridge* (New York: Harper & Row, 1979), pp. 17–18; James D. Boulger, *Coleridge as Religious Thinker* (New Haven, Conn.: Yale Univ. Press, 1961), pp. 34–35; Hough, "Coleridge and the Victorians," pp. 178–79, argues that the source of much of Coleridge's thinking was the Platonism and neo-Platonism that he had soaked up in his early school days.

16. Samuel Taylor Coleridge, *Table Talk*, ed. Carl Wooding, 2 vols. (Princeton, N.J.: Princeton Univ. Press, 1990), vol. 1, pp. 418f (August 14, 1833).

17. Ibid., pp. 242f (August 14, 1831). Alfred Cobban argued that in spite of his attacks on utilitarianism, Coleridge remained an advocate of the methodology because the legislative criterion was the utility of a policy. This seems strained because nobody ever advocates a policy without purporting to show its usefulness, and Coleridge was not shy in speaking of the moral and religious basis for public policy. Cobban, *Edmund Burke and the Revolt against the Eighteenth Century: A*

Study of the Political and Social Thinking of Burke, Wordsworth, Coleridge and Southey, 2nd ed. (New York: Barnes & Noble, 1960 [1928]), p. 175.

18. The French historian Louis Cazamian stressed Carlyle's opposition of French and German uses of reason and his partisanship for the latter. Cazamian, *Carlyle,* trans. E. K. Brown (n.p.: Archon, 1966 [1932]), pp. 54–55.

19. Thomas Carlyle, *Two Notebooks of Thomas Carlyle: From 23d March 1811 to 16th May 1832,* ed. Charles Eliot Norton (Mamaroneck, N.Y.: Paul P. Appel, 1972 [1898]), pp. 171–72.

20. Ibid., p. 145.

21. Thomas Carlyle, *Sartor Resartus,* ed. Kerry McSweeney and Peter Sabor (New York: Oxford Univ. Press, 1987 [1833]), pp. 158–59.

22. Ibid., p. 87.

23. Ibid., p. 12.

24. Ibid., p. 124.

25. Ibid., p. 158.

26. See the discussion of this in Donald D. Stone, *The Romantic Impulse in Victorian Fiction* (Cambridge, Mass.: Harvard Univ. Press, 1980), chap. 1.

27. Coleridge, *Table Talk,* vol. 1, p. 106 (April 20, 1830).

28. Paraclita Reilly, *Aubrey de Vere: Victorian Observer* (Lincoln: Univ. of Nebraska Press, 1953), pp. 39–41. Other arguments for the Christian orthodoxy of Wordsworth may be found in Edward Mortimer Chapman, *English Literature and Religion, 1800–1900* (London: Constable, 1910), pp. 65–66; John Clubbe and Ernest J. Lovell Jr., *English Romanticism: The Grounds of Belief* (De Kalb: Northern Illinois Univ. Press, 1983), pp. 2–3; J. R. Watson, *Wordsworth's Vital Soul: The Sacred and Profane in Wordsworth's Poetry* (Atlantic Highlands, N.J.: Humanities Press, 1982), pp. 7–8.

29. G. B. Tennyson argues that in explicating the religious dimension of nature Keble was largely making inferences from Wordsworth—as were most of the nineteenth-century nature poets. Tennyson, *Victorian Devotional Poetry: The Tractarian Mode* (Cambridge, Mass.: Harvard Univ. Press, 1981), pp. 68, 94, 101.

30. Martin Greenberg, *The Hamlet Vocation of Coleridge and Wordsworth* (Iowa City: Univ. of Iowa Press, 1986), p. 97.

31. John Tulloch, *Movements of Religious Thought in Britain during the Nineteenth Century* (New York: Charles Scribner's Sons, 1893), p. 16.

32. Stephen Prickett, *Coleridge and Wordsworth: The Poetry of Growth* (Cambridge, England: Cambridge Univ. Press, 1970), p. 105.

33. *Record,* August 21, 1834. Coleridge's actual deathbed scene was quite as pious as the common Evangelical ones, with a reaffirmation of his faith in Christ. See J. Robert Barth, *Coleridge and Christian Doctrine* (Cambridge, Mass.: Harvard Univ. Press, 1969), p. 235.

34. Tulloch, *Movements of Religious Thought in Britain,* pp. 13–17.

35. That is the argument in Pym, *Religious Thought of Samuel Coleridge.*

36. Coleridge, *Table Talk,* vol. 1, p. 333 (January 7, 1833).

37. R. W. Church, *The Oxford Movement: Twelve Years, 1833–1845,* ed. Geoffrey Best (Chicago: Univ. of Chicago Press, 1970 [1891]), p. 14. Newman said he had not read Coleridge before 1835, but he had met a number of the poet's disciples— including J. H. Frere, J. C. Hare, and John Sterling—and thus had imbibed his ideas secondhand. See John Beer, "Newman and the Romantic Sensibility," in Davies and Watson, *English Mind,* pp. 198–99.

38. That is the thesis of Stephen Prickett, *Romanticism and Religion: The Tradition of Coleridge and Wordsworth in the Victorian Church* (Cambridge, England: Cambridge Univ. Press, 1976). Prickett writes of the earlier view, that which divided the poet from the theologian, as having "hardened into a critical orthodoxy" from which only a minority deviated (p. 2).

39. S. T. Coleridge, *The Statesman's Manual; Or the Best Guide to Political Skill and Foresight: A Lay Sermon Addressed to the Higher Classes of Society* (London: Gale & Fenner, 1816), p. 38.

40. Ibid., p. 30.

41. *Christian Observer,* March 1845, p. 146.

42. Coleridge, *Table Talk,* vol. 1, p. 99 (April 13, 1830).

43. Ibid., p. 157.

44. Ibid., p. 275 (March 31, 1832).

45. Prickett, *Coleridge and Wordsworth,* p. 196; see also Boulger, *Coleridge as Religious Thinker,* pp. 20–24.

46. John Stewart Collis, *The Carlyles: A Biography of Thomas and Jane Carlyle* (London: Sidgwick & Jackson, 1971), p. 57.

47. Cazamian, *Carlyle,* pp. 14–15, 39.

48. Carlyle, *Reminiscences,* vol. 1, pp. 51–52.

49. Thomas Carlyle, *Letters of Thomas Carlyle, 1826–1836,* ed. Charles Elliot Norton, 2 vols. (London: Macmillan, 1888), vol. 2, p. 13.

50. See George P. Landow, *Victorian Types, Victorian Shadows* (Boston: Routledge & Kegan Paul, 1980), pp. 168–70, for an explanation of how Carlyle's use of Scripture owed much to the evangelical habit of interpretation. Landow shows how this was common for those of evangelical heritage, even after they rejected the theology.

51. See the explication of this in Richard E. Brantley, *Coordinates of Anglo-American Romanticism: Wesley, Edwards, Carlyle and Emerson* (Gainesville: Univ. Press of Florida, 1993), pp. 66–67. Brantley calls him an Arminian because he believed in social progress as a result of human action—for example, in Chartism.

52. Carlyle, *Reminiscences,* vol. 1, pp. 4–5.

53. Ibid., p. 65. Luann Walther believes that this filial piety of Carlyle's in his *Reminiscences* was something of a fiction. She thinks that a truer picture is given in autobiographical passages of *Sartor Resartus* that depict a stern father and a miserable childhood. See Walther, "The Invention of Childhood in Victorian Autobiography," in *Approaches to Victorian Autobiography,* ed. George P. Landow (Athens: Ohio Univ. Press, 1979), p. 70. Even if that is true, the religious sentiments he expressed in the *Reminiscences* are likely to have been genuine.

54. Carlyle, *Reminiscences*, vol. 1, pp. 277–78. A great scholar of the period comments on this passage that there is in it "no reliance upon grace or redeeming love, but on the contrary, much proud and passionate self-assertion. The emotion that follows release is hatred and defiance of the Devil, rather than love and gratitude towards God." Basil Willey, *Nineteenth-Century Studies: Coleridge to Matthew Arnold* (New York: Columbia Univ. Press, 1949), p. 115.

55. Collis, *Carlyles*, p. 66.

56. For example, Barry V. Qualls, *The Secular Pilgrims of Victorian Fiction: The Novel as a Book of Life* (Cambridge, England: Cambridge Univ. Press, 1982), pp. 38–47.

57. Willey, *Nineteenth-Century Studies*, p. 106.

58. D. C. Somervell, *English Thought in the Nineteenth Century* (Westport, Conn.: Greenwood Press, 1977 [1962]), p. 146.

59. Carlyle, *Past and Present*, pp. 23–27.

60. Carlyle, *Reminiscences*, p. 287.

61. This paragraph is based on the argument in Charles De Paolo, *Coleridge: Historian of Ideas* (Victoria, Canada: Univ. of Victoria Press, 1992), chap. 5.

62. Coleridge, *Statesman's Manual*, p. 3.

63. Ibid., p. 17.

64. John Stuart Mill, "Coleridge," in *Essays on Ethics, Religion and Society*, ed. J. M. Robson (Toronto: Univ. of Toronto Press, 1969), p. 153.

65. Carlyle, *Past and Present*, p. 73.

66. John Colmer, *Coleridge: Critic of Society* (Oxford: Clarendon Press, 1959), pp. 12–13.

67. Robert Hole, *Pulpits, Politics and Public Order in England, 1760–1832* (Cambridge, England: Cambridge Univ. Press, 1989), pp. 253–54.

68. David P. Calleo, *Coleridge and the Idea of the Modern State* (New Haven, Conn.: Yale Univ. Press, 1966), pp. 96–98. Stephen Prickett points to the paradoxical nature of Coleridge's National Church in that it was not necessarily a Christian Church. It was, rather, the name Coleridge gave to the spiritual values of the nation, and it could include considerable mythology. This interpretation is not held unanimously, but it is only natural to be uncertain about this when Coleridge's ideas on the subject are so ambiguous. Prickett, "The Religious Context," in *The Romantics*, ed. Stephen Prickett (London: Methuen, 1981), pp. 121–22.

69. There is an argument for the Tractarian dependence on Coleridge for their idea on the spiritual independence of the Church in Herbert Leslie Stewart, *A Century of Anglo-Catholicism* (New York: Oxford Univ. Press, 1929), p. 71.

70. Mill, "Coleridge," pp. 138–39.

71. The argument is in John T. Miller, Jr., "Private Faith and Public Religion: S. T. Coleridge's Confrontation with Secularism," in *The Secular Mind: Transformations of Faith in Modern Europe*, ed. W. Warren Wagar (New York: Holmes & Meier, 1982), p. 80.

72. Boris Ford, *Romantics to Early Victorians*, vol. 6 of *The Cambridge Guide to the Arts in Britain* (Cambridge, England: Cambridge Univ. Press, 1990), p. 81.

73. John Henry Newman, "State of Religious Parties," *The British Critic*, April 1839, p. 400.

74. Prickett, *Romanticism and Religion*, p. 260.

75. Michael St. John Packe, *The Life of John Stuart Mill* (New York: Macmillan, 1954), p. 83. See also Gertrude Himmelfarb, *On Liberty and Liberalism: The Case of John Stuart Mill* (New York: Alfred A. Knopf, 1974).

76. Willey, *Nineteenth-Century Studies*, p. 2.

77. Ibid., p. 31.

78. Barth, *Coleridge and Christian Doctrine*, p. 226.

79. Edward Norman, *The Victorian Christian Socialists* (Cambridge, England: Cambridge Univ. Press, 1987), pp. 24–25.

80. Prickett, *Romanticism and Religion*, pp. 264–67.

81. Pym, *Religious Thought of Samuel Coleridge*, p. 54.

82. The comparison is from Packe, *Life of John Stuart Mill*, p. 158.

83. R. J. White, *From Peterloo to the Crystal Palace* (London: Heinemann Educational Books, 1972), p. 91.

84. G. K. Chesterton, *The Victorian Age in Literature* (London: Williams & Norgate, n.d. [1913]), p. 54.

85. Tulloch, *Movements of Religious Thought*, pp. 204–5.

86. Willey, *Nineteenth-Century Studies*, p. 103.

87. Martineau to Fanny Wedgwood, in *Harriet Martineau's Letters to Fanny Wedgwood*, ed. Elisabeth Sanders Arbuckle (Stanford, Calif.: Stanford Univ. Press, 1983), p. 212.

88. Noel Annan, *Leslie Stephen: The Godless Victorian* (New York: Random House, 1984), p. 172.

89. David J. DeLaura, "Carlyle and Arnold: The Religious Issue," in *Carlyle Past and Present: A Collection of New Essays*, ed. K. J. Fielding and Rodger L. Tarr (London: Vision, 1976), p. 144. This essay describes Carlyle's influence on Matthew Arnold.

90. George Eliot, "Thomas Carlyle," in *Essays of George Eliot*, ed. Thomas Pinney (New York: Columbia Univ. Press, 1963), pp. 213–14. First published in the *Leader* 6 (October 27, 1855).

91. Qualls, *Secular Pilgrims of Victorian Fiction*, p. 85.

92. Katharine Chorley, *Arthur Hugh Clough, the Uncommitted Mind: A Study of His Life and Poetry* (Oxford: Clarendon Press, 1962), p. 132.

CHAPTER VIII

1. John Burnett, *A Social History of Housing, 1815–1985*, 2nd ed. (London: Methuen, 1986), pp. 31–32.

2. William Cobbett, *Rural Rides* (Harmondsworth, England: Penguin Books, 1969 [1830]), p. 254. Cobbett dated the conversation October 30, 1825.

3. A modern scholar describes Dickens's work of this genre as factually handicapped, which Dickens knew. So the novelist was "not only splendid, but from time

to time, splendidly unreliable." Norris Pope, *Dickens and Charity* (New York: Columbia Univ. Press, 1978), p. ix.

4. Edgar Johnson, *Charles Dickens: His Tragedy and Triumph*, 2 vols. (New York: Simon & Schuster, 1952), vol. 1, p. 451.

5. J. L. Hammond and Barbara Hammond, *The Village Labourer 1760–1832: A Study in the Government of England before the Reform Bill*, new ed. (New York: Augustus M. Kelley Publishers, 1967 [1913]), pp. 33–34, 332.

6. For a critique of Tawney's scholarship, see Jacob Viner, *The Role of Providence in the Social Order: An Essay in Intellectual History* (Philadelphia: American Philosophical Society, 1972), pp. 59–60; also A. M. C. Waterman, *Revolution, Economics and Religion: Christian Political Economy, 1798–1833* (Cambridge, England: Cambridge Univ. Press, 1991), pp. 2–3, 261–62.

7. See, for example, the critique of some of Hobsbawm's use of data in Peter H. Lindert and Jeffrey G. Williamson, "English Workers' Living Standards during the Industrial Revolution: A New Look," *Economic History Review* 36, no. 1 (1983): 13, fn. 38. Lindert and Williamson are critical of Hobsbawm's use of "primary materials shaky enough to make them unreliable even as testimony on purely local unemployment, let alone as national averages." The authors go on to specify where they think Hobsbawm went wrong.

8. F. M. L. Thompson, *The Rise of Respectable Society: A Social History of Victorian Britain, 1830–1900* (Cambridge, Mass., Harvard Univ. Press, 1988), pp. 177–78. "The mid-Victorian social tranquillity was indeed such a contrast [to the rhetoric of radical propaganda] that some historians have only been able to explain it by inventing a cunning and fiendishly successful conspiracy by the employers to subvert the true path of working-class consciousness" (p. 198).

9. The evidence is summarized by Ian R. Christie, *Stress and Stability in Late Eighteenth Century Britain: Reflections on the British Avoidance of Revolution* (Oxford: Clarendon Press, 1984), pp. 69–72.

10. These studies are summarized in Sara Horrell and Jane Humphries, "Old Questions, New Data, and Alternative Perspectives: Families' Living Standards in the Industrial Revolution," *Journal of Economic History* 52 (1992): 849–80. Lindert and Williamson conclude that after a period of stagnation, wages "nearly doubled" in the thirty years after 1820. "English Workers' Living Standards," p. 11.

11. Ferdinand Mount, *The Subversive Family: An Alternative History of Love and Marriage* (New York: Free Press, 1992 [1982]), p. 54.

12. J. L. Hammond and Barbara Hammond, *The Town Labourer: The New Civilization 1760–1832* (Garden City, N.Y.: Doubleday, 1968 [4th rev. ed. of 1925]), p. 7.

13. Douglas A. Reid, "Interpreting the Festival Calendar: Wakes and Fairs as Carnivals," in *Popular Culture and Custom in Nineteenth-Century England*, ed. Robert D. Storch (London: Croom Helm, 1982), p. 132.

14. G. E. Mingay, *English Landed Society in the Eighteenth Century* (London: Routledge & Kegan Paul, 1963), p. 254. Mingay took issue with the contention,

argued most notably by the Hammonds, that the enclosure movement that converted common lands to private ownership was a disaster for the poor. The results apparently were mixed (pp. 184f). Mingay elaborated further on this in *Rural Life in Victorian England* (London: Heinemann, 1977), where he highlighted the long-term improvement in rural fortunes as a result of enclosures. "The social and economic consequences of enclosure, therefore, varied widely from place to place in a largely random and unpredictable manner. On the whole the effects were much less pervasive and less damaging, and much more beneficial to employment and incomes than used to be supposed" (pp. 14f).

15. M. Dorothy George, *London Life in the Eighteenth Century* (Chicago: Academy Chicago, 1984 [1925]), p. 318, n. 18. See also pp. 112–13, 208, 302, and passim.

16. See the argument in Norman Gash, *Aristocracy and People: Britain 1818–1865* (Cambridge, Mass.: Harvard Univ. Press, 1979), p. 2.

17. Humphry House, *The Dickens World,* 2nd ed. (London: Oxford Univ. Press, 1960 [1942]), p. 34.

18. See T. S. Ashton, *The Industrial Revolution 1760–1830* (London: Oxford Univ. Press, 1970 [1948]), pp. 107–8.

19. This is discussed, along with fictional illustrations, in Asa Briggs, *The Age of Improvement 1783–1867* (London: Longmans, 1959), p. 58.

20. J. L. Hammond and Barbara Hammond, *The Age of the Chartists, 1832–1854: A Study of Discontent* (Hamden, Conn.: Archon Books, 1962 [1930]), p. 61.

21. Seymour Drescher, *Tocqueville and England* (Cambridge, Mass.: Harvard Univ. Press, 1964), p. 138; Friedrich Engels, *The Condition of the Working Class in England,* ed. and trans. W. O. Henderson and W. H. Chaloner (Stanford, Calif.: Stanford Univ. Press, 1968 [1845]), p. 313.

22. Thomas Arnold, *Thirteen Letters on Our Social Condition Addressed to the Sheffield Courant* (Sheffield, England: n.p., 1832), p. 9.

23. *Record,* March 22, 1838.

24. *Record,* March 15, 1830.

25. Cobbett, *Rural Rides,* pp. 41–42. The point to be made here is not that Cobbett's analysis was accurate but that the criticisms of the system came from every part of the political spectrum. I have cited above a tiny fraction of an enormous output of criticism. In recent years a body of literature has grown that concludes that the bad effects of Speenhamland were greatly exaggerated by contemporary sources and by traditional analysis. Two good studies of the issues with useful literature reviews are Gertrude Himmelfarb, *The Idea of Poverty: England in the Early Industrial Age* (New York: Random House, 1985 [1983]), and George R. Boer, *An Economic History of the English Poor Law, 1750–1850* (Cambridge, England: Cambridge Univ. Press, 1990). An older work that reinforced the traditional view is Karl Polanyi, *The Great Transformation* (Boston: Beacon Press, 1957 [1944]). Polanyi's conclusion: the Speenhamland system was extremely popular with direct beneficiaries and with farmers who perceived that their labor costs were lower, but that was all illusory. "In the long run the result was ghastly" (p. 80).

26. Carlyle, *Reminiscences*, ed. James Anthony Froude, 2 vols. (St. Clair Shores, Mich.: Scholarly Press, 1971 [London: Longmans, Green, 1881]), vol. 2, p. 190.

27. Alexis de Tocqueville, *Journeys to England and Ireland*, ed. J. P. Mayer, trans. George Lawrence and K. P. Mayer (New Haven, Conn.: Yale Univ. Press, 1958), pp. 57, 67.

28. For example, Mingay, *English Landed Society*, p. 115. Mingay points to the relatively responsible behavior of the nobility, its willingness to tax itself for the public good, and the very limited set of privileges it enjoyed.

29. Eugene L. Williamson, *The Liberalism of Thomas Arnold: A Study of His Religious and Political Writings* (University: Univ. of Alabama Press, 1964), pp. 185–86.

30. Arnold to Carlyle, January 1840, in Arthur Penrhyn Stanley, *The Life and Correspondence of Thomas Arnold, D. D.*, 6th ed. (London: Fellowes, 1846), p. 500.

31. Cobbett, *Rural Rides*, pp. 264–65.

32. Ibid., p. 41.

33. Ibid., p. 93.

34. Herman Ausubel, *John Bright, Victorian Reformer* (New York: John Wiley & Sons, 1966), pp. 7–8, 30–31.

35. Edward Miall, "The British Churches in Relation to the British People (1849)," in *The Evangelical and Oxford Movements*, ed. Elizabeth Jay (Cambridge, England: Cambridge Univ. Press, 1983), pp. 100–101.

36. Jerry Z. Muller, *Adam Smith in His Time and Ours: Designing the Decent Society* (New York: Free Press, 1993). See also Himmelfarb, *Idea of Poverty*, pp. 46, 63. For an argument that Smith and his contemporaries did not reflect the interests of industrialists, the common belief, but that of the preindustrial agricultural condition, see David McNally, *Political Economy and the Rise of Capitalism: A Reinterpretation* (Berkeley: Univ. of California Press, 1988).

37. Alfred Cobban, *Edmund Burke and the Revolt against the Eighteenth Century: A Study of the Political and Social Thinking of Burke, Wordsworth, Coleridge and Southey*, 2nd ed. (New York: Barnes & Noble, 1960 [1928]), pp. 204–5.

38. Southey to John Rickman, September 12, 1803, in *New Letters of Robert Southey*, ed. Kenneth Curry, 2 vols. (New York: Columbia Univ. Press, 1965), vol. 1, p. 327.

39. Raymond G. Cowherd, *Political Economists and the English Poor Laws: A Historical Study of the Influence of Classical Economics on the Formation of Social Welfare Policy* (Athens: Ohio Univ. Press, 1977), pp. 174–76.

40. Ibid., p. 67.

41. *Record*, April 1, 1833.

42. J. P. Kay-Shuttleworth, *The Moral and Physical Condition of the Working Classes* (Shannon: Irish Univ. Press, 1971 [1832]), pp. 55–57.

43. Valerie Kossew Pichanick, *Harriet Martineau: The Woman and Her Work, 1802–76* (Ann Arbor: Univ. of Michigan Press, 1980), pp. 54–81, 160–61; Stanley D. Chapman, *The Early Factory Masters: The Transition to the Factory System in*

the Midlands Textile Industry (Newton Abbot, England: David & Charles, 1967), pp. 198–99. Nevertheless, Martineau was so shocked by the material in Ashley's report on the exploitation of women and children in the mines that she supported legislation to correct the abuses. Pichanick, *Harriet Martineau,* p. 161.

44. Wilberforce to Lord Muncaster, November 5, 1800, in William Wilberforce, *The Correspondence of William Wilberforce,* ed. R. I. Wilberforce and S. Wilberforce, 2 vols. (London: John Murray, 1840), vol. 1, p. 218.

45. November 1, 1817, in William Wilberforce, *Private Papers of William Wilberforce,* ed. A. M. Wilberforce (London: T. Fisher Unwin, 1897), p. 179.

46. *Christian Observer,* August 1821, p. 500.

47. Boyd Hilton, *The Age of Atonement: The Influence of Evangelicalism on Social and Economic Thought, 1795–1865* (Oxford: Clarendon Press, 1988).

48. Lord Ashley wrote a letter to the *Record* bemoaning the lack of support received by both Michael Sadler and himself from evangelicals. The editor was chastened by this and promised to study the matter to rectify his own ignorance of the subject. *Record,* April 23, 1838. In the issues of March 5, 1840, and February 20, 1845, the *Record* made good on its repentance and backed Ashley's efforts at legislative reform. However, the *Record* had in fact supported Sadler's factory bill in 1832, citing "the wail of infantile misery . . . worse than that of the slaves in our sugar islands." *Record,* April 30, 1832. In the same issue, the paper claimed that the factory bill was compatible with political economy. The *Record,* in most respects very conservative and traditional, could take on a radical tinge on these issues. In its first months of publication it denounced the alliance of poor West Indian farmers with their creditors in the House of Commons (March 11, 1828) to the detriment of the nation. In supporting Ashley's factory legislation in 1838, it denounced wealthy and influential men who are "interested in the continuance of the system of cruelty and bondage" (July 16, 1838).

49. Waterman, *Revolution, Economics and Religion.*

50. Graham to Peel, April 13, 1843, in Robert Peel, *Sir Robert Peel from His Private Papers,* ed. Charles Stuart Parker, 3 vols. (New York: Kraus, 1970 [1899]), vol. 2, p. 560.

51. Peter Gaskell, *Artisans and Machinery: The Moral and Physical Condition of the Manufacturing Population Considered with Reference to Mechanical Substitutes for Human Labour* (London: Cass, 1968 [London: John W. Parker, 1836]), pp. 300–301. Gaskell made the same point in his earlier book, *The Manufacturing Population of England* (New York: Arno Press, 1972 [1833]), pp. 68–69.

52. Gaskell, *Artisans and Machinery,* p. v.

53. Catherine Gallagher, *The Industrial Reformation of English Fiction: Social Discourse and Narrative Form 1832–1867* (Chicago: Univ. of Chicago Press, 1985), p. 34.

54. Gaskell, *Artisans and Machinery,* p. ix.

55. Ibid., pp. 115–16.

56. Ibid., pp. 242–43.

57. Gaskell, *Manufacturing Population of England,* pp. 88–89.

58. Ibid., pp. 161–64.

59. Edwin Chadwick, *Report on the Sanitary Condition of the Labouring Population of Gt. Britain* (Edinburgh: Edinburgh Univ. Press, 1965 [1842]), pp. 204–7.

60. Ibid., pp. 422–23.

61. Asa Briggs, *The Collected Essays of Asa Briggs*, 2 vols. (Brighton, England: Harvester Press, 1985), vol. 2, pp. 132–33.

62. Thomas Chalmers, *On Political Economy: In Connexion with the Moral State and Moral Prospects of Society* (New York: Augustus Kelley, 1968 [1832]), pp. iii–v. Modern analysts commonly react to such a view with hostility. One, for example, regards it as a "Tory" view, which is wrong not only factually but also morally. See Jenifer Hart, "Nineteenth-Century Social Reform: A Tory Interpretation of History," *Past and Present*, no. 31 (July 1965): 39–61.

63. Kay-Shuttleworth, *Moral and Physical Condition*, pp. 4–6. As we shall see later on, Kay-Shuttleworth tried to infuse the evangelico-moral approach into the whole population by means of his influence over the teacher education institutions.

64. There is a good contemporary account of how these societies actually worked in Frederick M. Eden, *Observations on Friendly Societies for the Maintenance of the Industrious Classes during Sickness, Infirmity, Old Age and Other Exigencies* (London: J. White, 1801). As Eden explained it, the societies provided for their members "by means of the surplus of their earnings" (p. 1), which suggests that poverty was not considered the same as indigence.

65. Gaskell, *Artisans and Machinery*, pp. 300–301.

66. Norman Dennis and A. H. Halsey, *English Ethical Socialism: Thomas More to R. H. Tawney* (Oxford: Clarendon Press, 1988), p. 56.

67. David Roberts, *Paternalism in Early Victorian England* (New Brunswick, N.J.: Rutgers Univ. Press, 1979), pp. 43–47.

68. William C. Lubenow, *The Politics of Government Growth: Early Victorian Attitudes toward State Intervention, 1833–1848* (Hamden, Conn.: Archon Books, 1971), p. 53.

69. Michael Thomas Sadler, *Memoirs* (London: Burnside & Seeley, 1842), pp. 167, 224, 340–41, 505. One of Sadler's criticisms of Malthus was that he made no reference to divine authority (p. 512).

70. The view that working people were more or less estranged from religion, *pace* the Hammonds and others like them, is defended in K. S. Inglis, *Churches and the Working Classes in Victorian England* (London: Routledge & Kegan Paul, 1963).

71. Hugh McLeod, *Religion and the Working Class in Nineteenth-Century Britain* (London: Macmillan, 1984). McLeod has considerable material on the pitfalls of misinterpreting the sources due to the trickiness of the material (and the political agendas of the scholars).

72. E. D. Bebb, *Nonconformity and Social and Economic Life, 1660–1800: Some Problems of the Present as They Appeared in the Past* (London: Epworth Press, 1935), p. 11.

73. John Benson, *British Coalminers in the Nineteenth Century: A Social History* (New York: Holmes & Meier, 1980), p. 88.

74. Anthony Armstrong, *The Church of England, the Methodists and Society 1700–1850* (London: Univ. of London Press, 1973), pp. 209–10; Alan D. Gilbert, *Religion and Society in Industrial England: Church, Chapel and Social Change 1740–1914* (London: Longman, 1976), pp. 87–89.

75. James Obelkevich, *Religion and Rural Society: South Lindsey, 1825–75* (Oxford: Clarendon Press, 1976), p. 244.

76. Wellman J. Warner, *The Wesleyan Movement in the Industrial Revolution* (London: Longmans, Green, 1930), p. 144.

77. Robert Moore, *Pit-Men, Preachers and Politics: The Effects of Methodism in a Durham Mining Community* (London: Cambridge Univ. Press, 1974), p. 222. Moore compares Methodism in this later period with Calvinism in the seventeenth century, which prepared people for entrepreneurial roles.

78. Leslie Howsam, *Cheap Bibles* (Cambridge, England: Cambridge Univ. Press, 1991), p. 51.

79. Gaskell, *Artisans and Machinery*, p. 6.

80. Ibid., pp. ix, 1–2.

81. Ibid., p. 68.

82. Ibid., p. 115.

83. Graham Wallas, *The Life of Francis Place (1771–1854)*, 3rd ed. (New York: Alfred A. Knopf, 1919 [1898]), pp. 31, 14.

84. Francis Place, *The Autobiography of Francis Place (1771–1854)*, ed. Mary Thale (Cambridge, England: Cambridge Univ. Press, 1972), pp. 14–15.

85. Cobban, *Edmund Burke*, p. 225.

86. Barry Trinder, *The Industrial Revolution in Shropshire*, 2nd ed. (London: Phillimore, 1981), p. 223.

87. For a discussion of the misleading scholarship, see Norman McCord, "The Poor Law and Philanthropy," in *The New Poor Law in the Nineteenth Century*, ed. Derek Fraser (New York: St. Martin's Press, 1976), pp. 88, 106–7.

88. George, *London Life*, p. 26.

89. Margaret Maison, *The Victorian Vision: Studies in the Religious Novel* (New York: Sheed & Ward, 1961), p. 198.

90. Boyd Hilton, who has contributed much to our understanding of the evangelicals and social policy, went astray on this point. He generalized too quickly from the records of one evangelical society to conclude that the evangelical preoccupation with the spiritual reduced the provision of material goods to a merely symbolic presence. As we shall see, that was not so. See Hilton, *Age of Atonement*, pp. 98–99. A similar perspective may be found in Deryck Lovegrove, "Idealism and Association in Early Nineteenth Century Dissent," in *Voluntary Religion*, ed. W. J. Sheils and Diana Wood (Oxford: Basic Blackwell, 1986), pp. 303–17. Lovegrove's position seems to be drawn from a very limited selection of sources.

91. *Christian Observer*, April 1811, p. 260.

92. William Wilberforce, *A Practical View of the Prevailing Religious System of Professed Christians in the Higher and Middle Classes in This Country Contrasted with Real Christianity*, 2nd ed. (London: Cadell & Davies, 1797), p. 432. Wilberforce

prefaced that statement by saying, "I know that these sentiments will be termed uncharitable, but I must not be deterred by such an imputation."

93. Thomas Arnold, *Sermons,* 3 vols. (London: Rivington, 1829–1834), vol. 2, p. 352.

94. Stewart J. Brown, *Thomas Chalmers and the Godly Commonwealth in Scotland* (Oxford: Oxford Univ. Press, 1982), pp. 67, 190–91.

95. Ibid., p. 118.

96. R. A. Soloway, *Prelates and People: Ecclesiastical Social Thought in England 1783–1852* (London: Routledge & Kegan Paul, 1969), p. 130.

97. Frank Smith, *The Life and Work of Sir James Kay-Shuttleworth* (Bath, England: Cedric Chivers, 1974 [1923]), pp. 28–29.

98. Cobbett, *Rural Rides,* p. 230.

99. E. R. Norman, *Church and Society in England 1770–1970: An Historical Study* (Oxford: Clarendon Press, 1976), pp. 3–4, 135.

100. Diana McClatchey, *Oxfordshire Clergy, 1777–1869: A Study of the Established Church and of the Role of Its Clergy in Local Society* (Oxford: Clarendon Press, 1960), pp. 165–66.

101. For explanations of Chalmers's system, see Karl de Schweinitz, *England's Road to Social Security* (New York: A. S. Barnes, 1961 [1943]), chap. 11; Stewart Mechie, *The Church and Scottish Social Development, 1780–1870* (London: Oxford Univ. Press, 1960), pp. 52–54.

102. Brown, *Thomas Chalmers,* pp. 153–58. Chalmers was greatly admired by both Malthus (ibid., p. 116) and one of Malthus's fiercest enemies, Carlyle (*Reminiscences,* vol. 1, p. 157).

103. Leigh Hunt, *Autobiography,* ed. J. E. Morpurgo (London: Cresset Press, 1949 [1859]), p. 117.

104. Engels, *Condition of the Working Class,* p. 284.

105. For example, Theodore W. Jennings, Jr., *Good News to the Poor: John Wesley's Evangelical Economics* (Nashville, Tenn.: Abingdon Press, 1990).

106. Warner, *Wesleyan Movement,* p. 193.

107. Clive Field, "Methodism in Metropolitan London" (D.Phil. thesis, Oxford Univ., 1974), p. 252.

108. This is taken from Himmelfarb, *Idea of Poverty,* p. 31.

109. Richard D. Altick, *The English Common Reader: A Social History of the Mass Reading Public, 1800–1900* (Chicago: Univ. of Chicago Press, 1957), p. 5. See also M. G. Jones, *The Charity School Movement: A Study of Eighteenth Century Puritanism in Action* (Hampden, Conn: Archon Books, 1964 [1938]).

110. *Gloucester Journal,* May 17, 1784, Appendix A2 of Philip B. Cliff, *The Rise and Development of the Sunday School Movement in England, 1780–1980* (Nutfield, England: National Christian Education Council, 1986), pp. 328–29.

111. Henry James Burgess, *Enterprise in Education: The Story of the Work of the Established Church in the Education of the People Prior to 1870* (London: Society for Promoting Christian Knowledge, 1958), p. 132.

112. For example, L. E. Elliott-Binns, *The Early Evangelicals: A Religious and*

Social Study (Greenwich, Conn.: Seabury Press, 1953), p. 395: "The real weakness in the Evangelical doctrinal system was that it was too much concerned with the needs of the individual and neglected the wider needs of the community as a whole." Later on (p. 422), Elliott-Binns seemed to belie that contention by disagreeing with others who charged the Evangelicals with unconcern for the sufferings of their fellow countrymen; he cited Wilberforce's efforts on behalf of various reform movements.

113. Katherine Heasman, *Evangelicals in Action: An Appraisal of Their Social Work in the Victorian Era* (London: Bles, 1962), p. 292.

114. J. R. Poynter, *Society and Pauperism: English Ideas on Poor Relief, 1795–1834* (London: Routledge & Kegan Paul, 1969), pp. 91–95.

115. John Pollock, *Wilberforce* (New York: St. Martin's Press, 1977), p. 142.

116. G. B. Hindle, *Provision for the Relief of the Poor in Manchester, 1754–1826* (Manchester, England: Manchester Univ. Press, 1975), pp. 80–81.

117. John Roach, *Social Reform in England, 1780–1880* (New York: St. Martin's Press, 1978), p. 210.

118. Smith, *Life of Kay-Shuttleworth*, pp. 28–29.

119. Engels, *Condition of the Working Class in England*, p. 313.

120. Kay-Shuttleworth, *Moral and Physical Condition*, p. 65.

121. Hugh Evan Hopkins, *Charles Simeon of Cambridge* (Grand Rapids, Mich.: Eerdmans, 1977), pp. 47–48; John C. Bennett, "Charles Simeon and the Evangelical Missionary Movement: A Study of Voluntarism and Church-Mission Tensions" (Ph.D. thesis, Univ. of Edinburgh, 1992), p. 88. For numerous other examples of how women in particular visited the poor as a means of Christian ministry, see F. K. Prochaska, *Women and Philanthropy in Nineteenth-Century England* (Oxford: Clarendon Press, 1980); David Owen, *English Philanthropy, 1660–1960* (Cambridge, Mass.: Harvard Univ. Press, 1964), especially pp. 138–41; Donald M. Lewis, *Lighten Their Darkness: The Evangelical Mission to Working Class London, 1828–1860* (Westport, Conn.: Greenwood Press, 1986), pp. 40–43; also R. J. Morris, *Class, Sect and Party: The Making of the British Middle Class, Leeds, 1820–1850* (Manchester, England: Manchester Univ. Press, 1990), pp. 205–6.

122. Cecil Driver, *Tory Radical: The Life of Richard Oastler* (New York: Oxford Univ Press, 1946), pp. 13, 20–29.

123. E. M. Forster, *Marianne Thornton, 1797–1887: A Domestic Biography* (London: Edward Arnold, 1956), pp. 158, 224.

124. There is good material on this in Ian Bradley, "The Politics of Godliness: Evangelicals in Parliament, 1784–1832" (D.Phil. dissertation, Oxford Univ., 1974).

125. The *Record*, which had always opposed the Irish nationalist demands, insisted that efforts be made to help the Irish on the basis of Christian duty. *Record*, March 21, 1831.

126. For the ritualist component, see Nigel Yates, *The Oxford Movement and Anglican Ritualism* (London: Historical Association, 1983), especially pp. 25–28.

127. See Oastler's account of this conversation in Driver, *Tory Radical*, pp. 468–69; Brown, *Thomas Chalmers*, pp. 366–67.

128. Wilberforce to W. Hey, March 17, 1801, in Wilberforce, *Correspondence,* vol. 1, pp. 224–25.

129. Christopher Herbert, *Culture and Anomie: Ethnographic Imagination in the Nineteenth Century* (Chicago: Univ. of Chicago Press, 1991), p. 32.

CHAPTER IX

1. G. S. R. Kitson Clark, *An Expanding Society: Britain 1830–1900* (Cambridge, England: Cambridge Univ. Press, 1967), p. 34.

2. Crane Brinton, *A History of Western Morals* (New York: Harcourt, Brace, 1959), p. 351.

3. S. E. Finer, *The Life and Times of Sir Edwin Chadwick* (London: Methuen, 1952), p. 2.

4. John Eros, "The Rise of Organized Freethought in Mid-Victorian England," *Sociological Review* 2, no. 1 (1954): 100.

5. Leigh Hunt, *Autobiography,* ed. J. E. Morpurgo (London: Cresset Press, 1949 [rev. ed. of 1859]), pp. 435–36.

6. Leigh Hunt, *An Attempt to Shew the Folly and Danger of Methodism* (London: John Hunt, 1809), p. xiii.

7. This is the thesis of A. M. C. Waterman, *Revolution, Economics and Religion: Christian Political Economy, 1798–1833* (Cambridge, England: Cambridge Univ. Press, 1991).

8. Gertrude Himmelfarb, *Victorian Minds* (New York: Harper & Row, 1970 [1968]), p. 35.

9. Joseph Hamburger, "The Whig Conscience," in *The Conscience of the Victorian State,* ed. Peter Marsh (Syracuse, N.Y.: Syracuse Univ. Press, 1979), p. 25.

10. This is the argument in John Henry Lewis Rowlands, *Church, State and Society: The Attitudes of John Keble, Richard Hurrell Froude and John Henry Newman, 1827–1845* (Worthing, England: Churchman Publishing, 1989), pp. 216–21. Also William George Peck, *The Social Implications of the Oxford Movement* (New York: Charles Scribner's Sons, 1933), p. 94. Peck emphasized the utilitarian temper as a repudiation of the Augustinian heritage of Western Christianity.

11. *Record,* February 6, 1837.

12. See the argument in Catherine Gallagher, *The Industrial Reformation of English Fiction: Social Discourse and Narrative Form 1832–1867* (Chicago: Univ. of Chicago Press, 1985), pp. 188–90.

13. Samuel Taylor Coleridge, *Table Talk,* ed. Carl Woodring, 2 vols. (Princeton, N.J.: Princeton Univ. Press, 1990), vol. 1, pp. 242–43.

14. A. V. Dicey, *Lectures on the Relation between Law and Public Opinion in England during the Nineteenth Century* (London: Macmillan, 1905), p. 302. On the contrast between Bentham and Adam Smith and the move toward government control, see Ellen Franke Paul, *Moral Revolution and Economic Science: The Demise of Laissez-Faire in Nineteenth-Century British Political Economy* (Westport, Conn.: Greenwood Press, 1979), pp. 279–83.

15. John Stuart Mill, "Coleridge," in *Autobiography and Literary Essays,* ed.

John M. Robson and Jack Stillinger (Toronto: Univ. of Toronto Press, 1981), pp. 109–10.

16. John Stuart Mill, *Essays on Ethics, Religion and Society*, ed. J. M. Robson (Toronto: Univ. of Toronto Press, 1969), p. 125.

17. Richard D. Altick, *Victorian People and Ideas: A Companion for the Modern Reader of English Literature* (New York: W. W. Norton, 1973), p. 118.

18. Michael St. John Packe, *The Life of John Stuart Mill* (New York: Macmillan, 1954), pp. 181–82.

19. Ibid., p. 100.

20. John Roach, "Liberalism and the Victorian Intelligentsia," in *The Victorian Revolution: Government and Society in Victoria's Britain*, ed. Peter Stansky (New York: New Viewpoints, 1973), p. 329

21. Dicey, *Lectures*, pp. 399–401. Halévy's well-known belief that the two movements were consonant with each other was also based largely on his view that they were both individualistic. See Élie Halévy, *England in 1815*, vol. 1 of *A History of the English People in the Nineteenth Century*, trans. E. I. Watkin and D. A. Barker (New York: Barnes & Noble, 1961), p. 587.

22. Dicey, *Lectures*, p. 175. This has been argued in detail by a modern scholar, Mary Poovey, *Making a Social Body: British Cultural Formation, 1830–1864* (Chicago: Univ. of Chicago Press, 1995), chap. 5.

23. *Record*, February 7, 1831.

24. Brinton, *History of Western Morals*, p. 316.

25. Carl L. Becker, *The Heavenly City of the Eighteenth-Century Philosophers* (New Haven, Conn.: Yale Univ. Press, 1959 [1932]), pp. 96–97.

26. Mill, *Autobiography*, pp. 107–11.

27. For example, some on the left such as E. P. Thompson, *The Making of the English Working Class* (New York: Vintage, 1966 [1963]), pp. 740–42; also E. J. Hobsbawm, *Labouring Men: Studies in the History of Labour* (London: Weidenfeld & Nicolson, 1964), p. 373–75.

28. Edwin Chadwick, *Report on the Sanitary Condition of the Labouring Population of Gt. Britain* (Edinburgh: Edinburgh Univ. Press, 1965 [1842]), p. 193. Here one of Chadwick's investigators reports on visits to houses where overcrowded conditions led to mixed rooming and sexual immorality and thereupon to prostitution.

29. Packe, *Life of John Stuart Mill*, pp. 442–43. Packe based his judgment on the posthumously published *Three Essays on Religion* (1869), the last of which Mill wrote without the direct influence of Harriet Taylor, and which was orthodox enough to cause some consternation among Mill's followers. Evidently the old problem of theodicy presented the barrier to orthodoxy beyond which Mill would not go. There is a similar line of reasoning in Himmelfarb, *Victorian Minds*, pp. 151–53, which goes on to dispute some of the arguments that too quickly discounted Mill's turn to theism.

30. *Record*, March 9, 1835, and March 23, 1837.

31. Francis Place, *The Autobiography of Francis Place (1771–1854)*, ed. Mary Thale (Cambridge, England: Cambridge Univ. Press, 1972), pp. 198–99.

32. There is a good treatment of the place of literacy and literary productions in the early secularist movement in Edward Royle, *Victorian Infidels: The Origins of the British Secularist Movement, 1791–1866* (Manchester, England: Manchester Univ. Press, 1974).

33. Alexis de Tocqueville, *Journeys to England and Ireland*, ed. J. P. Mayer, trans. George Lawrence and K. P. Mayer (New Haven, Conn.: Yale Univ. Press, 1958), p. 87.

34. See the argument in Standish Meacham, "The Evangelical Inheritance," *Journal of British Studies* 3, no. 1 (1963): 93. On succeeding pages Meacham contended that this emphasis on experience became a source of weakness in the evangelicals, as the focus on the soul's experience degenerated into subjectivism and a sort of egocentricity.

35. For example, R. W. Dale, *The Old Evangelicalism and the New* (London: Hodder & Stoughton, 1889), pp. 18–20.

36. Paul Thomas Murphy, *Toward a Working-Class Canon: Literary Criticism in British Working-Class Periodicals, 1816–1858* (Columbus: Ohio State Univ. Press, 1994), pp. 68, 101.

37. See Michael Mason, *The Making of Victorian Sexual Attitudes* (Oxford: Oxford Univ. Press, 1994), pp. 2–3.

38. Hilton erred in supposing that utilitarian optimism could be contrasted with evangelical "backward-looking pessimism." Boyd Hilton, *The Age of Atonement: The Influence of Evangelicalism on Social and Economic Thought, 1795–1865* (Oxford: Clarendon Press, 1988), p. 245. Clapham's position, for example, was more like postmillennial optimism. As the years went by all Malthusians—utilitarian as well as evangelical—took on the pessimistic coloring of that philosophy with respect to economic prospects, but not necessarily as a general outlook.

39. G. M. Trevelyan, *Illustrated English Social History* (London: Longmans, Green, 1952 [1942]), p. 30.

40. Christopher Dawson, "The Humanitarians," in *Ideas and Beliefs of the Victorians,* no ed. (London: Sylvan Press, 1949), p. 251.

41. Mill, "Coleridge," in *Essays,* p. 146.

42. Ibid., p. 153.

43. Bentham to Wilberforce, May 22, 1798, in William Wilberforce, *Correspondence,* ed. R. I. Wilberforce and S. Wilberforce, 2 vols. (London: John Murray, 1840), vol. 1, p. 177.

44. R. I. Wilberforce and S. Wilberforce, *The Life of William Wilberforce,* 5 vols. (London: John Murray, 1838), vol. 2, pp. 170–71.

45. Brian Harrison, "State Intervention and Moral Reform in Nineteenth-Century England," in *Pressure from Without in Early Victorian England,* ed. Patricia Hollis (London: Edward Arnold, 1974), p. 293; Ian Bradley, "The Politics of Godliness: Evangelicals in Parliament, 1784–1832" (D.Phil. thesis, Oxford Univ.,

1974), p. 224. On succeeding pages Bradley describes differences between the Claphamites in Parliament and their radical colleagues, mainly over willingness of the former to countenance measures, such as the suspension of the habeas corpus, affecting liberty.

46. Packe, *Life of John Stuart Mill,* p. 87.

47. Wilfrid Ward, *William George Ward and the Oxford Movement* (London: Macmillan, 1889), pp. 294, 297.

48. Michael Ignatieff, *A Just Measure of Pain: The Penitentiary in the Industrial Revolution, 1750–1850* (London: Penguin Books, 1978), p. 67.

49. John Walton, "The Treatment of Pauper Lunatics in Victorian England: The Case of Lancaster Asylum, 1816–1870," in *Madhouses, Mad-Doctors, and Madmen: The Social History of Psychiatry in the Victorian Era,* ed. Andrew Scull (Philadelphia: Univ. of Pennsylvania Press, 1981), p. 166; Andrew T. Scull, *Museums of Madness: The Social Organization of Insanity in Nineteenth-Century England* (New York: St. Martin's Press, 1979), pp. 55–58.

50. John Rosselli, *Lord William Bentinck: The Making of a Liberal Imperialist 1774–1839* (Berkeley: Univ. of California Press, 1974), p. 86.

51. See the argument in John McLeish, *Evangelical Religion and Popular Education: A Modern Interpretation* (London: Methuen, 1969), pp. 66–71.

52. Harold Underwood Faulkner, *Chartism and the Churches: A Study in Democracy* (New York: AMS Press, 1968); David Jones, *Chartism and the Chartists* (New York: St. Martin's Press, 1975), pp. 51–53.

53. *"Northern Star,* April 3, 1841," in *Class and Conflict in Nineteenth-Century England, 1815–1850,* ed. Patricia Hollie (London: Routledge & Kegan Paul, 1973), p. 265.

54. Kenneth A. Thompson, *Bureaucracy and Church Reform: The Organisational Response of the Church of England to Social Change 1800–1965* (Oxford, Clarendon Press, 1970), p. 37.

55. Frank Smith, *The Life and Work of Sir James Kay-Shuttleworth* (Bath, England: Cedric Chivers, 1974), p. 20.

56. Patrick Brantlinger, *The Spirit of Reform: British Literature and Politics, 1832–1867* (Cambridge, Mass.: Harvard Univ. Press, 1977), chap. 1.

57. Bradley, "Politics of Godliness," pp. 225–32.

58. Mill, *Autobiography,* p. 111.

59. William C. Lubenow, *The Politics of Government Growth: Early Victorian Attitudes toward State Intervention, 1833–1848* (Hamden, Conn.: Archon Books, 1971, p. 22.

60. J. L. Hammond and Barbara Hammond, *The Age of the Chartists, 1832–1854: A Study of Discontent* (Hamden, Conn.: Archon Books, 1962 [1930]), p. 76.

61. Graham Wallas, *The Life of Francis Place (1771–1854),* 3rd ed. (New York: Alfred A. Knopf, 1919 [1898]), p. 105. The name of the society was changed from the Royal Lancastrian Association in 1813. This society was a rival of the National Schools Society, founded in 1811 and controlled by High Churchmen. Both associations used the monitorial system, and there was considerable mutual recrimina-

tion between them. See Henry James Burgess, *Enterprise in Education: The Story of the Work of the Established Church in the Education of the People Prior to 1870* (London: Society for Promoting Christian Knowledge, 1958), chap. 1. Also J. M. Goldstrom, *The Social Content of Education, 1808–1870: A Study of the Working Class School Reader in England and Ireland* (Shannon: Irish Univ. Press, 1972), pp. 39–41.

62. Arnold to A. P. Stanley, October 21, 1836, in Arthur Penrhyn Stanley, *The Life and Correspondence of Thomas Arnold, D.D.*, 6th ed. (London: Fellowes, 1846), p. 390.

63. Christopher Dawson in the introduction to [no ed.], *Ideas and Beliefs*, pp. 29–30.

64. Scholars on the left have laid much emphasis on this, but there is general agreement on the point. See, for example, Hobsbawm, *Labouring Men*, pp. 373–376.

65. Anthony Brundage, *England's "Prussian Minister": Edwin Chadwick and the Politics of Government Growth, 1832–1854* (University Park: Pennsylvania State Univ. Press, 1988), pp. 3–4. Edwin Chadwick's father was a Francophile radical and follower of Thomas Paine.

66. G. M. Young, "Portrait of an Age," in *Early Victorian England 1830–1865*, ed. G. M. Young, 2 vols. (London: Oxford Univ. Press, 1951 [1934]), vol. 2, p. 455.

67. See Norris Pope, *Dickens and Charity* (New York: Columbia Univ. Press, 1978), pp. 249–50.

68. Newman to R. H. Froude, January 17, 1836, in John Henry Newman, *Letters and Correspondence of John Henry Newman during His Life in the English Church*, ed. Anne Mozley, 2 vols. (London: Longmans, Green, 1891), vol. 2, p. 156.

69. Mill, "Bentham," (1838), in *Essays*, pp. 98–100. Mill says here that Bentham was mistaken in treating the business part of human life as the whole and that that was the failure of his moral system. But it would be truer to say that once the Benthamite materialist metaphysic is accepted, the rest follows naturally, as the organism strives to maximize its happiness. If there was an error, it was in the metaphysic, not the ethic, which only followed from the other.

70. Himmelfarb, *Victorian Minds*, pp. 287–88. She believes that the greatest influence of utilitarianism came about when Mill "diluted it with what was in effect evangelical ethics."

71. Mill, "Bentham," p. 90.

72. Gallagher, *Industrial Reformation of English Fiction*, p. 12.

73. Packe, *Life of John Stuart Mill*, p. 88.

74. William Hazlitt, *The Spirit of the Age: Or Contemporary Portraits* (London: Oxford Univ. Press, 1954 [1825]), p. 16.

75. Ibid., p. 1.

76. For example, David Roberts, "Jeremy Bentham and the Victorian Administrative State," *Victorian Studies* 2 (1959): 206; Norman Gash, *Aristocracy and People: Britain 1818–1865* (Cambridge, Mass.: Harvard Univ. Press, 1979), p. 46; Himmelfarb, *Victorian Minds*, pp. 285–87, believes that evangelicalism set the stage on which Bentham's influence could count for much. A dissenter from this view is

E. J. Hobsbawm, *The Age of Revolution, 1789–1848* (Cleveland, Ohio: World, 1962), p. 220.

CHAPTER X

1. Hannah More's disciple and biographer pointed out that More considered teaching the poor to read to be dangerous as well as beneficial because of the harmful literature to which they might be exposed. William Roberts, *The Life of Hannah More* (London: Seeley, Jackson, & Halliday, 1872), pp. 144–46.

2. T. B. Shepherd, *Methodism and the Literature of the Eighteenth Century* (New York: Haskell House, 1966), p. 94.

3. Edwin Wilbur Rice, *The Sunday-School Movement, 1780–1917, and the American Sunday School Union, 1817–1917* (New York: Arno Press & New York Times, 1971 [1917]), pp. 128–29.

4. David F. Mitch, *The Rise of Popular Literacy in Victorian England: The Influence of Private Choice and Public Policy* (Philadelphia: Univ. of Pennsylvania Press, 1992), pp. 126, 137–38; see also John William Adamson, *English Education, 1789–1902* (Cambridge, England: Cambridge Univ. Press, 1964 [1930]), p. 37.

5. Thomas Walter Lacqueur, *Religion and Respectability: Sunday Schools and Working Class Culture, 1780–1850* (New Haven, Conn.: Yale Univ. Press, 1976), p. 44.

6. J. S. Bratton, *The Impact of Victorian Children's Fiction* (London: Croom Helm, 1981), pp. 14–15. There is some disagreement about whether the Sunday school teachers were in fact working class. Philip B. Cliff marshaled evidence for the predominantly middle-class origin of the teachers in *The Rise and Development of the Sunday School Movement in England, 1780–1980* (Nutfield, England: National Christian Education Council, 1986), p. 151.

7. Raikes to Richard Townley, published in *Gentlemen's Magazine*, June 1794, and again in Cliff, *Sunday School Movement*, Appendix A1.

8. Henry Bryan Binns, *A Century of Education: Being the Centenary History of the British and Foreign School Society, 1808–1908* (London: J. M. Dent, 1908), pp. 94–95.

9. Denis Gray, *Spencer Perceval, the Evangelical Prime Minister* (Manchester, England: Manchester Univ. Press, 1963), p. 25. For Clapham's role in both organizations, see Robin Furneaux, *William Wilberforce* (London: Hamish Hamilton, 1974), p. 216.

10. James Kay-Shuttleworth, *Four Periods of Public Education* (London: Longman, Green, 1862), p. 387.

11. Ibid., p. 406. See also R. W. Rich, *The Training of Teachers in England and Wales during the Nineteenth Century* (Portway, 1933 [Cambridge, England: Cambridge Univ. Press, 1933]), pp. 64–66.

12. Richard D. Altick, *The English Common Reader: A Social History of the Mass Reading Public, 1800–1900* (Chicago: Univ. of Chicago Press, 1957), pp. 5, 82.

13. Louis James, *Fiction for the Working Man, 1830–1850* (London: Oxford Univ. Press, 1963), p. 8.

14. David Vincent, *Literacy and Popular Culture, England 1750–1914* (Cambridge, England: Cambridge Univ. Press, 1993), p. 64.

15. Paul Thomas Murphy, *Toward a Working-Class Canon: Literary Criticism in British Working-Class Periodicals, 1816–1858* (Columbus: Ohio State Univ. Press, 1994), p. 12.

16. M. G. Jones, *Hannah More* (New York: Greenwood Press, 1968 [1952]), p. 144.

17. Roger H. Martin, *Evangelicals United: Ecumenical Stirrings in Pre-Victorian Britain, 1795–1830* (Metuchin, N.J.: Scarecrow Press, 1983), p. 156.

18. Susan Pedersen, "Hannah More Meets Simple Simon: Tracts, Chapbooks, and Popular Culture in Late Eighteenth Century England," *Journal of British Studies* 25, no. 1 (1986): 84–113.

19. Martin, *Evangelicals United*, pp. 84–92.

20. John Henry Newman, *Apologia pro Vita Sua*, ed. A. Dwight Culler (Boston: Houghton Mifflin, 1956 [1864]), p. 21.

21. John Bright, *The Diaries of John Bright*, ed. R. A. J. Walling (New York: William Morrow, 1931), p. 5. The phenomenon is similar to that reported a century later by Eleanor Roosevelt, who grew up memorizing Bible verses and hymns as a daily practice. She thought it curious that even late in life, at crucial moments the appropriate passages would come to mind to give her guidance. See Eleanor Roosevelt, "The Minorities Question," in *Christianity Takes a Stand: An Approach to the Issues of Today*, ed. William Scarlett (New York: Harper & Row, 1946), p. 72.

22. T. Mozley, *Reminiscences; Chiefly of Oriel College and the Oxford Movement*, 2nd ed., 2 vols. (London: Longmans, Green, 1882), vol. 2, p. 367.

23. Southey to C. W. Williams Wynn (an old friend and long-time MP), January 9, 1830, in *New Letters of Robert Southey*, ed. Kenneth Curry, 2 vols. (New York: Columbia Univ. Press, 1965), vol. 2, p. 351.

24. *Christian Observer*, September 1832, pp. 596–97.

25. Leigh Hunt, *Autobiography*, ed. J. E. Morpurgo (London: Cresset Press, 1949 [rev. ed. of 1859]), p. 80.

26. Ernest E. Kellett, *Religion and Life in the Early Victorian Age* (London: Epworth Press, 1938), p. 122.

27. Heather Henderson, *The Victorian Self: Autobiography and Biblical Narrative* (Ithaca, N.Y.: Cornell Univ. Press, 1989), pp. 163–64.

28. Amy Cruse, *The Englishman and His Books in the Early Nineteenth Century* (New York: Benjamin Blom, 1968 [1930]), pp. 87–88. See also Marion Lochhead, *The Renaissance of Wonder in Children's Literature* (Edinburgh: Canongate, 1977).

29. H. D. Brown, *By Voice and Book: The Story of the Christian Colportage Association*, 2nd ed. (London: Christian Colportage Association, n.d.). This in-house history is strongly anti-Catholic, as was some of the literature the association distributed.

30. More to Wilberforce, January 1809, in William Wilberforce, *Correspondence*, ed. R. I. Wilberforce and S. Wilberforce, 2 vols. (London: John Murray, 1840),

vol. 2, p. 152. This letter includes the suggestion that at that point the lending libraries were new to the broad audience of novel readers but old hat to evangelicals.

31. T. W. Heyck, *The Transformation of Intellectual Life in Victorian England* (New York: St. Martin's Press, 1982), p. 35; Altick, *English Common Reader,* p. 296.

32. The principal work is Doreen Rosman, *Evangelicals and Culture* (London: Croom Helm, 1984).

33. Hugh Evan Hopkins, *Charles Simeon of Cambridge* (Grand Rapids, Mich.: Eerdmans, 1977), pp. 201–3.

34. See David Spring, "The Clapham Sect: Some Social and Political Aspects," *Victorian Studies* 1 (1961): 36–37.

35. *Christian Observer,* preface to the edition of 1810, p. v.

36. Ibid., pp. 376–82. This is a long review in double columns of fine type that is much more favorable toward the stylistic features of the poem than toward its philosophy. Byron's letter of December 3, 1813, is reproduced in Ernest Marshall Howse, *Saints in Politics: The "Clapham Sect" and the Growth of Freedom* (Toronto: Univ. of Toronto Press, London, 1952), p. 107. Byron wrote that he had not responded to public criticism for years but that he appreciated the "very able, and I believe just criticism [that] has been afforded me" in the *Observer.*

37. William Jay, *The Autobiography of the Rev. William Jay,* ed. George Redford and John Angell James (London: Hamilton, Adams, 1855), p. 122.

38. The modern scholar who has contributed most to our understanding of this is George P. Landow. See his book *Victorian Types, Victorian Shadow: Biblical Typology in Victorian Literature, Art, and Thought* (Boston: Routledge & Kegan Paul, 1980); for the outworking of this principle in poetry, see W. David Shaw, *The Lucid Veil: Poetic Truth in the Victorian Age* (Madison: Univ. of Wisconsin Press, 1987). For other illustrations in poetry, see George P. Landow, "Moses Striking the Rock: Typological Symbolism in Victorian Poetry," in *Literary Use of Typology from the Late Middle Ages to the Present,* ed. Earl Miner (Princeton, N.J.: Princeton Univ. Press, 1977), pp. 315–45.

39. George P. Landow, *William Holman Hunt and Typological Symbolism* (New Haven, Conn.: Yale Univ. Press, 1979), pp. 14–16.

40. Northrop Frye, *The Great Code: The Bible and Literature* (New York: Harcourt Brace Jovanovich, 1982), p. 74. Another critic says that since Frye's idea was published, "the Bible has been definitively recuperated as a, as *the* paradigmatic text, at least in Western literature." David Bevan, ed., *Literature and the Bible* (Amsterdam: Rodopi, 1993), p. 4. It is surprising that the world of literary criticism took so long to discover what lies on the surface of nineteenth-century texts, and it suggests that ideological factors blinded the scholarship to what was there all the time.

41. Frye, *Great Code,* pp. 217–18.

42. For example, Enid L. Duthie, *The Brontës and Nature* (London: Macmillan, 1986).

43. Stevie Davies, *Emily Brontë* (New York: Harvester Wheatsheaf, 1988). Another version has Emily as a mystic, to whom God spoke on the moors, in a way that little comported with orthodoxy; the evil in *Wuthering Heights* is a product of her ha-

tred for humanity. See Barbara Munson Goff, "Between Natural Theology and Natural Selection: Breeding the Human Animal in *Wuthering Heights*," *Victorian Studies* 27 (1984): 482–83; a softer but less convincing view may be found in C. Day Lewis, *Notable Images of Virtue: Emily Brontë, George Meredith, W. B. Yeats* (Toronto: Ryerson Press, 1969 [1954]), p. 10. Lewis believes that Emily Brontë was something of a moralist and was unconscious of the full moral significance of the novel.

44. Landow, *Victorian Types*, p. 97. Landow here gives the theological significance of Jane's expression as it would have been understood by Brontë's readers, indeed by any biblically literate readership.

45. Ibid., p. 153. Landow here discusses a passage in a Swinburne poem that uses "the prey of the serpent's tooth" (from Gen. 3) to show how the poet advances the notion of savior England as a substitute for Christ.

46. That is the thesis of Samuel F. Pickering, *The Moral Tradition in English Fiction, 1785–1850* (Hanover, N.H.: Univ. Press of New England, 1976).

47. John Harford was told this by one of Hannah's sisters. John S. Harford, *Recollections of William Wilberforce Esq.*, 2nd ed. (London: Longman Green, 1865), p. 274.

48. John Campbell Colquhoun, *William Wilberforce: His Friends and His Times* (London: Longmans, Green, Reader & Dyer, 1866), p. 123.

49. For example, Gene Koppel, *The Religious Dimension of Jane Austen's Novels* (Ann Arbor, Mich.: UMI Research Press, 1988); Warren Roberts, *Jane Austen and the French Revolution* (New York: St. Martin's Press, 1979); Marilyn Butler, *Jane Austen and the War of Ideas* (Oxford: Clarendon Press, 1975); Avrom Fleishman, *A Reading of Mansfield Park: An Essay in Critical Synthesis* (Minneapolis: Univ. of Minnesota Press, 1967).

50. Pickering, *Moral Tradition in English Fiction*, p. 100.

51. G. O. Trevelyan, "Macaulay and the Sense of Optimism," in *Ideas and Beliefs of the Victorians*, no ed. (London: Sylvan Press, 1949), pp. 46–47.

52. Donald D. Stone, *The Romantic Impulse in Victorian Fiction* (Cambridge, Mass.: Harvard Univ. Press, 1980), p. 19.

53. For example, Altick, *English Common Reader*, p. 124.

54. Paraclita Reilly, *Aubrey de Vere: Victorian Observer* (Lincoln: Univ. of Nebraska Press, 1953), pp. 39–40.

55. Jones, *Hannah More*, p. 225.

56. For example, Thomas G. Selby, *The Theology of Modern Fiction* (London: Kelly, 1896), p. 8.

57. Rosemarie Bodenheimer, *The Real Life of Mary Ann Evans: George Eliot, Her Letters and Fiction* (Ithaca, N.Y.: Cornell Univ. Press, 1994), pp. 37–44.

58. F. R. Leavis, *The Great Tradition* (New York: Doubleday, 1954 [1948]), p. 25.

59. Margaret Maison, *The Victorian Vision: Studies in the Religious Novel* (New York: Sheed & Ward, 1961), p. 189. The discussion here is of *Adam Bede*.

60. Mary Wilson Carpenter, *George Eliot and the Landscape of Time: Narrative Form and Protestant Apocalyptic History* (Chapel Hill: Univ. of North Carolina Press, 1986).

61. Elizabeth Jay, *The Religion of the Heart: Anglican Evangelicalism and the Nineteenth-Century Novel* (Oxford: Clarendon Press, 1979), p. 224.

62. George Eliot, "Silly Novels by Lady Novelists," in *Essays of George Eliot,* ed. Thomas Pinney (New York: Columbia Univ. Press, 1963). First published in *Westminister Review* 66 (October 1856): 442–61.

63. This is one of the themes of Humphry House, *The Dickens World,* 2nd ed. (London: Oxford Univ. Press, 1960 [1942]).

64. Walter E. Houghton, *The Victorian Frame of Mind: 1830–1870* (New Haven, Conn.: Yale Univ. Press, 1959), p. 275.

65. In 1868 he wrote to his son Plorn, about to depart for Australia: "You will therefore understand the better that I now most solemnly impress upon you the truth and beauty of the Christian religion, as it came from Christ Himself, and the impossibility of your going far wrong if you humbly but heartily respect it." Harland S. Nelson, *Charles Dickens* (Boston: Twayne Publishers, 1981), pp. 179–80.

66. For example, Andrew Sanders, *Charles Dickens, Resurrectionist* (New York: St. Martin's Press, 1982). See Sanders's historiographical note on this issue on pp. x–xi, showing what Sanders thinks is a growing belief that Dickens's religion was more orthodox Christian than has hitherto been generally recognized.

67. Nelson, *Charles Dickens,* p. 27.

68. Ibid., pp. 111, 128, 174.

69. See his characterization of Sir Mulberry Hawk in *Nicholas Nickleby* (1839), chap. 28. For a discussion on the dangers of assuming the author's views (specifically Dickens's views) from the opinions of a character, see Gertrude Himmelfarb, *The Idea of Poverty: England in the Early Industrial Age* (New York: Random House, 1985 [1983]), p. 453. Dickens, to cite her example, publicly favored training colleges and ragged schools, two institutions that he satirized in novels.

70. For examples on this point, see Pickering, *Moral Tradition in English Fiction,* pp. 121–28. Pickering also makes the case (pp. 110, 121f) that some of Dickens's characters were based on evangelical writings: for example, Little Nell bears strong resemblance to the heroine of Legh Richmond's immensely popular tract *The Dairyman's Daughter.*

71. *Nicholas Nickleby,* chap. 16.

72. Jerome H. Buckley, *The Victorian Temper: A Study in Literary Culture* (New York: Vintage Books, 1964 [Cambridge, Mass.: Harvard Univ. Press, 1951]), p. 38.

73. Janet Larson, *Dickens and the Broken Scripture* (Athens: Univ. of Georgia Press, 1985).

74. Clarence R. Decker, *The Victorian Conscience* (New York: Twayne, 1952), pp. 46–47. Trollope's novels had much material on the weaknesses of the Church of England, but there is considerable doubt about how conversant he was with it. On this, see C. K. Francis Brown, *A History of the English Clergy, 1800–1900* (London: Faith Press, 1953), pp. 201–2.

75. J. H. Newman, "State of Religious Parties," *British Critic,* April 1839, p. 399.

76. Georgina Battiscombe, *Charlotte Mary Yonge: The Story of an Uneventful Life* (London: Constable, 1943), pp. 13–14. For other examples, see Joseph Ellis

Baker, *The Novel and the Oxford Movement* (New York: Russell & Russell, 1965 [1932]).

77. Jay, *Religion of the Heart*, p. 7.

78. Hannah More, *Cœlebs in Search of a Wife, Comprehending Observations on Domestic Habits and Manners, Religion and Morals*, 2 vols. (London: Cadell & Davies, 1808), vol. 1, pp. 13–14.

79. Thomas Hughes, *Tom Brown's Schooldays*, 6th ed. (New York: Harper & Brothers, 1870), p. viii.

80. Kathleen Tillotson, *Novels of the 1840s* (Oxford: Clarendon Press, 1956 [1954]), p. 128.

81. See Thomas Vargish, *The Providential Aesthetic in Victorian Fiction* (Charlottesville: Univ. Press of Virginia, 1985).

82. Tillotson, *Novels of the 1840s*, p. 54.

83. John Clubbe and Ernest J. Lovell, Jr., *English Romanticism: The Grounds of Belief* (Dekalb: Northern Illinois Univ. Press, 1983), pp. 101–2, 146–47. Richard Brantley in *Locke, Wesley, and the Method of English Romanticism*, p. 184, argues that a "methodistical spirit of religion" informed Shelley's work, coexisting with the hostility to Christianity that was on the surface.

84. Hunt, *Autobiography*, p. 269.

85. Stephen Prickett, "Romantics and Victorians: from Typology to Symbolism," in *Reading the Text: Biblical Criticism and Literary Theory*, ed. Stephen Prickett (Oxford: Blackwell, 1991), p. 220.

86. Frank M. Turner, "The Victorian Crisis of Faith and the Faith That Was Lost," in *Victorian Faith in Crisis: Essays on Continuity and Change in Nineteenth-Century Religious Belief*, ed. Richard J. Helmstadter and Bernard Lightman (Stanford, Calif.: Stanford Univ. Press, 1990), pp. 15–17.

87. Linda H. Peterson, "Biblical Typology and the Self-Portrait of the Poet in Robert Browning," in *Approaches to Victorian Autobiography*, ed. George P. Landow (Athens: Ohio Univ. Press, 1979), pp. 238–39.

88. See Linda H. Peterson, *Victorian Autobiography: The Tradition of Self-Interpretation* (New Haven, Conn.: Yale Univ. Press, 1986). The Ruskin example is on pp. 1–2.

89. David A. Currie, "Cotton Mather's *Bonifacius* in Britain and America," in *Evangelicalism: Comparative Studies of Popular Protestantism in North America, the British Isles and Beyond, 1700–1990*, ed. Mark Noll, David Bebbington, and G. A. Rawlyk (New York: Oxford Univ. Press, 1994), pp. 72–89.

90. Kenneth Clark, *The Gothic Revival: An Essay in the History of Taste*, 3rd ed. (New York: Holt, Rinehart & Winston, 1962), pp. 219–21. On the influence of medievalism on nineteenth-century art, see Marcia Pointon, "Romanticism in English Art," in *The Romantics*, ed. Stephen Prickett (London: Methuen, 1981), chap. 2.

91. Melvin Waldfogel, "Narrative Paintings," in *The Mind and Art of Victorian England*, ed. Josef Altholz (Minneapolis: Univ. of Minnesota Press, 1976), p. 169; for an argument that many of the artists were religious themselves and not simply

reflecting the cultural norms, see A. Paul Oppé, "Art," in *Early Victorian England 1830–1865*, ed. G. M. Young, 2 vols. (London: Oxford Univ. Press, 1951 [1934]), vol. 1, pp. 129–30.

92. Tim Hilton, *John Ruskin: The Early Years, 1819–1859* (New Haven, Conn.: Yale Univ. Press, 1985), p. 13. Late in life, Ruskin apparently returned to a Christian, although not an evangelical, position. See Graham Hough, *The Last Romantics* (London: Gerald Duckworth, 1949), pp. 28–29.

93. See the argument in George P. Landow, *Ruskin* (Oxford: Oxford Univ. Press, 1985), pp. 39–45 and passim; an older work with a similar point of view is Henry Ladd, *The Victorian Morality of Art: An Analysis of Ruskin's Esthetic* (New York: Octagon Books, 1968 [1932]), p. 38.

94. Landow, *William Holman Hunt*, pp. 6–7. For an account of Hunt's calling together the group and giving it its marching orders, see G. H. Fleming, *Rossetti and the Pre-Raphaelite Brotherhood* (London: Rupert Hart-Davis, 1967), pp. 76–77.

95. William Holman Hunt, *Pre-Raphaelitism and the Pre-Raphaelite Brotherhood*, 2 vols. (London: Macmillan, 1905), vol. 2, p. 265.

96. Landow, *William Holman Hunt*, p. 19.

97. See Leslie Parris, ed., *The Pre-Raphaelites* (London: Tate Gallery Publications, 1994 [1984]), pp. 120–21.

98. The art of the Pre-Raphaelite Brotherhood may be seen most conveniently in the beautiful catalog produced for the 1984 Tate Gallery exhibition of the movement, *The Pre-Raphaelites*, ed. Leslie Parris (London: Tate Gallery Publications, 1984). The Tate has the best collection of Pre-Raphaelite Brotherhood paintings.

99. Norman Vance, *The Sinews of the Spirit: The Ideal of Christian Manliness in Victorian Literature and Religious Thought* (Cambridge, England: Cambridge Univ. Press, 1985), pp. 4–5.

100. Uncertainty in the work of Millais has been interpreted as stemming from "unsettled cultural assumptions, if not religious convictions." See Max F. Schulz, *Paradise Preserved: Recreations of Eden in Eighteenth and Nineteenth-Century England* (Cambridge, England: Cambridge Univ. Press, 1985), p. 261.

101. Patricia S. Kruppa, "'More Sweet and Liquid Than Any Other,': Victorian Images of Mary Magdalene," in *Religion and Irreligion in Victorian Society: Essays in Honor of R. K. Webb*, ed. R. W. Davis and R. J. Helmstadter (London: Routledge, 1992), pp. 128–29.

102. Susan S. Tamke, *Make a Joyful Noise unto the Lord: Hymns as a Reflection of Victorian Social Attitudes* (Athens: Ohio Univ. Press, 1978), p. 22.

103. Samuel Taylor Coleridge, *Table Talk*, ed. Carl Woodring, 2 vols. (Princeton, N.J.: Princeton Univ. Press, 1990), vol. 1, p. 150 (May 30, 1830).

104. Edgar Johnson, *Charles Dickens: His Tragedy and Triumph*, 2 vols. (New York: Simon & Schuster, 1952), vol. 1, p. 11.

105. Tamke, *Make a Joyful Noise*, pp. 2–3.

106. Hippolyte Taine, *Notes on England*, trans. Edward Hyams (Fair Lawn, N.J.: Essential Books, 1958 [1872]), pp. 190–91.

107. Tamke, *Make a Joyful Noise*, p. 78.

108. Donald Davie, *A Gathered Church: The Literature of the English Dissenting Interest, 1700–1930* (New York: Oxford Univ. Press, 1978), p. 59. Davie's book is on Dissent, but he is referring here to the generality of evangelicals; see also Robert W. Malcolmson, *Popular Recreations in English Society, 1700–1850* (Cambridge, England: Cambridge Univ. Press, 1973), pp. 6–8.

109. Charles Smyth, "The Evangelical Discipline," in [no ed.], *Ideas and Beliefs*, p. 98.

110. J. H. Clapham and M. M. Clapham, "Life in New Towns," in *Early Victorian England, 1830–1865*, vol. 1, ed. G. M. Young (London: Oxford Univ. Press, 1934), p. 243.

111. [W. J. Conybeare], *Church Parties: An Essay* (London: Longmans, 1854), p. 15. First published in the *Edinburgh Review*, no. 200 (October 1853).

112. *Record*, September 27, 1832. The paper elucidated further on this in the issue of October 4, 1832.

113. *Record*, September 1, 1836.

114. *Record*, September 29, 1836, and October 10, 1836.

115. *Record*, November 10, 1834.

116. *Christian Observer*, July 1817, pp. 425–29. The *Observer* had earlier wavered on this issue somewhat when it published a favorable review of Hannah More's anonymously published *Cœlebs in Search of a Wife* (1808) without realizing who had written it. This set a precedent for a milder treatment of the novel, which, however was reversed in 1816 when a weary Zachary Macaulay turned the editorship over to Samuel Wilks. See Pickering, *Moral Tradition in English Fiction*, pp. 83–87.

117. Louis James, *Fiction for the Working Man*, pp. 120–21; also Jay, *Religion of the Heart*, pp. 217–18.

118. Jay, *Religion of the Heart*, pp. 214–15.

119. Harry S. Stout, *The Divine Dramatist: George Whitfield and the Rise of Modern Evangelicalism* (Grand Rapids, Mich.: Eerdmans, 1991), pp. xix, 236–37, 245–46, and passim.

120. George Rowell, *The Victorian Theatre, 1792–1914: A Survey* (Cambridge, England: Cambridge Univ. Press, 1978), chap. 1.

121. *Christian Observer*, April 1805, pp. 234–43.

122. *Christian Observer*, May 1805, pp. 306–13.

123. *Record*, August 8, 1833.

124. Wilberforce to his sister, no date, in Wilberforce, *Correspondence*, vol. 1, p. 50.

125. Wilberforce to Samuel Wilberforce, June 11, 1832, in *Private Papers of William Wilberforce*, ed. A. M. Wilberforce (London: T. Fisher Unwin, 1897), p. 234.

126. Bunting to William Bird, December 12, 1820, in *The Early Correspondence of Jabez Bunting, 1820–1829*, ed. W. R. Ward (London: Royal Historical Society, 1972), p. 57.

127. *Record*, May 14, 1835.

128. *Record*, October 1, 1832. On worldliness in amusements, see the analysis in Malcolmson, *Popular Recreations in English Society*, pp. 103–5.

129. W. E. Gladstone, "The Evangelical Movement: Its Parentage, Progress and Issue," *British Quarterly Review* 70 (July 1879): 13–14.

130. On the development of an evangelical "language," see J. Elizabeth Elbourne, "'To Colonize the Mind': Evangelicals in Britain and South Africa, 1790–1837" (D.Phil. thesis, Oxford Univ., 1992).

131. Peter Francis Dixon, "The Politics of Emancipation: The Movement for the Abolition of Slavery in the British West Indies, 1807–33" (D.Phil. thesis, Oxford Univ., 1971), p. 88.

CHAPTER XI

1. *Christian Observer,* March 1804.

2. Southey to John Rickman, February 8, 1804, in *New Letters of Robert Southey,* ed. Kenneth Curry, 2 vols. (New York: Columbia Univ. Press, 1965), vol. 1, p. 350.

3. Gertrude Himmelfarb, *Victorian Minds* (New York: Harper & Row, 1970 [1968]), p. 102. Himmelfarb points out here the irony that "Malthusianism" came to imply reliance on artificial birth control, a strategy that Malthus always opposed.

4. Robert Colls, *The Pitmen of the Northern Coalfield: Work Culture and Protest, 1790–1850* (Manchester, England: Manchester Univ. Press, 1987), pp. 1–2.

5. Ibid., p. 131.

6. Francis Place, *The Autobiography of Francis Place (1771–1854),* ed. Mary Thale (Cambridge, England: Cambridge Univ. Press, 1972), p. 45.

7. Ibid., p. 57.

8. Ibid., p. 73.

9. Jerome H. Buckley, *The Victorian Temper: A Study in Literary Culture* (New York: Vintage Books, 1964 [Cambridge, Mass.: Harvard Univ. Press, 1951]), pp. 116–17.

10. Peter Laslett, *Family Life and Illicit Love in Earlier Generations: Essays in Historical Sociology* (Cambridge, England: Cambridge Univ. Press, 1977), p. 106.

11. Ibid., pp. 108–9, 130. See also Anthea Newman, "An Evaluation of Bastardy Recordings in an East Kent Parish," in *Bastardy and Its Comparative History: Studies in the History of Illegitimacy and Marital Nonconformism in Britain, France, Germany, Sweden, North America, Jamaica and Japan,* ed. Peter Laslett et al. (Cambridge, Mass.: Harvard Univ. Press, 1980), p. 141.

12. Laslett, *Family Life,* p. 113.

13. Most local and industry histories have illustrations of this. For example, see John Benson, *British Coalminers in the Nineteenth Century: A Social History* (New York: Holmes & Meier, 1980).

14. Donald Read, *Press and People, 1790–1850: Opinion in Three English Cities* (London: Edward Arnold, 1961), p. 33.

15. Hugh McLeod, *Religion and the People of Western Europe, 1789–1970* (Oxford: Oxford Univ. Press, 1981), p. 110.

16. Hannah More, *Thoughts on the Importance of the Manners of the Great to General Society and an Estimate of the Religion of the Fashionable World,* new ed. (London: Cadell & Davies, 1809 [1788]), p. 131.

17. Place, *Autobiography*, p. 61.

18. For arguments on this, see Kathleen Tillotson, *Novels of the 1840s* (Oxford: Clarendon Press, 1956 [1954]), pp. 57–64; also Peter Gay, *The Tender Passion* (New York: Oxford Univ. Press, 1986), pp. 49–51. Writing in the high Victorian years, an astute observer of society reported the departure of high society people from the morality of the pre-Victorian period, in order to wallow, as he thought, in degradation: "It is puritanism, it is morality, it is religion, it is the sense of duty, wedded to and regulating the fever of enterprise, which have made the English the race they are. Yet it is these obligations which society in London affects to ridicule." T. H. S. Escott, *Society in London,* 9th rev. ed. (London: Chatto & Windus, 1886), pp. 29–30.

19. Charles Astor Bristed, *Five Years in an English University* (New York: G. P. Putnam, 1852), pp. 352–53.

20. More, *Thoughts*, p. 78.

21. Hippolyte Taine, *Notes on England*, trans. Edward Hyams (Fair Lawn, N.J.: Essential Books, 1958 [1872]), p. 95. Taine's book was based on visits to England in 1858 and 1871.

22. Ibid., p. 116.

23. David Spring, "Some Reflections on Social History in the Nineteenth Century, *Victorian Studies* 4 (1960): 60–61.

24. Buckley, *Victorian Temper*, p. 118.

25. Élie Halévy, *The Triumph of Reform 1830–1841,* vol. 3 of *A History of the English People in the Nineteenth Century,* trans. E. I. Watkin (New York: Barnes & Noble, 1961), pp. 162–63.

26. Anthony Armstrong, *The Church of England, the Methodists and Society, 1700–1850* (London: Univ. of London Press, 1973), p. 92.

27. See, for example, James Obelkevich, *Religion and Rural Society: South Lindsey, 1825–75* (Oxford: Clarendon Press, 1976), pp. 208–9, 246–47, and passim; also Clyde Binfield, *Pastors and People: The Biography of a Baptist Church, Queen's Road, Coventry* (Coventry, England: Queen's Road Baptist Church, 1984), p. 35.

28. Max Weber, *From Max Weber: Essays in Sociology,* ed. and trans. H. H. Gerth and C. Wright Mills (New York: Oxford Univ. Press, 1946), p. 313.

29. T. Mozley, *Reminiscences; Chiefly of Oriel College and the Oxford Movement,* 2nd ed., 2 vols. (London: Longmans, Green, 1882), vol. 1, p. 284.

30. Southey to John P. Estlin, April 9, 1797, in Southey, *New Letters of Robert Southey,* vol. 1, p. 123. For a discussion of this, including Matthew Arnold's later use of such arguments against evangelicalism, see David J. DeLaura, *Hebrew and Hellene in Victorian England* (Austin: Univ. of Texas Press, 1969), pp. 13–14.

31. George Kitson Clark, *The Making of Victorian England* (Cambridge, Mass.: Harvard Univ. Press, 1963 [1962]), p. 126.

32. July 25, 1833, William H. Gladstone, *The Gladstone Diaries,* ed. M. R. D. Foot, 8 vols. (Oxford: Clarendon Press, 1968), vol. 2, p. 577.

33. Samuel F. Pickering, *The Moral Tradition in English Fiction, 1785–1850* (Hanover, N.H.: Univ. Press of New England, 1976), p. 41.

34. Joseph Ellis Baker, *The Novel and the Oxford Movement* (New York: Russell & Russell, 1965 [1932]), p. 72.

35. Peter Gaskell, *The Manufacturing Population of England* (New York: Arno Press, 1972 [1833]), p. 271.

36. William Holman Hunt, *Pre-Raphaelitism and the Pre-Raphaelite Brotherhood,* 2 vols. (London: Macmillan, 1905), vol. 2, p. 493.

37. Ibid., p. 361.

38. George Eliot, "The Morality of Wilhelm Meister," in *Essays of George Eliot,* ed. Thomas Pinney (New York: Columbia Univ. Press, 1963), pp. 144–45. First published in the *Leader* 6 (July 21, 1855): 703.

39. Hunt, *Pre-Raphaelitism,* vol. 1, p. iv.

40. That is a major thesis of Noel Annan, *Leslie Stephen: The Godless Victorian* (New York: Random House, 1984). On this issue, see Gertrude Himmelfarb "A Genealogy of Morals," chap. 2 of *Marriage and Morals among the Victorians* (New York: Alfred A. Knopf, 1986). By the next generation, at least in that family, the ripples had disappeared. Stephen's daughters Vanessa Bell and Virginia Woolf were members of the Bloomsbury "immoralists" (John Maynard Keynes's term for his own set).

41. David Large, "William Lovett," in *Pressure from Without in Early Victorian England,* ed. Patricia Hollis (London: Edward Arnold, 1974), p. 107.

42. Standish Meacham, "The Evangelical Inheritance," *Journal of British Studies* 3, no. 1 (1963): 88–104.

43. Rosemarie Bodenheimer, *The Real Life of Mary Ann Evans: George Eliot, Her Letters and Fiction* (Ithaca, N.Y.: Cornell Univ. Press, 1994), p. 64.

44. John Kucich, *Repression in Victorian Fiction: Charlotte Brontë, George Eliot, and Charles Dickens* (Berkeley: Univ. of California Press, 1987), p. 171.

45. Mary Thale, introduction to Place, *Autobiography,* p. xxi.

46. John Stuart Mill, *Autobiography and Literary Essays,* ed. John M. Robson and Jack Stillinger (Toronto: Univ. of Toronto Press, 1981), p. 45.

47. Annan, *Leslie Stephen,* pp. 16–17.

48. Ian Bradley, *The Call to Seriousness: The Evangelical Impact on the Victorians* (New York: Macmillan, 1976), p. 189.

49. See the description of the "religion of the hearth" in Deborah M. Valenze, *Prophetic Sons and Daughters: Female Preaching and Popular Religion in Industrial England* (Princeton, N.J.: Princeton Univ. Press, 1985), pp. 32–34.

50. See the accounts published in the *Morning Chronicle* in the period 1849–1851, a selection of which is in P. E. Razzell and R. W. Wainwright, *The Victorian Working Class: Selection from Letters to the Morning Chronicle* (London: Frank Cass, 1973), passim—for example, pp. 216, 226, 248, 264.

51. See the argument in F. M. L. Thompson, *The Rise of Respectable Society: A Social History of Victorian Britain, 1830–1900* (Cambridge, Mass.: Harvard Univ. Press, 1988), pp. 253–55. Thompson believes much of the stereotyping came from the interwar period in the twentieth century, when salaried social workers displaced

much of the volunteer effort of the preceding period. For the family life of prominent Evangelicals early in the century, see David Newsome, *The Wilberforces and
Henry Manning: The Parting of Friends* (Cambridge, Mass.: Harvard Univ. Press,
1966), passim.

52. See Tillotson, *Novels of the 1840s*, pp. 54–55; also E. E. Kellett, "The Press,"
in *Early Victorian England, 1830–1865,* ed. G. M. Young, 2 vols. (London: Oxford
Univ. Press, 1951 [1934]), vol. 2, pp. 48–49.

53. Taine, *Notes on England,* p. 88.

54. John Morley, *The Life of Richard Cobden* (London: T. Fisher Unwin, 1903),
pp. 90–92.

55. Maurice J. Quinlan, *Victorian Prelude: A History of English Manners, 1700–
1830* (New York: Columbia Univ. Press, 1941), pp. 157–58.

56. Trygve R. Tholfsen, "The Transition to Democracy in Victorian England,"
in *The Victorian Revolution: Government and Society in Victoria's Britain,* ed. Peter
Stansky (New York: New Viewpoints, 1973), p. 181.

57. F. K. Prochaska, *Women and Philanthropy in Nineteenth-Century England*
(Oxford: Clarendon Press, 1980), pp. 128–38.

58. Richard E. Brantley, *Locke, Wesley, and the Method of English Romanticism*
(Gainesville: Univ. of Florida Press, 1984), p. 201. A similar notion, defended in a
less sophisticated way, may be found in Frederick C. Gill, *The Romantic Movement
and Methodism: A Study of English Romanticism and the Evangelical Revival* (London: Epworth Press, 1954 [1937]).

59. Mark Pattison, *Essays,* 2 vols. (London: Routledge, n.d. [1908]), vol. 2, p. 3.
Pattison grew up in an Evangelical vicarage, became an ardent Tractarian as a student at Oxford, and later turned extremely hostile toward both expressions of faith.

60. John Rule, "Methodism, Popular Beliefs and Village Culture in Cornwall,
1800–1850," in *Popular Culture and Custom in Nineteenth-Century England,* ed.
Robert D. Storch (London: Croom Helm, 1982), pp. 48–63.

61. Hugh Cunningham, *Leisure in the Industrial Revolution, c. 1780–c. 1880*
(New York: St. Martin's Press, 1980), p. 40.

62. Obelkevich, *Religion and Rural Society,* p. 83. Obelkevich, it will be remembered from an earlier chapter, holds to a Feuerbachian view of religion as a product of purely material forces.

63. John Benson, *British Coalminers,* p. 169.

64. David Clark, *Between Pulpit and Pew: Folk Religion in a North Yorkshire
Fishing Village* (Cambridge, England: Cambridge Univ. Press, 1982), pp. 54–56.

65. Brian Harrison, "Pubs," in *The Victorian City: Images and Realities,* ed. H. J.
Dyos and Michael Wolff, 2 vols. (London: Routledge & Kegan Paul, 1973), vol. 1,
pp. 161–90; for details on the changes in drinking habits from the 1830s, see Brian
Harrison, *Drink and the Victorians* (Pittsburgh, Pa.: Univ. of Pittsburgh Press,
1971). See p. 31 for figures on the decrease of spirits' use after the 1830s.

66. Buckley, *Victorian Temper,* p. 118.

67. Alexis de Tocqueville, *Journeys to England and Ireland,* ed. J. P. Mayer,

trans. George Lawrence and K. P. Mayer (New Haven, Conn.: Yale Univ. Press, 1958), pp. 86–87.

68. R. K. Webb, *Harriet Martineau: A Radical Victorian* (New York: Columbia Univ. Press, 1960), pp. 64, 68–70.

69. Max Beer, *A History of British Socialism,* one-volume ed. (London: George Allen & Unwin, 1940 [1919]), p. 115.

70. I. D. McCalman, "Popular Irreligion in Early Victorian England: Infidel Preachers and Radical Theatricality in 1830s London," in *Religion and Irreligion in Victorian Society: Essays in Honor of R. K. Webb,* ed. R. W. Davis and R. J. Helmstadter (London: Routledge, 1992), chap. 3.

71. G. M. Young, "Portrait of an Age," in Young, *Early Victorian England,* vol. 2, p. 425.

72. Frank M. Turner, "The Victorian Crisis of Faith and the Faith That Was Lost," in *Victorian Faith in Crisis: Essays on Continuity and Change in Nineteenth-Century Religious Belief,* ed. Richard J. Helmstadter and Bernard Lightman (Stanford, Calif.: Stanford Univ. Press, 1990), chap. 1. Turner's thesis is that the anti-religious faiths in general were similar to the religion they were seeking to supplant.

73. John Henry Newman, *Apologia pro Vita Sua,* ed. A. Dwight Culler (Boston: Houghton Mifflin, 1956 [1864]), pp. 74–75.

74. Wilfrid Ward, *William George Ward and the Oxford Movement* (London: Macmillan, 1889), p. 423.

75. Ibid., p. 10.

76. Alfred (pseud.) [Samuel H. G. Kydd], *The History of the Factory Movement,* 2 vols. in one (New York: Augustus M. Kelley, 1966 [1857]), vol. 2, pp. 125–26.

77. Harriet Martineau to Helen Martineau, May 12, 1825, in Harriet Martineau, *Selected Letters,* ed. Valerie Sanders (Oxford: Clarendon Press, 1990), p. 7. This is one piece of evidence among many suggesting that R. K. Webb was hasty in his attempt to minimize the influence of evangelicalism by showing that some of the supposedly evangelical characteristics were present in the Unitarianism of Martineau's circle, which he thought "bore not a trace of Evangelicalism." Webb, *Harriet Martineau,* p. 88. There was hardly an institution or movement in England that was preserved from such contamination.

78. Friedrich Engels, *The Condition of the Working Class in England,* ed. and trans. W. O. Henderson and W. H. Chaloner (Stanford, Calif.: Stanford Univ. Press, 1968 [1845]), p. 313. This is in the midst of a passage in which Engels is explaining how the language of the English reveals their hypocrisy and secret motives.

79. Thomas Carlyle, *Past and Present* (London: Dent, 1912 [1843]), p. 59.

80. Michael St. John Packe, *The Life of John Stuart Mill* (New York: Macmillan, 1954), p. 243.

81. Michael Mason, *The Making of Victorian Sexual Attitudes* (Oxford: Oxford Univ. Press, 1994), p. 132.

82. Annan, *Leslie Stephen,* p. 153.

83. For more on this, see F. B. Smith, "The Atheist Mission, 1840–1900," in

Ideas and Institutions of Victorian Britain: Essays in Honour of George Kitson Clark, ed. Robert Robson (London: G. Bell & Sons, 1967), pp. 205–35.

84. This is the thesis of W. H. Oliver, *Prophets and Millennialists: The Uses of Biblical Prophecy in England from the 1790s to the 1840s* (Auckland, New Zealand: Auckland Univ. Press, 1978).

85. Harold Laski, "Fabian Socialism," in *Ideas and Beliefs of the Victorians,* no ed. (London: Sylvan Press, 1949), p. 80.

86. The best collection of information on these periodicals is Josef L. Altholz, *The Religious Press in Britain, 1760–1900* (New York: Greenwood Press, 1989).

87. Coleridge to Joseph Cottle, March 7, 1815, in Samuel Taylor Coleridge, *Selected Letters,* ed. Earl Leslie Griggs, 6 vols. (Oxford: Clarendon Press, 1956–1971), vol. 4, p. 546.

88. Francis E. Mineka, *The Dissidence of Dissent: The Monthly Repository, 1806–1838* (Chapel Hill: Univ. of North Carolina Press, 1944), p. 64.

89. Taine, *Notes on England,* p. 271. Something very similar was happening at the same time in the United States. A recent appraisal concludes that by the 1830s America had a *de jure* disestablishment of religion but "a *de facto* establishment of evangelicalism whose security lay in a common ethos, a common outlook on life and history, a common piety, and common patterns of worship and devotion." See Leonard Sweet, "Nineteenth-Century Evangelicalism," in *Encyclopedia of the American Religious Experience: Studies of Traditions and Movements,* ed. Charles H. Lippy and Peter W. Williams, 3 vols. (New York: Scribner's, 1987), vol. 2, p. 896.

90. W. E. Gladstone, "The Evangelical Movement: Its Parentage, Progress and Issue," *British Quarterly Review* 70 (July 1879): 6–7. In an earlier chapter I contrasted the High Church Gladstone's view that this cultural dominance occurred as a consequence of the Tractarian movement with Lecky's dissenting position that it occurred early in the century through the evangelicals. I think Lecky had the better of their public debate.

91. [W. J. Conybeare], *Church Parties: An Essay* (London: Longmans, 1854), pp. 2–3. First published in the *Edinburgh Review,* no. 200 (October 1853). By the 1850s, he thought the influence of the Evangelicals was slipping within the Church because of what he considered to be the excesses of its radicals, the Recordites (pp. 15–17).

92. W. E. H. Lecky, "The History of the Evangelical Movement," *Nineteenth Century* 6 (1879): 285.

93. Boyd Hilton, *The Age of Atonement: The Influence of Evangelicalism on Social and Economic Thought, 1785–1865* (Oxford: Clarendon Press, 1988), p. 219.

94. See John Wigley, *The Rise and Fall of the Victorian Sunday* (Manchester, England: Manchester Univ. Press, 1980).

95. *Record,* June 6, 1828.

96. That is the claim of a recent doctoral dissertation that links the colonies with the motherland. "The more powerful chain . . . was a shared language of evangelical Christianity, which concealed a multitude of differences but also brought Koi and Briton together in a variety of ways, from prayer meetings . . . to shared

magazines and mythologies. . . . The common language of evangelicalism made these linkages possible." Elizabeth J. Elbourne, "To Colonize the Mind: Evangelicals in Britain and South Africa, 1790–1837" (D.Phil. thesis, Oxford Univ., 1992), p. 18.

97. *Record,* June 8, 1837.

98. R. I. Wilberforce and S. Wilberforce, *The Life of William Wilberforce,* 5 vols. (London: John Murray, 1838), vol. 4, pp. 324–25.

99. See Ursula Henriques, *Religious Toleration in England, 1787–1833* (Toronto: Univ. of Toronto Press, 1961), pp. 216–17; also William H. Wickward, *The Struggle for the Freedom of the Press, 1819–1832* (London: George Allen & Unwin, 1972 [1928]).

100. Ian Bradley, "The Politics of Godliness: Evangelicals in Parliament, 1784–1832" (D.Phil. thesis, Oxford Univ., 1974), pp. 268–69. Bradley concludes that the Evangelicals indeed made a big difference for the better in the moral climate of the Parliament.

101. For example, *Christian Observer,* May 1802, p. 307.

102. W. E. H. Lecky, *History of the Rise and Influence of the Spirit of Rationalism in Europe,* 2 vols. (New York: D. Appleton, 1866), vol. 1, p. 351.

103. Crane Brinton, *English Political Thought in the Nineteenth Century* (London: Ernest Benn, 1933), p. 298.

104. Perry Miller, "The Garden of Eden and the Deacon's Meadow," *American Heritage* 7, no. 1 (1955): 55.

105. Mark A. Noll, "The Bible in American Culture," in Lippy and Williams, *Encyclopedia,* vol. 2, p. 1075.

106. Callum G. Brown, *The Social History of Religion in Scotland since 1730* (London: Methuen, 1987), pp. 136–37.

107. J. L. Hammond and Barbara Hammond, *The Age of the Chartists, 1832–1854: A Study of Discontent* (Hamden, Conn.: Archon Books, 1962 [1930]), p. 277.

CHAPTER XII

1. R. W. Dale, *The Old Evangelicalism and the New* (London: Hodder & Stoughton, 1889), p. 18.

2. *Record,* February 19, 1835, and September 14, 1835. This was some five years after the most recent revolution in France, to which the *Record* adverted, and which was far milder than the revolution of 1789 had been.

3. S. T. Coleridge, *The Statesman's Manual; Or the best Guide to Political Skill and Foresight: A Lay Sermon Addressed to the Higher Classes of Society* (London: Gale & Fenner, 1816), pp. 3, 38.

4. R. J. Morris, *Cholera 1832: The Social Response to an Epidemic* (New York: Holmes & Meier, 1976), p. 147.

5. Ian Bradley, "The Politics of Godliness: Evangelicals in Parliament, 1784–1832" (D.Phil. thesis, Oxford Univ., 1974), p. 42. This dissertation is the most complete study available on the subject, and I shall be making extensive use of it in this section. I am using *Clapham* to refer to the Evangelicals associated with Wilber-

force and his friends in that village. Wilberforce moved from there to Kensington in 1808, and others of the group moved away afterwards, but the group had sufficient cohesion to retain its identity for another quarter of a century, and so retains the name.

6. Ibid., pp. 115–16, 132–34.

7. Ibid., pp. 139–40.

8. Ibid, pp. 95–96.

9. Robin Furneaux, *William Wilberforce* (London: Hamish Hamilton, 1974), pp. 329–30.

10. See Charles Buxton, ed., *Memoirs of Sir Thomas Fowell Buxton* (London: J. M. Dent, 1925 [1848]).

11. For examples of this, see Denis Gray, *Spencer Perceval: The Evangelical Prime Minister, 1762–1812* (Manchester, England: Manchester Univ. Press, 1963), pp. 18, 25–27.

12. For this, see Boyd Hilton, *The Age of Atonement: The Influence of Evangelicalism on Social and Economic Thought* (Oxford: Clarendon Press, 1988), pp. 226–29. Hilton also cites the evidence of recent studies showing strong Evangelical influence among Whig politicians (p. 237) as well as the Tories.

13. Stewart J. Brown, *Thomas Chalmers and the Godly Commonwealth in Scotland* (Oxford: Oxford Univ. Press, 1982), pp. 244, 267.

14. G. M. Trevelyan, *Illustrated English Social History* (London: Longmans, Green, 1952 [1942]), p. 32.

15. Bradley, "Politics of Godliness," pp. 268–69.

16. Ibid., pp. 73–74, 98–99.

17. *Record,* May 10, 1830.

18. *Record,* August 27, 1832.

19. *Christian Observer,* 1839, p. v.

20. Francis Place, *The Autobiography of Francis Place (1771–1854),* ed. Mary Thale (Cambridge, England: Cambridge Univ. Press, 1972), p. 62.

21. *Record,* September 14, 1835.

22. *Record,* July 10, 1834.

23. Samuel Taylor Coleridge. *Table Talk,* ed. Carl Woodring, 2 vols. (Princeton, N.J.: Princeton Univ. Press, 1990), vol. 2, p. 291 (April 24, 1832).

24. *Record,* May 30, 1828.

25. T. R. Birks, *Memoir of the Rev. Edward Bickersteth,* 4th ed., 2 vols. (London: Seeleys, 1853), vol. 2, p. 29.

26. *Record,* October 17 and November 10, 1831.

27. *Christian Observer,* 1832, p. iv.

28. *Record,* February 4, 1833. A week later (February 11), the paper reverted to type and said there was not much hope for the Parliament, which was riven by hostilities and competing ambitions.

29. *Record,* August 12, August 19, and September 6, 1841.

30. Bradley, "Politics of Godliness," p. 217; Hilton, *Age of Atonement,* p. 246.

31. Ernest Marshall Howse, *Saints in Politics: The "Clapham Sect" and the*

Growth of Freedom (Toronto: Univ. of Toronto Press, 1952), pp. 58–59. Much of the following paragraphs is based on this work.

32. John S. Harford, *Recollections of William Wilberforce, Esq.*, 2nd ed. (London: Longman, Green, 1865), pp. 33–34.

33. For Grant's role in the reforming and religious movements in India, see Ainslie Thomas Embree, *Charles Grant and British Rule in India* (New York: Columbia Univ. Press, 1962), especially pp. 9–10, 142–47. For his cooperative efforts with Wilberforce and Henry Thornton, see pp. 151–55.

34. See John Rosselli, *Lord William Bentinck: The Making of a Liberal Imperialist, 1774–1839* (Berkeley: Univ. of California Press, 1974), passim, especially pp. 62–66, 126–27, 210–12.

35. M. Creighton, *Memoir of Sir George Grey* (London: Longmans, Green, 1901), p. 56.

36. For an example from Essex, see A. F. J. Brown, *Essex at Work, 1700–1815* (Chelmsford, England: Essex County Council, 1969), p. 139.

37. John S. Hurt, *Education in Evolution: Church, State, Society and Popular Education, 1800–1870* (London: Rupert Hart-Davis, 1971), p. 21.

38. For an extended argument of this thesis, see J. M. Goldstrom, *The Social Content of Education, 1808–1870: A Study of the Working Class School Reader in England and Ireland* (Shannon: Irish Univ. Press, 1972).

39. For example, Richard Johnson, "Education Policy and Social Control in Early Victorian England," in *The Victorian Revolution: Government and Society in Victoria's Britain*, ed. Peter Stansky (New York: New Viewpoints, 1973), pp. 199–277. Johnson cites in particular the writings of James Kay-Shuttleworth.

40. John McLeish, *Evangelical Religion and Popular Education: A Modern Interpretation* (London: Methuen, 1969), pp. 66–71. McLeish compares More's *Strictures on the Modern System of Female Education* (1799) with Wollstonecraft's *On the Education of Daughters* (1787) and finds them in agreement on a number of important points.

41. Thomas Carlyle, *Chartism* (London: Holerth, 1924), p. 84.

42. *Record*, December 15, 1836.

43. For the early history of the Establishment role in education, see Henry James Burgess, *Enterprise in Education: The Story of the Work of the Established Church in the Education of the People Prior to 1870* (London: Society for Promoting Christian Knowledge, 1958). At about the same time, Thomas Chalmers was behind a similar movement in the Established Church of Scotland. See Brown, *Thomas Chalmers*, p. 378.

44. Burgess, *Enterprise in Education*, p. 73.

45. Pamela Horn, *The Victorian Country Child* (London: Alan Sutton, 1990 [1974]), pp. 150–51.

46. Henry Venn, *To Apply the Gospel: Selections from the Writings of Henry Venn*, ed. Max Warren (Grand Rapids, Mich.: Eerdmans, 1971), pp. 196–97.

47. Venn to J. Long, March 24, 1845, in Venn, *To Apply the Gospel*, p. 198.

48. Brian Heeney, *Mission to the Middle Classes: The Woodard Schools, 1848–1891* (London: Society for Promoting Christian Knowledge, 1969), p. 14.

49. Burgess, *Enterprise in Education,* p. 43.

50. Maldwyn L. Edwards, *After Wesley: A Study of the Social and Political Influence of Methodism in the Middle Period, 1791–1849* (London: Epworth Press, 1936), pp. 108–9.

51. Anthony Lincoln, *Some Political and Social Ideas of English Dissent, 1763–1800* (New York: Octagon Books, 1971 [Cambridge, England: Cambridge Univ. Press, 1938]), pp. 66, 76–77.

52. Lord Shuttleworth in Frank Smith, *The Life and Work of Sir James Kay-Shuttleworth* (Bath, England: Cedric Chivers, 1974 [1923]), p. 331.

53. Ibid., p. 236.

54. Ibid., p. 6.

55. James Kay-Shuttleworth, *Memorandum on Popular Education* (New York: Augustus M. Kelley, 1969 [1868]), p. 9.

56. E. R. Wickham, *Church and People in an Industrial City* (London: Lutterworth Press, 1957), p. 90.

57. P. H. J. H. Gosden, comp., *How They Were Taught: An Anthology of Contemporary Accounts of Learning and Teaching in England, 1800–1950* (New York: Barnes & Noble, 1969), p. 13.

58. James Kay-Shuttleworth, *Four Periods of Public Education* (London: Longman, Green, 1862), p. 399.

59. Ibid., p. 406.

60. See, for example, Johnson, "Education Policy," pp. 206–7.

61. Smith, *Life of Kay-Shuttleworth,* p. 206.

62. Mary Sturt, *The Education of the People: A History of Primary Education in England and Wales in the Nineteenth Century* (London: Routledge & Kegan Paul, 1967), pp. 136–37.

63. Ibid., p. 91.

64. Peel to Victoria, June 16, 1843, in Robert Peel, *Sir Robert Peel from His Private Papers,* ed. Charles Stuart Parker, 3 vols. (New York: Kraus Reprint, 1970 [1899]), vol. 2, p. 561.

65. Owen Chadwick, *The Victorian Church,* 2nd ed. (London: Adam & Charles Black, 1970), pt. 1, pp. 345–46.

66. Hurt, *Education in Evolution,* p. 45.

67. Nicholas C. Edsall, *Richard Cobden, Independent Radical* (Cambridge, Mass.: Harvard Univ. Press, 1986), pp. 39–41.

68. Ibid., p. 221.

69. G. Otto Trevelyan, *The Life and Letters of Lord Macaulay,* 2 vols. (New York: Harper & Brothers, 1904 [1876]), vol. 2, p. 368.

70. Edward Norman, *The English Catholic Church in the Nineteenth Century* (Oxford: Oxford Univ. Press, 1984), pp. 160–61.

71. F. W. B. Bullock, *A History of Training for the Ministry of the Church of*

England in *England and Wales from 1800 to 1874* (Leonards-on-Sea, England: Budd & Gillatt, 1955), chap. 1; Michael Sanderson, *The Universities in the Nineteenth Century* (London: Routledge & Kegan Paul, 1975), pp. 31–32.

72. *Record,* March 11, 1833.

73. *Record,* June 24, 1828.

74. For example, Asa Briggs, *Victorian People: A Reassessment of Persons and Themes, 1851–67* (Chicago: Univ. of Chicago Press, 1955), pp. 147–48.

75. For example, Sturt, *Education of the People,* pp. 23–24.

76. For an argument showing this, see Burgess, *Enterprise in Education,* pp. 212–15.

77. John Howard, *The State of the Prisons,* 3rd ed. (London: J. M. Dent, 1929 [1784]), p. 41.

78. *Record,* February 22, 1828.

79. D. L. Howard, *John Howard: Prison Reformer* (New York: Archer House, 1963 [1958]), pp. 19, 28.

80. Michael Ignatieff, *A Just Measure of Pain: The Penitentiary in the Industrial Revolution, 1750–1850* (London: Penguin Books, 1978), pp. 58–59.

81. Howard, *John Howard,* p. 153.

82. Romilly to John Roget, May 22, 1781, in Leon Radzinowicz, *The Movement for Reform,* vol. 1 of *A History of English Criminal Law and its Administration from 1750* (London: Stevens, 1948), p. 314.

83. See Ignatieff, *Just Measure of Pain,* p. 67, for the similarities and contrasts between Howard and Bentham on prison reform.

84. Radzinowicz, *Movement for Reform,* pp. 313–14.

85. Ignatieff, *Just Measure of Pain,* pp. 146–48; Llewellyn Woodward, *The Age of Reform, 1815–1870,* 2nd ed. (Oxford: Clarendon Press, 1962), pp. 467–68; for an argument that the evangelicals were the party responsible for prison reform and that the utilitarians played almost no role in it, see David Roberts, "Jeremy Bentham and the Victorian Administrative State," *Victorian Studies* 2 (1959): 204–5.

86. Bradley, "Politics of Godliness," pp. 195–96.

87. Alfred (pseud.) [Samuel H. G. Kydd], *The History of the Factory Movement,* 2 vols. in one (New York: Augustus M. Kelley, 1966 [1857]), vol. 1, pp. 196f (from Deut. 24:14).

88. G. S. Bull, "Protest of the Rev. G. S. Bull, Addressed to the Commissioners for Factory Enquiry," in J. C. Gill, *The Ten Hours Parson: Christian Social Action in the Eighteen-Thirties* (London: Society for Promoting Christian Knowledge, 1959), Appendix A, p. 195.

89. Alfred, *History of the Factory Movement,* vol. 2, p. 237.

90. William C. Lubenow, *The Politics of Government Growth: Early Victorian Attitudes toward State Intervention, 1833–1848* (Hamden, Conn.: Archon Books, 1971), p. 162; for other examples of the rhetoric, see Richard Oastler, *Richard Oastler: King of Factory Children, Six Pamphlets, 1835–1861* (New York: Arno Press, 1972).

91. Cecil Driver, *Tory Radical: The Life of Richard Oastler* (New York: Oxford Univ. Press, 1946), p. 41.

92. J. T. Ward, *The Factory Movement 1830–55* (London: Macmillan, 1962), p. 34.

93. Driver, *Tory Radical,* pp. 467–69.

94. For this argument with supporting evidence, see Ward, *Factory Movement,* pp. 423–25.

95. For arguments along this line, see Gill, *Ten Hours Parson,* pp. 178–79.

96. Élie Halévy, *The Triumph of Reform 1830–1841,* vol. 3 of *A History of the English People in the Nineteenth Century,* trans. E. I. Watkin (New York: Barnes & Noble, 1961), p. 110.

97. O. O. G. M. MacDonagh, "Coal Mines Regulation: The First Decade, 1842–1852," in *Ideas and Institutions of Victorian Britain: Essays in Honour of George Kitson Clark,* ed. Robert Robson (London: G. Bell & Sons, 1967), pp. 58–60.

98. Alfred, *History of the Factory Movement,* vol. 2, p. 214.

99. David Roberts, *Paternalism in Early Victorian England* (New Brunswick, N.J.: Rutgers Univ. Press, 1979), p. 60.

100. Ward, *Factory Movement,* p. 219.

101. Nicholas C. Edsall, *The Anti-Poor Law Movement 1833–44* (Manchester, England: Manchester Univ. Press, 1971), p. 124.

102. David Roberts, *Victorian Origins of the British Welfare State* (New Haven, Conn.: Yale Univ. Press, 1960), pp. 59–61. An older work contrasted the Toryism of the countryside, the sort to which Oastler appealed, with that of the new moneyed classes in the city, much friendlier to political economy. In Oastler's view, the English had to choose between the apostle of Christ or the apostle of the market, between "the acknowledged master of each school—St. Paul and Mr. Huskisson." See R. L. Hill, *Toryism and the People 1832–1846* (London: Constable, 1929). The Oastler quote is on p. 13. For a modern exposition of the two types of Tory, see Hilton, *Age of Atonement,* pp. 220–22.

103. Ian Bradley, *The Call to Seriousness: The Evangelical Impact on the Victorians* (New York: Macmillan, 1976), pp. 130–31.

104. Brown, *Thomas Chalmers,* pp. 371–72 and passim.

105. Thomas Chalmers, *On Political Economy: In Connexion with the Moral State and Moral Prospect of Society* (New York: Augustus M. Kelley, 1968 [1832]), pp. iii–iv.

106. Patricia Hollis, *The Pauper Press: A Study in Working-Class Radicalism of the 1830s* (London: Oxford Univ. Press, 1970), p. 208.

107. Southey to Grosvenor Charles Bedford (a lifelong friend from their time at Westminster School), July 31, 1793, in *New Letters of Robert Southey,* ed. Kenneth Curry, 2 vols. (New York: Columbia Univ. Press, 1965), vol. 1, p. 31.

108. Coleridge, *Table Talk,* vol. 1, p. 187 (September 8, 1830).

109. William E. Gladstone, *The State in Its Relations with the Church,* 2nd ed. (London: John Murray, 1839), chap. 3.

110. For the changes in Gladstone's position, see E. R. Norman, *Church and Society in England 1770–1970: An Historical Study* (Oxford: Clarendon Press, 1976), pp. 102–3; Chadwick, *Victorian Church,* pp. 477–79. That may be called the established view of Gladstone's thinking on the Establishment. Alec Vidler's view was

that Gladstone never changed his convictions on the subject but in the interests of serving in high political office had to adopt the "lower" position with respect to the Establishment. See Vidler, *The Orb and the Cross: A Normative Study in the Relations of Church and State with Reference to Gladstone's Early Writings* (London: Society for Promoting Christian Knowledge, 1945).

111. For example, *Record*, January 31, 1831.

112. See the exposition in John Henry Lewis Rowlands, *Church, State and Society: The Attitudes of John Keble, Richard Hurrell Froude and John Henry Newman, 1827–1845* (Worthing, England: Churchman Publishing, 1989), pp. 221–26.

113. Alexis de Tocqueville, *Journeys to England and Ireland,* ed. J. P. Mayer, trans. George Lawrence and K. P. Mayer (New Haven, Conn.: Yale Univ. Press, 1958), p. 64.

114. T. Mozley, *Reminiscences; Chiefly of Oriel College and the Oxford Movement,* 2nd ed., 2 vols. (London: Longmans, Green, 1882), vol. 1, p. 184.

115. G. F. A. Best, *Temporal Pillars: Queen Anne's Bounty, the Ecclesiastical Commissioners, and the Church of England* (Cambridge, England: Cambridge Univ. Press, 1964), pp. 196–97. Best believes this form of pluralism was necessary for the bishops to do their jobs and was not a form of venality. But it seemed otherwise to many observers, particularly since pluralism in general was a great abuse.

116. *Christian Observer,* August 1821, pp. 502–3.

117. Owen Chadwick, *The Founding of Cuddesdon* (Oxford: Oxford Univ. Press, 1954), p. 1. For a picture, somewhat exaggerated, of the clerical profession's attraction to people of modest ability who sought a comfortable life, see W. J. Reader, *Professional Men: The Rise of the Professional Classes in Nineteenth Century England* (New York: Basic Books, 1966), pp. 11–13. Other indications suggest that between the 1830s and 1850s the Anglican clergy reached a level of standing not attained either before or since. For an argument on this, see Alan Haig, *The Victorian Clergy* (London: Croom Helm, 1984), pp. 360–61.

118. *Record*, January 4, 1830.

119. Best, *Temporal Pillars,* p. 60, believes that this relationship with the state delayed the reformation of the Church because the laity sitting in Parliament recognized that a reformed Church would be revitalized in such a way as to detract from the authority of the Parliament over it and therefore from the constituencies that elected them.

120. *Record,* March 12, 1832.

121. P. T. Marsh, *The Victorian Church in Decline: Archbishop Tait and the Church of England, 1868–82* (London: Routledge & Kegan Paul, 1968), p. 208. Marsh here describes Tait's appointing of relatives.

122. *Record,* June 29, 1829.

123. Raymond Chapman, *Faith and Revolt: Studies in the Literary Influence of the Oxford Movement* (London: Weidenfeld & Nicolson, 1970), p. 20.

124. Alan D. Gilbert, *Religion and Society in Industrial England: Church, Chapel and Social Change 1740–1914* (London: Longman, 1976), p. 126.

125. That is the conclusion of, among others, Norman Gash, *Reaction and Re-*

construction in English Politics: 1832–1852 (Oxford: Clarendon Press, 1965), p. 60. Halévy, *Triumph of Reform*, p. 208, missed this, believing that the short-lived hostility to the Church after the defeat of Napoleon had ushered in better days that still persisted after 1830. He evidently based this on the failure of Benthamism to gain a stronger hold on the English imagination along with the vitality of both the Evangelicals and the High Church. But the forebodings of both those parties suggest that they knew better.

126. J. L. Hammond and Barbara Hammond, *The Age of the Chartists, 1832–1854: A Study of Discontent* (Hamden, Conn.: Archon Books, 1962 [1930]), p. 218.

127. Thomas Arnold, "Principles of Church Reform (1833)," in *Miscellaneous Works* (London: Fellowes, 1845), p. 263.

128. *Record,* January 24, 1833.

129. *Christian Observer,* 1846, p. iv.

130. This suggestion was made by A. O. J. Cockshut, *Anglican Attitudes: A Study of Victorian Religious Controversies* (London: Collins, 1959), p. 11.

131. Butler, *Gladstone, Church, State and Tractarianism*, pp. 102–3.

132. [W. J. Conybeare], *Church Parties: An Essay* (London: Longmans, 1854), pp. 15–17. First published in the *Edinburgh Review*, no. 200 (October 1853).

133. Gilbert, *Religion and Society*, pp. 131–32. There is similar material in R. A. Soloway, *Prelates and People: Ecclesiastical Social Thought in England 1783–1852* (London: Routledge & Kegan Paul, 1969), pp. 433–34. Soloway's numbers are not identical with Gilbert's, but they point in the same direction, and for our purposes the conclusions are the same.

134. Best, *Temporal Pillars*, p. 235.

135. Ibid., p. 399.

136. See Esther de Waal, "Revolution in the Church," *Victorian Studies* 10 (1967): 435–39.

137. Best, *Temporal Pillars*, p. 261.

138. Desmond Bowen, *The Idea of the Victorian Church* (Montreal: McGill Univ. Press, 1968), p. 15.

139. S. Baring-Gould, *The Church Revival: Thoughts Thereon and Reminiscences* (London: Methuen, 1914), p. 174.

140. Chadwick, *Victorian Church*, pt. 1, p. 105.

141. Norman Gash, *Aristocracy and People: Britain 1818–1865* (Cambridge, Mass.: Harvard Univ. Press, 1979), p. 176. George Kitson Clark gave pride of place to Peel for what he too regarded as a monumental accomplishment. He believed it unjust to regard Peel as simply a slick politician. The prime minister was motivated by sincere religious feeling as well as compassion for what poor Englishmen were suffering. See *The Making of Victorian England* (Cambridge, Mass.: Harvard Univ. Press, 1963 [1962]), pp. 156–58.

142. Robert Currie, Alan Gilbert, and Lee Horsley, *Churches and Church Goers: Patterns of Church Growth in the British Isles since 1700* (Oxford: Clarendon Press, 1977), p. 59.

143. The figures come from Gash, *Aristocracy and People*, pp. 336–37.

144. M. H. Port, *Six Hundred New Churches: A Study of the Church Building Commission, 1818–1856, and Its Church Building Activities* (London: Society for Promoting Christian Knowledge, 1961), pp. 15–24. This book is, among other things, a defense of the esthetics and functionality of these churches.

145. See James F. White, *The Cambridge Movement: The Ecclesiologists and the Gothic Revival* (Cambridge, England: Cambridge Univ. Press, 1962). White believes the movement was misguided in absolutizing the thinking and architecture of a particular era.

146. Marsh, *Victorian Church in Decline,* p. 8. Marsh thinks that period came to an end after the publication of Darwin's *Origin of Species.*

147. Gilbert, *Religion and Society,* p. 138.

148. Soloway, *Prelates and People,* p. 431.

149. *Christian Observer,* 1846, p. iii.

150. *Record,* January 24, 1833.

151. *Record,* March 14, 1836.

152. Bradley, "Politics of Godliness," pp. 78, 85.

153. W. E. Gladstone, "The Evangelical Movement: Its Parentage, Progress and Issue," *British Quarterly Review* 70 (July 1879): 14–15.

154. Mark Pattison, *Essays,* 2 vols. (London: Routledge, n.d. [1908]), vol. 2, p. 3.

CHAPTER XIII

1. J. L. Hammond and Barbara Hammond, *Lord Shaftesbury,* 4th ed. (Hamden, Conn.: Archon Books, 1969 [1936]), p. 237.

2. John Stuart Mill, "Coleridge," in *Essays on Ethics, Religion and Society,* ed. J. M. Robson (Toronto: Univ. of Toronto Press, 1969), p. 125.

3. W. E. Gladstone, "The Evangelical Movement: Its Parentage, Progress and Issue," *British Quarterly Review* 70 (July 1879): 15; this theme is developed at length in Yngve Brilioth, *Evangelicalism and the Oxford Movement* (Oxford: Oxford Univ. Press, 1934).

4. B. I. Coleman, *The Church of England in the Mid-Nineteenth Century: A Social Geography* (London: Historical Association, 1980), p. 7.

5. A study of Sheffield, for example, concludes that between 1851 and 1881 the proportion of attenders increased among the populace. This was true among all classes and in both Church and chapel. E. R. Wickham, *Church and People in an Industrial City* (London: Lutterworth Press, 1957), pp. 141–42.

6. See the argument in John Roach, "Liberalism and the Victorian Intelligentsia," in *The Victorian Revolution: Government and Society in Victoria's Britain,* ed. Peter Stansky (New York: New Viewpoints, 1973), pp. 336–37. Roach believes that Carlyle was in more or less the same predicament. Both were Puritans in the moral sense, bereft of any doctrine to lend substance to their ethic.

7. George Granville Bradley, *Recollections of Arthur Penrhyn Stanley* (New York: Charles Scribner's Sons, 1883), p. 38.

8. E. Digby Baltzell's study of elites in the northeastern part of the United

States, *Puritan Boston and Quaker Philadelphia* (New York: Free Press, 1979), concluded that they drew their authority from the fact that people willingly followed their leadership out of admiration for their moral qualities. The same seems to have been true of England in the period covered by this book.

9. Gerhard Lenski, *The Religious Factor: A Sociological Study of Religion's Impact on Politics, Economics, and Family Life* (Garden City, N.Y.: Doubleday, 1961), p. 309. Robert Moore's study, *Pit-Men, Preachers and Politics: The Effects of Methodism in a Durham Mining Community* (London: Cambridge Univ. Press, 1974), which I have drawn upon in these pages, is in part an elaboration of Lenski's book in the nineteenth-century English context. Moore interprets his own work as a confirmation of Lenski's conclusion that the communal aspects of religious groups are more fundamental than their associational aspects; he demonstrates that the Methodists were a community as well as an association (pp. 226f). This suggests that the informal relationships of the past, which are much harder for a historian to ascertain, can be far more influential than the formal arrangements that are documented and more easily studied.

10. Herbert Butterfield, *Christianity and History* (New York: Charles Scribner's Sons, 1950), p. 131.

11. David Hempton and Myrtle Hill, *Evangelical Protestantism in Ulster Society, 1740–1890* (London: Routledge, 1992), p. xiii.

12. For an exposition of the social consequences of repentance, see Leo Raditsa in *Chronicles*, February 1991, pp. 49–50.

13. G. K. Chesterton, *Charles Dickens: A Critical Study* (New York: Dodd Mead, 1913), p. 8.

14. Hippolyte Taine, *Notes on England*, trans. Edward Hyams (Fair Lawn, N.J.: Essential Books, 1958 [1872]), p. 290.

15. D. C. Somervell, *English Thought in the Nineteenth Century* (Westport, Conn.: Greenwood Press, 1977 [1962]), p. 80. Somervell's thesis here is that it was not democratic sentiments that led to the passage of the Reform Bill or its successor a generation later. It was, rather, a general recognition that virtue "has spread further down the social scale."

16. Ernst Troeltsch, *The Social Teaching of the Christian Churches*, trans. Olive Wyon, 2 vols. (New York: Harper, 1960 [1911]), vol. 2, pp. 666–73 and passim. See also Ernest A. Payne, *The Free Church Tradition in the Life of England*, new rev. ed. (London: Hodder & Stoughton, 1965 [1944]).

17. John Stuart Mill, "The Spirit of the Age," in *The Emergence of Victorian Consciousness: The Spirit of the Age*, ed. George Levine (New York: Free Press, 1967). First published in the *Examiner*, January 1831.

18. William Hazlitt, *The Spirit of the Age: Or Contemporary Portraits* (London: Oxford Univ. Press, 1954 [1825]), p. 39. It may be that just as the poor will be always with us, so will intellectuals who believe that the intellect has reached the end of its period of innovation. In the twentieth century, as the science of genetics stood on the threshold of momentous discoveries, Gunther Stent, a distinguished geneticist,

opined that scientific progress had gone about as far as it could go and was approaching its end. See Gunther S. Stent, *The Coming of the Golden Age: A View of
the End of Progress* (Garden City, N.Y.: Natural History Press, 1969), pp. 110–15.

19. R. K. Webb, *Harriet Martineau: A Radical Victorian* (New York: Columbia
Univ. Press, 1960), pp. 296, 299. Webb believed it was inevitable that the English
social radicals would become dogmatic because they had no tradition to draw on,
given that England was the first industrial society. Thus they "turned from observation to extrapolation" (pp. 364f).

20. Bernard Semmel, *The Methodist Revolution* (New York: Basic Books, 1973),
p. 6, quoting from Tocqueville's work, *The Old Regime and the French Revolution.*

21. Edward E. Erickson, Jr., *Solzhenitsyn and the Modern World* (Washington,
D.C.: Regnery Gateway, 1993), p. 29.

22. See, for example, the discussion in Willis B. Glover, *Biblical Origins of Modern Secular Culture: An Essay in the Interpretation of Western History* (Macon, Ga.:
Mercer Univ. Press, 1984).

23. Keith Thomas, *Religion and the Decline of Magic* (New York: Charles Scribner's Sons, 1971), pp. 656–57. Thomas argued here that the rejection of magic due
to the theological revolution of the sixteenth century paved the way for the progress
of science and technology in the period following.

24. Jerome H. Buckley, *The Victorian Temper: A Study in Literary Culture* (New
York: Vintage Books, 1964 [Cambridge, Mass.: Harvard Univ. Press, 1951]), p. 125.

25. Owen Chadwick, *The Victorian Church*, 2nd ed., pt. 1 (London: Adam &
Charles Black, 1970), p. 386. Among other specialists in the period who have called
attention to the unities is Josef Altholz, *The Churches in the Nineteenth Century* (In-
dianapolis: Bobbs-Merrill, 1967), p. 103.

26. Newman to Dr. Jelf, canon of Christ Church, March 16, 1841, in Wilfrid
Ward, *William George Ward and the Oxford Movement* (London: Macmillan, 1889),
p. 159.

27. *Record,* October 7, 1830.

28. *Record,* January 1, 1829.

29. *Record,* August 4, 1831.

30. Michael Webster, "Simeon's Doctrine of the Church," in *Charles Simeon,
1759–1836,* ed. Arthur Pollard and Michael Hennell (London: Society for Promoting Christian Knowledge, 1959), p. 123, quoting from A. M. Ramsey, *The Gospel
and the Catholic Church.*

31. Vernon F. Storr, *The Oxford Movement: A Liberal Evangelical View* (London: Society for Promoting Christian Knowledge, 1933).

32. Michael Hennell, *John Venn and the Clapham Sect* (London: Lutterworth
Press, 1958), p. 122.

33. Charles Smyth, "The Evangelical Movement in Perspective," *Cambridge
Historical Journal* 7 (1941–43): 170.

34. J. H. Newman, *The Visible Church*, Tract #11, in *The Oxford Movement, Being a Selection from Tracts for the Times,* ed. William G. Hutchison (London: Walter Scott, n.d. [1906]), p. 43.

35. David Newsome, "The Evangelical Sources of Newman's Power," in *The Rediscovery of Newman: An Oxford Symposium*, ed. John Coulsen and A. M. Allchin (London: Sheed & Ward/Society for Promoting Christian Knowledge, 1967), especially pp. 25–26.

36. Robin Furneaux, *William Wilberforce* (London: Hamish Hamilton, 1974), pp. 427–28.

37. *Christian Observer*, March 1846, pp. 166–67. See also the testimony of J. K. Woodford, Samuel Wilberforce's chaplain for sixteen years and later Bishop of Ely, in David Newsome, *The Wilberforces and Henry Manning: The Parting of Friends* (Cambridge, Mass.: Harvard Univ. Press, 1966), p. 334. Pusey's disciple and biographer had the same opinion. See Henry P. Liddon, *Life of Edward Bouverie Pusey*, 4 vols. (London: Longmans Green, 1893–97), vol. 2, pp. 33–34.

38. S. Baring-Gould, *The Church Revival: Thoughts Thereon and Reminiscences* (London: Methuen, 1914), p. 110.

39. Edward Pusey, "Justification," in *The Mind of the Oxford Movement*, ed. Owen Chadwick (London: Adam & Charles Black, 1963 [1960]), p. 112.

40. Gladstone, "Evangelical Movement," p. 15. For the same point elaborated on by more recent observers, see Herbert Leslie Stewart, *A Century of Anglo-Catholicism* (New York: Oxford Univ. Press, 1929), p. 112; Sheridan Gilley, *Newman and His Age* (London: Darton, Longman, & Todd, 1990), passim; Peter B. Nockles, *The Oxford Movement in Context: Anglican High Churchmanship, 1760–1857* (Cambridge, England: Cambridge Univ. Press, 1994), pp. 321–23; also Roderick Strange, *Newman and the Gospel of Christ* (Oxford: Oxford Univ. Press, 1981).

41. Dieter Voll, *Catholic Evangelicalism: The Acceptance of Evangelical Traditions by the Oxford Movement during the Second Half of the Nineteenth Century, a Contribution to the Understanding of Recent Anglicanism*, trans. Veronica Ruffer (London: Faith Press, 1963), pp. 85, 122–23.

42. *Record*, February 21, 1831. In the issue of April 22, 1844, the paper noted that High Church publications were sounding more like the *Record* in opposition to the liberal influences of the Church.

43. This aspect of Arnold's thinking is emphasized by T. W. Bamford, *Thomas Arnold* (London: Cresset Press, 1960).

44. Thomas Arnold, *Sermons*, 3 vols. (London: Rivington, 1829), vol. 1, p. 53.

45. Richard Brent, *Liberal Anglican Politics: Whiggery, Religion, and Reform, 1830–1841* (Oxford: Clarendon Press, 1987), p. 259.

46. *Christian Observer*, March 1845, pp. 154, 156.

47. *Record*, January 30, 1845.

48. *Christian Observer*, April 1831, p. 221.

49. John Henry Newman, *Apologia pro Vita Sua*, ed. A. Dwight Culler (Boston: Houghton Mifflin, 1956 [1864]), pp. 273–74.

50. Ward, *William George Ward*, pp. 67–69.

51. Peter Hammond, *Dean Stanley of Westminster* (n.p.: Churchman Publishing, 1987), p. 27.

52. T. Mozley, *Reminiscences; Chiefly of Oriel College and the Oxford Movement,* 2nd ed., 2 vols. (London: Longmans, Green, 1882), vol. 1, p. 53.

53. Roger H. Martin, *Evangelicals United: Ecumenical Stirrings in Pre-Victorian Britain, 1795–1830* (Metuchin, N.J.: Scarecrow Press, 1983), p. 196.

54. W. R. Ward, *Religion and Society in England, 1790–1850* (London: B. T. Batsford, 1972), p. 234.

55. *Record,* December 4, 1845.

56. Newman, *Apologia,* p. 50.

57. These numbers are taken from Peter Toon, *Evangelical Theology 1833–1856: A Response to Tractarianism* (Atlanta, Ga.: John Knox Press, 1979), p. 2.

58. That is the thesis of Michael Hennell, *Sons of the Prophets: Evangelical Leaders of the Victorian Church* (London: Society for Promoting Christian Knowledge, 1979).

59. Basil Willey, *More Nineteenth Century Studies: A Group of Honest Doubters* (London: Chatto & Windus, 1963), pp. 188–90.

60. George Kitson Clark, *The English Inheritance* (London: SCM Press, 1950), p. 148.

61. G. S. R. Kitson Clark, *An Expanding Society: Britain 1830–1900* (Cambridge, England: Cambridge Univ. Press, 1967), p. 118. Kitson Clark here associated this evangelical failing with "the inherent weakness of all romanticism" and believed that it accounted for the evangelical lack of interest in scholarship and intellectual effort in general.

62. Richard E. Brantley, *Coordinates of Anglo-American Romanticism: Wesley, Edwards, Carlyle and Emerson* (Gainesville: Univ. Press of Florida, 1993), pp. 66–67.

63. Stephen Leacock, *Charles Dickens: His Life and Work* (Garden City, N.Y.: Doubleday, 1936), p. 135.

64. Henry Venn to James Stillingfleet, March 29, 1792, in *The Life and a Selection of Letters from the late Henry Venn,* ed. Henry Venn [the younger], 6th ed. (London: Hatchard, 1839), p. 475.

65. Gladstone, "Evangelical Movement," p. 5.

66. Clyde Binfield, *So Down to Prayers: Studies in English Nonconformity, 1780–1920* (London: J. M. Dent, 1977), p. xi.

67. John Foster, *On Some of the Causes by Which Evangelical Religion Has Been Rendered Unacceptable to Persons of Cultivated Taste,* 3rd ed. (London: Longman, 1806), p. 87.

68. Ibid., p. 110. Robert Hall, a popular Baptist preacher, more or less agreed with Foster but demurred to the extent of saying that "men of taste form a very small part of the community." Donald Davie, *The Eighteenth-Century Hymn in England* (Cambridge, England: Cambridge Univ. Press, 1993), p. 123.

69. Samuel G. Green, *The Working Classes of Great Britain and Their Present Condition, and the Means of Their Improvement and Elevation* (London: John Snow, 1850), p. 86. Green made his own beliefs explicit: "I take it for granted that the system of doctrines usually termed Evangelical is the truth" (p. 92).

70. E. M. Forster, *Marianne Thornton, 1797–1887: A Domestic Biography* (London: Edward Arnold, 1956), pp. 138–39.

71. *Record,* November 14, 1833.

72. Tim Hilton, *John Ruskin: The Early Years, 1819–1859* (New Haven, Conn.: Yale Univ. Press, 1985), p. 254.

73. Charles Dickens, *Pickwick Papers* (Signet Classic, 1964), p. xi, reprinted from the first cheap edition of 1847.

74. Desmond Bowen, *The Idea of the Victorian Church* (Montreal: McGill Univ. Press, 1968), p. 291. Some observers attribute the characteristic to Puritanism: e.g., John Marlowe (pseud.), *The Puritan Tradition in English Life* (London: Cresset Press, 1956), p. 116; Arthur Warne, *Church and Society in Eighteenth-Century Devon* (Newton Abbot, England: David & Charles, 1969), p. 128. But the social activism of Puritanism belies this. There is some definitional problem here, or perhaps these scholars are considering Puritanism transmuted, something analogous to the nineteenth-century evangelicals losing the vision of societal transformation.

75. Doreen Rosman, *Evangelicals and Culture* (London: Croom Helm, 1984), pp. 79–80.

76. *Christian Observer,* April 1840, pp. 195–96.

77. Standish Meacham, "The Evangelical Inheritance," *Journal of British Studies* 3, no. 1 (1963): 100.

78. Horton Davies, *Worship and Theology in England: From Watts and Wesley to Maurice, 1690–1850* (Princeton, N.J.: Princeton Univ. Press, 1961), pp. 236–37.

79. *Christian Observer,* May 1805, pp. 306–13.

80. Gladstone, "Evangelical Movement," p. 13.

81. Rosman, *Evangelicals and Culture,* pp. 79–80.

82. Standish Meacham, *Henry Thornton of Clapham, 1760–1815* (Cambridge, Mass.: Harvard Univ. Press, 1964), p. 154.

83. Baring-Gould, *Church Revival,* p. 93.

84. Henry Venn, *To Apply the Gospel: Selections from the Writings of Henry Venn,* ed. Max Warren (Grand Rapids, Mich.: Eerdmans, 1971), p. 130.

85. J. L. Hammond and Barbara Hammond, *The Age of the Chartists, 1832–1854: A Study of Discontent* (Hamden, Conn.: Archon Books, 1962 [1930]), p. 242.

86. Elizabeth Jay, *The Religion of the Heart: Anglican Evangelicalism and the Nineteenth-Century Novel* (Oxford: Clarendon Press, 1979), pp. 54–55.

87. William Jay, *The Autobiography of the Rev. William Jay,* ed. George Redford and John Angell James (London: Hamilton, Adams, 1855), p. 548.

88. Brian Harrison, *Drink and the Victorians* (Pittsburgh: Univ. of Pittsburgh Press, 1971), p. 31.

89. For a sociological analysis of modern American evangelicalism that exposes these characteristics, see James Davison Hunter, *American Evangelicalism: Conservative Religion and the Quandary of Modernity* (New Brunswick, N.J.: Rutgers Univ. Press, 1983), especially pp. 86–87, which, however, exhibits some of the determinism of its discipline. Hunter's later study, *Evangelicalism: The Coming*

Generation (Chicago: Univ. of Chicago Press, 1987), shows how the conformist tendency has grown, based on his analysis of trends in evangelical higher education.

90. *Record,* May 14, 1835.

91. Thomas Robinson to Henry Burder, December 22, 1787, in Henry Foster Burder, *Memoir of the Rev. George Burder* (London: Westley & Davis, 1833), pp. 138–39.

92. *Christian Observer,* May 1802, pp. 318–19.

93. R. W. Dale, *The Old Evangelicalism and the New* (London: Hodder & Stoughton, 1889), p. 29.

94. G. M. Young, "Portrait of an Age," in *Early Victorian England 1830–1865,* ed. G. M. Young, 2 vols. (London: Oxford Univ. Press, 1951 [1934]), vol. 2, p. 416.

95. *Christian Observer,* 1844, p. iv.

96. Leslie Stephen, *English Literature and Society in the Eighteenth Century* (London: Gerald Duckworth, 1904), p. 115.

97. Liddon, *Life of Pusey,* vol. 1, pp. 254–55.

98. Joseph John Gurney, *Reminiscences of Chalmers, Simeon, Wilberforce &c* (n.p., n.d. [1835]), p. 137.

99. *Record,* May 3, 1838.

100. *Christian Observer,* 1841, pp. iii–iv.

101. *Christian Observer,* 1846, p. iv.

102. The decline from the urbanity of a Charles Simeon to the relative crudity of later writers, especially in the heat of the anti-Tractarian years, has been argued by Elizabeth Jay, ed., *The Evangelical and Oxford Movements* (Cambridge, England: Cambridge Univ. Press, 1983), pp. 13–17.

103. Ward, *Religion and Society in England,* p. 177.

104. Ben Knights, *The Idea of the Clerisy in the Nineteenth Century* (Cambridge, England: Cambridge Univ. Press, 1978), p. 154.

105. Ibid., pp. 157–58.

106. "Appendix C of the Second Report of the Royal Commission on the Elementary Education Acts (1887)," in *How They Were Taught: An Anthology of Contemporary Accounts of Learning and Teaching in England, 1800–1950,* comp. P. H. J. H. Gosden (New York: Barnes & Noble, 1969), p. 60.

107. That is the argument, for example, of Walter E. Houghton, *The Victorian Frame of Mind: 1830–1870* (New Haven, Conn.: Yale Univ. Press, 1959), pp. 424–25.

108. Michael Mason, *The Making of Victorian Sexuality* (Oxford: Oxford Univ. Press, 1994), p. 4.

109. Christopher Hill, *The English Bible and the Seventeenth-Century Revolution* (London: Penguin, 1993).

110. David Vincent, *Literacy and Popular Culture, England 1750–1914* (Cambridge, England: Cambridge Univ. Press, 1993 [1989]), pp. 159–60, quoting from the *Suffolk Farm Labourer.* For similar descriptions from Lancashire in the same period, see John K. Walton, *Lancashire: A Social History, 1558–1939* (Manchester, England: Manchester Univ. Press, 1987), p. 184.

111. James C. Livingston, *The Ethics of Belief: An Essay on the Victorian Religious Conscience* (Tallahassee, Fla.: American Academy of Religion, 1974), pp. 36–37.

112. Noel Annan, *Leslie Stephen: The Godless Victorian* (New York: Random House, 1984), pp. 272–73. For a modern sociological analysis that seems to vindicate Stephen's expectations for the positive relationship between irreligion and lawlessness, see Christie Davies, "Moralization and Demoralization: A Moral Explanation for Changes in Crime, Disorder and Social Problems," in *The Loss of Virtue: Moral Confusions and Social Disorder in Britain and America,* ed. Digby Anderson (n.p.: Social Affairs Unit, 1992), chap. 1. A larger essay on the same subject is Gertrude Himmelfarb, *The Demoralization of Society: From Victorian Virtues to Modern Values* (New York: Knopf, 1995).

113. Gertrude Himmelfarb ends her essay "A Genealogy of Morals," with this in *Marriage and Morals among the Victorians* (New York: Alfred A. Knopf, 1986), p. 49.

114. James Connors, "'Who Dies if England Live?': Christianity and Moral Vision of George Orwell," in *The Secular Mind: Transformations of Faith in Modern Europe,* ed. W. Warren Wagar (New York: Holmes & Meier, 1982), p. 170.

Index